DRESSING
FOR
DINNER
IN THE
NAKED CITY

DRESSING FOR DINNER IN THE NAKED CITY

And Other Tales From The Wall Street Journal's "Middle Column"

Edited by Jane Berentson

New York

Library of Congress Cataloging-in-Publication Data
Dressing for dinner in the naked city, and other tales from the Wall Street journal's middle column / edited by Jane Berentson. — 1st ed.
    p. cm.
Articles published on the front page of the Wall Street journal from 1985.
ISBN 0-7868-8013-9
1. Newspapers—Sections, columns, etc.—Front pages.   [1. Wall Street journal.]   I. Berentson, Jane.   II. Wall Street journal.
III. Title: Dressing for dinner in the naked city.
AC8.D775   1994
081—dc20   93-6270
                                                    CIP

Designed by Levavi & Levavi, Inc.

First Edition
10 9 8 7 6 5 4 3 2 1

Contents

Introduction

Ahed

This is a collection of stories which have appeared on the front page of *The Wall Street Journal* since 1984. They're known as Aheds, and they usually have nothing to do with business, unless it's the business of running a rat restaurant in China or the ups and downs of selling frying pans on the streets of Warsaw. Aheds often are about strange animal behavior and eccentric characters. They can be poignant or heroic. The man who worships Bobby Thomson fits into this form. So does the sex life of a sea slug.

Aheds—so-called because of the headline style, which, with some imagination, looks like a capital "A"—have been published on and off since the 1940s. That was when Barney Kilgore, who designed the modern *Wall Street Journal,* decided to replace column four's spot news stories with quirky feature articles. Over the following decades, the price of aluminum or the rise in belt sales gave way to a paean to the carrot and the clothes problems of muscle-bound men.

Aheds now appear daily in the *Journal,* still in column four, just right of center. They are written by *Journal* reporters and edited by the page one staff. The purpose of an Ahed is to entertain readers with good storytelling and clever writing. We hope you enjoy them.

JANE BERENTSON
JUNE 1993

I

LOVE OF
LIFE

Gloom of Night
Can't Stay Her Hand
At the Bridge Table

Ruth Thorpe, Life Master,
Has Excelled at the Game
Since Its Very Creation

By James M. Perry

7/17/90

OSWEGO, N.Y.—Ruth Thorpe, a life master at the game, has played bridge through three fires, twice at the Pontiac Hotel here in Oswego and once at the Ithaca Hotel in Ithaca.

But worse still was the raging storm that blew out the windows at the Arlington Hotel in Binghamton, where she was playing in a tournament with Johnny Cullinan, another life master. The rainwater gushed in, and was soon an inch deep.

"It was so cold, I was shivering and could hardly hold the cards," says Mrs. Thorpe. "Johnny went to the bar and got me a ginger brandy. It's the only time he ever bought me a drink." The game, relocated hastily to a second-floor room across the street, rolled on.

And so has Mrs. Thorpe. Those old hotels all are gone now, but Mrs. Thorpe is still playing bridge. Serious bridge, too. Last February, she and her frequent partner, Audrey Johnson, finished first in a national tournament held simultaneously in more than 100 cities and involving 9,200 players. Mrs. Thorpe plays in Oswego tournaments three days a week and usually visits a sick friend for a social game Sunday nights.

Mrs. Thorpe, bridge champion, is 95 years old.

She began playing a card game called pedro before the modern game of bridge was devised (by yachtsman Harold S. Vanderbilt on a Caribbean cruise in 1926). The American Contract Bridge League believes she is the organization's oldest active player.

Mrs. Thorpe is a slender, gentle woman, known as Aunt Ruth to almost everyone in this upstate town on the shores of Lake Ontario. She is in good health, needs no medications, pays her own bills and bakes her own pies in the white frame bungalow she and her late husband, Walter, built themselves 62 years ago. Her depth perception isn't what it was when she was 90, and she is a little hard of hearing. "I must get younger," she says, as she stumbles a bit coming down her front steps. But at the bridge table, she is a tiger.

"At the level we play it, bridge is a serious game," says Mrs. Thorpe. She dismisses social bridge-rubber bridge, the kind most amateurs play—as "party" bridge or "kitchen" bridge. "They talk a lot and they miss all the slams [big winning hands]," she says during lunch at the Admiral Woolsey waterfront restaurant here. What she plays—what she has been playing since doctors thought she had tuberculosis years ago and she wasn't allowed to participate in outdoor activities—is duplicate bridge.

"It's hard to imagine her life without bridge," says her great-niece, Joan Braun. "It puts her in constant contact with people of all ages. It gets her up and moving."

Duplicate bridge is always played in a club or tournament setting, with a director certified by the contract bridge league in charge. Participants pay a nominal fee, from $2 to $6 per person, to play. Mrs. Thorpe directed the Wednesday afternoon tournament in Oswego for 37 years, donating her profit—as much as $750 in a good year—to the Catholic Daughters of America. Most days at her games, there were 12 or more tables. Now, she says, participation Wednesday afternoons is down to five or six.

In duplicate bridge, cards are placed in "boards," and every pair ultimately plays the same hands as everyone else. Top honors go to those who come closest to achieving the maximum potential of the cards they play. Partners will run up their score by making, for example, five hearts, when everyone else is making four. "It's that extra trick that counts," says Mrs. Thorpe.

"The whole idea," says Jane Johnson, a league official, "is to get the most out of each hand, whether declaring [playing the hand] or defending." Winning hands, or boards, is what counts; winning games or rubbers—the way conventional, social bridge is played—has no place in the heady world of duplicate bridge.

Serious players win master points for their successes in tournaments at the local, regional and national level. Mrs. Thorpe has accumulated 1,200 master points, achieving life master status in 1961. (She is No. 3,375 of 40,829 life masters.) Last February, in winning the national seniors event for players 55 and older, Mrs. Thorpe and her partner, Audrey Johnson, 67, scored an astonishing 79.1%, which means they played at nearly 80 percent of bridge perfection that day. It's a little like batting .800, a state of grace no baseball player has ever approached.

In tournaments, contestants must fill out cards saying which bridge-playing system they use. Mrs. Thorpe fills in the space with one word, "standard." That means she plays a sophisticated version of a basic system popularized by Charles Goren more than 50 years ago. But others keep trying to come up with more complicated systems. When Mrs. Thorpe encounters opponents who claim to use one of these innovations, she is delighted. "I know I'm going to fleece them," she says.

She is particularly contemptuous of systems that try to fool people. "They don't scare me," she says. "They lead from weakness, and I believe in dealing from strength. Did you ever scare anyone by being weak?"

The glory of duplicate bridge, and now its biggest problem, is its difficulty. "It takes at least a year of hard study, including lessons, to master the game," says Mrs. Thorpe. "Young people these days are very smart, but they have so many other things they want to do."

Also, the good players are sometimes rude and aggressive and scare off the novices. Mrs. Thorpe—a member of the league's national goodwill committee, which seeks to promote decorum and table manners—remembers with distaste a tournament in which a frustrated player picked up his chair and flung it against a nearby wall.

Because many of the serious players are growing old, the game tends to thrive in retirement communities, especially in Florida and California. The contract bridge league says it has 4,000 clubs and 190,000 members. No one has any idea how many Americans still play "party" bridge socially.

Oswego has always been a good bridge-playing town, and Mrs. Thorpe and her friend Mr. Cullinan are living legends in the whole central New York area. They still bask in the reflected glory of Oswego's greatest bridge player, a doctor named William Halsey, who used to teach nurses to play the game during idle moments in the operating room.

"He died at the bridge table in 1949," says Mr. Cullinan. "And when the tragic news reached Peg Weekes, our best woman player, her first question was, 'What was he in?' 'One spade,' she was told. Peg thought for a second or two and said, 'He probably should have been in four.' And, sure enough, when they went back and looked at the board, it became obvious he had seriously underbid his hand."

"It's probably what did him in," notes Mrs. Thorpe.

If We Told You Who This Story Is About, We Might Be Jinxed

Christopher C. Is a Curse, Say Dominicans, Who Knock When They Hear the Name

---

By José de Cordoba

4/22/92

SANTO DOMINGO—In a March speech to an Inter American Press Association convention, Robert Pastorino, the new U.S. ambassador here in the Dominican Republic, didn't dare say the name Christopher Columbus. Instead, he used a common local euphemism: the Great Admiral.

"We didn't want anybody diving under the tables during the speech," explains an aide to the ambassador.

The Great Admiral, many Dominicans believe, is fucu. Jinxed.

Whether Columbus, who discovered this island in 1492 and later asked that his body be buried here, brings bad luck is much debated. The Great Admiral's most stalwart champion has been Joaquín Balaguer, the 85-year-old blind president, who has built a massive, but squat, cross-shaped cement and marble lighthouse just outside Santo Domingo to honor him. In October, the metal urn that holds Columbus's remains will be moved from a local cathedral to the lighthouse. Mr. Balaguer, who admits to being superstitious, believes the Great Admiral brings good luck.

Many Dominicans disagree. Consider some of the evidence, compiled by a newspaper editor here:

On Aug. 4, 1946, at a ceremony commemorating the 450th anniversary of the founding of the city, during which Columbus's urn was opened, the country was struck by the worst earthquake in a century. Two towns slid into the sea.

In 1937, three planes—the Nina, the Pinta and the Santa Maria—taking part in a flight to raise money for the Columbus lighthouse project crashed in Colombia, killing their pilots. A fourth plane, named after the Great Admiral, survived.

In 1948, at the ceremony inaugurating the construction of the lighthouse, a dynamite charge dislodged a boulder that crushed the car of the official in charge of the project.

Then there's the Order of Columbus, one of the country's highest honors. Octavio Amiama, who runs the Central Bank's coin museum, says that in the 1940s a prominent politician was pricked by the medal's pin during the investiture ceremony and died from the infected wound. In 1969, says Mr. Amiama, he unsuccessfully tried to persuade the outgoing German ambassador, Count Karl von Spreti, to settle for a safer medal. In 1970, shortly after receiving the medal by mail in his new posting in Guatemala, the ambassador was kidnapped by leftist guerrillas, who executed him.

President Balaguer's lighthouse—which many Dominicans curse as a huge waste in such a poor country—is also widely believed to be cursed. Dominicans, already plagued by daily electrical blackouts, grimly joke that when President Balaguer throws the lighthouse switch, which will project a huge cross into the sky, at a ceremony for the 500th anniversary of Columbus's discovery, the whole country will go pitch black.

For the most part, believers in the curse are members of the country's intellectual, journalistic and political elite who have devoted hours of study to the history of the country and Columbus's own life.

"Zafa,"—literally, to untie—shouts Frank Marino, a financial consultant here, thrusting out the little and index fingers of both hands to demonstrate the antidote to any mention of the Great Admiral's name. For good measure, Mr. Marino knocks on a wooden conference table three times. "It happens daily," says Mr. Marino, who claims not to be a believer. "People say it jokingly, but they always say it."

Tempting fate, U.S. Ambassador Pastorino recently abandoned his prudent no-name policy and uttered the forbidden words not once but three times at a speech before a Dominican business group. "He screwed up," mutters a banker as Bernardo Vega, a publisher and former Central Bank governor, knocks on wood.

Not being as foolhardy as his U.S. colleague, Colombia's ambassador, José Pardo Llada, who is also a newspaper columnist, has decided not to write about the ill-fated 1937 flight. "Just in case," wrote Mr. Pardo Llada in a recent column.

He is not the only one who takes precautions. Newspaper owner German Ornes recalls being flattered but nervous about being named to the national Columbus Lighthouse Commission. So Mr. Ornes took it as an omen when, on his way to the swearing-in ceremony, he was challenged by a guard at the presidential palace, the first and only time that had happened. Mr. Ornes refused the honor. "I don't believe in the curse, but the best thing is not to defy it," he says carefully.

Mexico's octogenarian ambassador to the Dominican Republic, Fernando Benitez, has defied the Great Admiral's curse—and felt his wrath. A well-known writer who, to his Dominican friends' horror, loves to rail at the Great Admiral for his brutality against the Indians, Mr. Benitez has had two accidents, breaking numerous ribs and his hip, since he began to write a book that comments unkindly on the Great Admiral. "I don't believe in the curse," says Mr. Benitez, leaning on his cane. "But look at all that has happened to me."

Believers say the curse began with the life of the Great Admiral himself, who died penniless in Spain. Then the New World came to be known for a competitor. "He has what the Hindus call bad karma," says Manuel Manon Arredondo, a university history professor.

Controversy and bad luck followed the Great Admiral into his grave or, perhaps, graves. While most Dominicans swear he is buried here, some say Columbus's bones were moved first to Havana and later to Seville when Spain lost the Spanish American War. "The bones of the young Columbus are buried here while the bones of the old Columbus are buried in Seville," says José Israel Cuello, a book publisher, neatly solving that historical puzzle.

At any rate, the Great Admiral's stay here was particularly unfortunate. His first settlement on the island, La Navidad, was destroyed by Indians shortly after it was founded. In 1500, Columbus was arrested in a factional dispute with other Spanish colonists here and chained in a dungeon called the Well of Sorrows before being sent back in disgrace to Spain.

Some say the Great Admiral's bad luck has continued to plague the island. A few years after its discovery, the Indian population of Hispaniola, as it was then called, had all but disappeared, killed off by Spanish diseases, Spanish swords or suicide. Santo Domingo, the first capital of Spanish America, had to be moved to its present location after, according to hazy historical accounts, it was almost wiped out by a plague of ants.

Things went downhill from there. A brief season when Santo Domingo was the center of Spain's colonizing efforts in the New World was followed by centuries of stagnation, punctuated by civil wars, foreign interventions, coups and the bloody megalomania of the late dictator, Rafael Leonidas Trujillo.

Taking a puff of his cigarette, Mr. Manon Arredondo, the historian, says the Great Admiral, loving Hispaniola more than any other of his discoveries, spent more time here than in any other part of the New World. But Dominicans wish he had loved some other place more. "That great love of Columbus has brought great misfortune to the island," says Mr. Manon Arredondo, with a deep sigh.

What Else Is There?
Brooks Brothers Is
So Suitably Correct

————

Salesman Joseph Mancini, 80,
Has Served Up Good Taste
In Cuffed Pants for 66 Years

————

By Teri Agins

7/23/92

NEW YORK—Over the years, Joseph Mancini has suffered silently through Zoot suits, Nehru jackets, polyester leisure suits and countless other faddish detours from the impeccably correct. When others lost their heads to the whims of fashion, he resolutely held the line.

This Saturday, after 66 years of selling men's suits, the 80-year-old Mr. Mancini is retiring from the only job at the only store he has ever known: Brooks Brothers on Madison Avenue.

Mr. Mancini first walked through the store's mahogany portals in 1926, a 14-year-old lad in a gray knickerbocker suit. Jimmy Walker was the mayor then, and Calvin Coolidge was in the White House. It was the year Laurel and Hardy teamed up. Horses and buggies parked alongside Model T's in front of the store, discharging a steady stream of shoppers—from J. P. Morgan to Choate preppies.

For $13 a week, Mr. Mancini at first ran errands for the store's tailors, one of whom was his father. That same year he bought his first Brooks Brothers' suit, for $7.50 during an employee sample sale.

With his Churchillian jowls, natty bow tie and chipper elegance, Mr. Mancini is today the quintessential Man in the Brooks Brothers Suit, a voice of sartorial propriety. The Brooks Brothers' golden fleece logo adorns everything in his wardrobe, including his collection of fedora hats, oxford shoes, boxer shorts and his Brooks Brothers Formula 44 cologne.

In his cedar closet hang 25 Brooks Brothers suits, some more than 20 years old, that he wears in a fixed rotation. He favors subtle pinstripes, herringbones and muted glen plaids, and has a traditionalist's aversion to pattern-on-pattern. "The fella who does the windows here sometimes puts a striped shirt with a striped tie and a striped suit," he says with a shudder. Mr. Mancini always wears white shirts, first the buttoned-down-Oxford style that Brooks Brothers invented in 1900, and now that his neck is thicker, pointed collars.

The fastidious salesman virtually lives in a suit during the week. On weekends, he usually dons a blazer. He has his suits dry cleaned and pressed no more than once or twice a year. "Those tumblers beat the heck out of your clothes," he says.

Brooks Brothers could wish for no more impassioned booster than Mr. Mancini (though in 1941 he was a founder of the company union that brought higher wages and shorter hours). Not for him the high-fashion $1,500 Italian suits. Rather, he calls Brooks Brothers' classic styling the best buy in town, because in the long run the suits hold up, "and are always tasteful and correct."

But how would he know? This is a man who has never set foot in another haberdashery, not even J. Press around the corner or Paul Stuart half a block away. "We're No. 1," he says matter-of-factly. "You don't go to them, you let them come to you."

As for designer Ralph Lauren, who once briefly sold ties at Brooks Brothers and was recently quoted as saying he was "as Brooksy as you can get," Mr. Mancini admires him—but he won't visit his store. "Everything Ralph Lauren learned was right here," he says. "He's a smart fella. He made it pay off."

Such is Mr. Mancini's loyalty to his employer that 35 years ago, when his wife, Terry, announced that she was defecting to Barneys in search of a suit for their then-chubby 16-year-old son, Mr. Mancini was aghast. His wife recalls that he urged their son to go on a crash diet so he could squeeze into a Brooks Brothers suit. (In the end his wife and son went to Barneys.)

Last week, a scruffy young man in shorts, rubber thongs and a baseball cap worn backward wandered into the sixth-floor suit department. To Mr. Mancini, he was a "wrap-up," or sure sale.

"When a fella comes in dressed like that, you know he's going to buy—he needs clothes," Mr. Mancini explains. And indeed, Craig Phares, 27, a recent M.B.A., was outfitting himself for his first job, on Wall Street.

Mr. Mancini steered him to his personal favorite, the "authentic" Brooks Brothers' three-button sack suit, which has changed little since it made its debut more than 50 years ago. Mr. Mancini had no trouble selling the young Wall Streeter on an old-fashioned detail: a wide 1¾-inch trouser cuff.

Mr. Mancini is a great believer in wide cuffs. "The weight of the cuff helps hold the crease and makes your pants hang better," he says, recalling that during World War II, when wool was scarce, it was against the law for retailers to put cuffs in men's pants. He confides: "You know how we got around that? We hemmed the trousers a couple of inches too long. Then a man could take the pants to his own tailor and have the cuff put in."

Mr. Mancini's customer following is lengthy and loyal. So that they will be taken care of after his retirement, he is parceling out his 200-or-so regulars—known as "see yous" in the trade—to some of the other nine salesmen in his department, matching them by temperament.

Richard Bossone, the dean of the City University of New York, has been a client for 22 years. "Joe Mancini exemplifies good taste," Mr. Bossone says, adding that he calls him "Mr. Brooks." Mr. Bossone continues: "He is one person who treats you like a gentleman."

Richard Dresdale, a 36-year-old investment banker who has logged 15 years with Mr. Mancini, recently bought six new suits from him. Mr. Dresdale considers Mr. Mancini a conservative soulmate, one that won't easily be replaced.

In the fitting room, the avuncular salesman smooths his thick palms across Mr. Dresdale's shoulders and utters, "Richard, this looks great." While Mr. Dresdale ponders his reflection, Mr. Mancini slips away to attend another client.

Mr. Mancini's deft handling of customers has rewarded him well. He raised a family of four boys on his salary, based mainly on commissions. Last year, he earned $57,000, about average at the store.

Though he subscribes to many conservative dictums—preferring plain-front pants to pleated—he also believes that the customer, regardless of taste, is always right. "If a suit doesn't look right to me, I tell him so. If he agrees with me, fine. If not, he's paying for it—let him do it his way."

Brooks Brothers has a number of salesmen whose tenure exceeds 25 years. But as these old-timers retire—in Mr. Mancini's case to spend more time with his 80-year-old wife—they are increasingly hard to replace. "The problem with salespeople these days is that they are too grand, they think that the job is servile," observes Paul Smith, the director of North American operations for London-based Marks & Spencer, which has owned Brooks Brothers since 1988.

If Joe Mancini ever had such doubts, they were fleeting. Through all the years, rising each morning at 5:30 A.M., his zest for the work has rarely flagged. He rarely talks shop at home, but his wife says that before big sales he talks in his sleep: "Joe would say things like '39 long, 40 regular, herringbone.' "

One of his proudest moments was during New York City's 1965 power blackout, when the store went dark, and everyone evacuated. Everyone, that is, except Mr. Mancini and a fussy client, who chose two suits by the glow of a cigarette lighter.

Tale of a Whale: Mysterious Gambler Wins, Loses Millions

A Shy Japanese Duels Trump In a Kind of 'Moby Dick At the Baccarat Table'

By Robert Johnson

6/28/90

ATLANTIC CITY, N.J.—The most feared gambler on the boardwalk is a mysterious Japanese baccarat player known as "The Warrior." He bets $200,000 a hand—$14 million an hour—in spans up to 14 hours. A private chef prepares his favorite foods: BLT sandwiches and marinated monkey meat.

Yet so little is known about him that a credit review circulated among casino officials lists his profession as "Business." No one knows how he made his money. And even Donald Trump, his host in an oceanfront casino penthouse, says, "I don't really know where the hell he comes from."

His name is Akio Kashiwagi and he is high risk incarnate. He won $6 million at the Trump Plaza Hotel and Casino in February, then lost $9.4 million in May when Mr. Trump lured him back—after hiring consultants to figure out how to beat him.

Mr. Kashiwagi, 53 years old, is Mr. Trump's reclusive opposite, avoiding interviews and photographers. He runs his Tokyo real estate business from a shabby two-story building far removed from the glamour of Trump Plaza. Sipping tea amid tuxedo-clad barracat croupiers, Mr. Kashiwagi, in his rumpled blue-striped shirt and plain black slippers, has the the look of a quarter-slot-machine player just off the bus from Hoboken.

He throws around $5,000 casino chips with the composure of someone playing penny pinochle. Flanked by a bodyguard, he often smiles even when losing. "He plays only for fun," says Darryl Yong, an aide to Mr. Kashiwagi. Yet he bets more in an hour than 100,000 typical visitors wager collectively.

Mr. Trump ordered his guest's private table roped off in red velvet. He provided hot face towels and allowed him exclusive use of a nearby casino bathroom. "He's great, the best in the world," says Mr. Trump.

Mr. Kashiwagi is a steady player, never varying his bet whether winning or losing. At one point in last month's marathon, he lost 11 straight hands at $200,000 each without flinching. He takes notes describing the results of each hand, and casino officials rate his skill as excellent. But unlike many baccarat players, he often seems to bet on hunches—without any pattern or concern about how the cards are going.

In the parlance of the casino industry, a huge bettor like Mr. Kashiwagi is a "whale," which surely makes Mr. Trump his Ahab. Call him crazy, but Mr. Trump wants his croupiers to play another baccarat marathon with Mr. Kashiwagi. For how much? "Unlimited. Anything he wants to do," says Mr. Trump—although his employees say there would certainly be limits.

The ideal date for the contest would be Dec. 7, the anniversary of Japan's 1941 attack on Pearl Harbor, says Edward Tracy, president of operations at Mr. Trump's three casinos in Atlantic City. For advice on making that a day of infamy for Mr. Kashiwagi, Mr. Tracy is being advised by Jess Marcum, a mathematician he says "helped develop the atomic bomb. If he's that good, he can help us beat Kashiwagi."

Mr. Marcum, nicknamed "The Atheist" by gambling industry officials because he doesn't believe in luck, only in his calculations of odds, says he actually helped with the neutron bomb after World War II. Close enough, says Mr. Tracy.

Mr. Trump has also hired Al Glasgow, a gambling industry consultant, to help size up Mr. Kashiwagi. "He's a real samurai. He craves a challenge," says Mr. Glasgow. "When he's taking a break, he'd just as soon sleep on a cot."

But Trump Plaza provides better: a penthouse suite with three bedrooms, three baths—sauna, two butlers and a pianist. The living room features a smiling jade Buddha valued at $800,000.

Not bad, considering that virtually nothing is known about the true size of Mr. Kashiwagi's bankroll, where it comes from or how good his credit really is. He was born the son of a carpenter in a small city near Mount Fuji. One of his first jobs is said to have been guiding tourists around the mountain. An older brother, who works for a textile company, says he doesn't know how his sibling became rich.

His modest combination house and office near a busy Tokyo intersection is just down a hill from the offices of Japan's Diet. Only a small gold-colored sign indicates there's a business inside. Foreign luxury cars are often parked nearby. In his hometown, Kawaguchiko, he lives in a huge house known locally as "Kashiwagi Palace."

He claims $1 billion in assets and income of about $100 million a year. He describes his company, Kashiwagi Shoji Co., as a real estate and investment concern in which he is the only principal. His assistant, Mr. Yong, politely brushed aside a request by this newspaper for details.

A 1988 report by Tokyo Shoko Research Ltd., a data base of companies in Japan, shows Mr. Kashiwagi's company with sales of just $15 million and five employees. An official at the company says it has about 30 workers now; he declines to discuss sales. Mr. Kashiwagi isn't listed among the top 30 taxpayers in his district last year, according to Japanese government records, and tax officials won't talk about individuals' payments.

Mr. Kashiwagi took up his heavy gambling hobby about three years ago, according to Mr. Yong. His biggest win, $19 million in a week, came last February at the Diamond Beach Casino in Darwin, Australia.

There, too, he played baccarat, a card game similar to blackjack in which the winning hand is the one closest to a point total of nine. Face cards and tens aren't counted. Baccarat has snob appeal because it has higher minimum bets than other casino games—typically $20. But minimums don't interest Mr. Kashiwagi: Mr. Trump's casino is the only one in Atlantic City that granted his request for $200,000 a hand.

Smarting from his $6 million loss to Mr. Kashiwagi in 10 hours last February, Mr. Trump sought a better strategy in May. His consultants, Messrs. Glasgow and Marcum, suggested enticing their guest to play longer this time. They proposed a so-called freeze-out agreement, under which Mr. Kashiwagi wouldn't quit until he either doubled an initial $12 million or lost it all. The arrangement isn't binding—New Jersey gaming laws permit a player to quit at any time.

But the freeze-out agreement psychologically snared Mr. Kashiwagi, says Trump Plaza's Mr. Tracy: "His nostrils were wide open; he was hooked and going down."

Mr. Marcum calculated that the casino's risk doesn't increase with the size of the hand. All that matters, given the slight 1.25% advantage the rules give the casino in each hand, is that the customer play long enough to lose everything. Mr. Marcum's pages of handwritten charts show that after one hour of play, or about 70 hands, the customer has a 46% chance of being ahead. After 75 hours, or 5,250 hands, the customer's chance of winning falls to 15%.

Sure enough, Mr. Kashiwagi was ahead $5.5 million on his third day at the table. "It was beautiful," recalls Mr. Yong. But by 4 A.M. on the sixth day, after 5,056 hands in 70 hours of play, Mr. Kashiwagi was $9.4 million behind.

Mr. Kashiwagi then left in a huff, tipping poorly and threatening to burn his autographed copy of Mr. Trump's "The Art of the Deal."

Mr. Kashiwagi's people contend that Trump officials broke the freeze-out agreement by ending the game while they were ahead. Trump officials say Mr. Kashiwagi quit.

The Trump casino had advanced Mr. Kashiwagi a $6 million line of credit to be used only for gambling. But on the way to his limousine, Mr. Kashiwagi quietly cashed in $474,000 in chips. He has agreed to pay back everything except that. (He has also recently paid up for $3 million in losses at the Las Vegas Hilton.)

Sources close to Mr. Trump say he'll agree to let his whale keep that money in hopes he'll return and blow his stake again. They say Mr. Kashiwagi probably can't resist a chance for revenge, and Mr. Trump is extending an open invitation.

But Mr. Yong says Mr. Kashiwagi will never forgive the indignities he suffered. For instance, he says, Mr. Trump's guarantee of credit at Macy's in Atlantic City proved worthless. Mr. Kashiwagi left the department store in humiliation without his $5,000 in clothes and other purchases. Trump officials insist it was a misunderstanding and say the items were delivered later to their guest's suite.

"Not good enough," says Mr. Yong, slipping in a dig at their debt-ridden host. "We pity Mr. Trump's creditors," he says. "No wonder if they panic."

Mr. Young says all this has left Mr. Kashiwagi disenchanted with baccarat, and his new hobbies will be golf and a Japanese version of chess. How much he'll bet on those isn't known.

Yumiko Ono in Tokyo contributed to this article.

Father of Accounting
Is a Bit of a Stranger
To His Own Progeny

———

Luca Pacioli's Seminal Work
Gets a Promotional Boost:
A 1994 Bookkeeping Fest

———

By Lee Berton

1/29/93

Doctors have Hippocrates and philosophers have Plato. But who is the father of accounting? Knowing that accountants have long had inferiority complexes, two Seattle University professors have decided that the profession should have a father and that he should be Luca Pacioli.

But their anointing of the Renaissance scholar occasions an identity crisis. Hardly anyone—accountants included—has ever heard of Pacioli (pronounced pot-CHEE-oh-lee).

"Luca who?" asks Stephen I. Gilman, a certified public accountant and vice president of a marine insurance company in New York. Mr. Gilman has been an accountant for 38 years. The name, he says, "is a mystery to me."

Even John Hunnicutt, the group vice president for governmental affairs of the 300,000-member American Institute of Certified Public Accountants, is among the incognoscenti about Luca. "The name just doesn't ring a bell," he says.

But Luca Pacioli's name-recognition problem hasn't stopped accounting Profs. William Weis and David Tinius. They are planning a big celebration next year in Sansepolcro, Italy, the birthplace of Pacioli. The occasion: the 500th anniversary of the publication of his seminal work on double-entry bookkeeping.

The professors are pulling out all the stops. They have produced a costly video on Pacioli titled "Unsung Hero," in which Messrs. Weis and Tinius themselves play characters in his life story—to keep expenses down, they say. They have asked some of Sansepolcro's 20,000-odd residents to compete in Renaissance costumes with crossbow and acrobatic flag tossing at a fete next year in late May or early June. A Carrara marble statue of Pacioli is to be permanently installed in the town square.

Messrs. Weis and Tinius dreamed up the Pacioli quincentennial in

1986 on a ski trip to Austria. "Things were sort of dull and we were goofing around, so we decided to zip over to Italy." There, they decided that a Pacioli fete "could be fun and get some prestige for the profession," which Prof. Tinius says has "a terrible image."

Prof. Weis recalls that the pair at first discussed such "harebrained events as book-juggling and tugs-of-war between personnel from different big accounting firms." He adds: "But we finally got serious."

The pair persuaded four of the six biggest accounting firms, among others, to cough up $125,000 to make the 27-minute video. They were also going to commission a formal portrait of Pacioli, in hopes of promoting it onto a U.S. commemorative stamp. But the Postal Service turned them down, Prof. Tinius says, because a commemorative stamp celebrating the 100th anniversary of accounting in the U.S. that was issued in 1987 "didn't sell very well." The anniversary stamp, picturing a quill pen and ledger, "wasn't very exciting," he adds.

In the video, the name Pacioli is linked with famous artists, writers and political figures of his day. They include Pope Sixtus IV, the Duke of Urbino and renowned Renaissance painter Piero della Francesca, who put Sansepolcro on the map (in the rugged Apennine mountains 60 miles southeast of Florence).

Five centuries ago Pacioli published "Summa de Arithmetica, Geometria, Proportioni et Proportionalita." It contained a slender tract for merchants on double-entry bookkeeping, which had been in wide use in Venice for years. Because of that, some accounting historians, including Profs. Weis and Tinius, credit Pacioli with codifying accounting principles for the first time. That would seem to establish paternity.

But others are skeptical, and even go so far as to question Pacioli's links to luminaries of his day. "It's hard to believe that Pacioli knew all the famous people attributed to his circle," says Richard Vangermeersch, an accounting professor at the University of Rhode Island and former president of the Academy of Accounting Historians. "Since his life has been re-created from scanty references of that day, some historians like myself feel that some tales about his acquaintances are apocryphal."

Prof. Vangermeersch says the origins of double-entry bookkeeping are open to question. "If you're crediting people of past centuries for contributions to accounting, you should include Leonardo of Pisa, who brought Arabic numerals to the West; James Peele, who initiated journal-entry systems, and Emile Garcke and J.M. Fells, who applied accounting to factory use," he says. All these men have another thing in common, he adds: They are just as obscure as Luca Pacioli.

Profs. Weis and Tinius concede that Pacioli's fame is tenuous even in Sansepolcro. "Residents there care a lot more about Piero della Francesca," admits Prof. Weis. "Until now, Pacioli hasn't been a big deal."

Prof. Tinius insists that the tribute to Pacioli is deserved because his "Summa" contained the first complete textbook on accounting. The other reason is his fancy friends: Della Francesca—and Leonardo da Vinci (imagine that), who illustrated Pacioli's work on proportion.

"The central message for today's accountants is that a thinker of Pacioli's stature who hung around with Leonardo for years saw accounting as important," says Prof. Tinius. "This lifts the intellectual roots of accounting off of Bob Cratchit's dusty desk and deposits them in the fertile intellectual milieu of the Italian Renaissance." Pacioli helps accountants be "less apologetic" about their work, he adds.

To help spur interest in the Pacioli quincentennial, Profs. Weis and Tinius have joined forces in Sansepolcro with a local showman, Giuseppe Del Barna. Mr. Del Barna heads a troupe of acrobats in historical garb who toss big flags in the air at medieval festivals in old castles. The professors hope the performers, who call themselves Gruppo Sbandieratori, will help attract several hundred accountants from around the world to attend the 1994 events.

Judging from response to the preliminaries, the Pacioli fest may be a tough sell. A preview tour of Sansepolcro last September was a dud. Only a dozen accountants signed up, so it was canceled. "The timing just wasn't good, as college semesters had already begun, but we're much more sanguine about the real thing next year," says Prof. Tinius.

If the current state of knowledge among accountants about Pacioli is any portent, the real thing may flop, too. Even Eugene Flegm, general auditor of General Motors Corp. and a member of the quincentennial committee, concedes the general state of ignorance. "I showed the Pacioli video to about 30 accountants at my company and only two or three had ever heard of him," he says.

University of Rhode Island Prof. Vangermeersch recalls the tepid reaction of 25 members of Beta Alpha Psi, the accounting fraternity, to the video when it was shown on campus in Kingston. "There were lots of yawns and shuffling feet," he recalls. "It's hard to convince accounting students they have famous forebears."

Even in literature, says Prof. Vangermeersch, the only famous accountant was Daniel Defoe, who wrote "Robinson Crusoe." Unfortunately, Defoe was a terrible businessman and failed in a series of ventures, the professor observes. "Even as a dissenter and pamphleteer, he was tarred and feathered by the public."

Meet Jacques Coe:
He Goes to Wall St.
For a Wonderful Life

A 98½-Year-Old Broker Puts
Stock in Being Contrary
And Needling the Mighty

By Michael Siconolfi

5/15/92

NEW YORK—Being one of the world's oldest stockbrokers means never having to sell memories short.

And Jacques Coe, 98, has plenty of them. As he sits in his small cubicle at Cowen & Co.'s midtown office, he ticks off a few of the high points. He boasts of his secret formula for market success, and he claims (and others grudgingly agree) to have fathered the use of charts on Wall Street, back in 1916 or so. Pinned to one wall is a rotogravure from the New York Times, January 1926. It is of him and another youngish broker, and the caption reads ". . . on the road to success."

Mr. Coe points out he had wavy brown hair then. Now, the surviving strands are white. He is slightly stooped. But no matter. "At 98½, I've got all my buttons and all my marbles," says the sprightly limited partner, dressed nattily in a blue blazer, gray slacks and a blue tie emblazoned with golden bulls and bears.

Mr. Coe is one of the few Wall Street brokers to have been alive for nearly half the life of the Big Board, which celebrates its 200th anniversary this Sunday. In fact, Wall Street historians can't think of anyone older who is still active. As he nears his own second century, colleagues and clients agree that he has a zest for life and the markets. "He has tremendous insight into the market," says Leonard Kline, branch manager of his office. "His greatest asset is his brain—and it's still working at that age."

Of course, being an oldster does pose some problems. Mr. Coe, a widower, frets about what will happen to his business when he passes on. He suspects his secretary of vying to snatch his clients when he dies. "She may have aspirations," says Mr. Coe, "but I'll be passing them on to Jack." That is his son, a broker at Oppenheimer & Co., who, Mr. Coe notes, is "72—he's no chicken."

Mr. Coe's 62-year-old secretary got her broker's license about a year ago and doesn't yet have any clients. "I certainly would like to stay in the business," she says. "But I'm not looking forward to his demise." Jack Coe doesn't expect to inherit much business, anyway: Some of the clients are nearly as old as the elder Mr. Coe himself.

While Mr. Coe rattles off details of Wall Street in the '20s, he concedes he has some trouble recalling the recent past—like whether he has read "The Over the Hill Test: A Humorous Way to Face the Truth About Your Age," which sits on a dresser in his apartment. His health is not perfect, either. He had to cancel an appointment one recent day because his teeth had been removed for what he calls "upgrading." He sometimes uses a cane. Long known as a ladies' man, he freely grouses that he hasn't had sex since age 90.

But he still hammers out a respectable "Embraceable You" on his Steinway grand piano, awakens to an imposing nude hanging above his bed and squires dates to the theater. He also reckons the callow youth coming to Wall Street today could learn a thing or two from his life.

For one, he says, be a contrarian: He likes to buy stocks that are out of favor. For another, don't be intimidated by power. He is a prankster who lampooned Wall Street's elite through the years by helping to edit the Daily Muse (a now-defunct parody of the Daily News) and the Bawl Street Journal (a spoof of, well, you know).

In one 1930s gag for the Daily Muse, he took a photo of financier Arthur Lipper—grandfather of mutual-fund guru Michael Lipper and investment banker Arthur Lipper—shaking hands with a colleague. But Mr. Coe cut off the colleague's head and replaced it with Al Capone's. The headline: "Lipper Opens Chicago Office." Mr. Lipper was not amused. Then Mr. Coe says he compounded the slight by telling Mr. Lipper's son: "I had to apologize to Mr. Capone" for the incident. Mr. Lipper's grandson Arthur now says: "My grandfather was stuffy as hell—he was the stereotypical pompous Wall Street guy of the period—which to my eyes makes it even funnier." Michael Lipper calls the spoof "inflammatory."

Needling high-and-mighty Wall Streeters is "natural" for Mr. Coe, says his son, Jack. "He was not one of the inside group on Wall Street— the fact that he was an immigrant, the fact that he was poor, the fact that he was Jewish was always driving him," he says.

Indeed, Mr. Coe is the prototypical self-made man. Born on Nov. 19, 1893, in Amsterdam, Holland, he moved with his parents to Brooklyn when he was eight. He quit high school after a year and, taking a cue from Horatio Alger books, went to Wall Street to make his fortune. Despite his immigrant past, he says, "my English is better than the supergraduates of Harvard, Princeton or Yale." He adds, "I never split an infinitive."

He started as a runner on the Big Board in 1908. The pay was $5 a week. He eventually was hired by Jules Bache, founder of what is now Prudential Securities Inc., and later launched his own firm, which subsequently merged with Cowen, a small New York–based brokerage firm. Now, he says, his net worth is more than $2 million. He gets a "minuscule salary" of less than $100,000 "just for my brains and being the oldest active broker on Wall Street."

Well, almost active. On a recent afternoon, Mr. Coe sits quietly in his small cubicle. The phone hasn't rung all day. (He goes to the office each day for several hours; the rest of the time he works at his five-room apartment at 65th Street and Madison Avenue.) "The last thing I am is a pusher," he explains, feet propped on his tidy desk. "I haven't called on a client today."

Of Mr. Coe's 30 or so clients, most are well-to-do widows or widowers who have known him for years. He rarely trades for them; most of their $30 million in assets are in tax-exempt bonds, he says. He currently recommends just two stocks: Bethlehem Steel Corp. and Armco Inc.

"He's very conservative," says Clair Morris, a 90-year-old widowed client. "He won't advise me to do anything wild or out of line." She has no qualms that his age will affect how he handles her account. "He's amazing," Mrs. Morris says. "His mind is very alert—he has almost total recall."

Mr. Coe crows about a secret formula that tells him whether stocks are a buy or sell. He tallies the difference between the Dow Jones Industrial Average and the New York Stock Exchange composite index—then adds a numerator that he refuses to disclose. "This spread is my own invention," he says, pointing to his head.

But it isn't foolproof. His two stock picks—Armco and Bethlehem Steel, or Bessy, as he affectionately calls it—haven't moved much. Still, he says, "These two stocks will make money for me and my clients—I am absolutely positive."

How now the Dow? Down, down, down, Mr. Coe says, citing the recent explosion of initial public stock offerings. "That, to me, having been on Wall Street for nearly 85 years, is an indicator that the market is very much overbought," he says. But it doesn't affect Mr. Coe much. He owns only 5,000 shares of stock; most of his own portfolio is in tax-exempt bonds.

What keeps him young at heart are two small vices, a daily cigar and a vodka and tonic (no ice), and his wide-ranging loves—piano, chess, reading, theater and women, especially women. "He likes the girls and the girls like him. He's clever, funny and sharp," says Allen Kaufman, a friend and chess partner.

Mr. Coe is optimistic he will make it to the century mark. When he recently wanted to buy some one-year Treasury bills, a Cowen colleague told him he was only able to buy three-year notes. Mr. Coe's response: "Buy the three years—I'll be around."

Bojidar Yanev Has
A Passion for Bridges
That Doesn't Quit

As Chief Inspector of Spans
In New York City, He Is
An Aerialist With a Ph.D.

By Daniel Machalaba

11/6/91

NEW YORK—With lights flashing and sirens wailing, six police cars raced
to the Williamsburg Bridge to investigate a report that a man was climbing to the top of the main cable.

Officers blocked two lanes of traffic. A patrol boat was positioned
below the bridge, just in case.

"Come down, slowly," an officer with a loudspeaker shouted to the
man perched 300 feet above the East River.

He did, too, but not gladly, and not all the way. When he got within
about 60 feet of the police, he dropped them his business card.

This wasn't the only time Bojidar Simeonov Yanev (his friends call him
Yanev) has been mistaken for a jumper: It has happened to him three
times this year on that one bridge between Manhattan and Brooklyn.

"It's a big nuisance, the police give me hell," says Mr. Yanev, who is
chief bridge inspector for the city's Department of Transportation. He is
in charge of the 40 inspectors who monitor 872 bridges owned by the city,
and he is out there himself acting like an aerialist.

The police aren't the only ones watching Mr. Yanev. With more than
half the city's bridges in an advanced state of decay, the Bulgarian-born
Mr. Yanev and his crew are the first line of defense against catastrophe.

New Yorkers may not know him and his daredevil style, but Mr. Yanev
is a celebrity abroad, where the decline and fall of New York's bridges is
a matter of amazement.

Mr. Yanev's slide shows of rusted beams, cracking girders and crum-
bling concrete pack meetings in Paris and his native Sophia. "New York
is the best laboratory in the world for studying the consequences of
deterioration," says Jacqueline Llanos, a research analyst at the Central
Laboratory for Bridges and Highways in Paris. Adds Iskra Nesheva, a
research associate in Sophia and a Yanev family friend: "There isn't any-

thing he loves as much as the bridges, except his mother."

A Japanese TV crew recently filmed him climbing cables like a circus performer (Look, Ma, no hands) for a show called "A Man Over Troubled Bridges." And he has played host to more than 30 tours of the city's bridges for the enlightenment of engineers, politicians, business leaders, reporters and visitors from as far away as Tokyo and Helsinki.

A Columbia University doctor of engineering science, the 44-year-old Mr. Yanev, Dr. Yanev really, has always been a showman. As a teen-ager, he toured Europe playing the violin with the Bulgarian Children's Philharmonic Orchestra. In New York, he has been known to play his violin on a Greenwich Village street corner; one night he made $30 from passersby. Now he teaches a graduate course at Columbia in "buckling," the science of forecasting when a structure will give way. A field trip to a buckled bridge is a must, he says, given the "rich field of examples" the city offers. His favorite is the Honeywell Bridge over railroad tracks in Queens.

Tagging along with Dr. Yanev brings out the acrophobia in a reporter who didn't know he was afraid of heights. Because of Dr. Yanev's lifelong fascination with acrobats and his irresistible urge to act like one, he is known as "Spiderman" among city officials.

At the dilapidated Madison Avenue Bridge over the Harlem River, the tall, lean, lithe Dr. Yanev scrambles up exposed reinforcing bars on a bridge pier, scattering bits of concrete as he goes. Coming down, he grasps a rusting bar like a swaying birch and glides to the riverbank. "Someone has been playing here," he says, explaining the damage. But structurally the problem "isn't so serious."

At the Manhattan Bridge, dressed in an orange jump suit and wearing rubber-soled wing tips, Dr. Yanev casually traverses a beam 120 feet above the East River, pointing out cracks. As usual, he wouldn't dream of wearing a hard hat and safety harness. "Does an airline pilot wear a parachute?" asks the longtime admirer of French tightrope walker Philippe Petit.

"Compared to the French acrobats, what I do is rather pedestrian," adds Dr. Yanev, who once invited Mr. Petit to join him on the cables of an East River bridge. Still awaiting the reply he never got from Mr. Petit, Dr. Yanev was arrested last summer attempting to scale the Pont Massena, 60 feet above Parisian railroad tracks. His interest was purely intellectual, he says: He wanted to learn more about cable-stayed design, of which the Pont Massena is a striking example. It looks, he notes, like a stylized Christmas tree.

Dr. Yanev's angular, rubbery features come alive when he talks about bridges. His office at the city's Bureau of Bridges is decorated with broken stanchions, rusted steel plates and concrete chunks gathered during inspections. The day last April he was mistaken by police for a jumper, Dr. Yanev was searching the cables of the Williamsburg Bridge for the source of a steel clip that had crashed through someone's windshield. The driver of the car was unharmed, but other bridge failures have cost lives. The city currently is defending itself against a suit brought by the family of a dental technician who was crushed under a falling 400-pound chunk of concrete on the FDR Drive.

Dr. Yanev has pictures of the Eiffel Tower and the Golden Gate Bridge on the walls of his Manhattan apartment. The windows afford a view of the Brooklyn, Manhattan and Williamsburg bridges. In his spare time, he reads the treatises of famous New York bridge designers.

"He's a bridge artist," says Samuel Schwartz, the former Transportation Department chief engineer who hired Dr. Yanev. Mr. Schwartz is in awe, not of Dr. Yanev's derring-do, but of his expert judgments: "He told me to restrict or close some bridges, and he was right. Other times, he told me to keep a bridge open. He was always right."

Dr. Yanev, en route, is no more predictable than Dr. Yanev aloft. He makes an abrupt U-turn in Harlem to wash his city-owned Chevrolet Celebrity in water from a gushing hydrant. He blocks traffic on the Kosciuszko Bridge when he stops the car to take a photo of cemetery gravestones against a backdrop of New York skyscrapers. "I shouldn't do this, but I want this shot," he says as horns blare. "The best view of the city is from the bridges."

New York City officials say a $3.3 billion rebuilding program will take care of the city's bridge problems by the year 2004. But by that time, Dr. Yanev observes, "we'll need a new bridge program."

For now, New York is where the action is in bridge decay. "No other city in the world built so much and neglected so much," says Dr. Yanev, who boasts that New York's data on how spans fall apart are unexcelled.

Dr. Yanev says he once had dreams of designing bridges; inspecting them he considered a "professional rock-bottom low." The son of Bulgaria's chief bridge and highway engineer, Dr. Yanev came to America in 1972 in search of freedom, opportunity and challenge. But after earning his doctorate in 1976, he found no work to love until 1990, when he found his métier in this dangerous, rewarding $64,900-a-year job.

Bridge inspection, he now feels, is "the best of all possible worlds. You get to look at all these excellent problems, and all of it is essential to the life of New York City itself," he says. "And you also get to walk on these bridges."

From a tower of the Williamsburg Bridge, Dr. Yanev takes in the sweep of downtown Brooklyn, the twin towers of the World Trade Center, the nearby Manhattan and Brooklyn bridges and a barge 30 stories below. When he steps onto the cable and grips the handropes and walks toward Manhattan, he says he imagines that "I'm holding the bridge by the reins and riding it into the city."

She Has Her Eyes
Open, Ears Flappin'
And a Nose for News

———

Marian Houghton, 78, Writes
Features by the Dozen
In Little Jaffrey, N.H.

———

By Ellen Graham

3/18/91

JAFFREY, N.H.—Let other reporters rake muck and chase Pulitzers. Marian Houghton is content to cover this pretty little town and its 5,000 residents like a blanket.

Chronicler of Grange and VFW meetings, antiquarian teas and bean suppers, the 78-year-old feature writer for the Jaffrey-Rindge Chronicle got her start in the news business just six years ago. But she is fast making up for lost time.

Open the 1,500-circulation weekly Chronicle, and there is Marian Houghton's byline splashed all over the front page, and most pages that follow. Her column, "Ear to the Ground," is on the editorial page—and another column contains tidbits she collects while gathering other news. And don't forget the photo credits: Mrs. Houghton fills the Chronicle with snapshots of local doings, taken with a Vivitar automatic slung on a chain around her neck.

"I try to limit myself to 10 stories a week plus the columns," she says, stressing that she's a part-timer.

It is only a few miles from Jaffrey to Peterborough, N.H., immortalized as Grover's Corners in Thornton Wilder's "Our Town." In these parts, a line from that play is as true today as it ever was: "In our town we like to know the facts about everybody."

To that end, Mrs. Houghton says, "I listen. I keep my eyes open and my ears flappin'." Jaffrey fairly crackles with news: not the sort that shakes the world, perhaps, but rather the homely routines and rituals that stitch a community together.

Townsfolk are forever calling her with tips, or stuffing press releases in her mailbox. "They say Marian, I've got a hot lead for you," she says, "when sometimes it's so lukewarm that you wish they hadn't wakened you." Like the night the stable called to report that a horse had kicked over the carriage it was pulling, injuring a passenger. But by then, the horse had run off and there was nothing to photograph but a broken horseshoe. "I wasn't goin' out for that at 7 o'clock at night!" she says, still indignant.

When she was 72 and working as a saleswoman at a local arts and crafts shop, Mrs. Houghton got her big break. The State Line News in Winchendon, Mass., offered her the job of Jaffrey correspondent. (The paper subsequently became the Jaffrey-Rindge Chronicle, and now is part of the Worcester County Newspapers chain.) Mrs. Houghton was recruited more for her longstanding roots in the community than for proven journalistic skill; though she had once written radio commercials, she had never before tackled a news story or operated a camera. But she rose to the challenge, dictating her own terms from the start.

Finding it "degrading" to be paid by the column inch (10 cents an inch, 12 cents if she made the front page), she held out for a salary. She insists on working out of her home rather than making the 20-minute drive each day to the paper's Winchendon editorial offices. Nor will she cover night meetings in winter if roads are slippery. "And I won't chase ambulances," she says. "The only thing we'd gain is me taking a grisly picture, and I don't think that's fair to the person, dead or alive."

Otherwise, she keeps a schedule that would exhaust many a cub reporter. Donning Reeboks on a recent icy morning, she heads out with briefcase in hand for the Jaffrey Grammar School, where a preliminary heat of the National Geographic Society's "geography bee" is in progress. A fifth-grader is puzzling over this question: "What four-legged animal is used by the Indians of the Andes as a beast of burden?" "A crocodile?" he ventures shakily. Mrs. Houghton snaps the contestants' picture in front of a map, and is on to her next appointment: St. Patrick's School, where they are celebrating National Catholic School Month.

Before heading for her afternoon assignment, a profile of the drama director at nearby Franklin Pierce College, Mrs. Houghton sits in her Dodge Omni and, as is her custom, writes up the morning's items on the fly. "That way," she says, "I come home with three stories ready to put on the word processor."

Evenings, she usually mulls over her column in her La-Z-Boy recliner. These range from humorous family anecdotes (a widow, she has six children, 10 grandchildren and three great-grandchildren) to tart commentary on the passing scene. (Here she is on wearing a flattering new scarf: "As I went out the door, I heard 20 years drop with a thud behind me and I skipped down the path." In another, she describes a bicyclist as wearing ". . . parachute boots and sheer green Spandex briefs, which exposed a shocking display of rear cleavage.")

Jaffrey doesn't lack for excitement. When an elderly local woman broke her hip on a visit to Montreal, the operator of the Jaffrey airport invited Mrs. Houghton along to help escort the woman home. She flew up and back the same day, delivering the invalid to a crowd of well-wishers waiting on the Jaffrey runway and delivering a story for the front page.

Then there was the day the local fireworks factory blew up. Mrs.

Houghton got to the scene ahead of the fire trucks. "I made believe I was deaf to get by the cops," she says.

But don't look to Mrs. Houghton for scandalmongering or sensationalism. "Living alone, I don't want to get into that," she says. "I might find myself under the bed instead of on it." She was just as happy to let others cover the town meetings about a local teen-age Satanic cult ("candles and dead cats," she says with a shudder). She did attend a meeting of the American Legion women's auxiliary where the police chief spoke on local crime. "He told it like it was," Mrs. Houghton says. "And those biddies almost dropped their teeth." The chief's remarks, she adds, were "too rough to print."

During the 1988 presidential primary, when Sen. Robert Dole made a swing through Jaffrey, Mrs. Houghton got to observe the big-time media firsthand. "I was walking into the high school and someone said, 'The press is upstairs,' " she recalls. "Well, there were the AP, the New York Times, and the TV people all piled in with their tripods, lights and video cameras. What a grubby bunch—and the women just as bad as the men!" She says she was "too stunned" to ask a question at the press conference, but she got the senator's picture afterward.

Mrs. Houghton takes pains not to ruffle feathers locally—though she admits that when friends see her coming they say, "Stop talking, here comes the snoop." Indeed, Jaffrey seems to embrace her precisely because she is so unlike the yapping news hounds they watch on TV. "People trust her," says Martha O'Connor, the Chronicle's publisher. "She covers what's really important in little New England towns."

Jaffrey innkeeper Barry Miller concurs, suggesting that abrasive reporters would strike out with the locals here. "They'd get the real Yankee 'Can't say not knowin' response," he says. "They wouldn't find out a thing."

Alfred P. Sawyer is one such "damned, arrogant Yankee," as he describes himself. His family settled in this area 13 generations ago, and as Jaffrey's state representative, his avowed purpose is "to prevent legislation." As he guides a horsedrawn sleigh through a snowy woods, he reflects on Jaffrey and Marian Houghton's place in it. "This town runs smoother than most," he says. "It's so conservative that there's not a lot of muck for even reporters to find."

Maybe so, but there are 5,000 stories in this town, and Mrs. Houghton is determined to ferret them out. "Everybody has a story in their own funny way," she says. "There's something in there that they didn't know they had until you let them talk."

II

CREATURES, GREAT AND SMALL

Einstein Bird Has Scientists Atwitter Over Mental Feats

He May Be an Avian Genius Or the Great Pretender; Polly Wants a Thesaurus

---

By David Stipp

5/9/90

EVANSTON, ILL.—It is always awkward for a reporter when a source stops answering his questions, moves closer and gently chews his ear. But allowances must be made for eccentric geniuses.

The biting intellect here is an African Grey parrot named Alex, a research animal at Northwestern University. For 13 years he has fraternized only with people and now regards them as members of his flock—sometimes even preening the scruffier ones about the ears. But identifying with humans isn't what makes him special.

Nor is his ability to whistle some Mozart and say things like "Tickle me." Parrots, after all, are uncanny mimics. But Alex isn't just a copycat. Asked the color of a bluish pen held before him, he cocks his head, ponders and expounds: "Baaloo!"

The Prof. Henry Higgins behind this former squawker is animal-intelligence researcher Irene Pepperberg. For 13 years she and her assistants have tirelessly acted out a kind of "Sesame Street" for Alex. Like Big Bird and friends, they perform simple word skits, day after day, while he watches in a small room stocked with toys, snacks and perches. They have slowly drawn him into the act.

Now he can name 80 of his favorite things, such as wool, walnut and shower. (Studiously copying Ms. Pepperberg's Boston accent, he says "I want showah" to get spritzed.) He knows something about abstract ideas, including soft, hard, same and different. He can tell how many objects there are in groups of up to six. When he says, "Wanna cracker," he means it: Handed a nut instead, he drops it and exclaims in his peevish old man's voice, "I WANT CRACKER." So much for the idea that our feathered friends are all just bird brains.

Some other animals, such as chimpanzees, have learned nonverbal communication. But Alex is the first animal to actually speak with a semblance of understanding. Ms. Pepperberg believes his conversational gambits prove that he can handle some simple abstractions as well as chimps and porpoises can.

When shown a group of varied objects Alex has learned to answer certain questions such as, "How many corners does the piece of red paper have?" with about 80% accuracy. That is, if he is in the mood. When bored, he tells his teachers to "go away" and hurls test objects to the floor. "Emotionally, parrots never go beyond the level of a three-year-old" child, sighs Ms. Pepperberg, a young 41-year-old, patiently picking up toys Alex has strewn about his room in an orgy of play.

Skeptics argue that Alex isn't as smart as he seems. He has "learned to produce a repertoire of sounds to get rewards," says Columbia University animal cognition expert Herbert Terrace. "The only thing distinguishing him from pigeons taught to peck buttons for food is that his responses sound like English."

But regardless of whether Alex grasps meanings as we do, he shows an "incredible, totally unexpected" power to make mental connections, notes Ohio State University psychologist Sarah Boysen, who works with chimps. Before Alex, scientists generally dismissed talking birds as mindless mimics.

For her part, Ms. Pepperberg sidesteps the fray, merely noting that Alex shows "language-like" behaviors. But she adds that parrots in the wild routinely perform mental feats—such as learning to sing complex duet with their mates—that prove they have a lot on the ball. Biologists sometimes call them "flying primates"—they have even shown evidence of using tools. Once when Alex couldn't lift a cup covering a tasty nut, he turned to the nearest human assistant and demanded crowbar style, "Go pick up cup."

Parrots tend to go loco and pluck out their feathers when caged alone, says Ms. Pepperberg, so they generally don't make good pets. Yet the talking-bird trade is booming, endangering many parrot species. Alex, whom Ms. Pepperberg bought for $600 in a Chicago pet store in 1977, may himself have been nabbed in the jungle. And he probably isn't an avian Einstein—he is just highly schooled. "It's possible I got a dingbat," his coach says.

If so, he proves how much inspired teaching can do for the dingy. Ms. Pepperberg, who took up bird research while getting her chemistry doctorate at Harvard University, has helped pioneer a new training strategy for animals that stresses human-like learning by social interaction. "There's been a lot of resistance to my work," she says, "because I don't use standard techniques." But not from Alex.

Standing on a chair, he is all eyes and ears as she and an assistant hand back and forth a date nearby—they're trying to add it to his lexicon. "I like date," says Ms. Pepperberg. "Give me date. Yum." Suddenly Alex ventures, "Wanna grain." "No," says Ms. Pepperberg, "date. Do you want date?" Alex preens, seemingly mulling it over. Then he says, "I want grape." That's good enough for now. She hands it to him and he takes a bite.

Another of her tricks resembles the way parents help tug their toddlers into verbal being—by acting as if babbling is meaningful. When Alex says something new, Ms. Pepperberg tries to "map" it to something he is likely to remember. After he learned "rock" and "corn," and spontaneously said, "rock corn," she got dried corn and began using that term for it. Similarly, "peg wood" was mapped to clothespin and "carrot nut" to the candy Boston Baked Beans. Alex no longer gets candy, though, for it makes him hyperactively "bounce off the walls, saying 'I want this, I want that,' " says Ms. Pepperberg.

Alex often seems to play with words like kids learning to talk. Overnight tape recordings revealed he privately babbles to himself, perhaps practicing new words. Once he saw himself in a mirror and asked, "What color?"—that's how "gray" was mapped. When a student blocked him from climbing on her chair, he uttered the only curse he's heard: "You turkey!"

These untrained signs of wit may be just "babble luck," says Ms. Pepperberg. Still, Alex sometimes seems to be groping for linguistic connections. Soon after first seeing apples, he called one a "banerry"—a word he hadn't heard. "No," Ms. Pepperberg gently reminded him, "apple." Alex persisted: "Banerry," he said, "ban-err-eeee"—speaking as his teachers do with new words. He still uses banerry, says Ms. Pepperberg, which after all makes sense: An apple tastes a little like a banana and looks like a big cherry, fruits he already knew.

Today, the gray eminence is again doing it his way. When Ms. Pepperberg holds up two keys and repeatedly asks, "How many?" he plays dumb. Finally, she calls a "time out," leaving the room. Moments later, Alex looks at me, eyes the keys, and spits out, "Two."

Not-So-Subtle Slugs
Have Many Lovers,
Including Scientists

Researchers Are Attracted
To Their Amazing Minds;
But the Critters Dig Sex

By Eric Morgenthaler

2/13/92

VIRGINIA KEY, FLA.—Although it is too early in this article to discuss orgies, suffice it to say that sea slugs are much more interesting creatures than they might at first appear.

That's good, for sea slugs resemble nothing quite so much as blobs of mottled wild-cherry Jell-O. They while away the hours nibbling seaweed and drifting lazily in a saltwater haze. When they are irritated, they secrete clouds of purple ink. The most complex thing about them is their name: Some people call them "sea hares," claiming their antennae resemble ears, while most call them sea slugs, although they aren't slugs at all. Their scientific name is Aplysia.

Even one of the creature's biggest fans, Columbia University neurobiologist Eric R. Kandel, says Aplysia—a mollusk with an internal shell—exhibits "limited behavior, even compared to other invertebrates." What he means is a squid would be livelier company.

Yet that helps explain why people such as Dr. Kandel are drawn to slugs. They love them for their minds.

It also is why the University of Miami, in cooperation with Dr. Kandel, is raising thousands of the creatures in a laboratory in a converted garage near a nude beach on this little island off downtown Miami. Scientists say the Aplysia Resource Facility, as it is called, is the world's only commercial sea-slug farm.

The sign on the front door, yellow and diamond-shaped like a traffic marker, reads "SLUG XING," with a silhouette of a snail. Staffers sometimes answer the phone, "Slugs R Us."

Every Tuesday, the lab sends out hundreds of live sea slugs to scientists around the globe. The creatures are sorted by size—most would fit in a person's hand—packaged in long plastic sacks, then put in boxes for overnight shipping. The recipients use the animals in some of the most cutting-edge research going on today in the biology of learning and memory.

"Aplysia has a simple repertoire of behavior—it does nothing but eat, rest and copulate—and that's what makes it important," says Thomas R. Capo, a biologist and manager of the lab here, which is funded by the Howard Hughes Medical Institute, in Bethesda, Md.

"If you get into something complex, like a mouse or a rat, it just makes life more difficult," he says. "The fact that this is so simple makes it a wonderful research model."

The slug, indeed, seems made for study. It has relatively few neurons, or nerve cells—only about 20,000, compared with billions in, say, a mouse—but those it has can reach a millimeter in diameter, or more than 1,000 times the size of human brain cells. Columbia's Dr. Kandel says Aplysia has the largest nerve cells of any animal known.

The combination of size and simplicity—the neurons are bunched into 10 groups, called ganglia—has enabled scientists to work out "wiring diagrams," showing the role of individual nerve cells in behavior. Researchers inject slugs with dye, then use electronic tracing devices to monitor everything from the "firing pattern" of individual neurons to the scene at the synapses, where nerve cells connect.

Although the slug's system is a primitive one, its lessons aren't. "Aplysia is very good for studying higher-order features, such as how synapses change as a result of experience, how they are modified in short- and long-term memory, and what molecular events underlie memory," says Dr. Kandel, who since the 1960s has pioneered the study of Aplysia as a research model.

"You may have to survive in life as a blob at the bottom of the ocean, but you do have to survive," he notes. "You have to distinguish food that's nutritious from food that's poisonous. You have to distinguish a predator from your sexual partner. The fact is, these animals show quite good learning capabilities."

Today's farming activities date to the early 1970s, when Dr. Kandel and a graduate student, Arnold Kriegstein, launched an Aplysia-breeding project as part of Dr. Kandel's work on the molecular foundations of learning and memory. Dr. Kandel wanted lab-bred slugs in order to guarantee a quality-control that wasn't possible with slugs gathered in the wild.

Successfully breeding the creatures, however, took a full decade—first in New York, then at Woods Hole, Mass., where the project moved in 1978. "The animals are very fastidious," explains Richard J. Bookman, a lab technician during the mid-1970s, who recalls years of frustration with "a zillion little details." The last breeding problems were solved in 1983, but feeding problems lingered. The lab couldn't grow seaweed in cold weather, and it had to buy hundreds of pounds of it each week. Finally, in 1989, the lab moved to south Florida, where it could grow its own seaweed all year long.

Today, the Aplysia lab is an efficient, cheerfully casual operation across town from the University of Miami's main campus. Tropical plants snake around the two-story structure, and a blue racing bike leans against the door. Inside, a radio blares the Rolling Stones, and a sign on a bulletin board reads, "The only difference between this place and the Titanic is they had a band." Six people work on the project, tending slugs and weekly harvesting 500 pounds of red seaweed, the sea slug's bread-and-butter.

The "grow-out lab" where the slugs are raised is clean and brightly lighted, with rows of three-gallon clear-plastic tanks in which slugs loll about. The number of slugs per tank varies from two to 300, depending on their size, and each tank is marked with a tape giving the age and lineage of the occupants. Each slug gets a daily shower—the tank-water level is lowered, and the creatures gently hosed off—and a weekly move to a clean tank.

The slugs act sluggish. "They don't really do anything," says Lynn Hiskey, who runs the grow-out lab. But, she adds, "I think they're kind of neat."

The lab keeps a brood stock of about 20 animals, but most slugs are shipped out before they reach sexual maturity. Slugs range in price from $3 (for the smallest) to $20 apiece; an egg mass—which looks like a tangle of string and contains as many as three million eggs—goes for $5. Last year, the lab shipped about 22,000 slugs.

The slugs' tanks are filled with filtered seawater from Biscayne Bay, cooled to 50 to 55 degrees to slow the animals' development. Mr. Capo says that if the water is too warm, the slugs won't do anything but have sex all day. "Sometimes they sit there for hours doing it," he says.

Which brings us, very carefully, to orgies.

Sea slugs are hermaphrodites, meaning that each has both male and female sex organs. A slug can't have sex with itself, but otherwise the possibilities are endless. "In the field, they have mating orgies which could involve thousands of animals," says Mr. Capo, as he notes several small-scale versions in the lab's tanks. ("Here's a good one," he says, pointing to what seems to be three animals.)

Dr. Kandel writes that "group sex" or "chain copulation"—often involving up to 10 animals and forming a complete circle—is Aplysia's "most complex social behavior." It is also, he says, an example of "higher-order social behavior." At this point, we introduce another form of higher-order behavior—leaving well enough alone—and suggest that if you want to know anything more about sea-slug sex, or sea slugs, you consult your local science library.

See Spot Appeal:
A Condemned Dog
Bites Back in Court

California's Judicial System
Grinds Slowly for a Pit Bull
Waiting on Death Row

By Joan E. Rigdon

10/24/90

SANTA BARBARA, CALIF.—The condemned prisoner whimpers in the damp cell block on death row.

Meet Spot, an 85-pound pit bull with a bad reputation, a homeless owner called "Crazy Ed" and a recent arrest for biting three people. In other cities, where pit bulls are generally reviled, feared and executed without much delay, Spot would have been a dog gone long ago.

But this is Santa Barbara, where professionals attend public pray-ins for rain and a scientist has sued for the right to be killed and have his head frozen so it can be revived someday and attached to another body when there's a cure for the tumor infecting his brain.

Here, few are fazed to learn that a dog has an attorney. Actually, Spot has had two attorneys, and the latest promises to take his case all the way to the California Supreme Court.

Spot is on his second stay of execution, this one from the state Court of Appeal. Meanwhile, a crack team from this city's prosecutor's office is plowing through a pile of papers filed on his behalf: more than 100 pages of testimony and appeals.

This is Spot's tale: His owner is a 38-year-old bearded homeless man named Ed Mannon, who is known as Crazy Ed because of his violent temper. Mr. Mannon got Spot as a puppy four years ago after Spot failed to prove his worth as a fighter in an initial bout with another pit bull. Mr. Mannon says homeless people need dogs. "The reason I got into a dog as a protection number is because there was a guy shot dead in his sleep," he explains.

One night in March, while Mr. Mannon and Spot slept at an encampment for the homeless, two pedestrians walked by. What happened next is in dispute. The pedestrians say Spot attacked them without warning; Mr. Mannon claims the passersby were trying to steal a radio.

Police say they arrived in time to see the pedestrians running from Mr. Mannon, who was yelling "Attack!" to an excited pit bull. The passersby and Mr. Mannon all suffered dog bites and were treated and released at a nearby hospital.

After police impounded Spot, Mr. Mannon hounded lawyers in search of counsel. Most laughed at him. But Steve Balash, a high-profile, $150-an-hour criminal defense attorney, agreed to take the case on what could be called a pro bone basis as a favor to a friend of Mr. Mannon. Without legal representation, says Mr. Mannon, "I would have been rolled by the bureaucracy."

Mr. Balash, a Marine Corps veteran who often rides his Harley-Davidson to work, says, "It just wasn't fair. Spot got a bum rap." He says a second pit bull did some of the biting. And noting Mr. Mannon's claim that the passersby were trying to steal a radio, he adds: "If someone stole something from my back yard, I hope my German shepherd would bite them."

Mr. Balash demanded a trial, called a vicious-dog hearing, for Spot. Normally, the hearing would take place at police headquarters. But with more than a dozen witnesses and dozens more supporters, it was rescheduled for a community center near downtown. Mr. Balash hired his own court reporter. The atmosphere was tense. Reporters stood by. The only one missing was Spot, who remained in his cell in the county dog pound 10 miles to the west.

Sitting behind a cafeteria table, the "judge," police Lt. A.N. Katzenstein, listened patiently as several police officers and animal-control officers recounted the fight. But none personally saw Spot bare his fangs, bolstering one of Mr. Balash's defenses: that Spot's ex-girlfriend, another pit bull named Tina, did some of the biting that night.

Then Mr. Balash called numerous character witnesses, including a retired woman who thinks Spot is as sweet as Lassie and the president of a local engineering firm who sometimes brings food to the homeless, who testified that Spot is a milquetoast compared to domestic poodles. The climax of Mr. Balash's presentation was a color videotape of Mr. Mannon frolicking with Spot in his kennel on death row.

Nevertheless, Lt. Katzenstein sentenced Spot to death or life without parole in a dog kennel. Mr. Mannon says he would rather kill Spot than have him live that way. Besides, without a home, he has no back yard in which to build a kennel.

Mr. Balash responded with a 28-page appeal to county Superior Court. He argued that Spot didn't get a fair shake because he was judged by police in a case that involved police. He said police seized Spot without due process and failed to prove Spot is vicious. And, he said, the police are prejudiced against Spot and Mr. Mannon. In one confrontation, Mr. Balash alleged, a police officer pulled an apparent bag of ashes from his pants and told Mr. Mannon, "This is your dog, Spot." (The officer says Mr. Mannon provoked him.)

The county judge, a self-professed dog lover, agonized over the case and then refused to overturn the ruling. But he granted Spot a 30-day stay of execution. By then Mr. Balash was embroiled in a human murder defense, so he handed Spot's case over to a second lawyer, Will Hastings of the nonprofit Legal Defense Center.

Mr. Hastings obtained a longer stay of execution from the state Appellate Court, where he has filed an appeal. If the court agrees to hear the case, Spot gets a court date. If not, Spot gets executed.

Mr. Hastings vows to take the case to the state's highest court, but city officials say it won't get that far because the defense's arguments have no foundation in law. Besides, they note, Spot's rap sheet goes way back.

Pamela Christian, an animal-control officer, complains that since 1986 she has often seen the dog illegally leashed to the city courthouse while Mr. Mannon has been inside contesting a wide range of charges from illegal camping to possession of marijuana. Moreover, she says, the dog is mean.

Two years ago, Spot was impounded after he broke loose from Mr. Mannon, bounded across a four-lane street and bit a pedestrian, Ms. Christian says. According to police reports, the victim was beating on a pickup truck when Spot ran over. (The victim later said he was in town to tell President Reagan that the FBI had kidnapped his family.) Frightened, the victim hit Spot, whereupon Spot bit him.

In court, Mr. Balash argued that Spot only bites when provoked. Mr. Mannon testified that Spot is "100% friendly" as long as no one hits him with sticks or does other "freakazoid" things. City officials aren't biting. "Freakazoid things happen in society," says city law clerk Denise Kale.

Those officials are determined to keep Spot off the streets, but he has his supporters. Among them is the gossip columnist for the local weekly newspaper, who goes by the pseudonym Trixie. The column uses the unusual heading "Angry Poodle Barbecue" and a picture of a poodle with a bow in its hair and a barbecue fork in its paw. Trixie says that he would support a law against homeless people owning pit bulls, but that Spot is an exception.

Mr. Balash estimates he donated about $6,500 of legal time to Spot's case. So far, the Spot Legal Defense Fund, which has attracted donations from local citizens, has paid him $500.

For his part, Mr. Mannon takes 40-minute bus trips to visit Spot at the pound three or four days a week. He keeps a file of legal arguments, court documents, news clippings and letters on the case. "The only reason I'm doing it is because I owe it to him," Mr. Mannon says, explaining that once, when he was about to face a rap for possession of marijuana, Spot stepped in and ate the evidence.

Desperately Seeking Bubba: Beer Swiller, TV Fan and Boar

After Pampering the Piglet, Owners Fear the Worst: The Pet May Be Schnitzel

By Robert Tomsho

5/10/91

CORPUS CHRISTI, TEXAS—With his oversized head, spiked hair and scrawny legs, some might think Bubba ugly. His behavior too could be seen as crude—as a teen-ager he chugged beer and wet the bed.

But none of these little flaws stops Buddy and Patsy Thorne from missing him so badly they keep his photo enshrined in their living room. Five years after his disappearance, they still spend almost every scrap of their free time crisscrossing the Rio Grande Valley in search of him, sometimes armed with his favorite chocolate bars, which they sprinkle enticingly near alleged "Bubba sightings."

Actually, it's a quest that for a time caught up much of Bubba's hometown of Corpus Christi. Bumper stickers plastered the fenders of pickup trucks asking, "Where's Bubba?" Billboards pleaded, "Bubba, Call Home." After a local columnist wrote about Bubba, concerned citizens marched on city hall and local radio stations began blaring "The Ballad of Bubba." A local bar held a "Bubba Aid" concert.

But for Patsy Thorne, a former coffeeshop waitress who now works in the office of a small oil company, talking about the adopted little one whom state authorities took from her back in 1986 is almost too painful. "I just get all choked up," she says, referring all questions to her husband. As the Thornes' silver pickup truck rumbles down an isolated ranch road on yet another search, she simply whispers, "I'll never forget him."

It would indeed be hard to forget Bubba, who, despite his almost-human attributes, is—or perhaps was—actually a wild boar-like creature known in these parts as a javelina. Belittled as "musk hogs" and "cactus pigs," the normally funky-smelling javelinas (Bubba had had his musk glands removed) don't get much respect in their native Southwest. Their fearsome tusks have spawned a host of tall tales, although in truth, javelinas are more likely to run at someone out of nearsightedness than fury. Ranch hands use them for target practice, hunters stalk them for trophies and some determined cooks even turn them into schnitzel.

To the Thornes, however, Bubba was family. Found by Mr. Thorne as a piglet during a rattlesnake hunt, the eventual 90-pound porker lived with the Thornes for a decade. They say the experience transformed him into what sounds like a Texas Good Ole Boy. While the typical javelina dines on cactus roots, Bubba developed a taste for scrambled eggs, spaghetti and barbecued chicken. He could be finicky, refusing to eat vegetables unless they were divided into neat little piles on his plate.

Bubba's leisure-time activities were likewise unusual for the breed. He watched cartoons in the living room, snoozed in Buddy's easy chair and attended the Thornes' annual New Year's Eve bash—suitably attired in a party hat. "He would drink so much beer and then he would quit," says a respectful Buddy Thorne, a former rodeo cowboy turned construction engineer. "He knew his limits."

Most of his drinking was social. On evenings when Mr. Thorne was out of town, Bubba used to sip cold beer with Mrs. Thorne and listen to all of her problems. "She would sit there and talk with him as if he was me," says Mr. Thorne.

The Thornes' daughters brushed his tusks regularly—"He had his own toothbrush," Mr. Thorne explains. He even slept with them. Mr. Thorne still recalls the night one of his girls woke up screaming after Bubba wet the bed. "That rascal acted just like he knew what she was hollering about," Mr. Thorne says. "He jumped right out of that bed, ran all the way upstairs and got into a dry bed."

But what Bubba apparently didn't know for quite some time was that he was a javelina. He didn't take the news well. After the Thornes held a mirror up to him one day, his neck hair bristled and he scurried off, apparently in shock.

His own shock, however, was nothing compared to that of a new neighbor, a Yankee just moved in from St. Louis, who had a similarly hair-raising reaction when she peered over the Thornes' back fence one day five years ago. By the time the Thornes got home, the game wardens were there with tranquilizer guns. Over the Thornes' protests, the authorities loaded Bubba into their trunk and dropped him, still groggy, beside a back road 35 miles south of town. The location was kept secret from the family.

Buddy Thorne was cleared of misdemeanor charges of keeping a wild animal without a permit. He subsequently lost a civil suit against the game wardens accusing them of illegally entering his home and causing his family mental anguish by denying it Bubba's companionship. But a sympathetic judge ordered the wardens to reveal where they'd dropped Bubba.

Unfortunately, by then the trail was three months cold, and Bubba was nowhere to be found.

Driven by their devotion, the Thornes have kept searching ever since. They've pushed the odometer on Buddy's truck up to 97,000 miles and estimate that they've spent nearly $12,000 on legal fees and travel on Bubba's behalf.

With upward of 150,000 javelinas roaming the Lone Star State, the Thornes' chances of finding the one and only Bubba are slimmer than he ever was. They're not even sure he could survive in the wilderness. Pampered since piglethood, Bubba wouldn't touch warmed-over roast beef much less the uncooked fare available to most of his kind. And while javelinas have lived for up to 24 years in captivity, at 16, Bubba would be pushing the envelope for one in the wild.

Against the odds, the Thornes keep looking, sometimes pursuing what turn out to be only javelina-shaped rocks and shadows. Along the way, they have endured many indignities, from an awkward breakfast recently at a roadside cafe decorated with stuffed heads of Bubba's kin, to the occasional insensitive "wild hog tamale" joke.

The couple's spirits were boosted in December when they received snapshots from some Houston bowhunters who'd befriended a sociable javelina on a ranch about 110 miles west of Corpus Christi. Despite having several arrows shot over his head, the animal ambled into camp, let the men scratch his snout and posed for pictures.

The Thornes say the elderly animal was the spitting image of their Bubba. "It looked so close it was unreal," says Buddy. "It was the expression on his face, you know? He had that gentle look about him."

But despite several three-hour treks to the ranch, they have yet to find the familiar set of tusks among the scrubby stretches of mesquite and prickly pear.

Hard though the truth is to face, the Thornes have begun to realize that they may be running out of time. And so they have taken the necessary steps to give Bubba a decent end, purchasing a grave site for him at the Corpus Christi Humane Society's pet cemetery.

Bubba's resting place will be beside the grave of Kirby, the 200-pound sheep who shared the Thorne's back yard and was Bubba's bosom buddy. Kirby died two years after Bubba was taken, and Buddy recalls, "When we lost Bubba, he sulked so bad it was just like his life was gone." But then, Kirby is a whole other story.

Heartbreaking Fight Unfolds in Hospital For Valdez Otters

Rescuers Battle to Save Them With Antitoxins, Prayers; Otter 76 Strains to Breathe

---

By Charles McCoy

4/20/89

VALDEZ, ALASKA—It is 9:32 last Thursday morning, and Otter 76 is fighting for her life. She is pinned to a makeshift operating table in a clammy elementary school gym, lungs scored by petroleum poisons. She rattles and gasps, slow spasms rolling up in waves from her hind flippers to her bewhiskered snout. She foams at the mouth and she excretes crude oil. It takes four men to hold her down.

"Come on babes, hang on," exhorts Jeanie Clarke, a volunteer otter attendant from England. Veterinarian Riley Wilson, also a volunteer, frantically pumps drugs into the animal. "Live, damn it," he mutters, and implausibly, Otter 76 does live. The seizure subsides. At 9:43, Otter 76 goes back into her pen, and Mr. Wilson shakes his head and tells a colleague: "I didn't think she'd win that battle."

There will be more battles for her a few hours later. Otter 76 is one of hundreds of otters plucked from Prince William Sound since Exxon Corp.'s tanker, the *Exxon Valdez,* ran aground March 24 and smeared the sound's emerald waters with 10 million gallons of oil. Of those otters, only 134 made it alive into the improvised otter rescue center set up here in a gym by a patchwork crew of top marine mammal experts, volunteer animal lovers and hired hands. Their struggles to keep dying otters alive are desperate, touching, occasionally maybe even heroic. Sixty-eight of their otters have died. And counting.

The otter slaughter has become the most striking symbol of the nation's worst oil spill; the animal's mortality rate here has shocked even otter experts. It is far above anything ever seen in previous oil spills, even though otter rescue may be the only postspill operation in which about everything that can be done is being done. Otters that make it to the rescue center are swiftly scrubbed clean, pampered and spoon-fed, given oxygen, antitoxins and antibiotics and tender love and tears and prayers.

And still, they die. In a pen 10 yards away from where Otter 76 lies exhausted and trembling, a lactating mother otter, its newborn gone, sprawls listlessly. A young pup, its mother gone, rests fitfully in another pen nearby. The pup begins to whimper and cry, the mother answers, and a great keening chorus of otters swells up. Someone suggests maybe bringing mother and pup together, but it can't be done: Mother's milk is probably poisoned. So the motherless child and the childless mother sing their strange song, off and on, for hours.

A day later, they die within two hours of one another.

As of yesterday, there were 46 otters checked in at the otter hospital, just a small piece of an environmental picture that seems to darken daily. Scientists now say that as many as 4,000 otters—more than a third of the sound's pre-spill population—are presumed dead.

Some 5 million gallons of oil remain on the water. On many miles of shoreline, oil has seeped through the gravelly beaches into subterranean cavities. Tides will leach that oil back into the waters where the otters swim, probably for years.

All of which means they will be busy down at the otter rescue center for a long, long time.

The center was thrown together in the first frantic days following the spill by a ragtag team of animal lovers and volunteer veterinarians under the loose direction of the Sea World Research Center of San Diego, which is affiliated with the same Sea World that runs the killer whale and porpoise shows. Exxon is footing the bill, and Sea World's marine mammal experts say they have a blank check.

In three sleepless weeks, the center has gone from tiny, suffocating quarters in a junior college administration building to the less tiny but still suffocating quarters at the elementary school gym. Six rows of wooden pens, 96 pens in all, stretch from beneath one basketball goal to the other. A mixmaster of copper and plastic pipes snakes underfoot and overhead. The place is wet and the temperature is 47 degrees and it reeks of marine life. And marine death.

Early in the disaster, as many as 50 boats were retrieving otters and bringing them in for treatment. That's down to five boats now, all manned by professional registered otter rescuers. The U.S. Fish & Wildlife Service last week ordered amateur otter rescuers to cease and desist because "otters are mean and they bite," a spokesman explains. Five boats on the vastness of Prince William Sound are like five ants on a parking lot, and a lot of people here find this an incomprehensible step that will only mean fewer otters saved.

In any event, capturing the otters and getting them back to land can indeed be tricky work. Until they become too sick to mount any defense, even oiled otters will scramble and dive to get away from human hands. Mike Lewis, a biologist with the state's Department of Environmental Conservation, displays a jagged gash that loops around the whole circumference of his thumb.

"Tried to catch an otter with bare hands and duct tape," Mr. Lewis says. "For the first and last time."

He opens the cargo hatch of his helicopter; the otter, which was finally captured and stuffed in there, chewed through a six-inch section of steel sheeting. Helicopter pilots say one chopper came within a split second and a few feet of crashing into the sound when a 100-pound otter the pilot thought was dead revived and rampaged through the cockpit before being subdued.

Otter 76 presented no such difficulties. She was snared on April 5 while lying in the snow 30 feet from the water's edge at Bay on Knight Island, where some of the heaviest concentrations of oil hit. She didn't look too bad then. Her coat, golden brown with veils of silver and gray along her neck and snout, was only lightly oiled.

Once caught, otters are brought to a small scrubbing station in the junior college building. This is stage one of otter triage and it can be wild. One day last week four otters arrive, yowling in cages like the ones people use to take their dogs on airplanes. Jeremy Fitz-Gibbon, a barrel-chested mammal expert from the Vancouver Public Aquarium, inspects the otters as otter nurses load syringes and pass out rain gear. "This guy's got oil on him," Mr. Fitz-Gibbon announces.

Neil Utkov, a vet from Memphis who came here as a volunteer, pumps two shots of anesthetic into the struggling otter. What about an injection of antibiotics, someone asks. "Wait until he's out," the vet replies. "I don't want this guy to feel any more hurt than he has to."

In 15 minutes the animal is unconscious and laid out on webbing suspended over a basin. A load of Toxiban, a black slurry of activated charcoal meant to absorb oil poisons and pass through the body, is pumped through a tube down the otter's gullet. Then, using Dawn dishwashing liquid and hoses with garden spraying attachments, otter attendants painstakingly knead the animal's fur. Greasy, gray-black stew bubbles up between their fingers. Oil.

It takes about an hour and a half to scrub and dry each otter—almost too long for this animal. Midway into the process, he pops up as if on a spring and begins snapping at his handlers. "Easy boy," Mr. Utkov coaxes. He injects another blast of Valium into the animal, but the otter continues to fidget and writhe for the remainder of the operation.

The otters brought in on this day wear relatively little oil, an encouraging sign, but no guarantee of survival. R.V. Chalam, a toxicologist and pathologist from San Diego, says one of the things that has shocked scientists here most is the number of different ways in which oil is killing otters. Otters were always known to be particularly vulnerable to oil because they have no blubber and can't float or stay warm for long once oil mats their fur. Most of the missing and presumed dead otters in the sound just sank.

At the rescue center, however, Mr. Chalam's autopsies show that "these animals have livers that are totally destroyed, that crumble in your hand like dust." Additionally, "their immune systems are completely defused, making them extremely susceptible to secondary infection. There is emphysema not only in the lungs but throughout the body."

Mr. Chalam says this means that otters are being violently poisoned by the benzene, toluene, xylene and numerous other toxins in oil, which apparently can invade their bodies through inhalation, ingestion or simple penetration of the pores. In other words, it means "incredible pain."

A few hours after her seizure on April 13, Otter 76 seems to stabilize somewhat. She even tugs at a towel; otters, it turns out, like towels and like to curl up and hide their heads in them. Henry Iverson, an Athabascan Indian who is tending Otter 76, uses tongs to dangle a shrimp in front of her snout and she takes it, a good sign. "Man, I'd like to see her kicking back on a beach with her shades on and a can of beer in her paw," he says. "This girl's been through too much." Otter 76 spends the rest of that day and night resting, trembling some but eating a bit. "Maybe she'll make it," Mr. Iverson says. "At least she's holding her own."

Other otters are not. Outside the gym, 10 mesh-covered pens have been set up. The otter doctors have found that moving outside sometimes perks an otter up; some otter attendants have even taken to calling the dimly lit gym the "Death House." But even outside, Otter 81, nicknamed Otto, lies shuddering in a blue cage. Jake Matulka. a volunteer from Anchorage, kneels motionless in front of the cage, resting his head against it. He watches silently for several minutes. "I think he's going down," Jake says finally, to no one in particular. "Come on bud, play with your towel. Come on."

Otter 81 lingers for about an hour more. He dies at 5:18 P.M. on April 13.

Not all the news at the center is so grim. On Friday, April 14, a handwritten sign near the center's entrance proclaims that six otters treated here and shipped out to Point Defiance Zoo near Tacoma, Wash., earlier in the week are still alive and doing well. "Yeah!!" the sign reads. It is a moment of accomplishment and of progress. The center shipped six otters out to Sea World two weeks ago, but only one survived.

Eventually, all the otters the center manages to save will have to be sent somewhere—and it probably won't be back into the wild. "They can't go home again," says Mr. Fitz-Gibbon. "They're better off in aquariums than in oil." Scientists say they may try transplanting some otters to other regions, but they fear the otters will swim back to their home waters, no matter how distant.

Those who work with the otters stow away the small victories to help them cope. Many of the otter handlers came as volunteers and stayed on as Exxon shifted to a paid staff. Some have been here for weeks, and they've seen a lot of melancholy things. Jeanie Clarke, the English volunteer, was vacationing in Anchorage when the oil spilled. She hitched the six-hour ride to Valdez to help otters; one day two weeks ago, she spent 17 straight hours nursing a pup. "I was sitting in the cage with it, holding it in my arms when it died," Ms. Clarke says. "Even after the tears, that stays in your gut."

Carolyn McCollum, a writer from Cary, N.C., also came to help the animals. "I drive a car, I use oil," says Mrs. McCollum, who is 30 years old and pregnant with her first child. "In a sense, I share in the blame for this. I had to do something." She has lost three otters, the most recent one on Friday night.

"She was moaning and crying, like a little girl on a Ferris wheel," Mrs. McCollum recounts. "It got to where I knew she was brain dead, but she was still breathing. You can't just put her in a bag and forget about her." So Mrs. McCollum cradled the otter in her arms until it stopped breathing, some time around 10 P.M.

At about the time Mrs. McCollum's otter died, one of the veterinarians checks up on Otter 76. She has been showing some signs of improvement, eating four shrimp and three pollack earlier that evening. The vet looks her over and scribbles two notations rapidly on Otter 76's chart.

The first is "Possible eyesight loss." The second is "Pregnant." Otter 76, it has been discovered, is fighting not for one life, but for two.

The scientists at the center say they're learning as they go. "We know a lot more than we did about the logistics of trying to save animals," says Terrie Williams, a research physiologist from Sea World who is running the day-to-day operations of the center. "We know it's a nightmare."

But no breakthroughs on how to actually save otters from oil—what drugs, if any, might limit the corrosive damage, for example—have been made. The scientists are talking with Exxon about establishing a permanent research facility here to keep searching for more effective treatments.

"That's the only good that could ever come out of this disaster—some knowledge that might help us save animals when this happens again," Ms. Williams says.

Ms. Williams stands near the pen where, just a few hours before, Otter 76 began heaving for breath again. The otter was given Regalan to reduce inflammation and more Toxiban, the poison absorber. She was force-fed, too, but soon she fell once more into short, jerky convulsions.

At 3:15 A.M. Saturday morning, Otter 76 shuddered one last time and died.

Stingrays Once Had An Image Problem, Now They're Cuddly

Which on Grand Cayman Cuts Several Ways for the Fish: Pat Kenney's Spoiled Idyll

---

By James P. Sterba

3/1/93

GRAND CAYMAN, BRITISH WEST INDIES—To understand how two dozen southern stingrays, four feet wide, overcame their trash-fish reputations, Stealth bomber looks and decades of human fear and loathing to become gregarious subsea celebrities worth millions of dollars to this island's economy, it helps to know something about the Wayne, Mich., police department, especially in winter.

There, through the 1970s and early '80s, toiled Lt. Patrick Kenney, a Detroit high-school dropout who grew up thinking stingrays had four wheels and hot engines. Having landed in Vietnam as a Marine in March 1965, survived, come home and fathered two children, he began to feel his job-satisfaction level sink with every petty drug bust and frigid, overcast February.

It got harder and harder to go home from diving vacations in the Caribbean. Finally, in 1982, Pat Kenney, then 35 years old, left Wayne's world for good. He settled on this island, 490 miles south of Miami, got work as a diving guide, met his second wife and began hanging around with some menacing-looking stingrays in a mangrove-fringed lagoon called North Sound.

Southern stingrays, one of many species of skates and rays, are flat, kite-shaped, cartilaginous cousins of sharks—drab gray on top, white on the bottom—that feed mainly on worms, crustaceans and shellfish. A poisonous (but not deadly) serrated stinger, several inches long, adorns their tail for defense, but they don't sting divers.

Stingrays tend to be skittish and avoid divers. But these rays were different. For years, Cayman fishermen had taken refuge from the open ocean in the lagoon's sandy shallows, just behind a barrier reef. There, they would clean fish and conches, and toss discards into the water where the rays and other fish would scarf them up. It happened regularly enough so the rays learned to hang around.

Gradually, divers began to anchor their boats there to rest and eat between dives on the outer barrier-reef wall.

"We'd have lunch and snorkel and three or four rays always hung around," says Mr. Kenney, who along with fellow dive master, Jay Ireland, was leading North Wall dive trips for Bob Soto's Diving Ltd. In 1986, in what Mr. Kenney says was a sort of epiphany, one ray began eating out of their hands. They named it "Hooray." Other rays quickly lost their shyness and joined in. It was thrilling, says Mr. Kenney, in part because "I didn't know whether the damned things had teeth." (They don't. They suck food into their softball-sized mouths and crush it with powerful jaws.)

Intrigued, Mr. Kenney began visiting them on weekends and days off. More rays showed up to be fed, covering him like sombreros and acting like puppies. He began to tell them apart, see different personalities, and name them "Jayray" and "Stubby"—male names because he didn't realize they were females. (Males are only half the size of females.)

Word spread. Underwater photographers, filmmakers and marine scientists arrived. So far as anyone knew, this kind of man-ray interaction hadn't happened before. Divers have long fed groupers, moray eels and even sharks, turning them into pliant photo models. But stingrays had previously kept their distance.

Like many misunderstood marine creatures, stingrays were long condemned because of their looks to "monster" status. Popular Mechanics magazine in 1930, before scuba-diving gear was invented, lumped stingrays, spotted eagle rays, manta rays, sharks and killer whales as "Outlaws of the Sea," calling them "vermin of the deep" and "vicious and valueless marauders" that governments should endeavor to wipe out.

Even when Skin Diver magazine put Cayman's rays on its cover in September 1987, its headline read, "Stingrays, Friend . . . Or Foe?" But the article itself stressed their friendly side, dubbing their haunt "Stingray City." Divers flooded Grand Cayman, already a scuba mecca, to frolic with the rays.

By 1989, the year the rays made the covers of both the Cayman Islands phone book and National Geographic, Stingray City—an otherwise boring patch of sand in just 12 feet of water—was on its way to becoming the single most popular dive site in the world. Dozens of dive-boat operators were running ray-feeding trips for groups of 10 to 25 divers. Some boats, catering to visiting cruise ships, brought 50 to 120 snorkelers at a time. Sometimes half a dozen boats anchored there at once. The rays were greatly outnumbered but didn't seem to mind.

David Vousden, who heads the government's Natural Resources Unit, which monitors Cayman's marine environment, estimates that Stingray City is visited weekly by nearly 1,700 divers and 1,200 snorkelers, who pay from $20 to $45 each to boat operators. By his calculation, the rays—which would sell for maybe $5 a pound as fish market fillets or fake scallops—bring in nearly $100,000 a week, or $5.2 million a year.

Mr. Kenney got neither rich nor famous. He did, however, have second thoughts as more and more people arrived. "I began to think I'd created a real monster," he says.

"Stingray hickeys" became badges of honor among divers. Since a ray's eyes are on its top side and its mouth is on its bottom, it can't see what it is eating and sometimes latches briefly on to a diver's skin, causing a bruise.

Lured by the food brought for the rays, the local population of yellowtail snappers exploded. The yellowtails, in turn, lured more sport fishermen. The rays went after the bait, too, getting hooked in the process. Usually, they are able to break the fishing line with ease. The result: lots of rays swimming around with hooks in their mouths and line streaming behind. Mr. Kenney started his own hook-removal service, carefully extricating hooks with wire cutters. He swears some rays approached him specifically to get their hooks removed—the same way big fish allow little fish to clean off their parasites. He has a collection of more than 30 removed hooks.

He also removed an underwater knife stuck in one ray. It got to a point a couple of years ago when rogue divers with videos would stab or gash a friendly ray to make it bleed in order to attract big bull sharks and hammerheads, which feed on rays, for filming.

The local dive operators association established rules for Stingray City: no gloves, which are like sandpaper on the rays' velvety skin; only dive guides are supposed to feed squid or ballyhoo, a baitfish, to the rays. But Mr. Kenney and others began to discover discarded plastic bags on the bottom—evidence of divers sneaking in food for the rays. The bags, still smelling of food, are also dangerous. Turtles, birds and fish, including rays, swallow them, can't digest or dislodge them, and die.

Dr. Tom Byrnes, a 36-year-old marine biologist who operates the Cayman Marine Laboratory, is a staunch conservationist who protects coral by banning gloves on the dives he leads. He isn't crazy about the circus aspects of Stingray City but says, "It's a small price to pay for educating all these people that these wonderful creatures aren't monsters."

Pat Kenney says dispelling myths is important—up to a point. For him, that point was October 1991. Bitter and disgusted by the hubbub he helped create, Pat Kenney not only quit going to Stingray City, he quit diving entirely. Now, he plays rugby for exercise. He and his wife operate two boutiques. Last month, he got laid off from his job with an import company.

Virginia Shell Game Foils Agents Trailing Escargot at Large

G-Men Fear a Voracious Snail That's a Delicacy to Some, A Driving Hazard to Others

---

By Erik Larson

9/25/92

BRYAN PARK, VA.—An albino ferret named Nikkie rockets through the gloom and smacks headlong into Buckwheat, the cat. A pacu, close cousin to the piranha, watches from its tank with infinite patience. The shuddery light of an afternoon TV cartoon plays across the faces of Debra and Earl Rea, who live here in perpetual dusk with a menagerie of swimming, crawling and slithering creatures.

Mr. Rea wants to relay a message to the federal agent who recently searched his home for a dangerous fugitive. "Tell him he's welcome to search it again," he says. "This time at our convenience." He stops. "And if they make a snail detector, tell 'em to bring that, too."

The fugitive in question is an enormous escargot. Specifically, Archachatina marginata, the dreaded giant African snail. It's big, hungry and prolific—so much so that when 1,012 of the creatures slipped past inspectors in New York last spring, they became the target of a nationwide snailhunt that brought federal agents to the homes and pet shops of hundreds of astonished Americans.

For Mrs. Rea, the dragnet is fast growing old. She doesn't have the snail, she insists. "Believe me," she says, "if I did have it I would have microwaved it myself."

"Oh, she's got it," says Frank J. Formichella, who heads the Virginia office of the U.S. Animal and Plant Health Inspection Service, or Aphis, the agency charged with protecting America's fields and herds from alien invaders. "The house had snakes in it, lizards, everything. Just the typical place where you'd expect to find one."

The giant African snail, long outlawed here, is the mother of all snails. Its shell can grow to the size of a softball. When it emerges to move, its body can extend as long as one foot, trailing a broad swath of shimmery slime.

Size isn't the problem, however. Giant African snails are hermaphrodites, and notorious for rapid reproduction. A single member of one species can generate 16 quadrillion relatives in just five years, according to Albert R. Mead, a malacologist, or mollusk expert. Just counting that many snails, he estimates, would take a person over half a billion years.

Thanks largely to Aphis's unsung efforts, the giant snail has yet to gain a beachhead on mainland America, although it's firmly established in Hawaii. In 1969, a Florida boy brought a few Hawaiian giants home in his pocket, launching an infestation that took seven years to eradicate.

The snails have invaded much of the Pacific, a legacy of Japanese troops who brought them along as food during World War II. Wandering masses of giant gastropods have consumed bean fields in the Philippines, rubber in Malaysia and cabbage in Saipan, becoming so populous in some places that they created a driving hazard. "On corners," says John B. Burch, a University of Michigan malacologist, "they'd be just like ice." A Dutch naturalist noted the same thing in Saipan in 1945, observing "dat de jeeps er slipten."

One man's pest, however, is another's lunch. In West Africa, the snails are such a popular food they've grown scarce. Snail ranchers in Taiwan export young African snails to France as escargot. "Believe it or not," says Mr. Burch, "some people like to eat them raw."

This is not a good idea. Giant African snails can carry rat lungworm, a parasite with a penchant for boring into human brains. "It's usually diagnosed in autopsy," Mr. Burch adds.

Cooking will kill the worms, but anyone harboring a fugitive snail still shouldn't eat it. As any snail rancher knows, snails are what they eat, and this snail eats dead rats. It also eats excrement, paint, stucco and its own dead kin, shell and all. Most worrisome to Aphis, however, is its voracious appetite for virtually every food crop grown in America.

The latest incursion was discovered by accident, when a vacationing agricultural inspector stumbled across one giant in a Florida pet store. Finding out where it came from was easy. The trail of slime led back to a dozen or so distributors, from there to New York, and ultimately to Lagos, Nigeria. But uncovering the snails' final destinations took a lot of detective work. Twenty investigators needed half a week to sift through records of just one distributor.

Aphis dispatched officers to every pet shop that had received a snail, establishments with such winning names as Critter Corner, the Doggie Bag, For Pet's Sake, and the Barking Lot. Its agents found that hundreds of the fugitive snails had already died. Most never had a chance. It seems that many pet-shop owners, unfamiliar with land snails, blithely popped them into water-filled fish tanks.

The snails drowned.

Agents captured 203 snails alive. Two were seized from the Nature of Things pet store in Wilmington, N.C., where owner Inez Stevens gave them up without a fight. "They're a right pretty animal," she says. "But, man, they could eat a head of lettuce in a heartbeat."

Kevin Conner, an Aphis agent, traced a snail to Chestertown, Md., where he learned it had been sold—and had died. Mr. Conner needed proof. "If it died, well, that's a shame," he says, "but we can't just take someone's word for it."

He made an appointment to view the corpse, which the owner had kept frozen in his refrigerator.

The most controversial snail wound up at Fish Tales in Laburnum Park, outside Richmond, Va. The giant spent six presumably happy months in a terrarium at the darkened rear of the shop, sharing the twilight with snakes, iguanas and huge spiders, before a young couple came in, saw it, and fell in love.

Aphis called two days later, only to learn the mystery buyers had paid cash and couldn't be traced. Word of the snailhunt spread through the local press. The commotion, says Debra Rea, brought the feds to her door. She is convinced her neighbors confused one of Mr. Rea's pets, a hermit crab, for the fugitive snail. "See, I think they saw me with some kids. I was holding the snail—"

Casting an empty glance at her husband, she rapidly corrects herself.

"—the hermit crab. And all they could see was the shell."

Aphis's Frank Formichella confirms that neighbors ratted on Mrs. Rea. "The neighbors described the snail right down to a T," he says.

After receiving the tip, Mr. Formichella dispatched a veteran investigator, Victor Hoyos, who found Mrs. Rea's father. He directed Mr. Hoyos to the exterminating company where his daughter worked as a receptionist.

It is here that things get murky.

Mrs. Rea says she returned from an innocent trip to the post office to find Mr. Hoyos at her desk. But the feds say her father tipped her off. Maybe she did go to the post office—but she also had plenty of time to speed home, hide her snail, then return.

The agents found nothing.

Mr. Formichella still hopes to nab the snail, but his agency has few coercive powers. Meanwhile, the dragnet continues. Another 119 giant African snails remain on the lam in 29 states—17 in Florida alone, where the climate is perfect for infestation.

An agency fact-sheet assures snailowners that surrendered snails will be disposed of "in the most humane method."

To Aphis, this means boiling.

Philadelphia Gorilla Has Led an Odd Life But a Prolonged One

———

After Africa-Brooklyn Trip, He Was Believed Female; He Carried On, Now Is 53

———

By Francine Schwadel

6/8/84

PHILADELPHIA—It is feeding time at the zoo, and Massa grunts rapidly. The old gorilla scoots to the rear window of his cage, squats and stretches a large leathery palm toward the metal bars. His keeper throws him a chocolate cupcake, a treat he quickly shoves into his mouth.

Then he eats an apple, some escarole, a celery stalk, and several oranges cut in chunks. He holds the orange peel at his lips, using his few remaining teeth to rip the juicy fruit from its skin.

Massa still has a healthy appetite, despite signs of old age. His hair is gray, his toes are curled by what appears to be arthritis, and his eyes are clouded by the early stages of cataracts. All but three of his teeth have fallen victim to decay and gum disease. His chest is a sunken landscape of wrinkled flesh and bones.

At age 53, Massa is the world's oldest known gorilla. Gorillas in captivity live 20 years on the average and practically never reach 40, and gorillas in the wild are believed to die younger. Massa has lived since 1935 at the Philadelphia Zoological Garden, where he has spent most of his days alone in a cage.

When he dies, scientists plan to pore over his brain, his heart and other organs in search of information about aging. Researchers aren't interested in studying his habits now because he has had such an odd upbringing that generalizations based on his behavior probably wouldn't be valid. Behavioral researchers are more interested in groups of gorillas, not individuals, and Massa doesn't mingle with the gorilla family at the zoo.

Born in the lowlands of western Africa in 1930, Massa was captured when he was an infant. A retired zoo official speculates that Massa's mother had been killed earlier and that he had been kept alive by a native woman who nursed him at her breast—sort of a reverse Tarzan story—before selling him to an animal trader.

Later, Massa was bought by a sea captain and was shipped to the U.S. to live in a mansion on Shore Road in Brooklyn. It was the home of Gertrude Davies Lintz, an animal lover who was the childless wife of a wealthy doctor. Massa weighed 18 pounds when he arrived, unconscious, in a cardboard box. He had pneumonia, and Mrs. Lintz nursed him back to health, pre-chewing his food and feeding him cod-liver oil. Later when Massa was struck by infantile paralysis, Mrs. Lintz rigged up an exercise machine for him. It was Mrs. Lintz who named him Massa.

Believing that Massa was female (gorillas are hairy and their genitalia are small), Mrs. Lintz dressed him in little girls' clothes. She taught him to wash her kitchen floor. She thought gorillas might make good servants—but rejected the notion because Massa was strong enough to scrub the linoleum off the floor, she says in her 1942 book "Animals Are My Hobby."

Massa spent four years at the Lintz home in a menagerie that included chimpanzees, a leopard, owls, St. Bernards and, later, another young gorilla, who became Gargantua the Great when he was sold to the circus in 1937.

Mrs. Lintz called the apes her foster children. Gorillas were a special challenge because many in captivity died of tuberculosis. (At the zoo, a glass wall separates them from visitors who might be carrying infectious respiratory diseases. Keepers and occasional visitors who venture behind the cages are screened first for tuberculosis.)

At the Lintz home, young Massa learned to drive a kiddy car. He went for rides on a tea wagon. He played tag. He giggled when Mrs. Lintz tickled him. He tried on her dresses, hats and shoes.

Anthony J. Desimone, an animal trainer who worked for Mrs. Lintz, says Massa used to cry after losing boxing matches with a chimp. "The chimp," he says, "would slap him all over."

Mrs. Lintz also took Massa on outings in her automobile. Once she powdered her nose at a red light, then discovered Massa with her vanity case, disappearing behind a cloud of cosmetics. These escapades help explain why Mrs. Lintz called Massa her favorite. In her book, she described Massa as "the quintessence of femininity."

But Massa grew strong and finally attacked Mrs. Lintz, inflicting wounds that required more than 70 stitches. He had been scrubbing the kitchen floor. Mrs. Lintz entered the room quietly, slipped on a patch of soapy water and knocked over his pail, surprising him with a bath that sent him into a rage. Massa sank his teeth into Mrs. Lintz's thigh, abdomen and arm.

Mrs. Lintz recovered but soon realized that she couldn't keep a 140-pound ape around the house. In 1935, she sold Massa to the Philadelphia zoo for $6,000 as a mate for Bamboo, a large male. A Philadelphia newspaper announced the betrothal of Miss Massa and Mr. Bamboo. But when the two great apes met, Massa nearly killed Bamboo, and it was soon determined that Massa, too, was male.

Massa has lived alone ever since. Robert L. Snyder, director of the zoo's Penrose Research Laboratory, says that Massa might have accepted a female gorilla as a companion after he arrived at the zoo, but that he probably wouldn't have copulated because he had never had a chance to observe the behavior of older apes. And by the time Massa was 10, he lacked the social skills to live with other gorillas, Mr. Snyder says.

Despite his odd upbringing, Massa was a magnificent muscular sight in his prime. He weighed more than 350 pounds, compared with about 175 now. He delighted zoo goers by hanging a burlap bag like a shawl around his shoulders or turning it into a hat. He tormented Bamboo, splashing water at the older ape who lived in the cage next door until his death from a heart attack in 1961.

Massa's life style has been quite different from that of the estimated 20,000 to 40,000 gorillas who live in the wild in Africa. Gorillas are gentle and live in family groups, according to scientists who have observed them. They spend about 40% of their time resting, 30% feeding and 30% in a combination of traveling and feeding. They eat mostly leaves, shoots and stems. They build nests to sleep on.

Massa now spends most of his time dozing in his tiled cage. The deep creases in his face and his intent stare give the impression that he is lost in thought. He plucks out his hair. "All he wants to do is eat and drink," says Ralph E. McCarthy, his keeper for 23 years. Massa perks up when Mr. McCarthy calls, "Yo! Mot Mot." Mot Mot is Mr. McCarthy's nickname for Massa.

Now in his twilight years, Massa is a celebrity. His birthday party in December drew about 400 guests.

Zoo officials attribute Massa's long life to his diet, which includes two pounds of zoo cake a day. The cake is a granola-like mixture of grains, held together by ground chicken, polyunsaturated fats and oils.

Modern medicine also has played a role in Massa's survival. In 1969, after a bout with sinusitis, he underwent surgery to clean his sinuses and to alter slightly the inner structure of his nose. Later that year, 17 of his teeth were extracted. Six more abscessed teeth were removed last November after Massa grew listless and stopped eating.

"The signs are that he's aging very rapidly, like an old, old man," says C. Dietrich Schaaf, the zoo's current curator of mammals. "It wouldn't surprise me if he died tomorrow. It wouldn't surprise me if he lived another year or two."

When Massa dies, Dr. Linda C. Cork, a pathologist in comparative medicine at Johns Hopkins School of Medicine, plans to study his brain in an effort to get a clearer picture of the way human brains change with age. In human brains, she says, it is difficult to distinguish between changes caused by aging and those caused by such things as alcohol or drug abuse. Primates like Massa don't have alcohol or drug problems.

But aging animals are creating new problems for zoo directors seeking to preserve endangered species. These modern-day Noahs are becoming proficient at breeding animals in captivity. Now they are asking what should be done with animals that are too old to mate but that fill zoo space needed for younger animals.

Some zoos use euthanasia as a solution. "We are producers of wildlife. We are no longer consumers of wildlife," says Steve H. Graham, chairman of the animal-welfare committee of the American Association of Zoological Parks and Aquariums. "We have to do what nature does. Nature culls."

With about 650 gorillas in captivity around the world, zoos still haven't reached their saturation point for these great apes. No one knows what will happen when they do, although it appears certain that Massa won't face the death penalty if he is still around. Even Mr. Graham gets sentimental about Massa. "I can't explain why," he says. "Maybe he looks like my grandfather."

Mammoths May Be Extinct, but They Save the Elephants

The Ancient Ivory Is Plentiful In Siberian Permafrost; Purists Who Prefer Plastic

By Barry Newman

7/16/91

The Convention on International Trade in Endangered Species does nothing for the woolly mammoth.

"It is not on our list," says Jacques Berney, the convention's deputy secretary general in Lausanne, Switzerland. As Ken Goddard of the National Fish and Wildlife Forensics Laboratory in Ashland, Ore., says, "It is not illegal to kill a mammoth."

Even so, nobody has killed one for some time. Mammoths have been out of danger for 10,000 years, buried in the Russian permafrost. Down south, though, their descendants have needed help. After much uproar, the African elephant made it onto the endangered list 18 months ago. Trade in ivory has since died off, and the elephant seems to have been spared. Now it's the world's ivory carvers that face extinction. But who wants to save them?

The Russians do. They're mining mammoths.

The effect is visible through a shop window in the "Ivory City" of Erbach, Germany, where Graf Franz of Erbach began carving ivory in 1783, and where the ivory business survives by the skin of its teeth. On the left stand white carved elephants. On the right, woolly mammoths, brownish with curly tusks. The elephants were carved from the ivory of African elephants, the mammoths from the ivory of Siberian mammoths. A sign below them reads, "Guaranteed at least 10,000 years old."

"Mammoth is our biggest mover," says Monika Reinelt, keeping shop inside, where business seems fossilized nevertheless. "We get demonstrators. Elephant killers they call us. But they can't call us mammoth killers, can they?"

For the Russians, mammoths are nothing new. Charmex, a state trading company, has sold foreign scientists mammoth tusks for ages. Where arctic cliffs crack or riverbanks erode, mammoths often roll free. Elephantine deposits are found in spots where Pleistocene ice was thin and mammoths fell through. In the deep freeze, mammoths keep nicely for 30,000 years. The experts guess that Siberia has 10 million of them in the cooler.

"We have industrial quantities to offer," says an eager salesman at the Charmex office in Moscow. "Our mammoths are all extracted in the frozen zone. They are very fresh, very very fresh."

With the elephant out to pasture, the mammoth's price has gone up. Elephant ivory sold for about $100 a pound before the ban, mammoth ivory for $3. Now elephant costs $3, and wholesale mammoth from $300 to $1,000, depending on the cut. That would put the value of Soviet mammoth reserves at about $1 trillion, enough to save not only the elephant but Mikhail Gorbachev and communism, too.

Like everything else in the Soviet Union, though, the mammoth is a bone of contention. Moscow grants mammoth-mining rights and fixes raw-mammoth prices. But the mammoth lodes lie in Siberian Russia, Boris Yeltsin land. And within Siberia, the autonomous Yakut Republic claims mammoth sovereignty for itself. Outdoing them all, claim jumpers pinch hot tusks for black-market mammoth rings.

"A bulldozer operator who extracts a tusk from the permafrost can get more for it than he could for 15 or 20 years of faultless work," marvels the paper Moscow News. But Alexi Yablokov, Mr. Yeltsin's scientific adviser, sees this as natural evolution.

"In the Soviet Union, we have such a strange situation," he says. "Our customs declaration says nothing about mammoths. But now we need some regulation. This is a problem for Russia. But why prohibit it? For what reason?"

Conservationists have a couple. From Southern Africa to Hong Kong, ivory merchants are stuck with tons of tusks once costing millions and now hardly worth a nickel to anybody but the tooth fairy. Clandestine elephant laundries could be set up to infiltrate the mammoth trade.

"The whole idea is that there is no legal ivory," says Suzie Watts of the Environmental Investigation Agency, which tracks ivory racketeers from an office in London.

The forensics lab in Ashland, Ore., may have a solution. The lab opened a year ago for just this sort of assignment: telling the difference, for instance, between an elkburger and a mooseburger. One of the first items it looked at was a mammoth tusk.

Its scientists measured the angles formed by crosshatches in the ivory. Elephant angles, they found, are acute and mammoth angles obtuse. But the surprise came when they began measuring ivory seized at U.S. ports of entry: Of the first several thousand carvings, 95% turned out to be mammoth.

"It's real clear to us that there's a tremendous volume of mammoth out there," says lab chief Ken Goddard. Yet conservationists worry. Untested elephant shipments, they fear, could still slip by in mammoth's clothing. They'd prefer that the white soapy stuff came from crude oil or South American bushes. Some of it already does.

"We do turtle, horn, hardwood, everything alternative," says Roy Stevens of GPS Agencies in Chichester, England. He also does "ivory," in "tusks" cast from petrochemicals. Artisans use it for inlaid guitars, harpsichord keys, baroque recorders. "Whatever you do with ivory you can do with this," he says. "Really, mammoth is not the answer."

Then there's the elephant plant. It grows in Colombia, Ecuador and Peru, yielding a white nut carved into jewelry and toys by the Quechua Indians. The elephant plant caught the eye of Robin des Bois, a group of French eco-guerrillas who, dressed up as elephants, raid ivory shops. They have imported four tons of "vegetable ivory" and sell it to pay for their outings.

But the elephant plant can't supplant the elephant. Big tusks lend themselves to ornate figures better than small nuts do. And Mr. Stevens's ivory has an image problem: No matter how finely carved, a plastic flute usually won't fetch $800. On the other hand, mammoth isn't perfect, either. Nobody spends 100 centuries under the permafrost without showing his age.

Ichiro Kanimaki was certainly disappointed. The Japanese carve more ivory than anybody, and Mr. Kanimaki's employer, Miyakoshishoji Co., hoping that mammoth would fill the elephants' shoes, imported 1,200 pounds of it from Siberia.

"Very bad quality," Mr. Kanimaki says in Tokyo. "You know, mammoths have been buried under ice. All tusks were cracked due to change of temperature or something. We sent the whole lot back."

It would take Japanese masters 20 years to learn to carve mammoth, Mr. Kanimaki thinks, but by then they themselves will have gone the way of the dodo bird. In Germany, the carvers of Erbach aren't waiting: their numbers have already dwindled to about 40 from 1,500. Last year, they bought a ton of mammoth from the Russians. This year, they bought another ton.

"My first thought was, is it worth carving this?" Jugen Schott says in his workshop one morning. "Then I touched it, got the feeling. The funny thing was that the worst of it was the nicest to look at. Such colors. I decided to think like a mammoth carver. With elephant, you make a drawing and follow it. With mammoth, the piece gives you the inspiration."

Over at the Ivory Museum, Erbach's biggest attraction, Ernst Gerbig gives a demonstration. On his workbench lie chunks of cracked tusk encased in rough bark. Mr. Gerbig has just finished a leaf. "I looked at this," he says, holding up the slice of ivory it emerged from, "and I said to myself, this can't be anything else."

He turns on a strong light and fits a fine file to the drill bit of a motor bolted to his bench. Among the scraps, he finds a morsel of mammoth smaller than his thumbnail. He studies it in the light, switches on the motor, and presses the ivory to the spinning file. A head soon appears, ears, four small feet, and a thin tail.

"There," says the mammoth carver, setting it on his counter. "A 10,000-year-old mouse."

The Maggot Test:
Bugs on Dead Bodies
Have Tales to Tell

Forensic Entomologists Find
Insects Provide Good Clues
To Who-Dunit and When

By Bill Richards

4/27/92

Would-be murderers, beware. There will be witnesses. Lots of them. And in the right hands, they will chew up just about any alibi.

Who are these rats? They are bugs.

For years, crime-scene investigators have regarded flies, maggots, mites and other creepy crawly creatures that swarm around dead bodies as a disgusting nuisance. But a band of bug experts are proving that even the most repulsive insects can provide clues that can crack a tough case.

Take maggots. When the police kicked their way into a Tacoma, Wash., townhouse two years ago, they found a gruesome mystery: The decomposing body of the occupant, a 34-year-old man, lay still tangled in his bedclothes with a bullet through his neck. The doors and windows were fastened—from the inside—and the man's gun was still in its holster on a dresser.

A suicide? The only weapon in the room was the gun, and it hadn't been fired. A murder? Nothing was missing and there was no sign anyone had tampered with the body or entered the place. A motive? There wasn't a hint.

"We had a puzzle on our hands," says Pierce County Sheriff's Department detective Arthur Anderson.

But there were plenty of clues. Before the investigators retreated from the room they scooped up a handful of maggots and bagged them for evidence.

The maggots ended up in the Washington State University laboratory of E. Paul Catts, who goes by the title of forensic entomologist, one of a dozen or so full-time operatives in the U.S. Mr. Catts, a genial Sherlock Holmes fan, keeps a hard hat inscribed "Bug Man" in his lab. He has worked on more than 50 homicides.

"Every case has a different wrinkle," Mr. Catts says. "Once you get past the repulsive part—that's the victim, not the bugs—it becomes an ecological puzzle."

In the Tacoma case, Mr. Catts found that two generations of maggots had hatched at the scene. Since it takes a generation three weeks to reach adulthood, depending on factors like weather and a body's location, he figured the body had been there a little longer than that. (Medical examiners usually can do no better than guess at time of death after a body has aged more than four days. When detectives are stumped over the time of death, they often are turning to entomologists for answers.)

Armed with Mr. Catts's finding, detectives questioned the victim's neighbors and learned of a nearby party about the time the man died. They also discovered a reveler had fired off a couple of shots at the party. When they traced the path of the bullet it led from the deceased man's bed back to the party house. The shooter pleaded guilty to manslaughter and got 27 months.

"That bug business was very helpful, and it was pretty interesting, too," says detective Anderson.

Interest in the secrets that bugs can tell is indeed increasing. Five years ago, says entomologist Wayne Lord, the idea of tapping insects for clues to a homicide was all but unheard-of. Last year, Mr. Lord, who plies his skill for the Federal Bureau of Investigation's forensic science research and training center at Quantico, Va., fielded calls for help on some 50 homicides around the U.S.

Bugs, Mr. Lord says, can tell a trained observer not only when a body died but whether it was moved (most fly subspecies stay within a mile or so of where they hatched) and whether the victim died during the day or night (certain flies rest at night, slowing decomposition). Forensic entomologists have gone so far as to match the leg of a grasshopper in a killer's trouser cuff with the rest of the insect found at a death site. Soon, Mr. Lord predicts, researchers ought to be able to tie a suspect to a corpse by matching the blood sucked by mosquitoes in the area.

"These days," says Mr. Lord, the FBI's lone bug man, "everything's a clue."

That is especially true when it comes to flies—death's seemingly ubiquitous companions. Newly dead bodies emit a faint odor, too slight to be immediately detected by humans but a five-alarm signal to flies, says entomologist Neal Haskell at Purdue University in Indiana. Within minutes after a body hits the ground, they will swarm from up to two miles away, he says.

Mr. Haskell's response time is nearly as quick. He roars to crime scenes in a maroon Dodge Colt sporting a license plate that reads "MAGGOT."

One of the Purdue researcher's best bits of detective work occurred a couple of years ago in Kentucky, where police found the skeletons of a pair of elderly women, still in their nightgowns, propped up in separate beds in a large old house. The bodies, both dead nearly 10 years, were discovered after the owner of the house, a 69-year-old man, died of natural causes.

Using the remains of beetles and flies found in each bed, Mr. Haskell established the season each woman had died. (Flies don't breed in winter, beetles do.) His estimate was supported by a diary and unopened Christmas cards recovered from the house.

Police finally figured out the man had kept the bodies so he could illegally collect the women's social security and pension checks after they died of natural causes in their beds. Mr. Haskell's testimony gave the government and the pension fund ammunition to successfully sue for reimbursement from the man's estate.

While forensic entomology is a relatively new science, crime-busters have been tipped off by bugs as far back as the 13th century. In a volume entitled "The Washing Away of Wrongs" Sung Tz'u, a Chinese "death investigator," related perhaps the first recorded effort at using insects to solve a crime in 1235.

According to Sung Tz'u, a local death investigator looking into a slashing in a rural village found no one who would own up to the murder. The investigator ordered the villagers to lay down their sickles. Flies swarmed to one implement which looked clean but still carried minute remnants of the victim's body tissue. The sickle's owner broke down and confessed to the crime.

The account is included in a book with the catchy title "Entomology and Death" that Messrs. Catts, Haskell and a half dozen of their colleagues published two years ago. So far, the 182-page volume has sold only about 500 copies, but one reviewer gave it a rave write-up in the FBI's Law Enforcement Bulletin.

Lee Goff, one of the book's authors, may be the flashiest operative in this generally low-key science. Mr. Goff, who teaches at the University of Hawaii's College of Tropical Agriculture and Human Resources, wears a police beeper and often cruises to death scenes on his motorcycle with a butterfly net tucked under the seat.

Among his entomological peers, Mr. Goff is regarded as something of a bulldog on the bug beat. He once bagged a killer, who wrapped his victim in blankets, by simulating the crime with a pig. Mr. Goff wrapped the pig up and left it in his back yard to figure out exactly how long it took flies to get at the body. The information led to the arrest of the victim's estranged husband and, Mr. Goff says, "I found out who my good neighbors are."

Mr. Goff isn't the only one to bring a little pizazz to the field of forensic entomology. The science popped up in "The Silence of the Lambs," this year's big Academy Award winner and a best-seller for author Thomas Harris.

Mr. Harris devised a plot with a crucial clue involving a death's-head moth. In the book, a pair of slightly eccentric entomologists from the Smithsonian Institution help the FBI pin down the moth's identity, which leads to a serial killer.

Mr. Harris doesn't give interviews, but Gary Hevel, manager of the Smithsonian's entomological collection, says he spent hours with the writer poring over insects. They chose a silkworm moth to star in the book, Mr. Hevel says. Mr. Harris later jettisoned the choice for the spookier-looking death's-head moth. "I suppose it is a better name, but I thought the silkworm moth was very colorful," Mr. Hevel complains. He says he hasn't gotten around to reading Mr. Harris's novel.

III

BUSINESS:
FROM CRADLE
TO GRAVEYARD

Aren't You Dying
To Know if a Phorid
Is in Your Future?

———

Cemetery Magazines Cover
Grave Topics and Aren't
For the Faint of Heart

———

By James P. Sterba

4/25/91

Bored by the new world order? Tired of books about future shock? Tomorrow doesn't have to be either a politician's pipe dream or a Tofflerian tornado of tumult, techno-shock and info-frenzy.

Another future is out there, a placid future of chirping birds, grazing deer, butterflies lilting over dewy morning glades, and the smell of freshly mowed grass. To read all about it you don't have to plunk down $22.95, either—the price of Alvin Toffler's latest, "Powershift."

For only $18 you can bury yourself, every month for a year, in American Cemetery, the magazine of cemetery management, and learn what lies ahead. Be forewarned, however: You will learn things from this magazine that you might wish you hadn't. Be doubly forewarned: If you keep reading this article, you will encounter things so gross that Madonna wouldn't even dream of putting them in a rock video.

Phorids, for example. "You probably have phorids in your future," says Robert Snetsinger, a Pennsylvania State University entomologist—at least if you plan on being stashed above ground.

Before we consider phorids, it should be noted that there are actually three national cemetery magazines. The other two are Cemetery Management, the magazine of the American Cemetery Association, and Catholic Cemetery, the magazine for Catholic Cemetery Administrators. From reading them you will learn that many fine people are devoting their lives to public service in the cemetery business. Cemeterians, they call themselves.

They are hardly a bunch of humorless stiffs. They invited Richard "Digger" Phelps, Notre Dame's former basketball coach, to speak at their last national convention. They respond well to this kind of advertising: "Make Money the Modern Way. Urn It!" Cemeterians are modern businessmen. They buy state-of-the-art Cemetery Software computer programming from a Nashua, N.H., company to keep track of where the bodies are buried.

Of the three magazines, American Cemetery seems the least grave. It prints Gary Larsen's ghoulish "Far Side" cartoons, and jokes about "The Loved One," the novel-movie that cemeterians love to loathe. It features "Funerals of the Famous." Houdini's was in October. Gen. Douglas MacArthur's was a recent four-part series.

In October the magazine profiled the cemetery where Edgar Allan Poe is buried, noting that on his birth date, Jan. 19, every year since 1949 someone has left three roses and a half bottle of cognac on his monument, ignoring the incorrect birthdate, Jan. 20, carved in the stone. The magazine also reports on headstone thefts and grave desecrations.

Stephen L. Morgan, the cemetery association's executive vice president, says there are more than 100,000 cemeteries in the U.S., of which 5,000 to 7,500 are "active"; each one of these has at least one interment a year. The industry's revenues run between $2.5 billion and $3 billion a year, Mr. Morgan says.

The industry's prospects look bright, mainly because the nation's roughly 77 million baby boomers will soon begin reaching middle age and dying in increasing numbers. Last year, only about 2,155,000 people died in the U.S. In 2010, an estimated 2,627,900 will die. That is 7,200 a day, 300 an hour, five a minute.

Not all of them will be buried. Cemetery space is a problem, so mausoleum interments are popular. Cremations are hot these days, too. The number of crematees is expected to double in 2010, to 703,000 from a "really impressive" 352,400 last year, says Jack Springer, executive director of the Cremation Association of North America.

Cremations are quick, easy, convenient, environmentally sound, cheap—and boring. That's why Pennsylvania funeral director Donna M. Falk advocates "creative cremations." She writes: "Not everyone wants the bare boned (pardon the pun) services that we have traditionally offered with cremation." She says that the tune "50 Ways to Leave Your Lover" inspired her to think up "50 Ways to Leave Your (Cremated) Lover." Here are just four: You can leave him or her on a favorite football field, or ski slope, or vacation-home back yard, or at sea. But at sea be aware that the Environmental Protection Agency forbids ash-scattering within three miles of the shore.

If your ashes—or "cremains," in industry terminology—aren't scattered, they probably will remain in a standard, 200-cubic-inch urn. But Superior International Corp., asserting in advertising that many cremains won't fit, advises buying its bigger, 300-cubic-inch urns. (Note to sensitive readers: A good place to stop reading is right here.)

Some of the magazines' advertising is devoted to hawking solutions for a little-publicized problem involving leaky caskets—and phorids, Megaselia scalaris. These tiny flies, about the size of fruit flies, congregate around natural science museums, hospitals, nursing homes, mortuaries and mausoleums. Cremains aren't bothered, and phorids won't bug you six feet under. But in the mushrooming mausoleum business, phorids are a problem.

The reason: Even gasket-sealed caskets, for which funeral operators charge a premium, eventually leak, or "burp." The natural process of decomposition and desiccation of organic remains produces quantities of four gases, hydrogen sulfide, sulphur dioxide, methane and ammonia, that create enormous pressure when confined and open minuscule cracks along seams of caskets.

Ancient Egyptians knew that remains stay preserved best when all the liquids are removed. In nature, desiccation takes a few months. In many modern caskets, it can take many years. Time and today's embalming methods are on the side of the phorid fly, one of nature's busy decomposers.

"The embalming fluids preserve the bodies to the extent that they keep out molds and other decays," Prof. Snetsinger says. This, he observes, "means the flies have more time to eat." (Note to sensitive readers: Perhaps you will take our advice next time.)

"The phorid fly . . . is by far the most predominant mausoleum pest species," Harry Katz, a pest-control consultant, wrote in Pest Control Technology magazine. "Corpses exposed for two or three days are readily inoculated by ovipositing (egg-depositing) phorids. Generations then develop in the casket where conditions are favorable; the heat from decomposition keeps the pests comfortable within the 'cavelike' cool surroundings of the mausoleum."

Even when the crack along a casket seal is too small for an adult phorid to squeeze through, an adult will lay its eggs along the crack to give the little ones a leg up in their journey through life. They can squeeze through and get you even when the big guys can't.

Pepcis Corp., of Green Bay, Wis., says in a magazine ad: "Assuming a normal survival rate of 98%, ONE PAIR of Phorid flies in a crypt could produce 55 MILLION adults in as short as 60 days." Pepcis markets "Crypt-Tech, a revolutionary pest control system developed exclusively for mausoleums."

Not to be outdone, Ensure-A-Seal, a Pittsburgh company, advertises a kind of casket bag made of plastic fiber with a one-way brass check valve.

This amounts to a variation on the Roach Motel strategy. The gases can check out. But the phorids can't check in.

Help Me, Clarence!
The Building & Loan
Has Lost Billions!

'It's a Wonderful Life' Indeed;
In the '90s, George Bailey
Doesn't Look So Benign

By Ron Suskind

12/14/90

"Where's the money? You realize what this means? It means bankruptcy and scandal and prison, that's what it means. One of us is going to jail. Well, it's not going to be me!"

That Charles Keating sure is a quotable guy. No, wait: That's not the indicted former head of Lincoln Savings & Loan talking. Those lines were uttered by George Bailey, embattled chief of the Bailey Bros. Building & Loan in Frank Capra's classic 1946 film "It's a Wonderful Life." Every year, holiday viewers are treated to seemingly continuous airings of the movie. But this year, as Christmas passes under the shadow of the savings and loan debacle, the film may look somewhat different.

How should we feel about our hero, played by Jimmy Stewart? Is he a good man whose prayers are answered—or just another incompetent S&L operator pleading for a bailout? "If you get past all the warm and fuzzy stuff, you realize Bailey was a real speculator. He got into real-estate development and granted mortgages with almost no down payments," says John Wood, chairman of Massbank for Savings in Reading, Mass., and one of eight experts called together to help reassess the movie in light of current events.

"These days, regulators would be swarming all over him," adds panelist Lawrence Connell, a former top regulator who was appointed chairman of the troubled New Hampshire Savings Bank, which became insolvent in September.

"It's a Wonderful Life" parallels real life for many modern-day S&Ls. Bailey Bros. was a plodding institution that stressed personal service and offered loans to questionable customers, like Ernie the cabdriver and Violet the floozy, who were turned down by the local commercial bank. But those sleepy rhythms bred casual management, loose loan policies and, ultimately, employee error—prompting the bank's insolvency and the appearance of angels, financial and otherwise.

As the movie begins, with a review of George's childhood of good deeds, it is clear that our panelists—five S&L or savings bank operators, two former regulators and one thrift consultant—share a certain ambivalence about Mr. Bailey. Nowadays especially, it is flattering for any industry to have a matinee idol—so long as one doesn't have to constantly be compared with the guy. "George Bailey is a perfect person," says panelist John H. Pramberg, Jr., president of the Institution for Savings in Newburyport and its vicinity (founded 1820), a quaint mutual S&L in northern Massachusetts that would fit nicely on a Christmas card. "It's a tough crucible for us normal humans to meet."

So, as the movie progresses, the panelists engage in a bit of long-repressed Bailey bashing. "George was clearly undercapitalized, and that got him into trouble," says Rita Fair, a former top staffer of the Federal Home Loan Bank Board and now an S&L consultant at Secura Group. "A good consultant, called in early, might have saved him."

As young George sees his father arguing with the building and loan's majority stockholder, the evil Mr. Potter, Mr. Pramberg says the Baileys foolishly kept the B&L a stockholder institution. "I never would have done that. All you're doing is talking on the phone to guys like Potter," he says. "They should have converted it to a mutual."

"Come on, that's really simplified," retorts Mr. Wood, whose institution remains stockholder-owned. "George shouldn't have got into real-estate development. He got overextended."

The movie continues to a scene in which George, now a young man, tells his father that he doesn't want to succeed him and become a prisoner of that "shabby little office." Two panelists recall similar conversations with their own banker fathers, and the group's sardonic tone begins to soften. Later, after George's father dies and Mr. Potter moves to dissolve the building and loan, George gives an impassioned speech about protecting this "one-horse institution" on behalf of the people "who do most of the working and paying and living and dying in this community."

Louis Fineman, who runs the small Pelham (N.H.) Bank & Trust Co., begins his own speech: "That's it exactly. It's about people, about really knowing the people in your town and their situations, and developing a kind of trust."

Bill Ferguson, a consultant who recently testified before the House Banking Committee, says, "I should have played this movie for them, to show what's right about small-town banking."

Generally, George is getting good reviews, especially when he saves the bank during the crash of '29. But when he receives a call from his old buddy Sam Wainwright, who has become a big-time New York investor and tries to lure George into stock and real-estate deals, the group erupts. "Oh, no! It's a sleazy developer on the phone. Don't take the call, George! That's what got Silverado into trouble!" yells Mr. Pramberg.

"Developer? Forget it. That's Michael Milken on the line," adds Mr. Connell. "Hang up!"

The movie progresses to its long final day—the day before Christmas—which starts with a surprise visit by the bank examiner and newspaper headlines about George's younger brother winning the Congressional Medal of Honor. When George tells the examiner his mother just had lunch with the president's wife, Mr. Connell says, "He's clearly pulling a Keating, trying to influence the examiner with the 'friends in high places' routine."

Then George hands cash to Violet, bad girl of Bedford Falls, in what Mr. Connell says is clearly an "off the record" loan. She responds with a kiss—in full view of the bank examiner. "Philandering. Goes under the confidential section of the examiner's report," says Mr. Connell.

"Hell, that's CRA [community reinvestment]," says Mr. Fineman.

Soon, though, things begin to go very sour. George's simple Uncle Billy goes to the local commercial bank to deposit $8,000 from the little B&L's safe, but he misplaces the cash. The loss leaves the B&L insolvent, and events quickly slide into crisis. Soon, George is on an icy bridge, ready to jump. "Problem is, well, this is just like what happened to Bob Lee," Mr. Pramberg says quietly, remembering his friend. Mr. Lee, then president of First American Bank for Savings in Boston, committed suicide two years ago when the bank's problem loans mounted. The savings bank was seized in October. "He had a wife, kids. Nice guy," says Mr. Wood. "Problem loans. He just got overwhelmed."

The dim screening room has fallen silent. Mr. Connell, the former regulator who has been appointed to preside over several troubled S&Ls, begins talking about the many desperate bankers he has seen. "A lot more Bob Lees out there than Charles Keatings," says Mr. Wood.

On screen, Mr. Bailey's guardian angel, Clarence, arrives to show the banker what the world would have been like if he had never been born. Mostly, it's a tour of a place called Pottersville, a nightmare version of Bedford Falls without George Bailey's bedrock values. It is a haven of debauchery, free spending, carelessness. Kenneth Abt, president of First Federal Savings and Loan of Middletown, N.Y., says Pottersville is "symbolic of the excessive 1980s, of those years of greed, which is what really got us into trouble."

Mr. Connell takes it a step further. "Pottersville may be what we'll have once all the George Baileys are gone, once the old small-town S&L disappears, when we only have big banks and those personal relationships are replaced by impersonal ones," he says as the panelists, who were strangers a few hours before, launch into a kind of group therapy session.

Eventually, George is returned to the bridge, acutely aware of life's value and of all the people he has helped. Bursting with revelation, he runs through the snowy streets. Townspeople, hearing of George's plight, arrive at his home carrying cash in hats, bowls, cookie jars. Spirits of our panelists finally seem to lift. "Those are core deposits; that money's there to stay," says Mr. Connell.

"It's the original bailout," adds Allan Virr, Mr. Fineman's deputy at Pelham Bank & Trust, as a giant basket of cash is dumped before George Bailey. "It's just what the taxpayers will do."

It's Tough to Own
A Theater in Malibu
During Oscar Season

———

Some of the Local Stars Insist
On Seeing Movies There
—Or at Least the Credits

———

By Richard Turner

3/30/92

MALIBU, CALIF.—Shortly after Scott Wallace bought what he himself describes as the "crummy little theater" here, one of his employees got an agitated phone call.

Warren Beatty was on the line. He had noticed that Barbra Streisand's "The Prince of Tides" had been playing at the Malibu Theater for weeks. What was "Bugsy"—chopped liver?

It wasn't a matter of ego—or not completely anyway. This was Oscar nomination season. Why couldn't Mr. Wallace play "Bugsy" and allow members of the Motion Picture Academy, who would be voting on the awards, to attend free of charge? And what about advertising that on the marquee? Mr. Beatty was . . . insistent.

Of the 23,814 theater screens in America, perhaps none is more quietly important than this one. Housed in a nondescript chunk of poured concrete in a shopping center in Malibu, the theater draws its audience from the largest concentration of movie stars and moguls in the country. Tonight, those celebrities will gather at the Dorothy Chandler Pavilion in Los Angeles to honor the movies many saw first at the Malibu Theater.

Although most stars can see movies at studio screenings or in home projection rooms, they like coming to the Malibu Theater, where they don't get hassled. "It's cozy and it's comfortable," says Olivia Newton-John. "We can slip in in our sweats, settle down with a tub of popcorn and see most of the people we know."

The Malibu Theater is a focal point of this isolated town, which is strung out along the undulating Pacific Coast Highway northwest of Los Angeles. Considering its dense population of stars, Malibu retains a small-town atmosphere, with few posh boutiques or hip nightspots. In Malibu, Andy Griffith's Mayberry meets Valhalla.

Working at the theater is something like slinging hash at the counter where the great chefs grab lunch. During one showing of the movie "Cape Fear," for instance, a technician who had worked on the film insisted on being taken to the projection booth to adjust the focus. The help knows not to ask for autographs.

Mr. Wallace, a 34-year-old entrepreneur who once ran a 533-screen theater chain, bought the Malibu Theater last fall. He's still coping with culture shock—and customers like Warren Beatty. Mr. Wallace was willing to book "Bugsy." But although most area theaters allow Academy members in free, Malibu is different. "If I accepted Academy cards," Mr. Wallace says, "my business would be cut in half."

Mr. Wallace called a top executive at TriStar Pictures, which released "Bugsy." "He called me back right away," Mr. Wallace marvels. Mr. Beatty, apparently, had been calling the same executive at home.

A print of "Bugsy" was soon on its way to Malibu, and Academy members—who later gave "Bugsy" 10 nominations—were comped. Mr. Wallace hopes that, in return, TriStar will give him a break on booking future movies, like allowing him to play first-run pictures without forcing him to screen them for a minimum of several weeks.

For 20 years, the theater's former owner ran it like a small-town business. Dave O'Meara, 62, still wanders in a few times a week after sundown. A self-described "stubborn Irishman," he lost the theater last year in a bitter legal battle with the owner of the shopping center. Martin Sheen, the actor and Malibu activist, told him at the time a protest could be organized. Mr. O'Meara declined. Mr. O'Meara, who has Henry Fonda eyebrows and wears a Tom Joad cap, still has breakfast at 6 P.M. and goes to bed at 6 A.M., the result of theater hours and general eccentricity.

Mr. O'Meara has a million stories: There was Cher's birthday party for then 11-year-old daughter Chastity that shocked some guests because the somewhat racy "The Blue Lagoon" was showing; the way Bob Dylan always seems to forget how many children he's buying tickets for; the time Jerry Brown only reluctantly bought popcorn for his hungry date, Linda Ronstadt.

One night, a woman showed up and said she and her son only wanted to see the closing credits, so did she have to pay? The ticket taker explained that if she went through the turnstile, she'd have to be counted as a paying customer. But she was welcome to go underneath. So Barbra Streisand crawled in on her hands and knees.

The Malibu Theater's marketing program has always been deceptively simple: a large white plastic sign with red stick-on letters and lights that flash a path around the circumference. Tonight: "Basic Instinct." In the theater's 20-year history, the sign has never featured an actor's name. That could spur jealousy, or, Mr. O'Meara says, "What if a letter fell off?"

A name did appear once on the sign, but it was the name of a studio executive. Mr. O'Meara had complained to him that he hadn't been able to book "Rocky," even though it had been playing elsewhere for months. A fresh print was delivered, and the marquee read, "Thank you, Mike Medavoy." Mr. Medavoy is now chairman of TriStar Pictures.

The lobby has changed some since Mr. Wallace took over. The parakeet is gone, along with the fish tank and the slightly grouchy signs Mr. O'Meara used to post, like "Student Tickets Are a Privilege, Not a Right" or, after a disagreement with one studio, "For Your Viewing Guidance, No Warner Bros. Films Will Be Exhibited In This Theater." Mr. Wallace swiftly added an afternoon show, recarpeted, painted everything and installed track lighting to replace the fluorescent fixtures. He also raised admission prices to $7 from $6.

The theater's lobby is so tiny that the doors are locked until the previous show lets out. However, when Neil Diamond was being harassed by an obsessed fan, he was let in early. But generally, even frequent customers like Johnny Carson wait in line among the surfers and skateboarders.

At the Malibu's refreshment counter, there's now Kerns Guava Nectar and Evian water. Mr. Wallace has plans to "twin" the theater. He's also arranging to have a "reservation hotline" installed at celebrity chef Wolfgang Puck's new restaurant, Granita, down the road. Box-office revenue in the last year has more than doubled, he says.

Unlike Mr. O'Meara, Mr. Wallace plays all the Hollywood angles. He got a $10,000 four-channel surround-sound system installed absolutely free, in return for a sign on the door advertising the system. Mr. Wallace does uphold one tradition: He plays only instrumental music between films. Still, he says, patrons ask him, "Will you play my new record?"

If Mr. O'Meara displayed a dogged ignorance of most celebrities, Mr. Wallace often courts them. One day last year, a young usher heard a man pounding on the door. It was Mel Gibson, who wanted to use the theater for a fund-raiser for his children's private school. But when Mr. Gibson telephoned the next morning, Mr. Wallace put him on hold for several minutes; he thought it was the Australian bricklayer working on his home.

Mr. Wallace at first was reluctant—the fund-raiser seemed like a lot of trouble—but he started musing, "This summer . . . 'Lethal Weapon 3' . . ."

Dreaming of a favorable deal, he gave his approval. "And," Mr. Wallace remembers happily, "I sold a lot of popcorn."

Elvis Merchandisers
Are All Shook Up
By a Federal Lawsuit

Sellers of Kingly Goods Owe
A Fee, His Estate Asserts;
Fans: 'Don't Be Cruel'

By Timothy K. Smith

6/30/88

MEMPHIS—In the United States District Court for the Western District of
Tennessee, on the ninth floor of the Clifford Davis Federal Building, in
the federal court clerk's file folder, there are three pairs of panties of
questionable legality.

The panties would be uncontroversial—ordinary cotton, one pair pink,
one white, one blue—but for what Sid Shaw has done to them. Mr. Shaw,
an entrepreneur who lives in London, has decorated them with a picture
of Elvis Presley's face.

Mr. Shaw runs a company called Elvisly Yours Ltd., and publishes a
magazine called Elvisly Yours, and signs correspondence Elvisly Yours,
but he is not a kook. He is a small-business man who happens to be involved in a legal dispute with Jack Soden, who runs Elvis Presley Enterprises Inc. here in Memphis and who also is not a kook. Mr. Soden is a
man with a fiduciary responsibility to protect the image of Elvis Presley,
even if it means suing Mr. Shaw, which is how the panties got into the file.

Mr. Soden, representing the King's estate, is trying to collect fees of up
to 14% of sales from Mr. Shaw and anyone else who uses Elvis Presley's
name, license or image. This might seem like a reasonable business request. But he is finding out that it is like asking Catholics to send a quarter to the Vatican every time they genuflect.

The argument is about whether a celebrity's "right of publicity" is inherited by his estate when he dies. Tennessee passed a statute in 1984
saying it is, retroactively. Mr. Shaw (who once ran unsuccessfully for the
British parliament as a member of the Elvis Presley Party) thinks the law
and the licensing fee are unfair and has countersued the estate. The hundreds, perhaps thousands, of Elvis entrepreneurs around the world are
watching with concern.

"They want to have their thumb on everybody," says Elena Tubbs, who is half of the mom-and-pop team that runs Souvenirs of Elvis, an independent vendor here, and who is in the business "because you meet so many nice people." Standing directly in front of a $29.95 Elvis muumuu, she says of the Elvis estate guardians: "They've made a mockery of this."

These people are involved in an argument over what is almost certainly the world's most valuable face. Mickey Mouse and Lenin may be better known in some parts of the world, but Mickey lacks sex appeal and Lenin is no fun. Besides, Elvis fans have a special degree of, well, enthusiasm for their idol. Not only do they buy garden-variety Elvis T-shirts, key chains, posters and demitasse spoons, they also buy $125 Elvis-shaped decanters full of bad whiskey, $495 two-foot-tall ceramic Elvis figurines, $1,300 package tours from London to Graceland and back. (As one of his many biographers puts it, "We don't have Lourdes, we have Graceland.")

The Elvis industry is like the universe: large, not fully understood, and expanding. The value of the Presley estate has grown to more than $50 million from only about $4.9 million on the day Elvis allegedly died at age 42 in 1977. (Most Elvis fans grudgingly accept the King's death but the tabloid newspapers have been filled with recent accounts, based on yet another Elvis book, that Elvis is alive and hiding out in Kalamazoo, Mich.)

Just last year, seven of his record albums went gold, platinum or double platinum. Some 605,000 people last year visited Graceland, his psychedelic Memphis house, and paid $7 each to take a tour. (When Graceland was opened to the public in 1982 at a cost of $560,000, it paid for itself in 38 days.)

And the industry extends far beyond Memphis and the core Elvis businesses, music and movies. At least 204 books have been written about Elvis, no fewer than eight of them called "Elvis" and one called "Elvis, Elvis, Elvis." Hundreds of Elvis clubs around the world serve thousands of fans who buy and sell everything from original Elvis souvenir lipsticks ($1 in 1956, about $800 today) to back issues of Elvis magazines from Thailand. Traveling Elvis exhibits, stopping at shopping malls, draw a half million people a week.

Even Mr. Soden, who as executive director of Graceland lives with this every day, is sometimes astonished by the power and ubiquity of Elvis. "One of the hostages in Lebanon was released a couple of years ago," he says in a voice of real awe, "and he reported that one of the rooms where he was kept for a while had a bed, a toilet and an Elvis poster."

It is no wonder, then, that Mr. Soden and the trustees of Elvis's estate want to collect a licensing fee every time an object bearing Elvis's face or name is sold—particularly since during his lifetime, Elvis never received his fair share of the billions of dollars he generated.

"Col." Tom Parker, the King's manager, kept 25% of his earnings initially, and 50% after 1967, a proportion so outrageous that it triggered a probate-court inquiry after Elvis allegedly died. Col. Parker, who never gives interviews, also arranged in 1973 to sell the rights to all of Elvis's songs to that date to RCA Victor for $5.4 million, a figure so small it "just makes your head ache," Mr. Soden says. And Elvis himself was one of the great pre-OPEC impulse shoppers; he once bought 14 Cadillacs in one night.

The upshot was that history's most successful entertainer left a pitifully small estate. Since Mr. Soden was appointed director of Graceland in 1981, he and the executors have been rebuilding the estate. They opened Graceland, they tracked down two of Elvis's airplanes and put them on display, and they sued Col. Parker, obtaining all his Elvis assets and rights in a settlement in 1983. Now they are going after licensing fees—and the suits are flying everywhere.

Besides Mr. Shaw of Elvisly Yours, for example, the estate is also suing Joe Esposito, who was one of two best men at Elvis's wedding and who has some home movies of the King he wants to sell. It has even gone after small operators for whom the Elvis business isn't a full-time job.

"I've been an Elvis fan ever since I was seven years old. I never dreamed that I'd be sued by the Elvis Presley estate," says Larry Patrick, a Conway, Ark., restaurant manager who admits he belongs to 23 Elvis fan clubs but says "the media people spotlighting guys who dress up like Elvis ought to be hung up by their toes." Mr. Patrick, who was threatened with legal action over a collection of Elvis video tapes he sells on the side, says, "You don't sue fans for selling and trading."

"The fans are the ones who keep it alive," agrees Susan Fetcho, who runs the Elvis Presley Memorial Society in Syracuse, N.Y. (but who is "not the kind who buys all the trinkets"). Ms. Fetcho expresses the frustration of many when she says, "I can't understand how they think they can come in and say, 'Okay, now all you people have to pay us.'"

Mr. Soden says he has no choice because of his fiduciary responsibility and argues that most fans understand that it is all for the benefit of Lisa Marie, Elvis's only daughter, who inherits the estate five years from now when she turns 25. But some fans suspect that it is all for the benefit of the lawyers, and they suggest that the estate's trustees may be jeopardizing the estate's value in the long run.

They may have a point. "Lots of fans are selling off their collections now," says Jimmy Velvet, curator of the Elvis Museum in Nashville. "They're saying, 'I'll keep his picture in my bedroom, but I'm not going to Memphis anymore, and I'm selling what I have.'"

The trouble is that with each passing year it becomes clearer that the Elvis industry, like the Kennedy industry and scientology, is basically a transcendental business. People build shrines to Elvis. In a fan magazine, a would-be pen pal identifies herself as a "very devoted Elvis fan who Elvis inspired to help her walk again after being crippled." This year's theme is resurrection—as evidenced by the reports of Elvis sightings in Kalamazoo.

But religion may be able to survive litigation after all. Stacy Shepherd, a researcher at Graceland, says, "I have 13- and 14-year-old girls write me who've given up Bon Jovi for Elvis."

What Goes Bump In the Night—if It Manages to Move?

---

*A Clunker Like a '70 Gremlin
Or a '77 Volare, to Name 2;
The Pussycat of a Jaguar*

By Robert Johnson

12/1/89

A stroll down memory lane in the auto industry usually inspires recollections of classics like the 1960 Cadillac Biarritz, with its sharklike fins, triple carburetors and baby-smooth leather.

Rarely does anyone pay any attention to those other automotive milestones: the great lemons.

Yet at a time when the American love affair with the car is once-again producing hysteria over such roadsters as the Mazda Miata and Chevy's big-engined Corvette, a splash of cold reality couldn't do anyone much harm.

So here is a tribute to the clunkers, the bombs that humble their manufacturers. No amount of wax can gloss over rust buckets like the 1977 Plymouth Volare, one of the most re-called jalopies in Detroit history. Or how about the 1972 Chevrolet Vega, whose styling was reminiscent of a small rocket. The car ran about as long as the first stage.

Some losers, like the 1984 Pontiac Fiero, are fairly recent offerings. Other vintage junkers can be found lingering on the back rows of car lots under strings of lightbulbs, pretending to be bargains. They are the good-for-nothing, the bad and the ugly.

But once upon a time, they were someone's dream car. As William Jeanes, editor of Car and Driver magazine, says: "The losers teach painful lessons. Lucky people learn from the car in the neighbor's driveway." The following sampling of 10 turkeys—by no means all-inclusive—is based on the bitter remembrances of consumers, mechanics and auto brokers, as well as on test results from various watchdog groups. Current prices come from used-car dealers and auction lots.

The 1970 American Motors Gremlin. Design critics complained that this car looked as if it had been rear-ended while on the showroom floor. The manufacturer advertised it as "pure and simply more fun to drive," but the Gremlin was so cramped that when passengers swung the front seat forward to get in back, the horn honked. The engine tended to conk out inexplicably on right turns. Seats were covered in vinyl so slick that the driver slid away from the steering wheel going around a corner. The windshield-wiper knob was right by the light switch and looked about the same—a hazard at night or in a rainstorm. New: $2,000. Now: $150, negotiable.

The 1969 Subaru 360. This car shook so hard at 50 miles an hour that the driver's inside mirror was unusable. In handling tests, the 360 seemed to have a mind of its own. Condemned by Consumers Union as unfit for the road. "It was a pleasure to squirm out of the Subaru, slam the door and walk away," the watchdog group summarized. The doors were designed with hinges at their rear edges instead of the front, meaning they opened into the wind. Thus, even at low speeds, the airstream could rip open a partly latched door and slam it against the exterior. The ineffectual defroster could clear only a tiny triangle of the windshield. New: $1,300. Now: $100, less than a Schwinn three-speed.

The 1977 Plymouth Volare. Guinness doesn't have a listing for most-re-called vehicle, but this would be a top candidate if it did. Re-called four times for engines that stalled and for faulty hood latches, front brakes and suspension systems. Two years out of the showroom, some bodies had deteriorated so badly that radio aerials simply fell off. One buyer complained that the back of the front-seat collapsed backwards. Another said his new Volare was delivered with black carpet up front and brown in the back; the dealer at first claimed it was designed that way. New: $4,400. Now: $300. Think of the bus tickets that will buy.

The 1975 CitiCar. Made by Sebring-Vanguard Inc. of Florida, this electric car was a shocking low point in automotive technology. One of the few cars to flunk tests performed by Consumers Union, its brakes were known to shear off when the driver applied them while going just 30 miles per hour. "The car rolled to a leisurely stop in a puddle of brake fluid, trailing plastic fragments," recalls Robert Knoll, head of auto testing for the watchdog group. The test car later blew a fuse, stalling in the middle of a busy intersection. New: $3,100. Now: $200 if all eight batteries are fresh. Sebring-Vanguard sold about 3,000 CitiCars. Now doing business under a new name, Sebring Auto-Cycle Inc., the company still makes electric cars.

The 1960 Chevrolet Corvair. General Motors Corp. proved that truth in advertising still exists when ads promised "the big surprise comes when you pull away from the curb." The Corvair was the first air-cooled, rear-engine U.S. car since the 1920 Franklin (there haven't been any since). Roughly 60% of Corvair's weight was on the rear. This meant that on sharp turns the inside rear wheel rim tended to pinch the tire, deflating it and sending the car into a spin or flip. "Unsafe at Any Speed," Ralph Nader's book, indicted the car. The Corvair also baffled mechanics. Volkswagen repairmen, among the few people familiar with rear-engine technology, refused to work on Corvairs because they weren't metric. New: $2,000. Now: $50 barely running. However, collectors who prize the car's sporty look are willing to fork over as much as $6,000 for a fully restored relic.

The 1978 Jaguar XJ6. An elegant pile of scrap, it inspired bumper stickers reading, "All Parts Falling Off This Car Are the Finest English Workmanship." The electrical wiring remains a mystery. The car was plagued by fires and failures of its lights and windshield washers. Some mechanics took to replacing the engines with ordinary Chevy engines. New: $16,000. Prices have plunged as low as $550, but some still manage to wring $8,000 from the unknowing who figure that is a bargain compared to new Jags at more than $40,000.

The 1980 Renault LeCar. French motorists have a saying that to own one of their cars is to shrink all other worries to nothingness. "LeCar—a terrible thing. When I see it coming, I feel a heart attack on the way," says Stanley Gordon, chairman of Great Western Systems Inc., which operates auto auctions in the Southwest. Blown head gaskets. Oil and water leaks. A mechanic's nightmare. The spare tire, squeezed under the hood, blocks the spark plugs, the air filter and other regularly serviced parts. Awkward controls meant drivers often turned off their headlights when signaling a left turn. Exhaust pipes tended to come loose, as did bumpers and driver's seats. New $3,200. Now: $50.

The 1984 Pontiac Fiero. Pontiac boasted that the fiberglass panels would help this car last forever. Unfortunately, the engines had the life span of a mayfly. The car was notorious for cracked engine blocks, oil leaks and engine fires. Pontiac killed Fiero this fall after only five years in production. To give this car its racy look, designers crammed the engine between the passenger compartment and the trunk. Tuck your grocery bags in the trunk? Don't think of it. Heat from the engine and exhaust would toast your wieners after a few miles. All that and slow, too. The Fiero lost to Volkswagen Rabbit GTI in acceleration tests. New: $10,000. They are asking $3,900 now, but a "best offer" should be $1,000 or less.

The 1971 Plymouth Cricket. Sold in Europe under the more fitting name Avenger. Cruising on the highway, the Cricket tended to jerk as if you were shifting gears. Consumers Union found 40 defects in its Cricket. "One of the many serious oil leaks from the engine and driveline soaked the clutch housing and probably caused the clutch chatter that we experienced," the auto test division reported. Shoulder straps were positioned to chafe your face. New: $2,000. Now: $100, but there is really no floor on the "best offer" for one of these babies.

The 1973 Fiat 124 Coupe. Fiat had so few good things to say about the 124 that ads merely touted radial tires and bucket seats. This car was the automotive version of a spaghetti Western: bad-acting, noisy and with a grim ending. Buyers really should have purchased a pair so as to have one for spare parts. Engines ran rough. Clutch cables repeatedly snapped. One former owner says Fiat agreed to repurchase his lemon on the condition the dealer would destroy it. Another owner says his dealer's mechanic expressed amazement he actually bought one. New: $3,200. Now: $150, or less than a pair of Italian loafers.

A Real-Estate Broker
Finds Success Selling
To Rich and Famous

Clients of Edward Lee Cave
Want Ballrooms, Gyms
In Manhattan Apartments

By Meg Cox

1/14/87

NEW YORK—"This is a great, famous, '20s building," says Edward Lee
Cave, escorting a fur-coated lady through a $5 million penthouse apart-
ment in Manhattan's River House. "There used to be a private pier down
there for parking yachts. That is Garbo's building, and over there is the
apartment that I.M. Pei designed for William Zeckendorf. Of course, this
tower looks down on all of them."

To the accompaniment of classical music from a sound system in the
library, Mr. Cave breezes through the dining room, with its wine cellar
("kept at 58 degrees, just as it should be"), and the restaurant-size
kitchen. He shows off the living-room balcony, from which string quartets
have serenaded parties, and the circular bathtub, with a view of the Empire State Building.

The six-room servants' suite, with sweeping views of midtown, prompts
him to say: "Staff quarters are as important as the front of the house, because if you don't have good staff, you don't have a nice life. Who cares if
you have a diamond tiara if you have to wash your own breakfast dishes?"

Edward Lee Cave is a real-estate broker the way Stanley Marcus is a
shopkeeper. His clients are movers and moguls. The apartments he sells
routinely come with libraries, ballrooms and gymnasiums, as well as six
or eight working fireplaces and a minimum of 10 closets. These places
are the reality that Hollywood sets are based on, the kind of apartments
where those who make it big move to prove it.

In recent years, prices have crept up or even declined for overbuilt,
cookie-cutter condominiums and co-ops in Manhattan, but the market for
vast and luxurious pre-World War II apartments has exploded. A few
brokers dominate the ultra-deluxe market. Mr. Cave is one of the most
successful of all.

"My market is the spectacular," says the 47-year-old Mr. Cave. "I feel like every apartment I walk into is a novel. These are the richest, most powerful people in the world. They can have anyting they want, and I find it for them."

Mr. Cave knows where to find a New York apartment with a tenth of an acre of land on the roof and one with a marble-lined gymnasium. For an orchid lover, he found the perfect conservatory. When prominent decorator Dorothy "Sister" Parish wanted a covered terrace on which to walk her Pekingese on rainy nights, Mr. Cave came up with just the turf: Gloria Swanson's old garden apartment.

Finding apartments to sell isn't easy. Competition among brokers is fierce for the small supply of fancy apartments with fancy addresses like Fifth Avenue and Park Avenue, and many brokers subscribe to an obituary service to spot vacancies. Mr. Cave's more experienced rivals include Douglas Elliman & Co., which also manages tony buildings, and Alice Mason, a hostess of celebrity-studded dinner parties, who has been at it for 25 years. To make things tougher, many fancy apartments change hands privately.

Knowing the right people is crucial, and it is one of Mr. Cave's best-developed talents. "His firm is smaller than mine or Elliman's," says Clark Halstead, the head of Halstead Property Co. and a former employee of Mr. Cave. "But in terms of megabucks deals, Edward is probably doing as well as anyone. Edward is a more successful knower of people in those circles than almost anyone."

Mr. Cave, who surrounds himself with old-money trappings and is listed in the Social Register, doesn't tell many people that his father was a Volkswagen dealer back in Virginia. He met many of the right people during an 18-year career at Sotheby's. He began there as a clerk cataloging art and became an expert in Oriental art and then a senior vice president.

"He likes money and expensive people, and he spent more time with people than objects," says James Lally, a former president of Sotheby's in the U.S. "To our English colleagues, he was the stereotype of the hard-driving New York businessman: three phones going and lunches booked three weeks in advance. He probably brought in more business than anyone."

In 1976, Mr. Cave helped start Sotheby's real-estate division. "We've sold them Monets," his argument went. "Now we'll sell them the walls to hang them on." The idea worked, but Mr. Cave left in 1982 to start his own firm, Edward Lee Cave Inc.

The market was wide open. "The real-estate market froze in 1968 because of all New York's municipal problems," Mr. Cave says. "You could have bought any apartment in the city for $250,000." After the city's turnaround in the mid-1970s, real estate took off. Says Mr. Cave: "I started selling apartments to people from L.A. and Chicago who were coming to New York to do deals and hated staying in the Waldorf. Europeans who were worried about unrest in their countries started paying $1 million for Fifth Avenue apartments. I realized they were right: Fifth Avenue will always be Fifth Avenue."

In 1982, the stock market took off, creating more new rich. "Two years ago, we started cracking the $5 million barrier regularly," says Mr. Cave. The Elliman firm says that the average price for one of its luxury co-ops in Manhattan has risen tenfold in 10 years to $630,000 from $60,000. The unique and huge bring up to $8.5 million, and Mr. Cave says that the going rate for the truly exquisite now exceeds $1,000 a square foot.

At the office, there is an art-filled drawing room for clients and space for some 20 brokers. Accompanied by his cocker spaniel, Travis, and dressed in his usual gray pinstriped suit, blue polka-dot tie and tortoise-shell glasses, Mr. Cave sits down to begin his daily calls. The first is to a European man whose apartment here isn't for sale.

"You're hardly ever there," coaxes Mr. Cave. "I know this very attractive couple who would be prepared very quickly to buy your apartment for an extraordinary amount. Can I take them to see it this afternoon? It looks best in the afternoon light. It will probably be sold by tonight." The owner agrees, but, alas, no sale. The apartment is on Park Avenue; the couple simply must have Fifth.

Many of the names in Mr. Cave's three fat Rolodexes are friends, not clients, but one can become the other. Says Richard Jenrette, the chairman of Donaldson, Lufkin & Jenrette Inc., who has spent weekends at Mr. Cave's 18th-century Connecticut house but has never been a client: "If I were looking to buy or sell a place in Manhattan, I would go to Edward for two reasons: He's a walking encyclopedia of high-end real estate, and, two, one likes to deal with a friend."

Felix and Elizabeth Rohatyn are a little disappointed that Mr. Cave hasn't found a buyer for their apartment after more than three months. But Mrs. Rohatyn calls him "charming and professional" and says she recommends him to her friends. Since she asked for his help in 1975, she says, Mr. Cave has been the volunteer auctioneer every year for the Lenox Hill Neighborhood Association benefit auction. "The auction provides about 25% of our budget," Mrs. Rohatyn says.

Mr. Cave is also a good salesman, as he demonstrates one afternoon as he shows four $5 million apartments. In each case, he has called ahead to have a housekeeper turn on lights. He generally starts with the plush, imposing rooms that will be used to entertain, then tours the living quarters and staff rooms. "Now that your friends are happy and you're happy," says Mr. Cave at one stop, "let's make the kids happy. They get their own fireplaces, and they have direct access to the kitchen so they don't interrupt your important dinner parties."

Pointing out architectural details, he says to a reporter, "I'm not a proper real-estate tycoon. I can never remember the maintenance costs for a building. But if there is a fake Louis XV mantelpiece, I can spot it across the room."

Before a sale, there is often a final obstacle: the building's co-op board. Even if the buyer agrees to pay cash and proves that his liquid assets are at least triple the purchase price—standard requirements—he can be shut out. In the late 1970s, a New York co-op board turned down former President Richard Nixon. Mr. Cave says he found Mr. Nixon a town house instead.

The board of an opulent building may require 10 or more business and social references. "Some buildings are very la-di-da and only want pretentious people with old money, while others want bright young doers," says Mr. Cave. "Some buildings won't take single women: Who knows whom they might marry? Some interview the children, and rude teenagers can scotch the deal."

Recently, Mr. Cave took extra pains to get a big man on Wall Street into the $5 million apartment Mr. Cave had found him. "I knew the place was perfect," says Mr. Cave. "But someone else was bidding. It was an estate [selling], and I knew the lawyer didn't have the final say. I looked in the Social Register and tracked down one of the heirs, who belongs to the same hunt club in Virginia as a friend of mine. I asked my friend to chat with the heir and let him know my man went to all the right schools and has a house in Maine."

The bid was accepted, and the co-op board approved. Says the buyer: "I'm illiquid but happy."

Rest assured, his name will remain in Mr. Cave's Rolodex. When the man's children are grown and gone and the apartment is too big, Mr. Cave will be in touch.

Lots of Magazines Write About Thin; Here's One for Fat

———

Rendering Industry's Organ Tries to Beef Up Morale During These Lean Times

———

By James P. Sterba

4/9/91

Frank Burnham fondly remembers when the nation's meat coolers bulged with corpulent pork chops girdled in thick belts of fat and stacked belly to belly like phalanxes of proud little Norman Schwarzkopfs. Today's butchers, he says, offer up skinny sirloins, tremulous T-bones and pork chops so unporcine that they look like rejects from a singles bar at happy hour.

McDonald's plans to go national this month with a low-fat seaweed-and-beef concoction called the McLean Deluxe won nutritionists' cheers. Mr. Burnham says the burger giant McKnuckled under to anti-fat fanatics.

America's war on fat has fat on the run, all right. Its retreats and defeats litter the food chain. "LOW FAT" labels dangle like surrender flags on supermarket shelves. "FAT FREE" declarations invite consumers into entire liberated zones of adipose-less edibles.

But isn't this good news? Not to Frank Burnham. For 20 years, he's been one of fat's quixotic defenders as editor and publisher of Render, the National Magazine of Rendering, the bimonthly bible of meat industry by-products. Animal fat, he says, is the much-maligned victim of vegetable oil propagandists. Fat isn't the problem, he says. Abuse of fat is the problem.

"Look, we have been consuming entirely too much fat in this country, and we need to reduce fat intake across the board," says the cheery, 67-year-old Mr. Burnham, who stands six feet tall and tips the scales at 240 pounds. "But we feel there's a place for animal fat."

Mr. Burnham goes to bat for fat in every 30-page, four-color issue of Render, which he puts together in his Calimesa, Calif., home under the auspices of the National Renderers Association (NRA), the industry's Washington-based trade group.

About 7,000 copies go out free to the people who make profit off fat:

rendering plant operators, meat packers and others associated with rendering in a dozen countries. Renderers produce beef fat called tallow, pork fat called lard and other fats and protein meals from meat, poultry and fish industry leftovers. Sure it's preaching to the choir, Mr. Burnham says, but the choir needs inspirational sermons these days: Fat's profits are thinning. And when renderers have a bone to pick, they know Render magazine will pick it.

Last fall, for example, McDonald's, Burger King and Wendy's began replacing beef fat with vegetable oil in their french fry cookers. Those three chains had gobbled up 30% of U.S. edible tallow production. Render said the chains "turned their backs on pure edible beef tallow after 50 years of fast frying" just when "new research indicates vegetable oils may be far worse for the human system than animal fats were held to be."

"Nonsense," says Bonnie Liebman, director of nutrition for the Center for Science in the Public Interest in Washington, D.C. "There is no question in the minds of any scientists I know that animal fats are worse for you than vegetable oils, with the exception of tropical oils," she says.

In the face of such assaults, Render tries to keep industry morale up with headlines such as "More Good News for Beef Lovers: And That Means Good News for the Renderer." But it isn't easy. The $2 billion-a-year rendering industry is besieged, even though America would be hard-pressed to do without it.

Renderers, going back to ancient Egypt, were among the world's first recyclers. Without the 350 or so rendering plants left in the U.S., landfills would both bulge and smell. The meat industry generates enough inedible meat by-products in a year to build a tower of fat, bones, viscera, hide and feathers 10 feet across and four and half miles high, Mr. Burnham says. That's because only 58% of, say, a slaughtered beef steer is used for food.

Renderers gather 36 billion pounds of what's left annually and either recycle it back into the food chain for people and animals, or turn it into industrial raw materials "without using a penny of public tax money," Mr. Burnham notes.

They produce 18 billion pounds of products: edible and inedible tallow, lard, meatmeal, bonemeal, bloodmeal and feathermeal. It's fed to chickens, put in pet food. It goes into a wide range of lubricants, lipsticks, paints, inks, cosmetics, plastics, tires and emulsifiers. (Feathermeal, made from the feathers of some of the six billion chickens and turkeys slaughtered annually, is the chic protein of the moment. It's sprayed with recycled fat and fed back to new generations of food birds and animals.) American beef tallow is added to lean, imported ground beef to give burgers made from it an "American taste."

But prices for these recycled fats and proteins have dropped so low that renderers who used to pay for meat leftovers and old restaurant grease increasingly charge shops and restaurants to haul it away. Restaurants, unwilling to pay, are increasingly, and usually illegally, dumping their leftover grease down sewers, clogging them and creating havoc at sewage-treatment plants.

Animal fats are simply "not welcome in domestic food production," writes K.R. "Dick" Ellis, a former fat buyer for Procter & Gamble who is a columnist for Render. Domestic demand for beef fat is less than half of what it was five years ago. Lard sales are so low that the U.S. Department of Agriculture stopped keeping figures.

The rest of the world gobbled up about 2.5 billion pounds of American-exported fat last year. Mexico is the biggest customer.

There are a few tiny signs of a comeback for "natural," tallow-based soaps. But at the moment, tallow's use in soaps is at a 45-year low.

Animal fat's biggest potential villain is a Procter & Gamble product called Olestra, an indigestible non-caloric fat substitute with many uses including deep frying. Render derides it as "fake fat." It still needs Food and Drug Administration approval, which could take years. But, says Render, "Wide use of a non-caloric deep frying fat could all but destroy the industry's single largest market."

Render isn't afraid to lard its readers with praise. "The rendering guy has always been looked down upon and on the back street," says Mr. Burnham. For one thing, rendering plants stink. "Traditionally, they've gotten as far away from people as possible, just like airports. But builders built right up to edge, and then people complain about noise, or the smell." But the plants don't emit hazardous wastes. "A rose is a rose is a rose. It's in the nose of the beholder," says Mr. Burnham. "You can live downwind of rendering plants. They're non-hazardous.

"But they make major contributions to society," Mr. Burnham says. It was, he says, an "invisible industry" until West Coast renderers asked Mr. Burnham to start the magazine in 1972, after careers as newspaperman, Air Force information officer and aerospace writer. Now, when he isn't defending fat, he's operations director of the California Civil Air Patrol.

Render is non-profit. The NRA puts up the working capital, but the magazine must break even annually. That means relying on ads, many of which are for "odor abatement equipment." One ad compares the Mona Lisa to the Svaertek Prebreaker, which promises "to solve your raw material crushing and grinding problems once and for all."

Ask him and Mr. Burnham will wax about fat's heroic past—when housewives saved it and Boy Scouts collected it for the war effort against the Nazis and Japanese; how stearic acid from it makes a great lubricant for extruding artillery shells and bullets.

Fat helped America when it was down. Someday soon, Mr. Burnham expects America to return the favor.

The PEZ Fancy
Is Hard to Explain,
Let Alone Justify

Dispensing With All Fanfare,
Candy Company Pezident
Is Shy About His Product

By Michael J. McCarthy

3/10/93

What is it with PEZ?

It is just a cheap, plastic gizmo that ejects candy bricks from the heads of Goofy, Miss Piggy and Dumbo, among others. PEZ hasn't been advertised in more than a decade. A lot of people seem to think it long ago went the way of the Edsel, its 1950s contemporary.

But PEZ isn't just a nostalgia thing.

Lately, in fact, PEZ is sizzling. Two years ago, PEZ Candy Inc. had to double the size of its Connecticut factory, now two football-fields big, with 120 people working inside. Sales are so strong the company recently pushed its dispenser price beyond the buck-barrier, to $1.29. It sells 10-pack candy refills for $1.39. Come summer, there will be two national conferences for PEZ collectors. And in June, auctioneers at Christie's will hold a PEZ-collection sale.

Inexplicably, the 41-year-old contraption, loaded with stacked, chalky, artificially flavored candy, has become a cultural icon. "It's a candy adults like to introduce their kids to, like teaching them how to eat an Oreo," says Pat Barnes, owner of Goodie Gumdrops, a candy store near Cleveland. That's part of the appeal.

Odder still, PEZ Candy has done nothing to whip up sentimental fervor. PEZ's 40th anniversary came and went last year, unobserved. Other companies gladly pay for product placement in movies, but PEZ won't. Yet PEZ often pops up, spontaneously as it were, in movies and TV shows from "Murphy Brown" to Jay Leno's "Tonight Show" and "Seinfeld," which gave a cameo to a Tweety bird PEZ.

Based in Orange, Conn., near New Haven, PEZ Candy purposely avoids its past. The very privately held company (it won't say who its owners are) has no archivist to answer inquiries from people searching for PEZ dispensers of their reveries. The letters are often forwarded to PEZ collectors. Despite requests, there are no factory tours for the public. PEZ executives won't attend PEZ fests.

Collectors feel snubbed. With so tightlipped a company, they are haunted by PEZ mysteries. Why, for example, did cherry PEZ disappear? Why did the Mary Poppins PEZ bomb? Asks collector Richard Geary, a 36-year-old disk jockey in Ohio: "Why did they make a Bullwinkle, but not a Rocky? Who makes those decisions?"

That would be the head of it all, Scott McWhinnie, a 53-year-old Harvard-trained M.B.A. known for the past decade as the "Pezident." A secretive CEO, who wears pinstriped suits and drives a blue Cadillac, he won't dwell on history, won't discuss the company's ownership or financial details and tries to keep works-in-progress close to the vest. Speaking of which, he wears a dignified, navy blue PEZ-tablet tie.

Mr. McWhinnie, a former kiddie-cereal product manager at General Mills Inc. and a Harlequin Books marketing vice president, will say this: "Our job is to create the collectibles of the future."

That leaves PEZ history to people like Maryann Kennedy, a 60-year-old nurse and grandmother in Minnesota. With four file drawers of old PEZ ads and sales lists, she may be the pre-eminent PEZ historian. And she is peeved at PEZ. "It's very aggravating that they don't share information," she says. "It seems kind of selfish."

PEZ's defining moments, it seems, were flukes. The candy was invented in 1927 by Austrian food-company mogul Eduard Haas. Tinkering with peppermint oil in Vienna one day, Mr. Haas accidentally concocted his recipe. He then crafted teeny bricks and named them "PEZ," abbreviating the German word for peppermint, Pfefferminz. He put PEZ in rectangular dispensers, the first of which had no figureheads. An avid antismoker, Mr. Haas sold PEZ in Europe as an adult mint, a cigarette substitute.

He brought PEZ to America in 1952, winning U.S. Patent No. 2,620,-061, which termed his treasure a "tablet dispensing receptacle." In no time flat, PEZ fizzled. So, he recast the dispenser as a children's toy, with the head of a cartoon figure on top.

What was the very first head? "There has been controversy about that," says Mrs. Kennedy, the PEZ whiz, who thinks but doesn't know that it was Mickey Mouse. Some say Popeye.

The cast of more than 200 coming-and-going PEZ characters is a gallery of American pop culture—Batman, Snow White, the Creature from the Black Lagoon, Charlie Brown, Uncle Sam, Bugs Bunny, you name it. Last year, about 40 different dispensers and candy refills amounted to $18 million in retail sales, according to Information Resources Inc., a research company.

To keep track of all the models, the Plastic Candy Dispenser Newsletter began publication last year. After three issues, the $18-a-year bimonthly has 233 subscribers, prints correspondence between "PEZ pals" and reports the going rates for rare PEZ. A green-haired Wonder Woman recently fetched $242.

It is hard to figure PEZ's lasting appeal. Pressed, one social scientist speculates that PEZ is one of the few things in life that melds twin delights of childhood: toys and candy. "It's a way to keep in touch with youth," offers Alex McIntosh, a Texas A&M University sociologist.

From the outside, PEZ Candy looks like any other company, except for the bushes out front pruned into a P, an E and a Z. Inside, PEZ production starts with two gigantic yellow silos, each holding 30,000 pounds of sugar. In large tubes, the sugar is blended with palm oils and artificial flavors (except for orange, which is natural) and colors, like Yellow 6. As grinding machinery thunders, the refined powder is rapidly punched into PEZ bricks and packaged. Visitors are rare, although two rabbis were recently in the plant monitoring production of the first kosher PEZ.

The dispensers are made overseas, which cuts costs but adds quality-control problems—complexion problems in the case of Flintstones characters (Fred, Pebbles and Barney Rubble) made variously in China, Hungary and Slovenia.

The real stress involves PEZ headhunting. PEZ Candy gets hundreds of requests. There was a groundswell of demand some years back for an Evel Knievel PEZ. Current lobbying is for Elvis Presley and Michael Jackson. "I had all kinds of pressure to do Alf," says Mr. McWhinnie. But with a costly design process that takes a full year, and with licensing agreements and permissions to be hammered out, he waits to be sure a cartoon character isn't just a passing fad. And he shuns depictions of real people, most especially living ones. They don't have "interesting heads," Mr. McWhinnie says, and they can get into messy scandals unbecoming to a child's toy.

He also tries to avoid PEZ bloopers. The Annie PEZ, rushed out as a tie-in, flopped right along with the movie. Then there was the cherry PEZ problem. In the early '80s, PEZ dropped cherry in favor of grape. Then came "Stand By Me," a nostalgic movie in which a youngster says, "If I could have only one food to eat for the rest of my life? That's easy. PEZ. Cherry flavor PEZ." PEZ Candy was then beset with demand it chose not to meet. Don't ask why.

Some people will do just about anything to get their paws on PEZ. Two years ago, somebody ran an ad in the New Haven Register, promising to "pay big money for old PEZ." Overnight, dozens of rare models vanished from PEZ Candy headquarters. On another occasion, Pezident McWhinnie dashed off a "cease and desist" letter after spotting display-stands for PEZ collections that used the PEZ name without permission.

The recipient sold the letter as a PEZ collector's item.

Atlanta Pupils Give Some Snack Makers F's in Cooperation

Nabisco Irks Mitch and Emily, And the Class Views Mars As the CIA of Companies

---

By Betsy Morris

4/28/86

ATLANTA—The kids at Paideia School are learning that Fortune-500 companies say and do the darndest things. In a research project on famous food brands, 11- and 12-year-olds at the private school have turned up the following.

—Pepperidge Farm Inc. apparently has no idea why it makes crackers in the shape of goldfish and not elephants or giraffes.

—Nabisco Brands Inc. doesn't seem to give a Fig Newton about the youngsters it counts on to gobble up its cookies.

—Some companies are awfully eager to please. Memphis Baking Co., for example, delivered six dozen marshmallow-filled Moon Pies to one class member's doorstep.

—Mars Inc., on the other hand, refuses to answer even the most innocuous questions about M&Ms or its other candies. It now is known at Paideia as the CIA of corporate America.

The project has been assigned for two of the past three years. Each child picks a favorite food brand, writes the manufacturer for information, and reports to the class. In the process, says teacher Peter Richards, the students learn that "different companies have different personalities."

Consider Nabisco: When Kafi Seidu wrote two years ago asking about the origin of Oreo cookies, "they said they don't answer questions," she recalls. "I guess they thought I was a child spy from Hydrox."

This year Nabisco was only a little more helpful. It sent Mitchell Hollberg a few facts about Oreos—it said that all the Oreos ever sold would reach to the moon and back, and that their name came from the Greek word for hill or mountain. That wasn't much to build a report on, Mitch thinks. (Paideia, pronounced pie-DAY-uh, also derives from a Greek word, a basically untranslatable one that means something like the transfer of knowledge.)

Mitch was luckier than Emily Fleischer. Nabisco told her it didn't have anything at all on Triscuits, and it sent her the same Oreo information it had sent Mitch. When Emily said that that wouldn't do, Nabisco sent her facts about Fig Newtons, which unfortunately aren't her favorites. "Ycch, I think they're gross," she says, wrinkling her nose. "Gag."

To make matters worse, the Fig Newton information was so scanty that her report wasn't long enough, so she padded it with as much as she could scrape up on the history of the fig tree—a trick she didn't succeed in slipping by her classmates. "I'm burning," she says.

Her troubles pale, however, compared with those of Jason Bussey, who had the misfortune of picking A.1. Steak Sauce, another Nabisco product. Mr. Richards and Jason's mother called Nabisco half a dozen times on his behalf, and Nabisco kept insisting the information was in the mail. Jason eventually stopped believing that. "Boy, that company is a real bummer," he says. (Some information finally did come, two weeks after Jason's deadline. But it consisted only of recipes and a letter that Mr. Richards says didn't give Jason much to go on.)

Informed of all this frustration, a Nabisco spokeswoman replies: "We really do try very hard to respond to everyone." But she says "it's very difficult, dealing with the number of people we do, to send them everything they want." Nonetheless, she adds, "we apologize."

Some of the companies that dragged their feet came as a big surprise. Campbell Soup Co. sent information only grudgingly after several phone calls, which surprised Ian Ingram, who thought, "Campbell's, it seems like it's for kids." The company told his mother it gets bogged down in calls from youngsters, but that didn't absolve it any in Ian's eyes. Even after prodding from the teacher, Campbell's Pepperidge Farm unit failed to shed light on the mystery of the goldfish.

Borden Inc. was surprisingly unenterprising in its response, considering that Jeremy Gould later found the company rich in history. "They just didn't want to get up and go anywhere to help," he says. Some of the students thought that modern-day Borden employees might learn something from the epitaph on the milk-can-shaped tombstone of the company's eccentric but persistent founder, Gail Borden. It reads: "I tried and failed. I tried again and again and succeeded."

And Jif Peanut Butter lost a big fan when its maker, Procter & Gamble Co., failed to supply anything more than a letter on peanut processing to Michael Haskell. "In my eyes, it did something to Jif's image," he says. His disillusionment hasn't tarnished his brand loyalty, however. "I like Jif too much," he says. "Nobody else has such good Extra Crunchy."

A number of companies, however, went out of their way to be helpful, and at Paideia, they have quickly been elevated to hero status. Borden was largely redeemed by its response to a query on Cracker Jack. Within a week, a whole package of colorful history and pictures arrived. But what really impressed the class was to find that the company electronically screens each box three times to make sure it contains a prize. "They really care about kids," says Michael Cottrell.

Jell-O also got high marks for its honest accounting of its shaky beginnings. "The public was just not impressed with it for a long time," says Darren Glass. One early owner handed out the stuff free at county fairs trying to drum up demand; another tried unsuccessfully to unload the Jell-O business on his janitor for $35, according to tales provided by Jell-O's current owner, General Foods Corp.

Some companies have spawned loyal new followings by sending along free samples. Elyse Weitman says her whole family is eating Brach's candy now because E.J. Brach & Sons Inc. showered her with sweets. "That's pretty amazing, considering my dad's a dentist," she says. Her friend Jennifer Spencer says she has a new appreciation for Chattanooga Bakery Inc. even though she has grown temporarily sick of Moon Pies. (Jennifer ate them daily after school for a week, passed them out to her class, and finally had no choice but to turn the rest of the six dozen over to her brother.)

In terms of sheer volume, Coke and Pepsi took the cake. Coke outdid Pepsi slightly by sending "Coke" stickers in Chinese and Hebrew and furnishing Bess Bryan with enough paraphernalia to fill an entire bulletin board. "I will be a buyer for life," she says.

With a little help from his uncle at Malt-O-Meal Co., Eric Sultenfuss became the only kid in the class to cadge a personal interview with a vice president. To his surprise, he thoroughly enjoyed it. He had expected the cereal executive "to be pretty strict and formal," the youngster recalls. "He was wearing a suit and tie and all," Eric says, "but he was pretty friendly."

Classmate Michael Haskell says the project has changed his view of corporate America altogether. "I used to think all companies were the same—just a bunch of drones going around doing work," he says. Now he knows that "they vary a lot."

And none, the Paideia students believe, is worse than Mars. The candy company's unresponsiveness has practically the whole school boycotting it. When Chris Lindsay wrote asking how the Milky Way bar got its name, "they said that was classified," he says. "Confidential," he recalls. "Everything was confidential." When Sarah Bianchi asked how many M&Ms were sold yearly and why there weren't any red ones anymore, "they sent me back a wimpy booklet that says 'buy M&Ms' and a coupon. It was really tacky," she says.

When an adult reporter sought a comment from the candy maker, the children's opinion that Mars was as secretive as the CIA seemed reasonable. No comment could be obtained, and a Mars switchboard operator wouldn't even divulge the name of the Mars official who would issue a comment if a comment were to be issued.

And the students promise they'll remember. "Forget it. I won't buy M&Ms," Sarah says. Says Elyse Weitman: "I'll never eat a Mars Bar again. I hate them, because they didn't help this class."

The King of Beers
And Beer of Kings
Are at Lagerheads

Legendary Czech Brewery
Tells Busch, This Bud's
Not Necessarily for You

By Roger Thurow

4/3/92

Just inside the creaking doors of the Masne Kramy beer cathedral in Ceske Budejovice, Czechoslovakia, there is a woman who sells potato pancakes. Take one, two if you are hungry, and make your way to the centuries-old great hall and its maze of wooden tables.

Sit anywhere; the regulars won't mind. Quicker than you can ask, a waiter will put a glass of one of the world's legendary brews in your hand.

Before long, amid laughter and cursing, you will hear a tale of two beers. Two Budweisers, actually. Bud East and Bud West.

"We've always had the better beer," says Ivan Kandela, an engineer, draining a glass of Bud East. "Even the Communists knew that." A waiter hurries over with another round. The story unfolds.

It is about a Cold War—Make that Ice Cold War—brewhaha that is finally coming to a head.

For much of the past century, the Budweiser of Anheuser-Busch in St. Louis and the Budweiser that flows from the Budvar brewery in this quaint Bohemian town (widely known by its German name, Budweis) have dueled up and down Europe over marketing rights to their common brand name. It has been a battle royal: The Beer of Kings (the Budvar Bud) versus the King of Beers (the Busch Bud).

Now, with the dawn of capitalism in Czechoslovakia, Budvar's days as a state-owned enterprise are numbered. It is up for sale. Busch, seeing the lucrative possibilities of a unified Bud, dearly wants to buy. Budvar, thirsting for dollars, knows that Busch's mug runneth over. The Buds are talking.

But the politicians in Prague as well as the stalwarts of Masne Kramy aren't so sure they want foreigners to control Budvar, especially the ones from St. Louis. Bohemian taste and pride are at stake.

To the discriminating taste buds of the local burghers, Busch Bud is to

Budvar Bud what store-bought bread is to homebaked. "It can be described as weak," says Jiri Altera, the Czech deputy minister of agriculture who is overseeing Budvar's privatization. He knows whereof he speaks. He reaches into his file cabinet and produces an empty bottle of Busch Bud. "To beer drinkers here, it is not very thick, not very heavy," he says.

He closes his eyes and conjures up the taste of Budvar Bud, which is aged for 90 days (about three times longer than Busch Bud) to achieve its robust, pleasantly bitter taste. "It is the strongest of Czech beers," says Mr. Altera—and one of the most profitable of Czech enterprises. "It is like our family silver," he boasts.

All these factors are giving Josef Tolar, Budvar's earnest brewmeister, a walloping hangover. He is a man skilled in striking a balance between hops and malt, not in reconciling corporate dilemmas. How, he wonders, can Budvar take on a foreign partner and still keep control over its product? (Budvar's output of 300,000 barrels a year is small beer compared to Busch's 90 million.) He and others in Bohemia fear that if they don't do business with Busch now, the world's largest brewery may one day launch the first hostile takeover known to Czechs and snap up all the Budvar shares like so many beer nuts.

"It is difficult to organize a march of elephants and insects in the same direction," says Mr. Tolar. "The insects can get crushed, even if it isn't intentional."

Once upon a time, there was joy in Budville. Back in 1265, King Premysl Otakar II founded the royal town of Ceske Budejovice in the forests of South Bohemia. To its citizens, he granted the privilege of brewing beer. It was such good beer that the town's brewing reputation spread far and wide. In 1531, King Ferdinand of Germany quaffed a glass and ordered that it be the beer of his royal court. Thus, the "Beer of Kings."

To the German-speaking overlords, the beer from the town they called Budweis was simply known as Budweiser beer. No one bothered to trademark the name; who, outside of Budweis, would use it? In 1895, the Budvar brewery was founded. It designed a logo and printed up labels. Soon Budweiser Budvar was being exported throughout Europe.

An ocean away, Eberhard Anheuser and Adolphus Busch were trying to revive a foundering St. Louis brewery. In 1876, Mr. Busch created a new brand, and, like many American brewers at the time, he borrowed a name from the Old World beer heritage—Budweiser. He duly registered it as a trademark, along with a new slogan, "The King of Beers." The brewery blossomed.

The two Buds first clashed at a turn-of-the-century trade fair. Lawyers were brought in, and, in 1911, the Budweisers came up with an agreement that essentially divided the world into two spheres of Bud influence. Basically, Busch got North America, Budvar got Europe.

While Budvar was content to remain a rather exclusive beer, Busch was expanding like yeast gone wild. By the 1950s, Busch had become the world's largest brewery, and the U.S. Budweiser was knocking on the doors of Europe. "The surface of the earth was too small for the two of us," says Mr. Tolar.

The Bud war was on. Busch attacked with spiffy marketing gimmicks, including a dog named Spuds. Budvar defended with Communist lawyers in colorless duds.

From Sweden to Spain they went at it, and beyond to Africa and Israel. Each won battles, but neither won the war. Busch triumphed in the British courts, which ruled that both Buds could be served in the same pubs. Budvar prevailed with exclusive rights in the big beer-drinking nations of Germany and Austria.

When communism fell in 1989 and free enterprise came to Czechoslovakia, Busch moved quickly and tried to beat the privatization rush. It made a proposal linking a settlement of the brand name dispute to a joint venture in the management of Budvar. The government was ready to bite when other offers started pouring in, more than 40 altogether, from breweries on four different continents. Prague decided to give Budvar's privatization time to ferment.

For the moment, Budvar is leaning toward keeping majority control in Czech hands, mainly by distributing shares to employees and residents of Ceske Budejovice. Busch, eager to add a European-style beer to its brand lineup to bolster its overseas sales, is lobbying for at least a 30% stake and promises a light touch on the controls.

"The last thing in the world we would want to change is the taste," vows Jack MacDonough of Anheuser-Busch International. "We want to make it one of the strongest brands in Europe."

First, though, Busch knows it must remove the bitter taste left from decades of fighting. Last October it donated $50,000 to South Bohemia University in Ceske Budejovice. But the people of Bohemia are a hard sell.

"Busch made a good effort," says Ceske Budejovice deputy mayor Miroslav Tampir. "But that was last year. If you love a girl, you don't do something one day and then nothing for six months. We are waiting."

The town, he says, could use a technical school. New heating systems would be nice. There are a couple of soccer and hockey teams in need of sponsors. It can be a good partnership, says Mr. Tampir.

"About the name Budweiser. They can use it, but only if they take Bohemian beer quality to America and not American quality to Bohemia," the deputy mayor says with a wink. He has an idea. "Busch can bring 2,000 Americans to Ceske Budejovice every day to try Budvar. Let them judge."

There is plenty of room at the Masne Kramy. The woman at the door will stock up on potato pancakes. The waiters will carry more beer. The regulars will offer their chairs. They have a tale to tell.

If You Don't Like Hearing All the Dirt, Don't Get a Scanner

Devices Tap Cellular Phones, Pagers and Baby Monitors; 'Better Than Soap Operas'

By Michael W. Miller

_10/9/90_

BRASSTOWN, N.C.—At nightfall in the Smoky Mountains, the only sounds inside Bob Grove's home are the wind in the sourwood trees, a chorus of crickets, and an intimate conversation between two people 60 miles away in Chattanooga, Tenn.

Male voice: "It's strictly platonic!"

Female voice: "I'm going to aerobics. . . ."

Male voice: "I know you think I'm lying, but it was all platonic. . . ."

Mr. Grove doesn't know these people he's listening to, and they don't know that their phone call is providing live entertainment on Mr. Grove's scanner radio. On a clear day, he can also pick up a nearby McDonald's takeout window, the local highway patrol helicopter, the neighborhood hospital's paging system, Georgia game wardens, various taxi dispatchers, Alcoholic Beverage Control field agents, 20 different sheriff's departments, several electric power companies, and beeps from the collar of a hunting dog down the road.

"It's better than soap operas, and there's no commercials," says Mr. Grove.

The air has become a rich feast for people like Mr. Grove, who are making a hobby of listening in. Americans all over the place are talking to one another on devices without wires: phones in cars, cordless phones at home, and mobile radios in government and private offices. This new technology has opened up a huge gap in the privacy of personal and business conversations, and thousands of radio buffs are happily diving in.

A former science teacher with the folksy manner of public TV's Mr. Rogers, Bob Grove has made Brasstown the capital of recreational snooping. Besides keeping tabs on his electronic neighborhood, he runs a profitable mail-order business in scanners, antennas and directories of cordless-device frequencies. He also publishes Monitoring Times, a 30,000-circulation monthly magazine of technical tips and tales of scanning. In the past three years his sales have doubled and now, he says, are over $1 million a year.

The proliferation of cordless phones in recent years has transformed Mr. Grove's business. Gone are the days when police groupies bought scanners just to listen to cops in squad cars speaking in code. "People call me and say, 'Bob, my neighbor is having an affair, I need a better antenna,'" Mr. Grove says.

An even juicier medium than the telephone is the baby monitor, a device many new parents use to transmit sounds from the crib to a speaker elsewhere in their home. "People don't realize it's just like planting a bug in your house," says Steve Douglass, an Amarillo, Texas, photographer and scanner fan. "Anyone in the neighborhood listening on that frequency can hear the whole house."

Mr. Douglass has his own way of pinpointing exactly which neighbor's baby monitor he is listening to. He wires his scanner to a tape recorder, drives by a suspect's house, honks his horn, and goes home to see if the scanner hears the honk. "Sooner or later, you can figure out which house it is," he says.

As hobbies go, eavesdropping can be about as cheap as hunting or fishing, and it is less regulated. An entry-level listener can get started with a $250 scanner. Once you get into it, you can spend thousands on antennas, timers and recorders. Federal law permits monitoring virtually anything broadcast over the air, on the theory that users of wireless devices knowingly forfeit their privacy. Cellular phone calls are an exception, theoretically off-limits thanks to a 1986 statute commonly flouted and never enforced. (Monitoring household cordless phones is perfectly legal.)

Whether this hobby is moral is a different question, one that the staff of Monitoring Times has wrestled with in its pages.

"Scanning requires that we exercise a degree of common sense and responsibility," wrote columnist Bob Kay in a recent issue. "Before you begin to monitor your neighbor's cordless phone, ask yourself if you really want to learn about his or her personal activities, sexual habits, and other intimate secrets."

Most hobbyists have thought about it and decided: absolutely.

"When we lived in Dallas, we used to listen to this one couple. He's married, she's divorced, he's seeing her on the sly," recalls Larry Van Horn, a Navy chief petty officer in New Orleans. "Whenever we'd hear them, we'd call our friends and say, '[They're] on, everybody tune in!' That was the bad part of leaving Dallas. I'd have to miss hearing [them]."

Not every conversation a scanner picks up is quite so compelling. The Wall Street Journal recently wandered around the Upper West Side of Manhattan with a portable scanner tuned to cordless-phone frequencies. It overheard an actor scheduling an audition, someone explaining how to get into Sticky Mike's Frog Bar and a conversation about health clubs. (She: "If I don't have my headphones, I can't concentrate." He: "That's so true!") Then there was the woman on 108th Street who was arranging to buy illicit drugs. She wanted some for her sister, too.

What voices a scanner pulls from the sky depends on which range of frequencies the device is built to receive from among the hundreds in use. Some offer up much more than chit-chat. Fred Anderson, an Exeter, N.H., anti-nuclear activist, found that his scanner could pick up conversations in the control room at the Seabrook nuclear plant. He taped them for several months last year and embarrassed the plant by publicizing the highlights: unsettling remarks like, "I've got a bad feeling about these valves."

Other listeners prefer to turn their dials to lighter fare. Kevin Coulter, a Chicago computer engineer, brings a portable scanner to car races and hears drivers talking to their pit crews. Mr. Kay, the Monitoring Times columnist, once parked his car outside a Pennsylvania dinner theater and enjoyed "Oklahoma" as the musical was transmitted to him via performers' wireless microphones.

Fast-food restaurants whose employees take drive-through orders on wireless headsets are popular with the scanner set. "You hear the teenagers joking among themselves, sexually harassing each other," says Robert Parnass, an Oswego, Ill., computer scientist who has taken his scanner to McDonald's. "They have a button they can press so the customer can't hear them, but a scanner can."

Fortunately for scanner buffs, it is quite cumbersome, not to mention costly, to keep a cordless conversation private. Devices to scramble calls cost hundreds of dollars, and both parties on the line need to have an unscrambler. The only people who invest in scrambling gear are high-security users like the FBI and the White House.

And even the president isn't completely out of range. Dick Stedman, a dental-supply marketing executive with a vacation home in Kennebunkport, Maine, has compiled a list of 35 unscrambled frequencies for "Bush watching." He says you can track President Bush at his house there by listening to the police setting up roadblocks and TV crews mapping coverage.

At home in his listening room, beneath a framed movie still of Dr. Frankenstein's laboratory, Bob Grove cheerfully admits that scanning, like so many other of life's pleasures, brings the occasional pang of guilt. At the same time, he thinks, anyone upset about privacy issues ought to be blaming the makers of wireless devices.

"The industry has been remiss in not providing a program of awareness for the hapless users of these two-way radios," he argues. Phone-makers respond that their manuals do indeed warn that wireless conversations are subject to eavesdropping.

It's possible that bigger-print warnings wouldn't make much difference anyway. "All your life you think of a conversation as having just two parties," Mr. Grove says. "Every time I use my cordless telephone, I forget that there might be someone listening. And no one in the U.S. should be more aware of that than me."

He turns up his scanner: "You never have gotten your checks, baby—stop by the bank where Daddy opened up your accounts. . . . They want a media package, films, the works. . . . Well, I've got to pick up some chemicals. . . ."

IV

MODERN
ROMANCE

Chelsea Vocational's First Prom in Years Boasts All the Frills

*Inner-City Students Try Out
Silver Tiaras and Tuxes,
Watch the Sun Come Up*

By Christine McAuley

6/29/90

NEW YORK—Dianne Soto teeters across the housing project courtyard in her three-inch white satin heels toward the waiting pink and white limousine. At $35 an hour, the limo is a splurge. But Miss Soto and her four girlfriends thought it was worth the money. After all, Chelsea Vocational High School is having its first prom in more than a decade, and its organizers should arrive in style.

Over the blare of calypso music, Schela Brun, 17, explains the absence of dates. With only 25 girls in a senior class of 133, it would seem that there are plenty of eligible bachelors. "You can't go with just one," Miss Brun observes as she adjusts her white-lace strapless dress, "or all the others would be jealous and fight."

Six years ago, Chelsea Vocational opened its doors to girls for the first time since its founding in 1920. This year, all the class officers are girls. And they are getting what they want—a prom with all the trimmings. A revolving mirrored ball. Balloon bouquets in blue and gold, the school colors. Party favors. A $60-a-plate buffet with crudités and dip, fruit salad, and top round of beef. So what if it is a month later than every other school prom?

"We've worked so hard for it," Miss Soto says. "At first everyone wanted a prom, but they didn't think we could do it. Once it was organized, some kids backed out at the last minute. We had to collect the money and make it work—and we did."

The hotel deposit was a big hurdle. The Summit Hotel in Manhattan had to have $250 by mid-May for the late-June event. So the girls went from desk to desk to raise the money. They managed to come up with $280. In the end, turnout was better than anyone expected: 60 total, 40 from the graduating class.

Chelsea's students come from all over New York City to this small high school in a residential section of lower Manhattan. For some, the school is an opportunity to learn a trade: computers, electronics, photocopier repair. For others, it is an opportunity to escape a tough or dangerous school in their own neighborhood. Miss Brun says that's one of the reasons she went to Chelsea: "Drugs."

Not that Chelsea is immune to problems. Steven Lopez, one of the six teen-agers indicted for the rape of a jogger in Central Park, is a sophomore here. Two members of the graduating class are teen-age mothers.

Class vice president Sabrina Soto's 5½-month-old daughter, Crystal Marie, is home with family on prom night. Miss Soto, who is not related to Dianne, is wearing a regal purple dress gathered at the hip and shoes dyed to match. "I had my daughter and finished school," she says proudly. "It was tough but I did it. And tonight we're all celebrating what we've achieved."

If the students are shy or awkward in this formal setting, it is not around each other or their teachers, but with the hotel staff. Tracy Noel, a soft-spoken young man who will join the Navy in September, finishes his dinner and spots a waiter eyeing his empty plate. "Excuse me, sir," Mr. Noel asks. "Where should I put this?"

It's not every day that a 17-year-old sports a tuxedo, so more than one young man glances in the ballroom's smoked-glass mirrors to make sure he got his money's worth. In those desperate few moments before the photographer's flash pops, Peter Willis practices his stance in a mirror. Should he smile or look oh-so-seriously into the camera? He orders an 8-by-10 print of himself in his rented tuxedo. "I'll also get one with my date and one with my friends," he says.

Most students arrive without dates, and the partners on the dance floor change as quickly as the beat. The music ranges from slow numbers by Whitney Houston to 2 Live Crew's controversial single, "Me So Horny." "Let's make a party!" shouts the deejay, a podiatry student who rushed in still wearing his hospital whites under a sports jacket.

In a few days, the senior class will scatter. A few members plan to go to college in the fall. Many more are thinking about getting jobs. Five have signed up to serve in the armed forces, including the valedictorian, Rhazine Brown. Kenneth Roberts says he is joining the Navy because recruiters promised he would see the world. "First, I'm going to Chicago," he says excitedly. "Then I'm going to go to Virginia."

Caroline Lavelle wants more for her students, more than Chicago, more than just any old job in Brooklyn. It frustrates her. "Maybe the hardest thing is that the kids are happy with so little," the English teacher says. "I say they could have done better and they say, 'But Miss Lavelle, I passed.'"

Under her picture in the yearbook, Noemi Rivera, 17, requested that "Lawyer" be listed as her ambition. "Everybody asks me why I'd go to school for seven more years, but for me the more I know the better I feel," she says. Miss Rivera says she is going to a local community college in the fall. Eventually, she wants to study criminal justice at John Jay College in Manhattan.

Seniors dedicated the prom to Nelson Mandela and to Ruth Rondon, class secretary, who helped organize the prom and whose father died only weeks before. Ruth told her friends she didn't want to go, but Dianne Soto and Miss Rivera say they knew it was because she didn't have the money.

So they took up a collection, and Miss Soto lent her a black-lace dress. Mr. Roberts wrote and performed—in white tails—a rap song in her honor: "The next lovely lady, her job is secretary, all respect due to Ruthie, the legendary."

To announce the students voted by the class to be the prom's royal couple, Robert Mitchell, a teacher who has volunteered to chaperon, takes the microphone in the center of the dance floor. "And the King and Queen of the Chelsea Prom are . . . Hector Ramirez and Dianne Soto!"

They lead the next dance, a slow one. Mr. Ramirez and Miss Soto wear their coveted tiaras for the rest of the evening. They hadn't arrived together, but they spend much of the remaining evening that way.

At midnight, after the last dance, the students agree to gather at Orchard Beach in the Bronx to watch the sun come up. Thinking ahead, someone loads a half-eaten sheet cake from the buffet into a limousine.

And what about next year? Will there be a second annual prom for Chelsea Vocational? "It's up to the next class," Miss Soto says. "We just proved it could be done."

Love Affairs Bloom
Amid Bits and Bytes
Of Home Computers

———

Cupid's Electronic Arrows Hit
Many Plugged-In Seniors;
Just Call It Dial-Up-a-Date

———

By Clare Ansberry

2/12/93

JoAnn Oakes and Mayer Solen fell for each other just before Christmas in 1991. She had been watching from a distance, as Mr. Solen flitted from one group of friends to another, greeting all the women as "Honey," and they matching him with "Dear."

Finally, the two began a conversation. They discovered they were both widowed—she after a 35-year marriage and he after 49½ years. Both loved Mexican food and ballroom dancing.

They talked on and on, never noticing that everyone else had left the party. At midnight, they said good night, turned off their computers and went to bed, Mr. Solen in Carson City, Nev., and Mrs. Oakes in Bainbridge, Wash.

From then on, they talked nearly every day over the computer. Last March, Mr. Solen visited Mrs. Oakes in Washington. In June, the 64-year-old Mrs. Oakes drove to Nevada to see Mr. Solen, 76.

"I came down here with the idea of just a visit. I haven't been back" to Washington since, she says. For Mr. Solen, it was love at first byte. "Before I ever met her, I had fallen in love," he says.

Computers are playing Cupid for what seems to be an unlikely target—a generation that didn't know the difference between a mouse and a modem until they reached 60. Now, older adults are plugged in to interactive networks like San Francisco–based SeniorNet, where they can exchange gardening tips, debate atheism or try to come up with all the lines of "I'm Forever Blowing Bubbles."

The marriage between seniors and computers is, in fact, perfectly natural. They grew up writing weekly letters and keeping journals and diaries: A computer is an easier, eraser-less way to do the same. And more. Without ever leaving Ohio, they can carry on one conversation with someone in Maine and New Zealand, and later meet the professed cousin of Harry Truman and a man who says he once kissed Elizabeth Taylor.

Some, like Mr. Solen, log on at 6 P.M. to SeniorNet's Wednesday night "cocktail party" and stay until midnight.

SeniorNet, which costs members $9.95 a month, has 6,000 members and 46 learning centers across the country. Mary Furlong, founder of the seven-year-old network, says it is a painless way to socialize, especially for those recently widowed and reluctant to go out alone and for the disabled.

Ever since a 1982 auto accident, Theodora Groothof, of Colorado Springs, has been confined to a wheelchair. She doesn't get out much to meet people, but struck up a friendship over the computer with Edward Junkin, a retired doctor from Calgary. He has spent the last three Christmases at her house.

With no risk of censure or rejection, grandparents can let their hair down. Church-going Baptists confess they are really agnostics. Once straitlaced, they are flirting shamelessly with someone 500 miles away named Texas Tom. If they don't like the company or the discussion, they don't have to be polite. "Just hit the control button and you're gone," says JoAnn Oakes.

Women find computers especially liberating. Jessie Askew, a 55-year-old active volunteer, relied on her husband to keep all of her volunteer groups' records on computer. When he died in 1985, she bought her own. "I had to teach myself how to use it, but it made me so confident," she says.

On the first New Year's Eve after her husband's death, she decided to go on-line and found herself in her Lynchburg, Va., home playing Battleship with a 14-year-old from Baton Rouge, La. "I thought this is so neat. Here I am playing games with a kid halfway across the country," she says. "It caught my imagination."

Having moved in with her parents in Texas to care for her ailing mother, Mrs. Askew became a computer groupie and joined several networks. During a Wednesday night cocktail party last year, she noticed a newcomer, Chuck Ramsey. She called up his biography, which along with hobbies described his computer. "Chuck," she typed, "I just read your bio and I think I'm in love with your computer."

A few seconds later, Mr. Ramsey wrote: "Well, I just read your bio, and I think I'm in love with you. Will you marry me?" Jessie turned to her 74-year-old father and asked, "What should I say?" "Tell him 'YES,' " she says her father ordered. She did, and the party broke into peals of "HAH HAH" over what seemed to be a joke.

A few nights later, Mr. Ramsey asked her to call him on an 800 number so he could hear her voice. She discovered that her new interest, who was curt on the computer, could only type with two fingers and was much more expansive on the phone.

Within a few months, Mr. Ramsey was waiting for her on her father's front porch. "By the time we got to the house, it was arm in arm," says 68-year-old Mr. Ramsey, who lives in Woodland Hills, Calif. He has made five trips since, and they are talking about taking a trip to Denmark in the spring.

"This is kind of a wild adventure for me," Mrs. Askew says. Earlier, when an infatuation with a computer acquaintance in North Dakota turned out to be only that, she introduced him to one of her friends in Florida. They corresponded by computer for months, and finally met. Three days later, they married.

Computers, it turns out, are much more revealing than they might seem. JoAnn Oakes says: "If you talk to someone long enough, you find out how deep they are, or whether they're self-centered." When she first encountered Mr. Solen, she thought he was a Lothario, with all his flirting. But then she saw his response to a reticent newcomer, who after minutes of silence, typed, "I just lost my wife of 40 years." The screens went silent until Mr. Solen logged on, talking about his own grief after his wife died.

That impressed her. Still, she had some reservations. What if he was sloppy or unshaven? She knew only from his description that he was fit, used to be 5-feet-11 but was now 5-feet-8½ and had silver hair. "I didn't fall in love until after I saw him," she says.

That convinced her. But convincing her children that she was going to Nevada to stay with a man she met over a computer was another thing.

"I felt like I was her mother," says 38-year-old Marilee Oakes. "I was saying, 'I know you've talked to him on the computer and mentioned his name a few times but WHAT? He's coming up here? Or what? You're going down there?' "

Yet she admires her mother's courage and is happy for her. "She was laughing again," she says, adding that her mother calls Mr. Solen her "soul mate."

He in turn, calls Mrs. Oakes his "dream," and composed a poem for her on his computer:

"You came into my life by chance and made my dream come true,
A dream that only you enhance, my dream of loving you."

Men Who Aspire
To Women Higher
Have Lots to Learn

*Ms. Sayles Teaches Males How
To Land a Sugar Mommy;
Brutal Sacrifices Made*

By Jane Mayer

6/4/91

The term "gold digger" has an unpleasant ring to many people, but to Ginie Polo Sayles, it is a professional compliment.

"Mer-cen-ary," she says, caressing each syllable in her seductive, West-Texas drawl. "I just LOVE that word."

If the eyes are the windows of the soul, then Ms. Sayles's big blues are a dazzling glimpse into a cash register drawer. And keeping that drawer filled these days is a product that may be perfectly pitched to the times. Ms. Sayles is selling courses (in various cities), tapes, private consultations and a soon-to-be-released book, all on a topic that seamlessly spans the distance between the Greed of the 1980s and the Family Values of the 1990s: "How to Marry the Rich."

In pre-liberation days this topic might have been thought the province of scheming females, like Lorelei Lee, the diamond-loving leading lady in Anita Loos's "Gentlemen Prefer Blondes." But Ms. Sayles, who is not one to deny herself half the market, has tapped a new, lucrative vein: fortune-hunting men.

"It's still a woman's game, more than a man's," she acknowledges, "but that is changing." In the three years she has been selling her introductory audio cassette, "How to Marry the Rich" ($24.95), she says the percentage of males buying her tape has more than doubled, to 30%, inspiring her to shape a large portion of her curriculum specifically to their needs.

"I think she's on the frontier of this whole sexual-relations thing," says one former pupil, Mario Morais, 30, a Dallas-based systems engineer who would prefer to spend his daylight hours "discovering myself and traveling." He adds, "I think there's a part of everyone that just wants to be taken care of. It used to be that women looked for a Sugar Daddy. But now the revolution has come, why not find a Sugar Mommy?"

The first hurdle Ms. Sayles faces with her clients is getting them to discard quaint American notions that marriage should be first and foremost about love, that honesty is the best policy, even among spouses, and that work is necessary for a full life. Instead, Ms. Sayles espouses deceptive dating, strategic coupling and total financial dependence if possible. The ultimate goal is virtual adult adoption.

Male pupils also must overcome sexual stereotypes casting men who sponge off women as either emasculated dandies, or vapid studs—what the Palm Beach set calls "lifeguards."

Certainly, Patrick Platner, 42, one of Ms. Sayles's recent graduates, is willing to risk the humiliation. As he puts it, "I have no problem being supported at all." An aspiring actor in Dallas, he wants the time and money to expand beyond such recent roles as that of a victim in the horror film "Goat Man." Letting a woman pay his way, he says, is no threat to his ego. "I've had many women try to spoil me—and I liked it just fine."

Ms. Sayles's three-hour course ($25, with an option of $125-per-hour private consultations) and her audio cassette have helped Mr. Platner clarify both his ends and his means. "My goal is to meet someone independently wealthy who would like to sponsor a younger man. I'm not exactly bad-looking," he notes, adding, "I've been told that I look like a young Marlon Brando" of approximately "The Wild One" vintage. And so, as he sees his romantic future, "It's sort of a trade-off I'm offering: her money for my interest."

For such willing novitiates, Ms. Sayles offers a step-by-step guide in the great tradition of American self-help manuals. And like a charismatic preacher who once was down, too, she offers her own life as testimonial that one can be born, as she was, "a poor barefoot girl playing with lizards in a tiny town in West Texas," and end up married, as she is, at least the third time around, to what she says is a bona fide "adorable" millionaire trading in oil and gas from a mansion in Little Rock, Ark.

But first beware: Every great ambition calls for sacrifice, and marrying a rich mate, or in her lexicon, an "R.M.," is no different. "Unfortunately," she warns, "there are some rather brutal choices you may have to make to achieve your dreams." You may have to move to a better neighborhood, even if it means renting an attic in a wealthy person's garage or taking a roommate; you may also have to dump your old friends and, as she puts it, "limit your exposure to parents or relatives who are holding you back."

This worked for Ms. Sayles. Her father, a retired government soil-conservation worker, and her mother, a housewife, "kind of wanted me to take care of them for the rest of their lives. They're sweet, good people," she quickly adds, "but I had to limit my exposure so that I didn't restrict my own thinking." Instead of continuing an early career as a schoolteacher, she became a stockbroker and, without telling her parents, moved out of town.

Once such a commitment is made, the rules are simple. First, Ms. Sayles advocates haunting all the classiest places in town, "getting used to having your body near the very best that money can buy," in order to learn about taste, style, and how to make yourself what she calls "elevateable." Try on the most expensive clothes, test-drive an expensive car and follow "impressive couples" out at night, to see where they go.

Next, try to mingle with a potential "R.M." For men, she suggests reading obituaries to spot wealthy widows, noting their religion, social clubs, hobbies and other data that might make it possible to engineer a meeting "after waiting six months," presumably for decency. Read the social columns for parties to crash, take sports lessons at a club too expensive to join (or better yet, become a pro and give the lessons), or join an Alcoholics Anonymous branch in a wealthy neighborhood to meet a few "100-proof millionaires." But before going to great lengths, she warns, make sure the targeted Sugar Mommy "lives on assets, not alimony."

Once wedding plans are made, move quickly and "don't announce anything to anyone. You may be lucky enough to get your R.M. to the altar before anyone has time to think of a pre-nuptial agreement." But don't get too used to breakfast in bed; since matrimonial bliss only lasts 18 months, "start researching countries that have safe, secret bank accounts, and start socking away whatever cash and gifts you can charm your R.M. into buying you."

Judging from the progress of Ms. Sayles's recent graduates, however, getting to easy street isn't always so easy. She says only one male graduate has married rich, and declines to give his name. Mr. Morais, the systems analyst, says he is thinking seriously of moving to a smaller place in a wealthier neighborhood where he might bump into the rich at a convenience store. "The rich shop at 7-Eleven just like we do," he says confidently. But has he met any yet? "No, not to actually know them," he confesses.

Warren Jinks, 46, a part-time cable television producer who took Ms. Sayles's course, also has yet to hit pay dirt. He has worked as an escort to rich widows, as a ballroom dancing instructor to wealthy older women and as a remodeler of expensive homes. But he found that "no matter what, they never invited me to their cocktail parties."

He also tried the Sayles suggestion of attending a church in a wealthy neighborhood. But "most of the other people didn't live there, either," he found. "They were all trying to move up."

Mr. Platner, the actor, has had a little more success. He says he now has "a different circle of friends" and has become "good at crashing parties," and has "sort of upgraded my life-style."

But although he has "met a few wealthy women," he laments, "I'm not engaged yet. The problem is that most of them just don't take me seriously."

This Is the Sad Tale
Of Lovers Parted
In a Modern War

An Egyptian Hears Nothing
From His Vietnamese Wife
Since She Fled Iraq's Bombs

By Peter Waldman

4/15/93

My Love Mustafa, You are my sun by day and my moon at night. How I
ask God to meet my heart again!
—BAN NHAN, IN A LETTER TO MUSTAFA WAGIH, JULY 3, 1991

BAGHDAD, IRAQ—That was the last time Mustafa Wagih heard from Ban
Nhan. Since then, whenever the 28-year-old Egyptian has dropped by the
Vietnamese Embassy here looking for mail from his true love, an Iraqi
soldier in front of the shuttered building has shooed him away.

The couple was married July 19, 1990, two weeks before Iraq invaded
Kuwait. They were wrenched apart six months later, with Western bombs
exploding in Baghdad. The Vietnamese ambassador drew up the divorce
papers himself, assuring the young lovers it was only for the best: Vietnam's contract to supply nurses to Iraq had been abrogated by war, he
explained; Ms. Nhan must go home. It was doubtful, the ambassador
added, that the two would ever see each other again.

At first, the newlyweds refused to sign. Their brief marriage had been
full of pleasures. By combining their lives they could begin to create what
most poor migrant workers can only crave: a home. With his savings as a
bartender and hers as a nurse, they planned to move to Egypt, to raise a
family in Mr. Wagih's childhood home, to start an interior-design firm in
an affluent suburb of Cairo.

When war came, the 60 or so Vietnamese workers in Iraq huddled at
their embassy, awaiting buses to take them to Jordan on a moment's notice. Ms. Nhan huddled at home with Mr. Wagih.

For a week, they wept. He begged her to stay, to ride out the war until
Iraq's currency—and thus his life's savings—regained its prewar value.
He had nothing to show for five years in Baghdad but fistfuls of now

nearly worthless Iraqi dinars. If they waited, he promised they'd leave in style.

Twice in those agonizing days the couple went to the Vietnamese Embassy to see off friends and consult with the ambassador. On the third trip, as the embassy staff itself boarded the last bus, Ms. Nhan broke down. Her cousins had been killed in the U.S. bombing of Hanoi, she told her husband, "And now I'm going to die like that, too?"

As Ms. Nhan sobbed wildly, the divorce was sealed. The ambassador eased her from Mr. Wagih's arms, onto the bus.

"I told her, 'Don't worry, these problems will end,' " Mr. Wagih says. " 'I'll come for you in Hanoi.' "

More than two years later, Mustafa Wagih is still reeling from the whirlwind of war, his heart heavier than ever. Overnight, he says, he lost his savings, his wife and his dreams. Now, the chances of recovering any of them are fading fast.

For several months, a friendly Iraqi attendant, who was guarding the closed Vietnamese Embassy, passed on letters from Ms. Nhan. She had returned to her village near Hanoi from Iraq. But one day the attendant disappeared, and a soldier on duty warned Mr. Wagih never to return. Ms. Nhan has no way of knowing that Mr. Wagih is working for a different hotel now, and living in a place owned by that hotel, so he hasn't heard from Ms. Nhan in nearly two years. He worries she may have moved and hasn't received his letters.

At first, Mr. Wagih set about saving up enough money by bartending in nightclubs to buy a plane ticket to Vietnam. But since the war, the United Nations' trade embargo has continued hammering the Iraqi dinar, and with it, hopes of earning hard currency for the long trip east. Prospects of Ms. Nhan returning to the Mideast are just as slim. The Vietnamese government keeps a waiting list for overseas jobs that is many years long, Mr. Wagih says.

So now he "works to eat and eats to work," he says, his life on hold. On the phone, his crying mother begs him to return to Cairo. He won't think of it.

"Going home now means I've lost, I'm beaten," says Mr. Wagih, as he waits for customers in an empty nightclub, while an Armenian organist plays "Raindrops Keep Falling on My Head."

"You get nothing from war, nothing," he says. "Only tears."

They met in Baghdad between the war with Iran and the war over Kuwait, a moment of hope in a city of fear. The nightclubs were hopping then. Mr. Wagih could squirrel away $1,500 a year in the late 1980s, plus send money home to his parents in Cairo. Roughly a million foreigners worked in oil-rich Iraq, population 18 million. At least half of them fled after the invasion of Kuwait. But thousands have stayed on or returned, particularly from Sudan, Egypt and other poor Arab countries, whose own economies are even worse off than Iraq's.

On the fateful night, Ms. Nhan came with a friend to the hotel lounge where Mr. Wagih was tending bar. She ordered a Campari cola, but a confused Sudanese waiter placed the order as gambari cola—shrimp cola in Arabic. Mr. Wagih went over to clear things up. After a good laugh, he offered the women a free drink. They spoke in English.

She came back the next night and sat at the bar. They talked for hours. She was 31, the third child in a family of 12. She had waited five years for a nursing contract in the Mideast.

He says he graduated third in his class in archaeology at Cairo University, but he was too broke to pursue advanced studies. After a year in the army, he worked as a carpenter, a tour guide and a joiner in a window factory, but the two-hour commute by crowded bus was miserable. He applied for visas to Italy and the U.S., but couldn't come up with $1,000 in "fixer fees" intermediaries demanded. He heard there was work in Baghdad, no visa needed.

It wasn't until Ms. Nhan's third or fourth visit to the bar that Mr. Wagih found out her name. She was turning 32 that night; he had the band play "Happy Birthday." The next week, she and her friend met Mr. Wagih for a walk by the Tigris River. They ended up at a riverside fish restaurant, where the conversation turned personal.

Are you married? asked the friend, who was also a nurse from Vietnam.

No, Mr. Wagih said. "I haven't found the right person—until now. But I'm afraid to ask her. Maybe she'll refuse me."

Ms. Nhan suddenly went off to the ladies' room. The friend said not to worry, to keep trying: Ms. Nhan had loved him since the day they met.

A few days later, when the couple was alone in the bar again, Ms. Nhan told Mr. Wagih how poor her family was, how they depended on her work in Iraq to get by.

"I told her, 'Keep your money for your family and live with me,' " he recalls. " 'I'll pay for anything you need.' "

That was the marriage proposal. The Vietnamese consul visited Mr. Wagih in his apartment to look things over. He asked the young Egyptian about his job, and checked up on him with Iraqi security officials. Over lunch, he explained that Ms. Nhan was a different religion, Christian, and that she would have to leave Iraq when her nursing contract expired.

"I said, 'No problem. It's love. Don't ask about religion or nationality,' " Mr. Wagih says.

The wedding was at the Vietnamese Embassy, with the consul reading the wedding vows, partly in Vietnamese, partly in English. Ms. Nhan's friend, choking back tears, was the only guest.

Mr. Wagih says he doubts he will ever marry again. Ms. Nhan was the only close friend he ever had, he says. "You can't trust people in this world."

He keeps her picture on his bedstand. Every night, before going to sleep, he wishes her sweet dreams.

Happy Endings:
This Marriage, Too,
Is Saved by Therapy

———

Ladies' Home Journal Tells
How to Work It All Out;
Wendy's Strange Fixation

———

By James S. Hirsch

1/14/92

Bob and Wendy were happily married for 20 years—until she fell in love with country music. Then all hell broke loose.

Wendy started going off to concerts, hanging out with roadies, joining fan clubs, playing Willie Nelson records too loud at home. She returned from one show with her shirt autographed above her left breast by a country singer. Bob was jealous; Bob felt ignored. He blamed the blaring music for his high blood pressure and threatened to move out.

What to do?

The couple's story appeared six years ago in Ladies' Home Journal's venerable column "Can This Marriage Be Saved?" For 39 years, the magazine (circulation 5 million) has been saving marriages monthly in what it calls "the most popular, most enduring women's magazine feature in the world."

Based on real-life stories, the column has been a peephole into decades of infidelity and odious in-laws. Not just that: While half of all marriages today end in divorce, here is an island of reconciliation.

Consider the depressed woman in a 1968 column who tried to end more than just her 17-year marriage. She took 45 sleeping pills and didn't wake up for three days. But there was an awakening. After months of therapy, which is always part of these stories, her husband began watching less television (one of their problems), she lost weight (that was another). She started feeling better about herself. The marriage was saved.

Then there was the real-estate salesman, featured in 1973, who dealt his wife a double blow. First he cheated on her, then he fired her as his secretary. A counselor, concluding that man and wife were bored, told her to fix herself up (she was dowdy) and told him to add romance to the relationship. Candlelight dinners and flowers were part of the prescription. Another marriage saved.

Ladies' Home Journal finds its troubled couples through a small stable of therapists—psychologists, marriage counselors, what have you—who have successfully treated the couples in question. Happy endings thus are assured.

It all usually begins with an unhappy wife. She describes how she met and married her husband, then how the relationship soured. The disgruntled husband then gets in his two cents' worth, and the therapist arrives to explain what's what and how the marriage was put right.

The story of love, disillusionment, desperation and renewal is crammed into 2,500 words. Only the names and details like number of children are changed to protect anonymity. The therapists' names are used.

"You read that column and you feel there's hope out there, and maybe what's happening to you isn't so bad," says Helen Gurley Brown, editor of Cosmopolitan.

The column has shown that, sexual revolution or no, marital problems have changed little over the years. Lack of communication is a major flash point. So are money, in-laws, sex, job stress and children (when to have them, how to raise them). Marriages have been sandbagged by impotence and alcohol, by dirty dishes and unrealistic expectations.

In recent years, "Can This Marriage Be Saved?" has reflected evident changes in the social landscape. More wives, for instance, seem to be having affairs. More husbands pout that working wives want to quit jobs to spend time at home.

Journal therapists frequently advise that the happy marriage requires blocking out time for conversation, sharing household chores and paying at least one compliment per day to one's partner. Does your marriage lack intimacy? Try cuddling.

To maintain a certain tone, the column avoids certain subjects, such as marital rape, domestic violence and child abuse, the sorts of problems that make saving a marriage a dubious proposition. Instead, the feature seeks out "empathetic" characters and gives practical advice on "the intermeshing of a relationship," says Editor in Chief Myrna Blyth.

A typical couple is Kathleen and Robert Loos, whose marriage was featured last year and who have agreed to let their actual names be used here. Three years ago, the Looses, who live in Arlington Heights, Ill., sought out a family counselor after quarreling over how to discipline their three children. (They now have four.) Adding to the stress: Mr. Loos, now a hotel controller, was unemployed for a while, and the family had to move in with his parents.

The column described how the Looses created a more structured environment for their children by sticking to a regular schedule for meals and bedtime, and how they grew closer by reserving Wednesday evenings for themselves—"kid-free time," the counselor says.

Theirs was still another marriage saved, but was the column realistic? "We had three years of therapy described in two paragraphs, and that's kind of diluted," Mrs. Loos says, adding that some of the discipline problems with the children are now recurring. But the column is still her favorite thing about Ladies' Home Journal.

The column, which is copyrighted by Meredith Corp., the magazine's publisher, has its detractors, particularly among those who regard divorce as sometimes preferable to a miserable marriage. Ann Landers, the syndicated advice columnist, thinks the Journal is a bit dated, particularly now that many women have more financial independence. "When I started writing in 1955, I had the naive notion that all marriages should be saved," she says. "Now, sometimes I'll just say, 'Throw the bum out.' " (Ann Landers herself is divorced.)

A nagging thing about "Can This Marriage Be Saved?" is that while the couples always reconcile, readers never hear what becomes of them—durable domestic bliss or divorce court? The magazine doesn't follow up.

Ms. Blyth, the editor, says the point of the column—offering advice on how to improve marriages—is as timely today as it ever was. "We're not being moralistic about it, and we're not saying that every marriage should be saved."

Back when women's magazines tended to dwell on fashion and home-making tips, this was the first feature to discuss the daily trials of marriage and, in doing so, to lift the stigma attached to marriage counseling, says Kathy McCoy, a Los Angeles human behavior specialist. "It gave readers a peek into what happens in marriage counseling, and it raised awareness that you just don't have to live with problems, you can solve them," Dr. McCoy says.

And, so it seems, there is a solution to every problem. In the January 1992 column, titled "My Husband Wanted a Sex Slave," wife Joan discovers during therapy that husband Jeff is sleeping with another woman—"a major setback" to wedded bliss, says the counselor. But Jeff is helped to rethink his ideas about sex with a video on tender lovemaking. Joan tells Jeff what makes her happy. He starts opening doors for her and doing household chores. "Little things," Joan says, "but they're important."

But what about Bob and Wendy, the couple driven apart by Willie Nelson? They had been ignoring each other's emotional needs for years. Wendy's obsession with country music was just her way of rebelling. Given some good solid advice, the two began talking, leveling with each other. Wendy cut back on her concerts. Bob's blood pressure came down. They decided to spend more time together. "Suddenly," Wendy confided to her counselor, "I'm in love with my husband again!"

V

THE HOME FRONT

Kids Acting Up?
Don't Yell, Validate
Their Tiny Feelings

Experts Say Empowerment Is Key to Tots' Self-Esteem; But Many Parents Rebel

---

By Cynthia Crossen

12/10/91

Beth Tulipan was trading shop talk with a fellow mother when the mother made this modern-day confession: "I almost said it," she told Mrs. Tulipan. "I almost said, 'Because I said so.'"

That would have been very grave indeed—worse even than telling a child that the picture he has drawn "looks like" something. Other modern offenses against small children include being negative, criticizing, screaming, threatening, spanking, bribing or uttering any of the following phrases: "You're too big a boy to cry"; "It's on your plate, finish it"; "Don't be sad"; and "You don't hate your sister, you love her." In fact, sometimes it seems as though there isn't much parents can say to their kids these days without sentencing them to hours on an analyst's couch.

"It's like being politically correct—only you have to be psychologically correct in your parenting," says Mrs. Tulipan, of Hinsdale, Ill., who has a five-year-old son and an 18-month-old daughter. "Sometimes I say something, and I'm sure he's going to become a serial murderer or she's going to become a prostitute."

It has never been easy being a parent, but today's parents have it rough. They face not only the traditional problems—biting, whining and hitting, for example—but also a veritable tower of Babel of expert advice on child-rearing. Earlier generations of middle-class mothers learned from one another as they passed time on park benches or front porches. Today, the next-door neighbor has been replaced by thousands of books, magazines, seminars, newspaper columns, videocassettes and early childhood experts, advising parents on every facet of raising children. The book titles—"Loving Your Child Is Not Enough," "When Parents Love Too Much"—can intimidate parents, who thought if they knew one thing about children, it was that love was enough and never too much.

"We're all a little paralyzed," says Tracy Barnes, a Providence, R.I., mother, who knows that modern children are supposed to learn to use the toilet because it is something they feel proud of. "I bribe him with M&Ms anyway," she says, but then feels guilty about it.

Experts have been telling people how to be parents in the U.S. since the early 19th century, but most theories were tried out on the poor, in settlement houses, for example, and then through programs like Head Start. The middle and upper classes haven't completely escaped child-rearing fads and fashions, either, including one early 20th-century expert who recommended parents show affection with a brisk handshake.

But traditionally, raising children has been "intuitive and spontaneous," and parents were encouraged to "do what came naturally," says David Elkind, professor of child study at Tufts University. "Today, there's more information, parents are more isolated, and parenting has become a matter of technique."

Much of the current advice arises from a growing recognition that almost from the beginning, children have much more mature feelings and thoughts than they were traditionally given credit for. So strong is the emphasis on children's feelings that parents sometimes feel children must be tended like hot-house flowers. "Say that during play, your son makes the baby doggy bite off the head of the daddy doggy," writes Susan Golant and Mitch Golant in their book, "Getting Through to Your Kids." "Instead of jumping in with, 'Oh, that's terrible' . . . name your child's feeling by saying, 'Wow! It looks to me as if the baby doggy is really angry at the daddy doggy.' "

Some parents embrace the new philosophy of validating feelings. "Our parents didn't know what they were doing," says Erin Leider-Paliser, a mother of two children and a graduate of parenting classes. "We don't know what we're doing either, but we're sure getting some help and we're trying harder."

Ms. Leider-Paliser says some things she used to do are now no-nos. For example, her two-year-old is having a tantrum about leaving a toy store. "Before reading or taking seminars, I'd say, 'I'm leaving without you, goodbye.' So the child feels he's going to be abandoned or someday you will abandon him. Instead, you have a conversation, say, 'I know you'd really like a toy today, but your birthday's coming up; let's put that on your list.' "

For other parents, the sheer volume of child-rearing advice is unnerving. "They keep inventing new rules," says Nicki Norman, a Berkeley, Calif., mother. "I'm a firm believer that you could find a book saying just about everything you do is a terrible mistake."

A favored word among child-development experts today is "empower," which means giving children as much control over their lives as possible. In extreme cases of empowerment, children are treated as though they have a vote, and a good campaign can win it. "A woman told me how she and her husband and young child were trying to leave the house to go to a party," says Marlene Bloom, a New York mother. "But the kid had a temper tantrum. The parents actually tried to talk the child into going. Of course, they all missed the party."

The other big concept in modern child-rearing theory is building self-esteem. That comes from treating children with respect. "It's like being in a grocery store, and your child says, 'I want that,' and you might say, 'You don't want that,' " says Piper Smith, a mother of two. "Well, the child wants it. You're denying their desires. You have to acknowledge what they want. That's what promotes healthy self-esteem."

As for saying that the drawing of the sailboat looks like a slide, or vice versa, that, too, is verboten. "Please do not say their art work looks like something," admonishes a New York preschool to parents. Say something like, "I noticed you put a red triangle next to a blue one." The reason? Budding artistic sensibilities should not be crushed by the weight of parental expectations.

Yelling at children is now considered a form of child abuse. (In Germany recently, a commission of the parliament even proposed a law against constant nagging of children.) The state-of-the-art discipline in America: time-outs, where the perp is sentenced to several minutes of calming down. And when the five-year-old boy grabs his three-year-old sister's cookie, instigating a fight, instead of saying, "Knock it off," parents are supposed to say something like, "Annie, you were so angry when Howard took your cookie. Howard, do you see how angry she is? But Annie, when you hit, it's hard for Howard to understand what you're feeling—when people get hit, all they want to do is protect themselves. Tell Howard how you feel in words," according to "The Preschool Years" by Ellen Galinsky and Judy Davis.

Even the experts acknowledge that advice like this has a nice theoretical ring but is worthless when one whiny child is grabbing a pantleg and the other has just wrestled a chair over to a second-floor window. "Haim Ginott [a forefather of modern child-rearing theory] had a 10-minute dialogue on what you're supposed to say when your kids won't put on their boots in the morning," says Susan Ginsberg, director of the Work and Family Life Seminar at Bank Street College in New York. "No one has time to do that. Sometimes you just have to say, 'Put the damn boots on.' "

Whatever methods parents adopt to raise their children, it may already be too late. A new movement among obstetricians emphasizes the importance of preparing for parenthood before a couple is even expecting. It's called preconceptual counseling.

The Work Ethic Is
A Living Thing
To the Morgans

Florida Family Had Means—
Spiritual Not Financial—
To Raise 18 Children Well

By Eric Morgenthaler

2/26/92

MARIANNA, FLA.—When she got married 46 years ago, Annie Morgan thought she and her husband, Walter, would have two children. Then she had a dream.

"I was sitting on a back doorstep," she says, recounting the dream. "And the yard was just full of children, like in a Sunday-school class. And I knew they were all mine."

Mrs. Morgan took the dream as a sign from God, for the Morgans recently had become born-again Christians. Over the next two decades, despite sometimes grinding poverty on their small farm near this Florida Panhandle town, the Morgans pursued their calling: They had babies.

First came Betty. The next year Elijah arrived. Then Isaiah and Walter, and then came the twins: Daisy and Hezekiah. Next was Zechariah, then Paul and John and Marie and Joseph. Then Samuel and Nepton and Randolph and Nadine. And Patricia and Geraldine. Finally, Nehemiah, who was born in 1968—the year Betty, the oldest, graduated from Bethune-Cookman College in Daytona Beach.

In all, the Morgans had 18 children: six girls and 12 boys.

"Lots of noise, lots of noise," Mrs. Morgan says, clasping her hands and laughing gaily, as she describes life with a houseful of kids—all born at home except Betty, who was born in a hospital. "Whenever they would go out and go for the school bus, it seemed like a storm had blown through. Lots of noise, lots of laughter, lots of chatter. But I endured it."

She did better than that. All 18 of the children graduated from high school. Ten went on to do at least some college work, largely with grants and loans. Today, even in a recession, all have good jobs. There are two brick masons, a carpenter, two chefs, an Army and a Navy noncom, a beautician, a postal clerk, a computer operator, a teacher and a corrections officer. Elijah, Isaiah and John are ministers in the Church of Christ Written in Heaven, the Pentecostal sect to which their parents belong. The four eldest of the Morgans' 46 grandchildren are now in college.

In 1978, after Mrs. Morgan got the last of her own children into elementary school (and thus out of the house) she went back to school herself, for she had dropped out of high school to marry. In 1980, she graduated from the local junior college, then began working in special education. Her husband, who is 76, is retired from his last wage work, as a custodian, but he still farms their 40 acres.

"The Lord blessed me," says Mrs. Morgan, a gracious, soft-spoken 65-year-old. "I have much to be thankful for."

The Morgans are notable for having successfully raised such a large family under difficult conditions. But their life also is a lesson in values. "We were raised different than a lot of families," says Nehemiah. "We were raised to work."

"I would go by that house and see them in the fields, and they were so little that when they hit that hoe they would bounce," says their 83-year-old neighbor Pandora Merritt.

The children were rousted out of bed as early as five in the morning, to do chores before school—milking cows, chopping peanuts, shelling peas, cleaning house. After school, there was more work to do. The boys, as well as the girls, ironed clothes and cooked; even the toddlers didn't get off scot-free.

"As soon as they started walking, when they threw something down, I'd teach them to pick it up," says Mrs. Morgan. "Because if they didn't do it, I was going to have to. I sure wasn't going to live in a dirty house."

The Morgans raised their family, and live today, deep in the pine woods, down a red-dirt road about six miles south of this little town near the Alabama line. Moss-draped live oaks shade the property, and near the house are pear, pecan, fig and peach trees. Mustard greens, English peas, broccoli and cauliflower are growing in the garden. Mr. Morgan still has a field of sugarcane, from which he makes syrup.

The farm is part of a close-knit black neighborhood known, after a church nearby, as the Jerusalem Community. As many as 40 families live in an area of about two square miles. Mr. Morgan's family has been in the county for at least three generations. He, himself, was one of 18 children. He and his wife settled here, on 40 acres he had purchased next to his father's farm, soon after their marriage. (They had met and married in Waco, Texas, her hometown, when he was in the Air Force.) Six of Walter and Annie's children have homes on family property, as do Mr. Morgan's three sisters.

Although the Morgans had some very hard years, their basic needs were always met. "We didn't have a lot of money, but we always had food to eat, because we raised it," says Elijah, the oldest son.

However, they lived in something of a time warp. They plowed their fields behind mules until the 1950s, when they got a tractor. They took their corn to a mill to be ground; they put up canned goods. They had no electricity, running water or central heat until the 1960s, and they didn't have a telephone until nearly the end of that decade. When Mrs. Morgan wanted to get a message to a neighbor, she would send a note with one of the children. They got their first TV set in the early '70s.

They used to do their laundry on washboards—a big job with all those babies. "You talk about diapers," says Mrs. Morgan. "Oh man, we went through some diapers in those days. And when the weather was bad, we had to dry them indoors." Even when they got a washing machine, they had to haul well water to fill it.

The children bathed in a big tin tub, with water heated on the kitchen stove. They never had bicycles and had few toys. They amused themselves outdoors, making castles of pine needles, or rolling old tires down country paths. "It was a lot of fun," says Elijah. "We always had someone to play with."

In 1957, just before Christmas, a kerosene stove exploded and the Morgans' house burned down. Nobody was injured, but Mrs. Morgan, who was seven months pregnant with her 11th child at the time, recalls the fire as "the worst thing that ever happened." The family moved into a tiny two-room house, with a tin roof and tar-paper siding that looked like brick. The six oldest boys slept in one bed.

The Morgans lived in the little house for two years, and two babies were born there. As the Morgans saved money, they bought and stock-piled materials to build a new home—the four-bedroom ranch-style house they live in today. They were hard years, but the children have happy memories.

"Even in that little house, we didn't feel poor or that we were missing anything," says Isaiah, "because we were all together and the bond of love was there—and that made the difference."

The children give their parents the credit for that. The Morgans were strict but loving. "Mamma was a person you could always talk to," says Zechariah. "She always had her arms open." The family always had daily prayers and Bible reading, went to church on Sunday and conducted an at-home service every Wednesday night.

(Mr. Morgan was a disciplinarian. Recalling the only time a child of his ran away from home, for two or three days, he says: "He wanted to do his own thing. I said you won't do it here.")

The parental guidance extended to racial matters. "They taught us to love everyone," says Zechariah. "They never taught prejudice and hatred."

Before the civil-rights era, the Morgan children had few contacts with whites. Aside from the occasional visit to town, where segregation was strictly enforced, "Our only encounter was at the school-bus stop, when the white bus would pass and the kids would yell things at us out the window," says Zechariah. Betty says segregation "was something we just accepted, until the change came."

Daisy was the first in the family to attend school with whites, in the first year of integration at Marianna High School in the mid-'60s. "Someone would make a slur or a comment, and you'd fight back," she says. "But I had double trouble because when I got home, I had to deal with Mom and Dad."

Now that her children are grown, Mrs. Morgan is still mothering. She works as a teacher's aide in a program for handicapped adults. "They need the same thing children at home need," she says. "They need love. They need to know somebody cares."

A New Tradition: Making Mincemeat Of Tom Turkey

He May Not Want to Hear It, But Dad Can't Be Trusted With the Carving Knife

By Gary Putka

11/27/91

The blade is sharp, the linen crisp. The big fork gleams like a trident. As the oven cools, expectant faces take their places in the familiar dining-room tableau.

And the carver?

Probably inexperienced, Thanksgiving analysts say. Inept with knives, knife makers chime in. So untidy, eyewitnesses testify, that the kitchen is fast displacing the dinner table as prime slicing site.

In an age of micro families and microwaves, carving skills are falling into desuetude. To some, a cherished holiday rite has become a fowl mutilation.

"A hack job," says Anthony Ambrose, chef at Seasons restaurant in Boston. "When I go into houses as a guest, there's no common sense of what to do with the bird."

Walter Gardiner, president of Imperial Schrade Corp., a big cutlery maker, agrees. "Nobody knows how to carve," he says. "We've spent a lot of time trying to educate America about the right way to carve turkeys—unsuccessfully, based on what's left of them on Thanksgiving."

Even some professionals can't cut it. "I'm awful at carving," confesses TV's Frugal Gourmet, Jeff Smith. "I just yell at the bird and hope the meat will fall off."

Carving "is a lost art," complains Beatrice Snyder, who speaks for the Norman Rockwell Museum, in Stockbridge, Mass. Mr. Rockwell's "Freedom From Want," which hangs in Stockbridge, evokes an idealized Thanksgiving, perhaps just a bit out of sync with contemporary reality. The oft-reproduced painting has grandma lowering a mountainous bird onto a bountiful table surrounded by happy faces. The carving set rests just inches from grandpa's hand.

To many Americans, this is Thanksgiving as it was meant to be. More important, anthropologists say, it is the Thanksgiving we always try to have. Amy Shuman, a folklore professor at Ohio State University, says Thanksgiving gives Americans a chance to act out, if only for a few hours, mythic ideals of family and hearth—and traditional sex roles. The lack of carving skills is one thing wrong with the picture, and not the only thing.

So while the average household is 2.6 people, grandma is in the rest home, and dad gets more practice ordering burritos at Taco Bell than he does boning birds, tomorrow we will eat in large groups, have grandma home for the day, cook a bird bigger than we can eat, and tear it to shreds.

Ms. Shuman says that inexperienced males insist on carving, even when the womenfolk at the celebration can do it better, because the carving ritual makes them feel like hunter and provider.

"There is a mythical head-of-family, top-of-the-table symbolic role played by the carver," says David Saxton, president of the company that owns the Chicago Cutlery line of knives. Men covet the part of paterfamilias, he says, "even though they're generally incompetent."

Mr. Saxton calls himself "a confident carver," but he has a certain humility about it. "I cut my thumb badly" several years ago, he says. "It bled all over the white meat." Mr. Saxton prefers to cut in the kitchen, "where you have the freedom to put your fist around the drumstick and yank it." Also, he says, with nobody watching, you get to eat the bad pieces.

Half of all carvers have been similarly maimed, according to a statistically insignificant survey of a dozen who wield blades on Thanksgiving or loiter around, hoping for scraps. The turkey gets its revenge, albeit posthumously.

Arlene Sarappo, who manages cooking schools for Kings Super Markets in New Jersey, says tradition dictates "that my father-in-law carves the bird," although his lack of regular practice sometimes shows. "One year carving the turkey, he threw out his back," says Ms. Sarappo of the rusty carver. "We sat him down and took the knife away. . . . My husband carved in his stead. He didn't do very well."

Jack Ubaldi, a former butcher and author of "Jack Ubaldi's Meat Book," says that as the guest of a priest one Thanksgiving, he saw the pastor attack the bird so aggressively that "it bounced off the plate and onto the table and was rolling around like a ball. You hate to say anything. You can't take over, because people get offended."

Food writer Holly Garrison, in her new "Thanksgiving Cookbook," says that "learning to carve at the table was a mandatory lesson for all young men a generation ago. Nowadays, more often than not, the bird . . . is carved in the kitchen by whoever has the most skill—or courage—and is brought forth in that rather unceremonious state to the table."

Lack of practice isn't the only problem. Cooks like Ms. Sarappo note that carvers must often contend with birds toughened by overcooking, or falling off the bone in dry shreds. A sharp blade is essential, in any event, but "the drawers of America are full of dull knives," says cutlery man Mr. Gardiner.

Carvers who want to get better at it must also sort through conflicting, and sometimes dubious, advice. Experts generally agree that the bird needs to cool before cutting, that the drumstick should come off first and that a well-carved bird yields many large, thin, uniform slices of breast meat. There is little agreement about anything else.

Ms. Garrison and Imperial Schrade's 1989 instructional carving video advise carvers to begin the breast by making a deep horizontal cut at the base of the bird to release the slices when the vertical cutting begins.

Roberta Dowling, of the Cambridge School of Culinary Arts, in Cambridge, Mass., says a release cut isn't necessary if the carver cuts at an outward angle to make elliptical slices.

"Talking About Turkey," the official U.S. Department of Agriculture guidebook on such matters, just adds to the confusion. It contains not one, but two techniques—the "Traditional" and "Kitchen Carving" methods. In the former, the knife wielder is urged to place the dismembered drumstick, fat end down, on the plate, "tilt drumstick to convenient angle," and slice "toward table" for good dark-meat removal.

That, says Mr. Ubaldi, is crazy. "You cannot slice the drumstick. There are 14 different tendons inside, and they're all like wires." He advises keeping the drumstick intact, and let somebody gnaw on it. That is a Thanksgiving tradition, too.

Mr. Smith, the TV cook, cares little for advice that's too precise. "I don't do this routine of trying to cut it off the bird in nice slices," he says. "The bird doesn't appreciate it, and neither will you. I reach in there with my hand and grab off the breast, then cut across the grain. Otherwise it will be tough."

Preparing for a carving lesson in an evening cooking class in Cambridge, Ms. Dowling's students truss, roast and baste a turkey. After the bird cools awhile, Ms. Dowling picks up a knife, quickly severs the drumstick, thigh and wing joints, and peels off two thin, juicy slices. "It's so easy, it's ridiculous," she says.

"Do you want to finish this up?" she asks an onlooker. He picks up the blade, explains that he doesn't carve much at home—and proceeds to chop the rest of the bird up into chunks and wedges.

The slices "could have been a little thinner," observes Ms. Dowling, shaking her head, "a little bit thinner."

She Might Have Inherited Millions, But for Her Mother

While Ralph Falk II Received A Fortune, His Sister Was Cut Off: Now She's Suing

By Jeff Bailey

11/25/91

CHICAGO—Ralph Falk, the founder of Baxter International Inc., left a generous legacy when he died 31 years ago.

To his widow, Marian, and his son, Ralph II, Dr. Falk bequeathed Baxter stock that would grow to be worth nearly $200 million. Marian lived the life of a wealthy socialite until she died last December at age 95. Ralph II, meanwhile, succeeded his father as chairman of Baxter, which went on to be the nation's biggest hospital-supply concern. Retired 11 years ago, he is 69.

But there is another Falk, one the family apparently tried its best to forget. Her name is Carol, the only daughter of Ralph and Marian. Dr. Falk's will left Carol $100. Her mother's will didn't mention her at all.

Why did the elder Falks provide so lavishly for their son and leave next to nothing to their daughter? Because she was fat, Carol says.

Mrs. Falk was a svelte and striking beauty, and her daughter's obesity, beginning around age 8, became an obsession. According to Carol, now Mrs. Lopacich, her mother marched her nightly into the bathroom and onto the scale, reading off the little girl's weight disapprovingly.

"I got small, tiny, bird-like portions" to eat, says Mrs. Lopacich, now age 66. "And I always had to leave a little on my plate." But the more she was denied food, she says, the more she ate, sneaking and stealing to get it. Shipped off to a succession of boarding schools, juvenile fat farms and psychiatric clinics, she became estranged from her rich parents and eventually ate her way to 340 pounds.

Now, Mrs. Lopacich is suing her brother for "infliction of emotional harm." She has also made claims against the family fortune. She wants $37.5 million or more.

The lawsuits, in federal and state court here, reveal a bizarre family drama. William Graham, Baxter's chief executive officer for 27 years and a close friend of the Falks, says in a deposition that neither of them ever mentioned their daughter.

"It's tragic," says Eppie Lederer, better known as Ann Landers, the advice columnist. A friend of Mrs. Falk's, Ms. Lederer once asked her about her daughter: "She said, 'I have no daughter.' She'd written her off completely."

Ms. Lederer says of Ralph Falk II: "He's got all that loot. Doesn't he think he should cough up something?"

Mr. Falk declines to be interviewed. His lawyer, Melvin L. Katten, says of Mrs. Lopacich's account of her life—her weight problems, her estrangement, her childhood grief: "I don't know of any source" of information that would dispute her story. He adds that her suit has no merit.

Dr. Falk was a prominent Boise, Idaho, surgeon who founded Baxter in 1931. The company, now based in Deerfield, Ill., a suburb of Chicago, pioneered the mass production of intravenous fluids. In Boise, and later in Chicago, the family moved in wealthy circles. Mrs. Lopacich remembers playing checkers with a nice man at Sun Valley; it was David Niven.

Mrs. Falk was a remote figure, her daughter says, rarely hugging or kissing her children. She let the servants bathe and dress the children and put them to bed. But when Carol showed a tendency toward obesity at about age 8, Mrs. Falk got personally involved and ordered a strict diet.

Carol rebelled. She would sneak downstairs early in the morning to get food before the cook was awake. She stole money from her mother and the servants to buy chocolate eclairs, "the lemon-filled ones," she says. At camp, she rowed across a lake early one morning to buy candy.

She grew fatter and unhappier, and repeatedly ran away from home to avoid the scale. At age 14, her parents sent her to the Annie Wright school, in Tacoma, Wash. There, she says, she stole another girl's blouse, ran away and ended up spending about two weeks with a man, having sex in exchange for a place to stay.

While at a Milwaukee weight-loss clinic, she learned to be a masseuse. At one psychiatric clinic, she says she was chained to her bed. As a young adult, she met the first of four husbands, Karl Syfrig, through a personal ad. He worked on an airline cleaning crew in Seattle.

Driving from Milwaukee to his Washington home, the newlyweds stopped in Boise, where Mrs. Falk still lived. "I called mother. I said I'm married; I want you to meet my husband." She says her mother replied: "What do you weigh?" Carol said she was still fat. "Then she said she couldn't see me. She had guests."

As early as 1944, Dr. Falk did set aside for Carol 3,000 shares in then closely held Baxter which would be worth about $16 million today. But, Ralph Falk II explains in a deposition, the young company's shares were then considered "risky," and Carol's shares were replaced by "more conservative investments." The trust is worth about $212,000 today, says Mrs. Lopacich's lawyer.

Before Dr. Falk died, Mrs. Lopacich says he sent her a letter. "He and mother wished me well but they didn't love me," she says he told her. Carol learned of her father's death about two weeks after the fact. A letter from her brother's wife explained that the funeral had been "a small private affair for immediate family only," Mrs. Lopacich says. She cried all night long.

She reached out to her mother once more. Mrs. Lopacich's son, Nathan Syfrig, was musically precocious. When he was about 5, she says she called her mother on Mother's Day and told Nathan to play his violin into the phone. "Mother wouldn't let Nathan finish," Mrs. Lopacich says. Hand the phone to your mother, Mrs. Falk told the boy. She asked Mrs. Lopacich: "What do you weigh?"

Mrs. Lopacich gave up after that.

Ralph Falk II grew up trim and, by all accounts, accepted by his parents. They sent him to Culver Military Academy in Indiana and then to Dartmouth College in New Hampshire. After a World War II stint in the Navy, he went to work at Baxter. He is still a director.

Mr. Falk became an architecture buff; he built a house in Lake Forest that, even by the standards of that old-money Chicago suburb, is extravagant: a replica of an 18th-century Georgian mansion, on five acres, built from scratch beginning in 1976. It also includes modern touches like ice-melting cables in the rain gutters, an elevator and tennis court.

"It's the most outstanding house built in this town in 30 years," says Genevieve Plamondon, a Lake Forest real-estate agent.

Later, Mr. Falk bought a three-story pink Mediterranean-style house on Lake Michigan. He is also building in Salt Lake City what his designer says will be the nation's finest South African Cape Dutch-style house; there are only three others.

The Georgian home cost $8.5 million to build, according to Carol's suit, but it sold for not quite $4 million. He donated a $200,000 scale model of the house to Chicago's Museum of Science and Industry.

Mr. Falk has sold more than one million Baxter shares, for $36.4 million over the past eight years, according to Securities and Exchange Commission filings. He paid settlements of $12 million and $6.5 million, respectively, to his first and second wives, according to his sister's suit.

From 1972 to 1985, the years of Mr. Falk's second marriage, his mother "had barely more to do with me than she did with my sister," he says in a deposition.

During that time, Mrs. Falk grew old and fragile. Her closest companion during the latter part of that period was Mark Mannino, a loquacious former elevator operator at the Drake Tower, where she lived. They met while walking their dogs on Michigan Avenue, says Mr. Mannino, now 32. "She fell in love with me instantly. Me, too."

Mrs. Falk was "cheap," he says, buying her pantyhose, for instance, in bulk when the local drugstore had a sale. But she was generous to Mr. Mannino. She bought him an apartment building (he videotaped her signing it over in case the family protested) for more than $400,000, a car and a piano. And the surgeon's widow introduced him to her friends as "Dr. Mark," he says, because he helped her put in her contact lenses.

By 1986, Mr. Falk was married to his third wife. He began seeing his mother again. Already 90 years old, she had told many people—Mr. Mannino, a bank trust officer who handled her affairs, and a niece—that she wanted to die at the Drake Tower.

While her housekeeper was out of town in March 1988, Mr. Falk and his third wife drove down from Lake Forest, packed up his mother's belongings, and moved her into their home.

She needed help, Mr. Falk testified later at a hearing that resulted in his being named her guardian: Her teeth were all gone and she was "subsisting almost totally on hot chocolate"; she told a court-appointed guardian that she was between 200 and 300 years old.

Mrs. Falk's trust bought his Mediterranean fixer-upper and paid for about $1.5 million in improvements. Her trust also paid for flights on the Baxter jet, because, her son testified, "I couldn't afford it."

Meanwhile, Mrs. Lopacich had done something amazing. She had dieted down to 142 pounds and wanted to show her new figure off to her mother. "It was her lifelong wish to have a slim daughter," Mrs. Lopacich says.

Her brother wouldn't allow a meeting at his house, so one was arranged at a Presbyterian church. Mrs. Lopacich was nervous. She wore a new yellow dress and a wig to cover her thinning hair. Nathan Syfrig played the piano. But it was too late. Mrs. Falk, in a wheelchair, had little idea what was going on.

She died last Dec. 28 during a nap. On Jan. 25, a memorial service was held in Lake Forest, and Mrs. Lopacich says her brother did his best to ignore her. Mr. Falk had some people back to his house for lunch; Mrs. Lopacich, her son and Mr. Mannino went to a local pancake house.

Back in her home near Seattle, Mrs. Lopacich, now at about 180 pounds, looks wrinkled and old, but her eyes are childlike. She spends most of her time alone in her two-bedroom house.

She talks about her lawsuits as if they were the state lottery. If she won "the money," she says, she would buy a new motorhome and travel. She would have the windowsills painted. She would have eyelift and tummy-tuck surgery. "And most important," she would get "psychiatric care" and go to a first-rate introduction service, she says. "I'm not pretty and I'm not smart, but there must be someone who would want me."

A Holiday Hint:
Dustbusters Aren't
Forever, Jewels Are

Men Who Buy Women Gifts
That Plug In Are Not
Plugged In to Gift-Giving

By Ellen Graham

12/11/90

I will make a clean breast of it. Once my husband gave me a strainer for Christmas. This revelation staggers gift consultants, who busy themselves at this time of year selecting extravagant baubles for their clients.

To gift experts, the strainer misses on several counts. It is utilitarian. It's cheap. It's not romantic. And it's ugly. Linda Barbanel, a Manhattan psychotherapist, even sees a hidden message in my strainer. She describes it as a "know your place" present. "I bet he never used it," she astutely observes.

But I am not alone. Once, Sunny Bates received a manhole cover from her husband, Scott Campbell. "He found it on the beach covered with tar," says Ms. Bates, who runs an executive-recruitment firm in Manhattan. "It had my initials on it." That was when they were newlyweds, and as far as gift-giving goes, she says "he hasn't improved over time."

Coaxed to recall presents best forgotten, women have long memories. Gift-giving between couples can backfire in either direction, of course. It's just that women tend to make a big deal out of gifts, and men don't. This can spell tension amid the tinsel.

Ms. Bates's manhole cover was followed, on other festive occasions, by a pickup truck, a front-end loader and a toilet bowl. "He buys me exactly what he wants," she laughs. "I think most men do. He just happens to lust after heavy machinery." Her computer-salesman husband also comes through with books of IOUs: "You know," she explains, "like when you were little and you promised your mother one vacuuming." But she hasn't redeemed many of his coupons. After all, she says, "It was never 'IOU a diamond.'"

Ms. Bates, who says even former boyfriends with impeccable taste always gave her insulting presents, bets that Zsa Zsa Gabor always gets exactly what she wants. "Some women are the kind that always get flowers," she says. "Other women get humidifiers." Long ago she took the advice of a friend and became what she calls "self-basting." When she wants to be lavished with something frivolous or extravagant, she buys it herself.

In some households, the ritual gift exchange is fraught with dark subplots. Bettie Bearden Pardee of Boston, an author and authority on entertaining, now laughs about one "catastrophic" Christmas in her youth that escalated into a sort of Yuletide night of the long knives.

"It was always a bone of contention in our house that my father couldn't carve," Ms. Pardee says. That year, her mother hit upon a solution: She gave him an electric carving knife. Her luckless father—a jokester who had steadfastly resisted learning how to carve—reciprocated with an expensive, bone-handled carving knife. "It was the final blow," Ms. Pardee says. "He was rubbing my mother's face in it, making it easier for her to continue doing something she hated—carve the meat."

Hours later, after what Ms. Pardee calls "the boudoir murmurs," her father came sheepishly to his daughter's room and implored, "Do you have anything in your jewelry box?"

"I was in my early teens," she says. "What would I have that my mother would want?" Instead, she thrust forward a favorite baby doll. "He got this look, and said, 'That could backfire.'"

Not only must a gift impress the recipient, in some circles it must withstand the scrutiny of finicky friends. "It's like show and tell," Ms. Pardee says of these post-holiday comparisons. Ruthie Watts, an Atlanta muralist, remembers the time she breathlessly told a friend that her husband had given her a microwave oven for Christmas. "I could see the concrete veil coming down over her eyes," Ms. Watts recalls. "She said, 'I always tell my husband never to give me anything that plugs in.' That's when I knew that one woman's perfume is another woman's poison."

Indeed. When a friend mentioned to New York socialite Mai Hallingby that she had been given a Range Rover by her husband, Ms. Hallingby joked: "That's like getting an electric knife."

Dawn Bryan, author of "The Art and Etiquette of Gift Giving," says that the hunger for gifts is a "hunger for approval, importance, affection and love." To the extent that women are insecure in these areas, she suggests, gifts assume a loaded significance: "Women are saying I'm of equal value, and you aren't paying." Men—probably because they have traditionally enjoyed greater economic status—"don't see gift-giving as so important and vital," she says.

When given gifts they hate, men generally shrug it off and get on with their lives. But they do resent chronic ingratitude. Don Kollmar, a New York therapist, finally broke up with a woman who consistently belittled the expensive jewelry he gave her. "She couldn't receive," he says. "I wound up feeling gypped."

On his 10th wedding anniversary, New York attorney Gerald McMahon raced out during a break in a trial and bought his wife an engagement ring, which he couldn't afford to buy before they were married. "It was a half-carat diamond," he says. "I figure she'll go crazy. She says, 'A half carat after 10 years?' I was aghast."

How do men lumber into these minefields? One way is to confuse what a woman needs with what she wants. "It may be congenital," Sunny Bates speculates, "to be able to listen when she says she wants a humidifier and know she really wants maribou slippers."

When she was first married, Kevin White, an interior decorator in Santa Rosa, Calif., came home one Christmas after a long trip. Noting that there was nothing for her under the tree, she inquired about her gift. With great ceremony, her husband led her to her closet.

"My eyes were covered," she recalls. "I thought, this is wonderful—he's never bought me clothes before." But the visions of furs and filmy negligees evaporated when he unveiled the new lighting system he had rigged up for her closet. The next year he gave her a Dustbuster. "I didn't tell anybody," she confesses. "It was like high school—just make something up."

She has mellowed. "He was trying to make my life easier," she says. "When I thought about it that way, it was touching." Besides, she says, "it got better after that—he's moved on to jewelry." Nor are her own gift selections always on the mark. Her husband, an eye surgeon, routinely returns the clothes she buys him. He says he doesn't need them.

The worst gifts, consultants agree, are those that scream thoughtlessness. Author Dawn Bryan remembers that her ex-husband twice gave her expensive pierced earrings. The trouble was, her ears aren't pierced.

Such gifts provide plenty of grist for the therapy mill. Linda Barbanel says she uses gifts to assess "what's cooking" in her patients' relationships. She recalls a patient who had always received silver jewelry from her husband until the year he gave her a plastic barrette purchased from a street vendor. "Her initial reaction was that their relationship was going down the tubes," Ms. Barbanel says, adding that the patient brought the gift in to show her. "It wouldn't stay in her hair," Ms. Barbanel says. "This was an added insult." The patient now can laugh about the incident, Ms. Barbanel says, "but it took a year." The couple has now "settled into middle-aged marriage," she explains.

Sunny Bates may not be a therapist, but she offers a theory about why so many gifts go awry. Men, she contends, learn about gifts from their mothers, and those lessons are cemented for all time. "Think about it," she says. "The boy asks, 'Mommy, what do you want for Christmas?' Now, you don't tell a 10-year-old you want a feather boa. You don't say a ring—you're afraid you might get something made out of Popsicle sticks. So you say, 'Sure honey, those cookie cutters would be swell. Go down to the dry goods store and charge them to my account.'"

Shopping for Men
At Christmastime
Is So Unrewarding

All They Seem to Want Are
Power Tools, Fishing Gear
And Truly Expensive Stuff

By Clare Ansberry

12/18/92

Shopping for men is as dull as white socks.

And men (let's generalize) seem to like it that way. "All they want is socks, ties and shirts," says Lisa Howard, of Westlake, Calif. Her husband, David, admits that, indeed, ties are his favorite Christmas gift.

Some men want white shirts, navy ties and black socks—no other flavors, please. Janet Lubic, an independent wardrobe consultant in Pittsburgh, spent years trying to get plaid socks on her husband. He would open the package and exclaim: "What's this? What's this?" she says. He relented and wore them after his wife finally was able to convince him that two-tone socks are just as comfortable as solid black ones. But the triumph hardly turns her on. "Really, how exciting are socks? Do you ever see them? They're hidden under pant legs."

Even hobbies hold little gift potential, and not much of a thrill to the gift-giver. Hunting and fishing seem decidedly unfestive, so do power tools like chain saws and the places that sell them. There are no red-robed choirs and department-store Santas at Ace and True Value. Besides, do men really need these things?

On the other hand, not all men are sheep. Some have strong, unrealized desires. Every year, Paul Hoppe of Lexington, Mass., gets gloves from his in-laws. His secret fantasy is to be dropped by helicopter in British Columbia so he could ski down a mountain. That would be the perfect Christmas gift.

Brian O'Neill let it be known to his entire family last year that he desperately needed soft luggage to replace his 12-year-old hard stuff. He received instead the usual ties, gloves and scarves, which tend to be cheaper than Tumi ballistic nylon carry-on bags. He repeated his request this year, and he expects another round of ties, gloves and scarves. "All I want in life is soft luggage," he says.

Mr. O'Neill, a Pittsburgh writer, dismisses his plight as one of demographics. As the "generic bachelor uncle," he says, he gets short shrift in the competition with adorable nephews and nieces. But he may have dried up his dear ones' creative gift-giving juices. A brother-in-law bought him a beer-making kit, which he never used, and when his sister told him she was buying him dishes for pasta, he said he didn't want them, he already had cereal bowls. "Maybe it was a test and I failed," he says.

Men have always been a problem. You could give her Arpege. But for dad, it was soap-on-a-rope, Old Spice, English Leather and a black magnetic Hide-a-Key. Men are a veritable black hole, accessory-wise, unless they happen to be the cuff-link type or smoke a pipe.

Marlene Bloom's husband is a New York artist who works at home, doesn't wear ties, jewelry or cologne. She bought him a ratchet set one Christmas, which he loved, but that used up her one tool idea. And she just gave him a wallet for his birthday. "About this time of year, I want to die," she says, perhaps alluding to what professionals call "seasonal affective disorder."

Fads are a ready source of new ideas. Bill Cosby's $1,500 hand-knit sweaters created a boomlet in flashy knockoffs. Rowing machines had a vogue but are now in the attic with the exercycle.

Hobbies are a problem because only the aficionado himself really knows what will come in handy. Bettie Bearden Pardee, a Newport, R.I., author and authority on entertaining, is reluctant to buy her fly-fishing husband a lure to catch salmon in Scotland, for fear of buying the wrong one. "I just know I can't do it," she says. Her husband's other sport—court tennis—is a relatively exotic game whose heyday was in 14th-century England and France. For gear she scouts auctions and antiques stores.

Lefty Wilson, the operations manager of Soldier of Fortune magazine, knowing women's plight, suggests that women buy their men gift certificates at gun shops. "I would think it's nearly impossible to shop for men," he says.

It's certainly impossible to shop for him. He buys himself everything he needs. His son bought him a cart to push around his golf clubs in last year. It sits unused in the garage. When his daughters introduced him to lavender workout suits, he introduced the suits to the back of his closet. He wears black or gray. "It's not their fault," he says. "I'm 50 years old. I'm not going to change."

Mr. Hoppe, of Lexington, loves the unusual Christmas gift, including the juicer he got last year and a "stunning" 25-inch TV set from a Christmas past. He already has this year's Christmas present: a 1974 chocolate-colored Triumph with a white top.

That suggests yet one more problem for the woman trying to buy for a man. Gifts so often seem to be priced in a feast or famine range, that is, under $50 or over $5,000. To judge from the ads in Sports Illustrated, men want either a Jaguar, a Rolex, batteries or a smoking patch.

"The men I buy for don't have enough cheap vices," says Julie Agnew, of Midland, Ky. Her father likes cars and boats. Her fiancé would love a trip to New York to see a Knicks game. "It's torture buying for them," she says.

Linda Barbanel, a New York psychotherapist, says women want personal things, men expensive ones. Her own husband wants a Jacuzzi this year. "Women need to feel more loved," she says. "Men want high-tech, costly gifts that reflect their status and the respect of the gift-giver."

Ms. Barbanel suggests women get into the mood by shopping for themselves first. "That's how I got my mink earmuffs," she says.

In the end, the perfect gift is something a man wants—be it a $19.95 magnifying glass to use with a stamp collection or a pair of ugly $45 pants to garden in. Doug Hall, president of Richard Saunders International, an inventing and market-research firm, says women should think about Three Stooges movies, scuba-diving lessons and anything with parts: a coffee grinder with 15 pounds of coffee, or a pizza-making kit with paddle and stone.

And don't forget dumb gifts. "It's something they can talk about for years," he says. This year, he's sending out chia pets—ceramic animals that seem to grow green hair when watered. They are going to everybody who ever sent him a salad shooter.

VI

FADS 'N' FASHIONS, A PARTIAL ACCOUNTING FOR TASTE

Hair Is Big in Dallas, And That Troubles Roger Thompson

Transplanted New Yorker Isn't Teasing About Plans To Change the Local Do

---

By Kevin Helliker

1/29/91

DALLAS—When Roger Thompson opened a hair salon in a North Dallas shopping mall last August, women here had great expectations. Mr. Thompson, of New York, is world famous in hair circles. He was artistic director for Vidal Sassoon. And he's big in hair.

Hair is big in these parts, very big. But Mr. Thompson doesn't think that's any reason for the women of Big D to hold their heads high. He thinks their heads are too high already—with hills of hair, bleached, lacquered and stiff as a board.

That's definitely not his style. He prefers a more natural look—short, straight and done without gels, sprays and teasing combs. He had plans to sell the beautiful women of Dallas on it. He refused to do "big hair," even though, he says "you see so much of it walking around here."

Mr. Thompson couldn't have caused more of a stink had he called the men at the Alamo sissies. In the months since his arrival last summer, he has found it hard to find stylists willing to work for him, let alone customers willing to forsake big hair for the Thompson look. And, he says, he has become a pariah socially among the hairdressers of Dallas.

Nevertheless, he promises to stick it out until the Dallas do is done for. Mr. Thompson's daughter, Sara, his partner in crime, says, "the Dallas do will go out of style before we lower our standards." She runs the new salon for her 49-year-old father.

In Texas, those are fighting words. Julia Sweeney, a local public-relations executive and former society columnist for the Dallas Times Herald, rejoins: "Dallas women will never be separated from big, blond hair."

Linda Ivy, a well-dressed socialite whose hair is big and sometimes blond (except when it is red), considers big hair an identifying characteristic of a Dallas lady, and a good thing, too. "Wherever I go, people seem to know I'm from Dallas," she says.

Ms. Thompson, who wears her own red hair short, puts a different spin on the phenomenon: Dallas men like big, blond hair on their women, and "Dallas women are so dependent on their men."

And so the battle rages—New York arrogance vs. Lone Star intransigence. Local hairdressers, stung by the Thompson salon's criticism of their work, have fought back by calling Thompson stylists "twits" and "snobs," and by snubbing them in hairdresser hangouts such as the Inwood Lounge. When Thompson hair colorist Miguel Fernandez goes out on the town, he says, "I say I'm a construction worker." Says Michael Lederer, who operates the Lasting Impressions salon in North Dallas: "This is a pretty cliquish town for hairdressers, and the Thompson salon has offended it."

The popularity in Dallas of big, blond hair has been attributed to the sunny local climate, to a historical paucity of dark-haired European immigrant groups in Dallas, and to a peculiar reluctance among women here to renounce their youth, when big, blond hair was "de rigueur." But Dallas pediatrician Caryn Halpern, a big-haired blonde, says it's simpler than that. "I like a lot of hair," she says, "because it's sexy and it feels good."

Hair-color makers such as L'Oreal say Dallas is one of the biggest markets anywhere for bleach. And Glemby's, which operates salons across the nation, sells twice as much blond coloring in Texas as elsewhere. "Blond is the Dallas color," says Debbie Blackstone, who runs a local Glemby's.

Indeed, the hair of many Texas leaders, all the way up to Ann Richards, the new governor and a Democrat, towers over John Tower. And it gives women's heads all the immobility of an office tower. In an interview with the Dallas Morning News, gubernatorial hairdresser Gail Huitt disclosed the secret to Ms. Richards's relentlessly upstanding hair: "I rat the tar out of it. I spray the hell out of it. We get it up there. We defy gravity."

Women here defiantly defend the Dallas do against Yankee interlopers. "New Yorkers have such an attitude," sniffs Christie Cunningham, a Dallas blonde without big hair, who is in the clothing business. She and others ask why the Thompson salon ever bothered coming to Dallas if the styles here are so "backward."

Thompson stylists respond that they made the trip at the behest of Barneys New York, the department store that is home to Mr. Thompson's Manhattan salon. If Barneys didn't have an exclusive arrangement with the Thompson salon, "we would never have come to Dallas," says Ms. Thompson, saying she would have preferred "a more sophisticated" city like Chicago.

With that attitude, critics say, the Thompson salon could go the way of a Vidal Sassoon shop that opened and closed in Dallas in the mid-1970s. "They had that same superior attitude about Dallas blondes, right up until they packed their bags and left," says Dallas hairdresser Paul Neinast. Sassoon's public relations agency attributes the salon's demise to "the wrong location" and says Vidal Sassoon may return to Dallas some day.

The Thompson beauticians have tried, a little late perhaps, to mend fences. Ms. Thompson joined a committee of the Cattle Baron's Ball, the biggest social event of the year. Alas, at her first meeting, Ms. Thompson recalls, "a lady came and yelled in my face for 10 minutes about how there was nothing wrong with big, blond hair."

Likewise, attempts at peace with other hairdressers have come to naught. The Roger Thompson Salon invited its local competitors to a holiday cocktail party, but "they didn't come," says Mr. Thompson. On another occasion, Mr. Thompson, spotting two competitors in a restaurant, waved a white napkin in a playful gesture of surrender. "They just got up and walked away," he says.

Five months after the salon opened, Ms. Thompson says, "We can't get any hairdressers to apply" for jobs. Which may be just as well, because the salon isn't busy anymore. It had six stylists but has let three of them go. Mr. Thompson says that's because they failed to meet his standards. A hairdresser who left, Ahmed Hammourri, says the three were let go for lack of business. Whatever the case, Mr. Thompson and his daughter concede there are lots of blank spaces in the appointment books. "Money is not an issue when you believe in what you're doing," says Ms. Thompson.

Indeed, Mr. Thompson, who was born in Britain, says he has never hesitated to reject customers if he disapproves of their hair styles or even their professions. He won't do psychologists' hair, for instance. They are "crazy," he says, and incompatible with him. "It's important for me to have clients with whom I can establish long-term relationships."

In the long run, he believes, he will benefit from the controversy, and customers will come around. The difference between him and his competitors, he feels, is the difference between art and commerce. And Dallas women will eventually appreciate the virtues of a stylist who won't give them—for any amount of money—a hairdo that looks terrible on them. "We're already seeing women we turned away come back and tell us we were right," he says.

Sue Eudaly isn't one of them. Persuaded by a Thompson stylist to try something new, she found herself staring at brown hair she didn't like—and a $225 bill. "It was very depressing," says Ms. Eudaly, who left without leaving a tip.

A few weeks later, Ms. Eudaly, the wife of a Dallas investment banker, got another hairdresser to bring back the blond. "The Roger Thompson Salon is very definitely New York," she says. "But they need to understand that this is Dallas, Texas."

Unhappy Redheads
Of Botkins, Ohio,
Have a Solution

It Is Known as 'The Works,'
And It Gets the Rust Out;
It Is Meant to Clean Toilets

By James S. Hirsch

2/10/92

BOTKINS, OHIO—Angie Cisco got it after her water softener broke down. Becky Thatcher came down with it while working as a lifeguard.

Their malady: orange hair. And it's going around. Some cases are minor-split-ends turning copperish, and such. More severe attacks, mainly experienced by blondes, turn flaxen locks a brassy red. This isn't pretty.

"I used to dye my hair red, but I don't have to here," sighs Sara Kjellmert, a 17-year-old exchange student from Sweden.

But don't call in the Food and Drug Administration. This is one condition with a known cause (though it also has a dubious cure). The culprit is hard water, water with a heavy mineral content found in wells throughout rural America. The stuff, they say, is safe to drink, but in the shower minerals latch onto strands of hair and leave deposits of iron, lime or magnesium.

Like garden tools or an old Chevy, hair can oxidize, redden and rust. The heavy buildup develops particularly among women who have had perms full of chemicals or who use highlighting paste on their hair. Teenagers, who wash their hair a lot, are particularly prey to the orange peril.

Battling rust buildup is a daily struggle for the four beauty salons in Botkins, a tiny farming town 50 miles north of Dayton. Put on a little perm solution and rinse, and just watch the deep-purple water flow like Manischewitz. One young woman had her blonde hair highlighted and saw it turn gray. "It's scummy, it's dandruffy, and there's no shine to the hair," says Darla Berning, who owns the Village Salon.

The problem is by no means unique to this area. High concentrations of hard-water minerals stretch from upstate New York to Montana, and particularly around the Great Lakes region. For people who live in cities where water is treated, this is a non-issue.

That's even the case for the 1,200 residents of Botkins. It's those who live outside of town who tend to develop this red badge of corrosion. Getting a water softener and calling the Culligan man helps, if you can afford the tanks and the chemicals and the regular servicing.

Still, there's a Rust Belt that cuts a swath through the hair curlers of rural America.

"I don't like being a redhead," says Shelly Zitzelsberger of Stockbridge, Wis., whose true hair color is light brown. "I mean, it's not that color makes a difference, but I want my color back."

What to do? Ah, there's the rub.

Many things have been tried, including vinegar, baking soda, skin cleansers, hydrogen peroxide, shampoos, conditioners and clarifiers. Missy Grieves, a Botkins High School junior with flowing blonde hair, has had limited success with distilled water, lemon juice and salt. Miss Thatcher, a 19-year-old blonde who became a redhead, has since dyed her hair brown, voiding the issue.

Some Botkins residents are resigned to their fate. Red hair is just part of living in a community where a big feed mill spews corn dust and the only motel is next to a pig farm.

But other people are desperate to get the rust out. And in recent years, some people in these parts of south-central Ohio have been using a product called The Works, which contains just enough hydrochloric acid to do the job. It's controversial, among other reasons, because the product is made to remove toilet-bowl rust, and, besides that, it is poisonous. It says so in bold, black letters across the bottle, and the label expands on the theme: "May Be Fatal If Swallowed. Causes Severe Burns. Vapor Harmful."

But it would take more than dire warnings to deter Sharon Klosterman, who has been shooting The Works on her hair every six months for several years. Wearing rubber gloves, the 33-year-old mother of three mixes two ounces of the toilet-cleaner with two ounces of water, then sluices it through her rusty blond hair.

She doesn't let the solution touch her scalp. "I just put it in and rinse it out," she says. "It's never done any damage to my hair." It's toxic, but it gets the rust out.

Mrs. Klosterman, who works in quality control at a nearby Honda plant, says many of her friends have also taken the cure. One 26-year-old blonde, who lives outside Botkins, says she started using the toilet-bowl cleaner on her hair four months ago after she tired of being called "carrot top." The friend who recommended The Works to her, she says, told her not to be concerned if her hair started to smoke. She says that hasn't happened.

The testimonials go on and on, from people pleased with the results and blasé about the peril.

But the product's manufacturer is very concerned about its misapplication. Lime-O-Sol Co. in Ashley, Ind., said it first heard that The Works was being used as a personal-care product last month, and the only reports the company has had have come from south-central Ohio.

"We prefer that our cleaning products only be used for cleaning, and we encourage people to read labels," says Therese Stantz, supervisor of sales and customer service. "This was definitely a first for us."

It isn't clear where the innovative new use for The Works came from, or if that matters. Some attribute it to teen-agers, others to Botkins beauticians. But the issue came to a head last year when a beautician in Botkins, Connie Mielke, was asked by a high-school student about using toilet-bowl cleaner to get the red out. Mrs. Mielke, who owns the Hairitage House here, says she was shocked. "Some of these kids have used it for three years, and they say their hair is fine, but believe you me, their hair is not fine." It has lost protein, for one thing, she maintains.

Mrs. Mielke began a crusade to discourage using The Works—then created a rhubarb when, in a local newspaper, she called people who do "stupid." Some salon owners say she is just trying to drum up business for herself.

And many people hereabouts don't see much wrong with the rust remover. Bartending at Meyer's Tavern, Rita Dorsten says she figures beauticians have probably used toilet-bowl cleaner on her blond tresses. "It's no worse than perm solution," she says, taking a drag on her cigarette. "That stuff will burn your skin." In her opinion, "Anything that's going to strip (the rust) out of your hair will be just as hard" on it as something that burnishes porcelain.

A product was introduced last year that is meant to get mineral deposits out of hair. It is called Malibu 2000 and is available only in salons. It is touted by its manufacturer in Southern California as "a whole new approach to hair," and it is endorsed by Jan Hodgin-States, the manager of a J.C. Penney Styling Salon in Muncie, Ind. "It's the most effective product I've ever used," she says.

And it is now being pushed aggressively in the beauty parlors of Botkins. But Mrs. Berning, of the Village Salon, doesn't think it will necessarily catch on with the inadvertent redheads who have come to rely on The Works. "They're not going to pay for expensive products," she says, "when they've been using that for years."

These Thieves Are
Partial to Sequins,
And Pretty in Pink

Gangs of Florida Transvestites
Steal Millions in Dresses;
Police Call It 'Frustrating'

By Eric Morgenthaler

1/23/92

WEST PALM BEACH, FLA.—It seemed to be a routine traffic violation—a car going the wrong way on a one-way street—until the cops discovered that one of the guys in the car had two rhinestone tiaras in his purse.

The tiaras turned out to be hot. The guy with the purse turned out to be Rodney Lowery, who police say is part of a shadowy band of transvestite burglars who knock over boutiques like they were bowling pins. Mr. Lowery also goes by the name Dior. When police stopped him, he was wearing short shorts, a wig of flyaway brown curls, and a black feather boa, flung around his neck.

Mr. Lowery showed up for his tiara-theft trial, in state court here in mid-1990, wearing a flowing green crepe-de-chine pantsuit, by Naturally Yours of Hawaii. Police Detective Michael Roggin, in court to testify, thought he recognized the outfit. Sure enough, it had been grabbed in a boutique heist he had investigated the night before. Mr. Lowery got 4½ years for the tiara theft, with some of the time also counting for purloining the pantsuit, which he admitted.

Even by the balmy standards of Florida—where the everyday crime scene includes drug lords, arms smugglers and money launderers—there is something special about a big-time burglary ring manned by female impersonators. For several years now, such a group—involving more than 100 transvestites, police say—has been preying on upscale women's shops in dozens of Florida towns.

The gang members steal pricey gowns and dresses—and the occasional tiara—for their own use, as well as for fencing. They seem partial to beading and sequins, and, says Pepper Cain, whose Pepper's Bridal Boutique in Boynton Beach was hit three times last year, "They know labels." Sometimes they dress as women for the heists, sometimes as men, and sometimes as a bit of both—wearing makeup and perhaps wigs, but men's clothing.

They are very adept burglars. "I would estimate that their take, throughout Florida, is in the millions and millions of dollars," says Detective Roggin, who says he has apprehended "40 or more" ring members in his three or four years on the case, without putting any noticeable crimp in their operations. He adds that last year in West Palm Beach—a focal point for the thieves—he linked "at least 25" break-ins to the gang or gangs, with a haul of about $400,000. "It's very serious," he says.

Merchants use stronger language. "It's horrible," says a woman whose boutique in Boca Raton was hit six times in eight months, despite ever-increasing security measures. "You just don't know what to do." After she installed a metal anti-burglary grate inside the front window last spring, gang members drove a car through the glass, in an attempt to break the bars. They failed, and they have since left her alone. She requests anonymity, because "I would just like to go forward."

Others don't have that option. Carole Chase last year closed her three Global Treasures boutiques, in Cocoa Beach, Vero Beach and Indialantic, after her insurance company dropped her following eight break-ins during what she calls "a year of torture and hell for me." She says during the first burglary, a $51,000 heist in April 1990, the fleeing thieves dropped a jeweled pink gown. Two days later, gang members struck again, taking another $22,000 worth of clothes—"and they hand-picked that same jeweled gown out of a rack," she says. "They wanted that dress."

The ring's signature break-in is a lightning-fast "smash-and-grab" burglary, involving perhaps four or five people, during the early-morning hours. The thieves typically throw a cinder block through a shop's front window, dash in and scoop up armloads of clothes, throw them into the trunk of their car—which usually is newly stolen—and speed off. "The crime takes no more than a minute or two," says Guy Di Benedetto, a police detective in Boca Raton, where the ring was linked to 20 break-ins last year—none of them solved. "By the time the alarm goes off and the police respond, they're gone."

"It's very frustrating," says Police Sgt. Robert Smith, who heads Fort Lauderdale's burglary squad and links the transvestites to nearly $1 million of stolen merchandise in the last year or so.

It does, however, make for some interesting police work. Detectives believe the thieves recruit new members—and wear, sell and trade stolen outfits—at transvestite beauty pageants. Thus, last May, six law-enforcement professionals—from three cities and four agencies, including the state attorney's office—hauled out to the little town of Pahokee, in the Everglades, to attend a show.

The law enforcers didn't make any arrests, but they videotaped, photographed and took notes on the proceedings. "The host, or hostess, of the event—he was a male, but in drag—spoke openly about police being in the audience," says Detective Di Benedetto, who was there. "He made the comment that not all their clothes were stolen. Then he looked down at the gown he was wearing and said, 'Well, maybe they are.'"

(Detective Di Benedetto says the law-breaking few shouldn't give a bad name to the law-abiding many. "These are criminals who just happen to be transvestites," he says of the burglars.)

Police say they have identified scores of ring members, but seldom have enough evidence to bring successful cases against them. Even with evidence, the cases are often settled with plea-bargains and light sentences. Police say some of the transvestites are street prostitutes. Almost all use aliases.

"This is a guy they call Large Marge," says Detective Roggin, pointing to one of perhaps 100 mug shots in a thick black notebook of suspected ring members. "I've arrested him three or four times" on various charges. Marge is dressed as a man in this photo. The notebook says he is 6-feet-2 and weighs 250 pounds. "But he's larger than that now," Detective Roggin says. "Probably 275 or 80."

He flips to another mug shot, of a slender young person with teased hair and careful makeup. "They call him Farrah," he says.

Despite years of work, there is a lot the authorities don't know about the boutique burglars. They are not even sure whether they are dealing with one ring or several. They have had scant success in getting informants. "They're a pretty tight group," says Boynton Beach Police Detective Paul Valerio. Police don't seem keen to go undercover themselves.

Some think the trouble started in the West Palm Beach area in the mid-1980s, then spread. Although the thieves prefer upscale boutiques, police say they aren't averse to hitting other retailers, as well. Because burglaries are usually a local-police matter, news of gang operations doesn't always travel quickly among law-enforcement agencies around the state. "They're a lot more organized than we are," says Cathy Whitaker, a crimes analyst for the Fort Pierce police department. "And they capitalize on this."

Crooked transvestites aren't unique to Florida. "I've had calls from Missouri" about similar crimes, says Detective Roggin. But it may be a commentary on the times that a large bunch of men who dress as women can run a criminal enterprise that is—of all things—elusive.

"If this were 20 years ago, they'd stand out like a sore thumb," says Fort Lauderdale's Sgt. Smith. "But in today's society, you know, it's become second nature to see all sorts of people out walking around."

Egad! Why Plaid?
A Partial Accounting
For Taste This Fall

———

Fashion Retailers Believe
Tartans Old as the Hills
Will Add to Bottom Line

———

By Teri Agins

9/6/91

NEW YORK—It's a plaid, plaid, plaid, plaid world.

To the delight of some, tartan plaids—bold, crisscross patterns that make you think of kilts—will be here with the autumn leaves, a fashion statement old as the Scottish Highlands, but new for the fall of 1991.

Others think plaid is too ugly or ordinary to bother with.

Stewarts and Gordons and other clans too numerous to mention surely shudder that the extended-family colors are turning up on boxer shorts, baseball caps, sequined cocktail dresses and a $9,286 Ralph Lauren mahogany highboy with tartan drawers.

Harry Lindley, a consultant to Kinloch Anderson, a big tartan retailer in Edinburgh, finds it "disgusting" that U.S. designers are adding loud colors, even pinks, to traditional tartans of red and green and the rest. But why not? There are 2,200 registered tartans. Send in your surname and the Scots, for a fee (150 pounds), will register an official tartan for you, or for your company.

In pushing plaids, anxious retailers probably are assuming that slaves to fashion currently have closets full of taupe and black but nowhere near enough tartan to go around in a rage of plaid.

But egad! Why plaid? It isn't new—and it has a checkered past. Junior Leaguers pretty much doomed it to dowdiness after years and years of wearing floor-length tartan hostess skirts and velvet headbands at Christmastime. Golfers with a penchant for goofy prints made a plaid situation worse.

Boxy and busy, plaids have always been hard to wear without coming across like an overstuffed chair or a rec-room couch that doesn't show dirt. Hips seem to double in size when clad in plaid. Like horizontal stripes, plaids make people look fat, or so says Jenny Craig, who advocates not just dieting and exercise but solid colors.

People named Madge and Ethel on TV comedies go in for plaid house-dresses in a big way. But even this year under pressure from Seventh Avenue, television's fashionable anchor people aren't likely to go tartan. Plaid, you see, upsets the camera lens, causing a blur and jiggle—a moire pattern that is distracting to the plaid-couch potato at home.

Of course, clotheshorses have long lumped wool plaid weaves with Hawaiian prints and double-knits as best avoided. "You never saw Audrey Hepburn or Babe Paley photographed in plaid," says fashion historian Caroline Rennolds Millbank.

But fashion marketers can concoct a rationale for anything. Plaids, they say, are wholesome and honest, durable and economical, the perfect back-to-basics couture for people who are fed up with frivolity and artifice but still willing to spend a few bucks on new duds.

"Taking things like tartan that have a timelessness and making them look new has always been part of what I do," says the designer Mr. Lauren, who is at the cutting edge of plaid this year, slapping tartans not just on apparel but on china, bed linens, wallpaper, luggage and napkin rings.

Indeed, in fashion circles there are all sorts of revisionist theories about plaid. For example, Karen Erickson, part owner of Eric Beamon Inc., a Manhattan maker of funky wide tartan bracelets, dangling earrings and handbags, says "classic plaids have the naughtiness of a Catholic schoolgirl."

And so it is that tartans are blaring like bagpipes from shelves this season. Saks Fifth Avenue's latest mail-order catalog, called "The High Road to Style," has 13 dizzying pages of women's suits in tartans, tweedy plaids and houndstooth checks. Vogue's big September fashion number includes a 24-page spread of model Linda Evangelista romping through the heather in plaids. Dan River Inc., a marketer of plaid fabrics, estimates that its 1991 sales have surged (or is it serged?) 30% over last year's.

And some people who care a lot about what they wear actually like plaid. Houston socialite Lynn Wyatt became entranced with the ball gown in yellow and black MacLeod tartan taffeta she saw at the couture fashion show of Paris designer Emanuel Ungaro. To party in the spartan '90s, she immediately ordered the $20,000 strapless dress with cascading train. Tartan "makes it less formal," she says. "Considering the troubled times that we are in, anything that is overdone is inappropriate." She wore her new dress last week at Count Giovanni Volpi's ball in Venice.

That tartan has the common touch comes as good news to Loni McKown, fashion editor of the Indianapolis News. It won't be hard to explain or justify to Hoosier readers, she says. "This is one trend that even people out here will get."

Of course, some who disdained plaid still don't like it and say so. "Plaids are too brash and make men look like boys," says designer Joseph Abboud. Marshall Blonsky, a semiotician, has a conspiracy theory to explain plaid's resurgence: "The tartan explosion is a clandestine wink between the apparel maker, advertiser and retailer to get people to throw their money after fashion jokes." Mr. Blonsky thinks the plaid fad is a case of "conspicuous disposability." In other words, consumers will buy the new uniform only to then throw it out.

New York fashion publicist Erin Owens has already turned against the fall suit she ordered last month from the I. Magnin catalog. "I've seen so much plaid in the last few weeks that I'm sick of my suit already—and I haven't even worn it." Still, you would never know that a plaid backlash is a-building from the way Seventh Avenue is carrying on.

Plaid is hardly a sometime thing in Scotland. Tartans date back to the 13th century when the Irish and British wore them to represent district or clan. By the 18th century, the Highland military regiments had adopted tartans as their official uniform. Traditional tartans consist of colored bands or lines of a certain width and crossing at right angles. Since 1963, tartans have been registered under family names with the Scottish Tartan Society, in Comrie, Scotland.

Registered patterns are, in theory, protected, and just a handful of designs, including the popular dark-green Black Watch tartan and the red Royal Stewart, are in the public domain. No self-respecting Scot would wear somebody else's tartan.

But Americans don't stand on ceremony. Ruth Greene, the manager of Scottish Products Inc., a New York importer and retailer of tartans, is dismayed that U.S. customers request them by color instead of by name. And Mr. Lindley, the tartan consultant, sniffs at the "made-up tartan" jacket from Ralph Lauren that adorns the latest cover of Vogue. He says Mr. Lauren has used purple and yellow where green and blue belong.

Since Seventh Avenue has always believed in imitation, it isn't certain just who was first to go plaid this time. But Isaac Mizrahi, the 30-year-old New York designer known for his witty creations, is getting most of the credit. He wowed fashion editors with his plaid designs in 1989, especially a strapless gown in cashmere.

Later, he did shirtwaist dresses and matching barbecue mitts that would have been just right for June Cleaver in "Leave It to Beaver." Twyla Tharp thereupon hired Mr. Mizrahi to design tartan tutus for her ballet "Brief Fling." Says Mr. Mizrahi: "There's nothing quite like a good tartan. They are so precious and rich looking and played down."

So it's a case of "the good, the plaid and the ugly"—a line borrowed from President Bush's favorite Off-Broadway musical, "Forever Plaid." With plaid, ugly can be a big problem; most tartan clothes on shop floors today look as if they were stamped on fabric, certainly not dyed in the wool and matched at the seams.

And whatever the quality of the craftsmanship, dressmakers haven't figured out how to minimize plaid's baleful effects on thunder thighs.

Unless, that is, one heeds the fashion tip of a Bloomingdale's saleswoman to those heavyset women she tries to sell red plaid stretch pants: "Wear them with a long black top."

Christie Brinkley
Need Not Apply
For This Model Job

---

*The Ideal 'Fitting Model' Has
An Off-the-Rack Figure
And Plenty of Opinions*

By Teri Agins

1/9/90

NEW YORK—Exotic to look at—as you might expect from their names—
Aly and Dalma draw rubbernecking stares when they sashay through
Manhattan's garment district. Karen Perkins—who, at 5-foot-3 and
40ish, looks like a sitcom-type mom—turns few heads.

Aly, Dalma and Ms. Perkins are models. Aly, who is from Ireland, and
Dalma, from Brazil, work the international runways and fashion magazines. Ms. Perkins, from a New York suburb, works on Seventh Avenue.
She is a fitting model, a combination mannequin, critic and sounding
board for apparel makers. Her average body proportions help designers
and manufacturers fashion clothes for those who may aspire to be, but
will never be, an Aly or Dalma.

The ideal fitting model is perfectly ordinary—with a 35-inch bust, 26-
inch waist and 37-inch hips. "When you are working in fittings for production . . . your measurements can't be too long-waisted or broad-shoul-
dered. In a fashion show, that stuff matters, but not in production," says
Ellen Harth, president of the runway division of Elite Model Management
agency in New York.

The fitting model is, in this sense, the transition from the fantasy of the
runway—the drama of décolletage and skirts hiked to midthigh—to the
actuality of the more wearable dresses found on department-store racks.

On one day recently, Ms. Perkins shuttles among five Seventh Avenue
showrooms for one-hour fitting sessions.

In the cramped executive suite at Michael B. Petites Ltd., she is facing
a full-length mirror, stripped down to a silk camisole, pantyhose and
black patent-leather pumps. It is much like a department-store fitting
room, except that the suite is full of men—two executives, the pattern
maker and a production manager—along with one female assistant.

Ms. Perkins slips on a droopy rayon coat-dress that looks pretty hopeless. "This dress isn't living," she says with a sigh. Solomon Hanan, the production manager, peers over his half-frame glasses and points out that the buttons are pulling it down. He starts pinning. Ms. Perkins pinches a sleeve a quarter of an inch. "The neckline needs to be picked up," she says. They dicker over the front placket.

The flaws in this sample dress would jump out at anybody, but problems are often subtle, indistinguishable to the untrained eye.

At the Maggy London showroom, a jumpsuit seems perfect. It isn't. "This pant leg is sloping forward just a little," Ms. Perkins volunteers. She sits in a chair, separates her legs and stands to test it for comfort.

"Doesn't it look a little tight? Let's release it about a half of an inch across the hips," says Milton Cahn, the owner. Now he notes that the crotch seam is dipping to one side. An assistant takes the jumpsuit to the workroom and reappears a few minutes later. Ms. Perkins tries it on again. She leans and bends in different directions and they pin some more.

There isn't much glamour in this kind of modeling, but there is money—up to $300,000 a year. In one of Ms. Perkins's first jobs on Seventh Avenue, crunching numbers as a buying-office assistant, she watched the models work. "They were making a lot of money, and they weren't working as hard as I was," she recalls.

She signed up with a modeling agency and started fitting for junior-sized clothes for JCPenney & Co. Now, she fits petite sizes for such popularly priced labels as Maggy London International Ltd., Donnkenny Inc. and C. S. F. Alexandria Blouse Inc. She commands up to $150 an hour. Michael B. Petites is so attached to Ms. Perkins that they have a plaster cast of her body, used for fittings when she isn't there in the flesh.

Good fitting models, unlike plaster casts, speak out, offering opinions on how short a skirt should be or whether a jacket should close with snaps or buttons. David Myers, an owner of Michael B. Petites, claims that Ms. Perkins's insistence on moving a chain decoration on a dress "really did work better on a short torso." Ms. Perkins says, "I know when something works."

In apparel making, fit is on a par with style, and it is essential in developing a following. "You hear women say they wear Liz Claiborne because they have happily stumbled on a fit that works for them," says Marjorie Deane, the chairman of Tobe Associates Inc., retail industry consultant.

But that fit has little to do with size. Despite what the tags say, there are no standard sizes. The last apparel production standards sponsored by the government were done in the 1930s; only now are they being updated. Meanwhile, people have grown larger.

"What used to be a size 14 back then could now be more like a size 10 or an 8, depending on the manufacturer," says Sirvant Mellian, chairman of a committee updating the size specifications. Apparel firms also play to vanity. "They call something that is really a 10 an eight," says Ms. Deane, the consultant. This is especially true when it comes to expensive clothes for older women.

Fashion manufacturers choose fitting models who conform to their interpretation of size and who can "test-market" their styles. At Gap Inc.'s Banana Republic division, model Carole McCarroll is doing what the company calls a "looks" session.

Around a long conference table, four female production-staff members drink diet sodas and chatter like sorority sisters while Ms. McCarroll, a 5-foot-9 blonde, tries on sweaters, shirts and other sportswear pieces.

The banter ("that's very Banana," and "Cute. That's really cute, Carole") sounds silly, but this session—weeding out the weaker styles in preparation for an important sales meeting—is in earnest. "Carole gives a sporty stance, she gives attitude to the clothes," says Etta Granata, Banana Republic's product director for women's clothing. "When Carole is in the clothes, we really feel we see our customer walking down the street."

All too often, clothes look suspiciously alike. Alan Millstein, a retail consultant who spent many years working at a coat firm on Seventh Avenue, says, "It's no accident that designers come up with similar ideas in the same season." Fitting models, he says, are a part of the "underground railroad," of fabric salesmen, button peddlers and overlapping sources that spread information from showroom to showroom.

Though apparel firms deny they pump models for intelligence about the competition, snippets of information do slip out. "If a model has been doing a certain sleeve for one designer, at another fitting the designer may ask her how she thinks the sleeve should look . . . she's likely to fold the sleeve back the same way without even thinking about it," says Luiz Lopez-Cepero, owner of Les Girls modeling agency.

But a fitting model who wants to stay in the business won't divulge the details of a designer's collection that's still under wraps. "A couple of times I've been asked what's so-and-so doing this season, but I would never say anything," says Ms. McCarroll. "You'd never last long in this business if you did."

Fitting models don't have to worry about growing older, as do most runway and fashion models. Experience is highly prized. The silver-haired Ulla Mancini, who formerly did runway fashion shows for designers like Halston, has spent most of her 25-year modeling career doing fittings. Regular exercise, diet and not having children have helped her maintain her size; she even does fittings for strapless lingerie.

Ms. Perkins, who has two children, says that like customers her age, her body has "spread." No matter. She simply upgraded, from juniors to women's petites.

But there is one threat to a model's career: competition from the dozen or so other top models on Seventh Avenue. Ms. Perkins says that she is afraid to take a vacation for longer than a week. Several years ago, she lost several accounts when she took maternity leave. "Replacements are the kiss of death in this business," she says.

Enlightenment Is
Fine, but for Now
A New Car Will Do

Buddhist Sect Members Chant
For Very Specific Aims;
2 Tickets in Front, Please

By Kathleen A. Hughes

5/9/86

LOS ANGELES—Seven bouncing young women in white and purple se-quined miniskirts are waving white pompons and leading a cheer. It is Sunday afternoon and the amphitheater is packed.

"We can do it, we know we can. Can we do it? Yes we can. How do we stand? Hand in hand. Unite! Fight! Win!" The crowd goes wild.

But wait. This isn't a UCLA pep rally. This is the young women's divi-sion of a Buddhist sect—devoted to chanting for success.

Does it work? Diane Reichard from New Mexico steps to the micro-phone. "I chanted to live courageously on my own," she says. "Soon, I talked to my boyfriend and he moved out. He left me the car, the apart-ment and the stereo, I couldn't believe it!"

The crowd goes wild again.

The 6,000 women gathered here belong to Nichiren Shoshu Soka Gak-kai of America, a controversial sect of Buddhism that has fused that an-cient religion with some very 20th-century values. The group is gaining popularity fast, especially in California.

The sect, founded in 1960, claims 500,000 members, up 100,000 from a year ago. Its parent group is Soka Gakkai International, a Japanese um-brella organization for Nichiren Shoshu Buddhist sects in more than 100 countries.

Chanting isn't new, of course, nor is praying for a better lot in life. But this group encourages its members to chant for rather concrete goals. While some seek noble aims like world peace or spiritual calm, many focus right in on the here and now. They chant for a better job, a new coat, a white BMW.

The words they chant don't say anything about their objective. Mem-bers simply kneel before an altar and recite over and over an ancient Buddhist chant, "Nammyoho-renge-kyo" ("Hail to the Lotus sutra"). Besides this daily ritual, they sometimes meet in small groups called "hons" to chant together and relate their successes.

Much of this irks many more traditional followers of Buddhism, a religion that identifies craving and attachment as the cause of human suffering. "Even if you do get your car, it has little to do with enlightenment," says Masao Kodani, a minister in the Jodoshinshu sect of a prominent school of Buddhism known as Pure Land Buddhism.

But some in Lotusland clearly find success very enlightening. Heidi Bergman, a 20-year-old college student, says she has chanted for a new car, relationships, better grades, cheaper auto insurance and the recovery of a notebook she lost. She also chanted for good seats at a concert by the rock group the Police.

She says it works, most of the time. Her father bought her a new Dodge Colt, even though she had smashed up his car not long before. She received an A in a writing class, despite having missed an assignment. And she got to sit close to the stage at the rock concert because she ran into a friend and was able to share his seat. She is still chanting for the cheap car insurance.

Miss Bergman usually chants for an hour a day. But sometimes she is a little worried she won't be able to find a parking place, so to be on the safe side she chants an extra 10 minutes. "Every time I chant with real determination and I push myself, I get the parking space," she says.

In the freeway megalopolis that is Los Angeles, chanting has taken on a decidedly vehicular slant. Followers chant for new cars, for their old cars to keep running, and for recreational vehicles.

Virginia Feingold, a 38-year-old career counselor, chanted for "a wonderful new car" after first her purple Volkswagen and then an old yellow Honda broke down. "I chanted for the wisdom to pick the right car and for a salesman who would allow me to get the best deal possible," she says.

Ms. Feingold decided on a Nissan 200SX. Then she picked two car dealers and began playing them off against each other, until finally one offered a good deal on a white 200SX with a sunroof and digital dashboard. Now "I love my car," she says.

Then there are those who chant for RVs, such as Mary Pat Kuppig and her husband. "We chanted for a VW camper in decent shape, the kind that sleeps five with a stove and the beds," says Ms. Kuppig, who sells advertising. Before going to the bank to apply for a loan, they chanted for an extra 20 minutes.

They got the loan, and they quickly found someone selling just the right sort of camper, only the seller wanted $1,000 too much. But the Kuppigs detected an engine problem and got the seller to cut the price. "Chanting helped us get exactly what we wanted with the least amount of effort," Ms. Kuppig concludes.

So how does it work? Many chanters aren't quite sure. Some chanters ascribe their good fortune to confidence, focus and positive energy. Some say harmony with the universe. Some say "rhythm."

Officials at Nichiren Shoshu decline to be interviewed. But the group's literature explains that chanting activates one's Buddha nature—which in most people is asleep. Living in a state of Buddhahood allows one to use the "power, fortune and wisdom" of that state to be more effective in achieving goals.

For about $15, chanters get a Gohonzon, a scroll said to embody what Buddhists call Mystic Law. The group's handbook says the writings of Nichiren Daishonin, a Japanese Buddhist priest of the 13th century, "clearly attest to the power of the Gohonzon."

However, the literature warns members not to view the Gohonzon as a "wish-fulfilling magic lantern," and it says chanting should always be followed by "courageous action." Material gains, called the conspicuous benefits, reinforce faith and thus pave the way to the deeper "inconspicuous" spiritual benefits that spring from "indestructable happiness."

A waiter who aspires to being "a personality in the entertainment industry" says he chants primarily for personal growth, consistency, courage and confidence. He does, however, also chant for his old Chevy to keep running. It has 98,000 miles on it, after all. "It's working," the waiter says. "I feel like my car has attained Buddhahood."

Chanters don't chant just any which way. The group's literature warns that a hurried chant can lead to a harried day. And a sloppy chant can make you feel at the mercy of everything. But, it says, a robust chant "in a clear voice at crisp, galloping pace" will result in "victory after victory."

Devotees also are advised not to tumble out of bed and start right in chanting. Out of respect, the handbook says, "you should not face the Gohonzon in your sleepwear."

For many, the group offers a network of support. On a recent Friday night in Hollywood, members told of getting better high-school grades and, in one case, a job at Warner Brothers. Speakers were greeted with wild applause and a special cheer combined with an arm motion something like that of a baseball pitcher.

Sometimes, chanters say, the results can be spectacular. Following a separation from her husband, Kathy Ferris, a vitamin distributor, drew up a list of 300 things she wanted. After a year of chanting, she had 280 of them. That included a suede coat with a belt and a certain kind of buttons. A friend gave her such a coat because it had been a gift from an ex-boyfriend.

Some believe that even when chanting fails, it succeeds. "There's a guarantee with chanting that you will get exactly what you want," says Ms. Kuppig, who got the VW camper. "And if you don't, you will find out why and be glad."

Consider what happened to Ms. Ferris. One of the few things she wanted that she didn't get was a Camaro that her uncle, a car dealer, had on his lot. She says she was devastated when he sold it to his other niece. But that isn't the end of the story.

Before long, the niece's Camaro's radiator fell out on the freeway, causing an accident in which the car was banged up. Later, one of its axles cracked. Eventually, the Camaro simply burned up.

"I ended up with a Rambler," Ms. Ferris says, "but I had that car for eight years and no problems."

Putting On the Dog
Just Comes Naturally
In Fey Marin County

At a Popular Sunday Brunch,
Chow Hounds Pack It In
And Network With Peers

By Carrie Dolan

9/20/85

LARKSPUR, CALIF.—It is Sunday morning, and the fun lovers of Marin County are gathered for their monthly outdoor brunch. A vase of pink rosebuds and pale yellow gladioluses adorns the table. Glass dishes and wicker baskets hold fresh-baked treats. A lilting breeze from the bay brushes the lace tablecloth.

The temperature is warm and the tone is casual, yet all the guests wear fur. That is because all the guests are dogs.

While other brunches around this fashionable Northern California county offer a marvelous chance to put on the dog, this brunch is put on for the dogs. For the past three years, about 60 chic chow hounds mingle here at, one hopes, the world's only Sunday brunch for dogs.

"We get out all the dog finery for Sunday," says Marilyn Ascher, who wears a gold beagle necklace. Her white poodle, Nicole, wears a jaunty red cap and emits a high-pitched yap. "Oh darling, shut up," she says to her dog. She says to her husband, "Honey, give her another piece of quiche, will you? Quiche is the only thing that keeps her quiet."

Gastronomically speaking, Marin mutts don't ride the same gravy train that more pedestrian pooches do. This brunch features such canine cuisine as "kibble quiche," liver pâté cake and cream-cheese tidbit rolled in health food, called "wheat germ woofies." Owners sip chilled champagne while their doggies dine. A few folks nibble on the all-natural dog biscuits. "They're really not bad," says one woman. "No salt, no sugar, no preservatives."

Patricia Monahan, who says she has been "into Marin and into dogs my whole life," holds the free bashes outside her pet boutique, known as For Paws. The boutique features pastel jogging suits, hand-knit sweaters from London and brass beds for dogs. Ms. Monahan says the brunches promote her shop and provide "a lovely way to spend the day with my friends—my four-legged friends."

Owners say it is a great way for pets to network with their peers. "It's a socialization process," says Rupert Jernigan, accompanied by his wife, Cynthia, and his 105-pound Newfoundland, Gabriel. "A lot of dogs don't get enough of it. They're too people-oriented. Without socialization, they don't know what they are."

Gabriel lunges forward and runs his tongue over the mug of a young, two-pound poodle named Crescendo, attending his first brunch. "Clean the baby's face, Gabriel," coos the owner. "He's very good with babies."

The relaxed brunch atmosphere inspires such puppy love, says Mrs. Jernigan, who wears a button-down shirt and a green skirt, both embroidered with spaniels. "All the dogs are here on equal footing, having fun. Here, they all have the same status."

Dogs from the humble origins of pounds, or of uncertain parentage, are now pampered socialites. Each dog has a tale. Lakme, an Afghan, was born a "mistake," the offspring of a purebred mother who strayed. Mingling at brunch "has made a real change in her behavior," says Beth MacArthur, her owner. "She used to be very shy." Bitten Orth, a 22-year Marinite, finds such stories inspiring. "I would rather listen to people talk about their dogs than their lives," she says. "Actually, I'd rather listen to their dogs."

News of the brunch has flowed like Perrier through the county. Bruce Bacheller says she was just walking her dog Charlotte on the bike path in Tiburon, where she lives, "when a complete stranger stops me and says, 'You have a gorgeous dog, and you just have to take her to this cocktail party in Larkspur.' I ran home, put it on the calendar, and here we are." Her dog, like most guests, licks the plate clean. (Usually, all the brunch-eon fare is eaten. Any leftovers, of course, are taken home in doggie bags.)

A dachshund from Greenbrae suddenly leaps toward a plate of cookies, bumping a table and spilling a bit of the bubbly. A few guests begin barking. "Razzberry didn't mean it," says her owner, Helen Holden, "she's a totally passive dog, she's just obsessed with food." Ms. Holden says, "I have a harness for her, but it's not dressy enough for brunch."

She thinks her salami-shaped pet, who wears a deep-blue, rhinestone-studded collar, has a "very expressive, photogenic face." She has already contacted Paw Productions, a local pet modeling agency about a screen test for a dog-food commercial.

Such pride is common among the attendees. Dora Moreaux included her English sheepdog, Kaddy, in her wedding party. She brings out Kaddy's photo album, showing snaps of him in the bathtub with her, opening up a box from Tiffany's and frolicking at Lake Tahoe in his snow boots. "Dogs do a lot for people," she says.

When Jean Oeverndiek goes shopping, she won't leave home without her poodle, Blackberry Brandy, carrying him into even the trendiest shops. "If they ask Berry to leave, I just cut up my credit card and hand it back to them."

Berry hasn't missed a brunch in two years. Mrs. Oeverndiek, a native Californian who's never been east of Arizona, notes that while other communities have special events for pets, "Marin has really taken the lead in this area."

Those who live in Marin, where folks commute on ferries and dwell among the redwoods and gelato shops, brim with boosterism. "There's a whole different, healthy mental attitude in Marin," says resident Pamela Lawrence. "That peacock-feather image is just not true."

Ms. Lawrence wears a pink and lavender jogging suit, clutching a glass of champagne in one hand, and a leash to Glory in the other. "Glory's so mellow," she says. "She gets along with everybody."

Other gala events are held here too, such as the recent puppy shower, thrown for a pregnant Great Dane. This summer, Valerie Ceredwin Chebre Pupey Snydale Pudsey had a birthday bash with some 300 guests, many wearing party hats. Val (as her friends call her) arrived in a limo. She was accompanied by her owner, David Seely, a one-time Silicon Valley software writer, who wore a tux.

Last month, there was a beach party, with palm trees, a plastic pool, patio tables and a pianist. A fund-raiser for the Humane Society, the day was a howling success, with over 200 canines in fashionable beach togs. A Labrador wore a sarong, a wolfhound donned a Hawaiian print shirt and a lei, a pair of Siberian huskies wore sunglasses and swim fins around their necks. Some mutts sported life jackets. One wore a snorkel mask. A 100-pound "lifeguard" named Marvin wore orange trunks, a whistle and a glob of white cream on his nose to protect it from the sun.

More than 50 dogs competed for the title of "Ms. Marin," judged on their poise, congeniality and fit of costume. Edging out a cute Maltese in a pink bikini, the winning pooch and her owner wore matching swimsuits. "The people may look like fools," says Diane Allevato, executive director of the Marin Humane Society, "but somehow, the animals manage to keep their dignity."

Next month, Ms. Monahan will hold a Halloween Party for dogs. However, there won't be any black cats at that event. "Kitties don't do well at parties," she says. "They're too smart."

You Wish Your Pet Could Talk to You? Who Says It Can't?

For Fee, California 'Psychics' Will Hold a Conversation And Tell You All About It

---

By Kathleen A. Hughes

12/17/87

PALOS VERDES, CALIF.—If only pets could talk. They could say whether they're happy. Whether they like liver more than beef. Why they bite the pets next door. How much they care about their owners.

Most pets, of course, never utter a word. But in—where else?—California, some pet owners say their pets are talking up a storm. That's because the owners have consulted pet psychics—people who claim they can tune into a pet's innermost thoughts and feelings using psychic powers and then spill all to the owner. The fee is usually $40 to $60 an hour.

Unlike pet psychologists, who focus on more banal behavior problems such as a pet's refusal to stop chewing on guests, most animal psychics claim they actually read a pet's mind using extrasensory perception. And pet owners lap it up.

Witness the four housewives in this wealthy neighborhood who have called in a pet psychic to have a serious talk with their four horses, seven dogs, two cats and a parrot. The entire group assembles at the palatial home of one of the housewives on a sunny Friday afternoon, and the pet owners have some very specific questions.

Ann Leatherbury, for example, would like to know whether Wham, her champion female golden retriever, wants to continue her career in dog shows or have puppies. Listen as the pet psychic, Beatrice Lydecker, seated on a living-room couch, discusses Wham's inner thoughts:

"She wants to be a show dog. She doesn't really want puppies," says Ms. Lydecker, after a penetrating look across the room at Wham, who appears to be concentrating entirely on the other pets. "She says, 'I've seen other dogs with puppies and I don't want that. It's too confining and restricting. I want to learn more, and I want to do more obedience training.'"

Many veterinarians take a dim view of the handful of self-styled pet psychics. "People want to believe that animals have a very humanlike thought process," says Benjamin Hart, a professor of physiology and behavior at the veterinary school at the University of California at Davis. "If someone comes along and tells them pets can talk, there's a predisposition to want to believe them." But Dr. Hart adds, "It's really nonsense."

Pet owners, however, frustrated by years of one-way conversations, often take a less cynical view. Consider Jean Roper of Lomita, who asked pet psychic Lydia Hibby to chat with her white spaniel, Didi. The result: "Didi wanted to know what happened to the big black dog I had six years ago," says Ms. Roper. "We thought Didi was stupid, but evidently she lies around and thinks a lot."

As it happens, Ms. Roper did have a big black dog. That isn't uncommon, but pet owners are often impressed by such tidbits of information. Margaret McCall, an advertising executive in La Crescenta, asked a psychic to find out how Tanya, her taffy-colored Labrador mix, felt after Ms. McCall's children moved away. "Tanya wants you to lighten up," said pet psychic Carol Gurney. "And she said something about golf."

"I come from a family of professional golfers and Carol had no way of knowing that," says Ms. McCall. "She hit upon things that were uncanny."

Pet owners often call a pet psychic because a pet is sick and they want a detailed account of how it's feeling. And some pet psychics claim they can chat with pets from a distance. For example, Gay Travers, a former publicist, called pet psychic Penelope Smith when her cat, Sebastian, was very ill. Ms. Smith told her to hang up while the psychic talked to Sebastian. Three minutes later she called back with some bad news.

"All that was on Sebastian's mind was skulls and bones," recalls Ms. Travers. "All he could think about was death. It was a kind of a depression."

Ms. Travers doesn't doubt that the psychic chat took place. For one thing, Sebastian looked "very disturbed" during the chat but perked up afterward. "I watched him for a few days and he was a lighter cat," says Ms. Travers. "Some burden had been taken off him."

Other pet owners have been told that their pets are facing a type of existential crisis. Lauren Glassman consulted pet psychic Gurney when her cat, Fannie Marie, stopped eating and veterinarians weren't helping. After a 45-minute tête-à-tête, Ms. Gurney broke the news: Fannie didn't feel she had a sense of purpose. She also wanted to go outside more.

Fair enough. Fannie Marie was allowed to spend more time outdoors, and she did seem to like that. But she still wasn't eating. Finally, another veterinarian pinpointed a more down-to-earth problem: bladder stones. The pet needed surgery, not philosophy. Since the operation, Fannie Marie has been downing large quantities of turkey-and-giblets cat food.

Pet owners frequently want to ask a pet directly why it is being so difficult. For example, Ms. Roper, the owner of Didi the spaniel, asked psychic Hibby to find out why Snapper, a brown and black combination of German shepherd and Akita, refused to wear a collar.

The answer wasn't pretty. "She said that when he was young he watched his mother be choked to death, and when he has a collar on he feels like he is going to die," recalls Ms. Roper.

Ms. Roper stopped trying to put a collar on Snapper.

Above all else, owners want to know whether their pet is happy. Rochelle Weitzen, a film producer, asked Ms. Gurney to find that out in her chat with Little LuLu, a black briard puppy. "Someone I live with is moving out and I wanted to make sure the puppy was feeling OK," she says. She also wanted to know whether LuLu wanted another puppy around.

LuLu was feeling fine, the psychic said, but forget another pooch. LuLu also seized the opportunity to ask that her owner not sneak out of the house and pretend that LuLu doesn't notice.

How do pet psychics explain their professed ability to chat with pets? Most say that when they mentally ask questions, they receive images from the pet. And they say that anyone can do it. Ms. Lydecker even offers a one-day class on how to talk to pets for just $60. It has been the training ground for several other pet psychics. On a Saturday afternoon in Chatsworth, 14 hopeful pet owners show up for the class with almost as many dogs and cats in tow.

Ms. Lydecker allows a reporter to attend only on the condition that her "top-secret techniques" won't be detailed. But she does allow the results to be noted.

After three hours of lectures, the group has its first opportunity to practice by forming a circle around a large basset hound named Wally. The assignment: Find out what Wally's yard looks like, what Wally's home is like, what Wally likes to eat and what makes Wally angry—then check it all with Wally's owner.

"Won't it be confusing for the dog to answer so many questions?" asks Judy Johnson, a cat owner in the class.

"No, it's like a radio station," says Ms. Lydecker. "He's always sending out those signals."

Maybe so. But the group's first stab at telepathic communication with Wally, who happens to have his eyes closed and his nose in the air, seems to hit some type of atmospheric disturbance:

"Wally has a small yard," says one woman.

"No," says his owner, Deborah Gelson, a video producer who says her yard is fairly large.

"He has a friend who's a small child," the woman continues.

"He doesn't know any children," says Ms. Gelson.

"He likes canned food," says the owner of a Hungarian pointer.

"He doesn't eat canned food," frowns Ms. Gelson.

Wally, it seems, isn't talking.

The Radium Water Worked Fine Until His Jaw Came Off

Cancer Researcher Unearths A Bizarre Tale of Medicine And Roaring '20s Society

---

By Ron Winslow

8/1/90

In 1927, a steel mogul and socialite named Eben MacBurney Byers tumbled from the top berth of his private Pullman compartment en route home to New York from the Harvard-Yale football game. He was apparently engaged in some vigorous post-game revelry at the time.

What happened next led ultimately to his gruesome death 4½ years later—and to his place as a central character in a bizarre episode in U.S. medicine.

The saga of Mr. Byers is the subject of a report in today's Journal of the American Medical Association. While it has timely implications for contemporary medicine, it also provides an evocative look at a period in medicine before regulators and lawyers spoiled the fun.

"Byers was the personification of the Roaring '20s," says Roger M. Macklis, principal author of the report and a radiation oncologist at the Dana Farber Cancer Institute in Boston and the Harvard Joint Center for Radiation Therapy. "He was into everything."

The chairman of A.M. Byers Steel Co. and a director of Westinghouse Electric & Manufacturing, Mr. Byers was also a U.S. amateur golf champion, a horseracing enthusiast and, by reputation, an ardent ladies' man.

Dr. Macklis's interest in Mr. Byers was provoked in part by the doctor's acquisition late in 1989 of four mostly empty bottles of a patent medicine called Radithor. It was a status drink: At $1 a bottle, only the well-to-do could easily afford it. And it was a health drink—marketed by an entrepreneur named William J. A. Bailey, it promised to cure more than 150 maladies.

Mostly, Mr. Bailey sold it as an aphrodisiac. "Improved blood supply sent to the pelvic organs and tonic effects upon the nervous system generally result in a great improvement in the sex organs," touted a pamphlet entitled "Radithor, the New Weapon of Medical Science," which was mailed to doctors in the mid-1920s.

Radithor's magic ingredient was radium. The concoction rode the crest of the Mild Radium Therapy movement, a phenomenon in U.S. social circles shortly after the Curies discovered radium at the turn of the century. It was based on the premise that radiation, taken in minute doses, provided a metabolic kick to the body's endocrine system and infused depleted organs with energy.

Dr. Macklis says Mr. Bailey "was a born con man" who had been peddling various miracle cures, especially for impotence, for years. But none achieved the success of Radithor, an over-the-counter tonic he asserted was the result of years of laboratory research, but which was really just distilled water laced with one microcurie each of two isotopes of radium.

He sold more than 400,000 bottles for $1 each—a 400% profit, says Dr. Macklis, adding: "He was the chief impresario in the radioactive patent medicine field."

Mr. Byers was 47 when he fell out of the berth and injured his arm. Over the next several weeks, he complained of muscular aches and a run-down feeling that undermined his performance both athletic and, it was rumored, sexual, Dr. Macklis reports. A Pittsburgh physiotherapist recommended Radithor.

For the next two years, Mr. Byers gulped two or three bottles a day. His activities while under its influence aren't well documented. But initially, he was apparently so satisfied with the results that he sent cases of it to business partners and girlfriends, and even fed it to his racehorses.

The science of the day gave at least a measure of support to Mr. Byers's faith in radium water. And U.S. regulatory agencies at the time were more concerned about truth in advertising than about potential harmful effects. The Federal Trade Commission, for instance, took action against makers of potions that lacked advertised levels of radioactivity.

Over two years, Mr. Byers guzzled perhaps 1,400 half-ounce bottles of the potion, Dr. Macklis says. He finally quit in October 1930, complaining to his doctor then that he'd lost "that toned-up feeling." He began to lose weight and experience headaches; many of his teeth fell out.

By 1930, the FTC had begun to raise questions about another advertised claim of radium-water medicines: that they were harmless. It asked Mr. Byers to testify at hearings in 1931, but by then he was too sick. An agency lawyer dispatched to take his statement at his mansion on Long Island was aghast.

Mr. Byers's "whole upper jaw, excepting two front teeth, and most of his lower jaw had been removed," the lawyer reported. "All the remaining bone tissue of his body was disintegrating, and holes were actually forming in his skull."

By the end of the year, the FTC ordered Mr. Bailey's operations closed. And on March 31, 1932, Mr. Byers died in a New York City hospital. He was 51. The next day, a front-page headline in the New York Times proclaimed the medical examiner's initial autopsy findings: Mr. Byers died of radium poisoning.

The news alarmed some members of the upper class, although James J. Walker, then mayor of New York City and an avowed user of radium water, at first resisted warnings to stop. In Pittsburgh, there were whispers in the press that a lady friend of Mr. Byers had also died of a mysterious ailment. Health officials in some cities ordered store shelves cleared of such potions. And some doctors stepped forward with evidence of other cases. A doctor went on a New York radio program and held radioactive bones of one victim in front of a Geiger counter to demonstrate "the deadly sound of radium," Dr. Macklis says.

Dr. Macklis bought his bottles of Radithor from a dealer in medical antiques; he's not saying how much he paid. Then he and two colleagues at the Harvard Joint Center, Marc R. Bellerive and John L. Humm, conducted a radiochemical analysis of the Radithor. It confirmed that Radithor was laced with significant amounts of radium isotopes.

Using a complex computer program, the scientists reconstructed the radium's life cycle through dozens of generations as it decayed to form new isotopes, and calculated the level of Mr. Byers's exposure. "He took enough radium to kill four people if he took it all at once," Dr. Macklis says. "The mystery is how did Byers survive so long, feeling so good, and have such a super-lethal burden in his body?"

He speculates that despite Mr. Byers's macabre demise, it is possible that chronic, low-level doses of powerful "alpha" radiation really do have at least a temporary stimulative effect, probably by provoking a defensive response that triggers production of fresh blood cells within the bone marrow.

Dr. Macklis and his colleagues also believe if alpha radiation could be safely harnessed, it could become a precise medical weapon that would attack cancerous cells without damaging nearby healthy tissue. Two years ago, Dr. Macklis succeeded in accomplishing that in mice.

It was his search for information on the impact of alpha radiation on people that led Dr. Macklis to the lost story of Mr. Byers, which he pieced together from medical literature, press accounts and historical documents.

In the end, Mr. Byers's death caused the collapse of the radioactive patent medicine industry. But all along, Mr. Bailey insisted that his potion was safe. After all, he said, he had probably drunk more Radithor than anyone else, and he felt fine.

Nearly 20 years after Mr. Bailey's death in 1949 of bladder cancer, medical researchers exhumed his remains. They had been ravaged by radiation. They were still "hot" when pulled from the ground.

VII

FOOD,
GLORIOUS FOOD

Waiter, There's A Rat in My Soup, And It's Delicious!

A Restaurant in China Serves Rat 30 Different Ways; We Suggest the Kabobs

---

By James McGregor

5/31/91

GUANGZHOU, CHINA—The Cantonese people of south China are legendary for eating anything that moves—and some things that are still moving. The food market here features cats, raccoons, owls, doves and snakes along with bear and tiger's paw, dried deer penis and decomposed monkey skeletons.

Now, this rich culinary tradition, along with rising disposable income in this most prosperous city in China, has inspired kitchen utensil salesman Zhang Guoxun to open what is believed to be China's first restaurant dedicated to serving rat.

That's right: Rat. Rat with Chestnut and Duck. Lemon Deep Fried Rat. Satayed Rat Slices with Vermicelli. In fact, the menu lists 30 different rat dishes, even including Liquored Rat Flambé, along with more mundane dishes such as Hot Pepper Silkworm, Raccoon with Winter Melon and Sliced Snake and Celery. And in the six months since the doors opened, customers have been scampering in at all hours to the euphemistically named Jialu (Super Deer) Restaurant.

"I was always eating out, but I got bored with the animals that restaurants offered," Mr. Zhang says during an interview over a plate of Black-Bean Rat. "I wanted to open a restaurant with an affordable exotic animal. Then I was walking home one night and a rat ran across in front of me and gave me this idea."

Mr. Zhang's restaurant is as trendy as they come in China. The 15-table, two-story eatery is a mixture of blond wood furniture, stucco walls and wooden lattice laced with plastic vines. Tonight's crowd includes a young couple who stroll in hand-in-hand and nestle in a quiet corner for a romantic rat dinner. Other groups include engineers, office clerks, salesmen and factory workers.

Tonight's special is Braised Rat. Garnished with sprigs of cilantro, the morsels of rat meat are swaddled in crispy rat skin. The first nibble reveals a rubbery texture. But the skin coats one's teeth with a stubborn slime. The result is a bit like old chewing gum covered with Crisco.

But other dishes are better. German Black Pepper Rat Knuckle (rat shoulders, actually; the knuckles are too small) tastes like a musty combination of chicken and pork. The rat soup, with delicate threads of rat meat mixed with thinly sliced potatoes and onions, is surprisingly sweet. Far and away most appealing to the Western palate is Rat Kabob. The skewers of charcoaled rat fillet are enlivened with slices of onion, mushroom and green pepper and served smothered in barbecue sauce on sizzling iron plates that are shaped like cows.

Also on the menu: a Nest of Snake and Rat, Vietnamese Style Rat Hot Pot, a Pair of Rats Wrapped in Lotus Leaves, Salted Rat with Southern Baby Peppers, Salted Cunning Rats, Fresh Lotus Seed Rat Stew, Seven-Color Rat Threads, Dark Green Unicorn Rat—and, of course, Classic Steamed Rat. Generally, the presentation is quite elegant, with some dishes served with lemon slices or scallions forming a border and others with carrots carved into flower shapes.

Experienced rat eaters, however, warn that this is no meat to pig out on. "Watch out," warns Wei Xiuwen, a factory manager eating at an adjacent table. "If you eat too much rat, you get a nosebleed." Several customers take off their shirts halfway through the meal because eating rat, like dog, seems to raise the body temperature for some reason. That's why rat is considered a winter food. In the summer, the restaurant does most of its business during the late-night and early-morning hours, after the weather cools down.

The restaurant is popular—Mr. Zhang claims profits of $2,000 a month—because it brings people back to their roots. The restaurant's cooks, and most customers, are originally from the countryside, where as children they ate air-dried rat meat. "If dried by a north wind, it tastes just like duck," Che Yongcheng, an engineer and regular customer, says wistfully of his favorite childhood snack.

For newcomers, Mr. Zhang has color brochures, featuring a photo of Rat Kabobs alongside a bottle of Napoleon X.O. In both the menu and brochure, the rats are referred to as "super deer" because Mr. Zhang says he wants to separate his fare from the common sewer rats that even Cantonese might find unappetizing. Mr. Zhang says his restaurant serves only free-range rats, wild rodents that feed on fruits and vegetables in the mountains a couple of hundred kilometers to the north.

The brochure explains why rats are the health food for the 1990s. It says the rats are rich in 17 amino acids, vitamin E and calcium. Eating them promises to prevent hair loss, revive the male libido, cure premature senility, relieve tension and reduce phlegm. A rat's "liver, gallbladder, fat, brain, head, eye, saliva, bone, skin" are "useful for medical treatment," says the brochure.

The restaurant's basement kitchen is a Dante's Inferno where shirtless cooks sweat over huge woks atop howling gas-fueled stoves that shoot flames five feet in the air. Dozens of fat, ready-to-cook rats are piled in a bamboo basket next to a crust-covered pump that noisily slurps up a small river of scum that runs off the stove and across the floor.

The senior chef is not here tonight. An understudy, Huang Lingtun, clad in rubber sandals and pants rolled up to his knees, explains how the rats are rounded up. They're captured and cleaned by farmers who freelance as rat bounty hunters. Some smoke the rats out by setting fields on fire and snaring the fleeing rats in nets attached to long bamboo poles. Others string wires across fields to stun unsuspecting rodents with high-voltage charges. The rats, each about a half-pound, arrive at the restaurant freshly gutted, beheaded and de-tailed.

Mr. Zhang says that the traditional recipes on his menu were suggested by Tang Qixin, a farmer honored as a model worker by Mao in 1958 for his prowess as a rat killer. Rat eradication campaigns have been a staple of Chinese life since Mao declared war on the four pests—rats, flies, mosquitoes and bed bugs—in the 1950s.

In 1984, the last Year of the Rat, the government launched an all-out crusade in which an estimated 526 million rats were killed. In 1985, the government tried to maintain the momentum by promoting rat meat as good food, explaining that "rats are better looking than sea slugs and cleaner than chickens and pigs."

Like most successful entrepreneurs during these times of shifting political winds in China, Mr. Zhang is quick to highlight the patriotic nature of his business rather than the personal economic benefits. "I am helping the government by eliminating some pests and helping enrich some farmers," he says.

Mr. Zhang says he's too new to the business to think about a chain of rat restaurants. But he says he's unconcerned about anyone stealing his idea. "My quality is tops," he says, "so I'm not worried about competitors."

Why the Pimento In Your Olive Seems To Lack Something

Chances Are It's Just Paste From Mechanical Stuffer; Portugal Keeps Tradition

---

By Barry Newman

1/16/85

MOURA, PORTUGAL—Long ago, after the nuns left, the convent of Santo Antonio da Pipa became a sausage factory. When the sausage makers left—it has been 40 years—the olive stuffers came.

Behind the convent's walls, across a cobbled court, in the old chapel's darkened narthex, stands a wooden table covered by a cloth of fine lace. On it rests a large glass jar of stuffed olives on display:

Olives stuffed with capers, hazelnuts, hot peppers; olives stuffed with anchovies and resealed with tiny plugs of olive flesh; olives stuffed with red, piquant pimentos; with pickled onions; with almonds; with almonds and pimentos; with pimentos and pickled onions.

From high on the water-stained wall, a bust of Santo Antonio da Pipa gazes down in reverence.

"It is so difficult, so very difficult to stuff an olive by hand," says Antonio Mesa Garcia, tapping his cigarette over an ashtray decorated with a drawing of a martini glass. He is a Spaniard in a white coat and manager of the olive-processing company, Fabrica de Conservas Patria Ltd.

"We prefer university students," says his Portuguese wife, Antonia Patinho, the personnel manager. "With the others, you must explain it time and time again."

The labor of 120 green-smocked, green-kerchiefed women in Fabrica de Conservas Patria clarifies one of the earliest mysteries of condimentology: how the pimento got into the olive. The human hand did it first. In Moura, except when a crisis strikes, the human hand does it still. But in Spain, 15 miles away, some sly engineers have taken the humanity out of olive stuffing. Subliminally, olive eaters know about this already.

Take a long look next time the bartender puts a plate of olives in front of you. Pick one up by the toothpick. Pluck out that red thing. Notice the glassy sheen, the even thickness? That's no pimento. That's rubbery goo flecked with pimento bits. That's paste.

Tastes like it, too. Over the past 10 or 12 years, olives stuffed with zesty pimentos—which are much like red bell peppers, only sweeter—have gone the way of vine-ripened tomatoes and freshly squeezed orange juice. In America, 97% of olives that appear to be stuffed with pimentos are stuffed with paste. Buyers may not know quite why, but they eat fewer olives now and more pickles instead.

Olive-stuffing economics made it happen. A human olive stuffer can stuff about 18 olives a minute. The Spaniards built a machine that stuffs 1,800. It put legions of olive stuffers out of work. But the machine works only on coils of pimento paste. It can't handle the natural fruit. A machine hasn't been built yet that can stuff an olive with real pimento.

A few stuffers have stayed on in Spain, filling orders from the wealthy and well-informed. They put olives in jars one by one, with the pimento facing out to look pretty, and they get paid plenty. In Portugal, by contrast, olive stuffers earn $100 a month. They haven't priced themselves out of a profession. This country may not be rich, but none of its old-time products have to put up with phonies.

Port wine, which hails from Portugal, still stands fast against fakes from Spain and dubious doubles from California. Half of the world's cork also comes from Portugal; as wine booms and stoppers grow scarce, cork does daily battle with screwtops. Now a French company, St. Gobain, has invented a stopper that looks like a cork, feels like a cork, and has to be yanked out of a bottle like a cork. It is made out of plastic. The company named it after the Tagus River, which runs through the middle of Portugal.

"Most people will know it isn't cork only if they focus their attention on it," says Alain Viricel of St. Gobain. Portugal's cork makers remain calm. A survey they give out says 90% of the French believe that only a cork stopper "really makes a wine." The Amorin Group, Portugal's biggest cork maker, produces 1.1 billion cork stoppers every year. Mario Cruz, its export director, says: "We aren't afraid of plastic."

Olive-stuffer confidence hardly runs so high. Paste seems poised for total victory. Yet real pimento has its champions—Morgan and Bernard Spencer of the Spencer Fruit Co. in Los Angeles, for example. The Spencers import stuffed olives, mainly from Spain, have them put into bottles in Houston and sell them in Southern California. They hate paste.

"We specialize in pimento-stuffed olives," Morgan Spencer says on the phone from Houston. He has been in the stuffed-olive business for almost four decades. His younger brother runs the business.

"Green olives have been stuffed for many, many years," says Bernie Spencer. "It goes back to when boats carried olives over here as ballast. You'd buy them for practically nothing. That's what started the stuffing business."

As Mr. Spencer tells it, America gave birth to the stuffed olive. History seems to support him. Sophocles wrote about olives. So did Homer, Virgil, Ovid, Horace, Plutarch, Cato and Pliny the Elder. Not one of them mentions pickled onions, much less pimentos. Even today, in Spain and Portugal, hardly anyone will eat an olive with anything in it apart from the pit.

When the olive went to America in ballast loads, though, and consumers offered practically nothing for them, promoters decided they needed a gimmick. First they tossed out Europe's numbered olive grades and introduced an American hierarchy: sub-petite, midget, petite, standard, select, small, medium, large, extra large, jumbo, colossal and super colossal.

Still, olives were drab. They lacked appeal. Black olives, which are ripe green olives, had it hardest. They have to be cooked at high heat and sealed in cans to ward off botulism. "Even if you put something in them that looked good," Bernie Spencer says, "shoppers couldn't see it."

But green olives had hope. Preserved in brine, they could be packed in glass. All they needed for greatness was one stroke of entrepreneurial inspiration, and this was it: Push out the pit and stick a pimento in the hole. The green olive became an object of beauty; the taste surpassed the sight.

Then prosperity swept America and economic development came to Spain. Olive stuffers went on to better things. And the pimento gave way to goo.

"I can pull that thing right out," Morgan Spencer says, "And the flavor will seem about the same to me—maybe better, because I'm not eating all that junk. There's no taste to paste."

Not even Fabrica de Conservas Patria is sheltered completely from the new technology. Behind the old chapel, at the end of a puddled passageway, a small room harbors a set of obsolete Spanish stuffing machines. Mr. Mesa, the manager, puts them to use only when he must stretch the Portuguese pimento supply. Today, however, he provides a demonstration.

Having blended pimento bits with water and a powdery chemical from Denmark, one of Mr. Mesa's workers pours the mixture into the paste machine through a funnel that leads to a series of tubes. From the other end emerges a continuous, milky-red noodle.

Two workers feed the coiled paste into a stuffing machine, a jumble of chutes and hoses, while olives drop from a hopper. A plunger jabs each one, grabs the pit, and jams in a slice of paste. Olives drop into a bucket at a rate of 60 a minute. Mr. Mesa offers a sample. The taste barely registers on the piquancy meter.

"To make paste, we have to take the salt out of the pimento," Mr. Mesa says. "Otherwise, it won't coagulate."

The factory's only other electrical contraption is the pimento slicer. It stands at the entrance to the stuffing room, across the courtyard. Halfway down the long room, women sit at small tables, pumping the pedals of machines that pluck out the pits and leave a uniform pouch. At the far end, 75 more women sit at one narrow table, heaps of sliced pimentos and pitted olives before them. They are the olive stuffers.

With her right hand, Isabel Valerio flips a finished product into a tub as her left hand reaches for the next olive. Her right hand chooses a pimento slice and the thumbnail trims it to size. Her hand doubles the pimento and inserts it, and her thumb shoves it in with a faint "squish." Her thumb and forefinger grasp the olive and flip it into the tub. Her left hand reaches for the next one.

Mrs. Valerio has done this 18 times a minute, 8,640 times a day, every workday for 21 years. "I can't explain it," she says, but her supervisor, Maria Antonia Santos, can.

"When you pick up the olive," she says, "you must judge how long the pimento has to be. Each pimento is custom-cut. The important thing is to pay attention. You can make a mess of it. You can push the pimento too hard so it goes through the other end. Or you could leave the pimento hanging from the front. You've got to bend it exactly in half or else it will slowly unfold. Then the worst possible thing could happen: The pimento could fall out."

If You Really Cut
The Mustard, You
Will Relish This Job

Driving a Wienermobile Means
That Almost Everyone
Will Be in Love With You

By Carrie Dolan

7/7/92

SAN FRANCISCO—As she drives through the city on a sunny morning, people notice Erin O'Shea. Construction workers applaud, a homeless person waves and a garbage man flashes an enthusiastic thumbs up. At a stoplight, a red convertible pulls alongside, and a man with slick blond hair makes an off-color remark about her vehicle.

Ms. O'Shea turns to her passengers and says with a shrug, "Welcome to Wienerworld."

For the past year, Ms. O'Shea's world has been consumed by an Oscar Mayer Wienermobile, a 23-foot fiberglass hot dog in which she and her partner, Brian Soifer, have traveled about 50,000 miles. "After this, there's not much you won't do," she says.

Six Wienermobiles roam the nation, attending parades, stopping by schools and grocery stores, and escorting couples from their weddings, with banners reading "Just Linked" and "For Better or Wurst." Each is driven by a pair of college graduates who spend about 340 days on the road, covering a region of the country. They hand out wiener whistles and try to create excitement about meat products. More than 1,000 people applied for the 12 Wienermobile driver slots this year, a response the company says is "somewhat reflective of today's job market." Applicants must have a good driving record, a taste for bad puns and no shame.

The latest crop of hotdoggers, as the company calls them, has just taken over. Michael Ellgass graduated from Indiana University with a degree in finance, but says he sees driving a wiener as "a challenge. I felt banking would always be there." Most are thrilled just to be working. Tim Young, a West Coast hotdogger, says he is the only one among his friends to find a good job—a salary of $19,500, plus $50 a day for lodging and $15 for food.

On his first day at work, Mr. Young is greeting giggling preschoolers outside the Sunset Chinese Baptist Church, dressed as a bottle of ketchup. "Think I can pick up girls in this outfit?" he whispers. He entertains the children by biting a happy face into a slice of baloney.

The youngsters are delighted. The director says the preschool serves hot dogs about once a month, "but not Oscar Mayer ones—they're too expensive." Later, the Wienermobile maneuvers past a cable car, for a stop in San Francisco's financial district, where people in suits jostle for wiener whistles.

Before hitting the road, drivers go to Oscar Mayer headquarters in Madison, Wis., for 10 days of indoctrination. A fatherly fellow named Russ Whitacre reads inspirational words from John Steinbeck and Jack London, praises the class for "cutting the mustard" and grills them with questions. "Remember, we do it all for a reason. And what is that reason?" The group shouts back, "Sell more meat!"

Drivers learn about the company's products: new ones (Baloney Light), old ones (head cheese) and failed ones (peanut butter and bacon spread). Discreet vehicle behavior, they are told, is a must. "People know when it's parked in front of a bar," Mr. Whitacre says. "There are no secrets. You can't hide in a Wienermobile."

Most important, they learn how to drive. "It's scary," says Brittne Eickman on her first time behind the wheel. "Pull out far enough around the corners, so you don't scrape your buns on the curb," says the driving instructor.

Training also addresses "partner relations." An attractive, unmarried pair on the road for a year in a big hot dog "was a concern," says Mr. Whitacre. "We thought some people might be offended." So far, on-the-road romances haven't been a problem. A few drivers, citing irreconcilable differences, have been switched to new partners.

Ms. O'Shea says her folks weren't worried about her taking off with a young man. "My parents said we'd definitely not be attracted to each other after that much time together." Her partner, Mr. Soifer, in a quest for romance, appeared on the TV show "Love Connection," treating his date, Suzanne Patterson, to cold cuts in the Wienermobile. She thought it was very original, and the two are still seeing each other.

The Wienermobile first rolled in 1936, manned by a midget billed as "Little Oscar—the world's smallest chef." Wienermobiles toured the U.S. in the 1950s and '60s, then were retired in favor of more TV commercials. Four years ago, a new fleet was launched. The program, which costs more than $1 million a year, is a "relatively inexpensive" form of marketing, says Richard Searer, vice president and general manager. "It's more efficient than buying media."

Today's Wienermobiles seat six, and feature a sunroof, microwave, refrigerator, cellular phone, and a stereo system, which can play "I wish I were an Oscar Mayer wiener" in 21 styles, including Cajun, rap and bossa nova. Mileage is low (10 miles to a gallon), top speed is about 65, and—at 5,800 pounds—Wienermobiles are sturdy. In a recent mishap, "we practically ate an Acura," says driver Cathleen Dumbaugh. The car was totaled; the Wienermobile was merely nicked.

People usually warm up to the Wienermobile, though adults tend to like it more than teens. The lead singer of ZZ Top recently flagged down one Wienermobile, and took its drivers out for sushi. "That was so cool," says hotdogger Dennis Lee. "Someone like that's not going to stop you in a normal car." But when a meat buyer asked Ms. Dumbaugh to drive a group of seventh graders to school, she says the kids were embarrassed. "They begged us to drop them off behind the school."

Having to be perky for an entire year isn't easy. "You can't be rude if someone cuts you off while you're driving," says Alisa Delaney. "If you park at a restaurant, people will come in and ask you about the Wienermobile. You can't say, 'Leave me alone, I'm eating.' " After a long day of talking about hot dogs, "you'd rather walk a mile to the store than go in the Wienermobile," says another driver.

There are other troubles. Wienermobiles tend to boil over in hot weather, and sometimes break down in places where mechanics have never worked on a wiener. Scheduling conflicts can result in long hauls on short notice. Last month, Ms. Delaney had to drive 1,000 miles by herself in order to make an appearance at Wal-Mart's annual meeting.

After delaying real life for a year, most hotdoggers go on to careers, in areas like public relations, advertising, sales or marketing. One got a job as Kool-Aid man in Alaska.

But getting potential employers to appreciate their experience is tough. "Everyone thinks you're a hot-dog vendor," complains Rob Strasberg, who nevertheless views Wienermobile driving as a "giant stepping stone" into advertising. Jennifer Rahn, who wants to be a teacher, says after a year of spewing puns, "I can't stop. I'll have a job interview, then say, 'I'd relish the opportunity to work here. Get it?' It's going to take time to adjust."

Still, at the end of the road, the retiring drivers are nostalgic. "It's just a hot dog, but I have feelings for it," says Mr. Strasberg. "It's like your girlfriend. I went to movies in it, ran errands with it. I have so many memories." Doug Salva agrees. "You experience so much with it; the whole range of emotions. It almost becomes alive."

"The biggest bummer is you aren't famous anymore," says Ms. Rahn. "You go to the mall and no one cares."

Its Eye on Fries, Poland Pursues Potato Parity

Its Agronomists Slowly Learn To Raise a Tuber Worthy Of the Golden Arches

---

By Barry Newman

10/9/86

GUZOW, POLAND—In the staff dining room of the Guzow Vegetable Experiment Station, Marian Dobrowolski watches, expressionless, as the waitress crosses the bare tiles and sets before him a platter of french-fried potatoes.

The potatoes are deep brown, thick cut and of irregular lengths and shapes. Mr. Dobrowolski frowns. Seated to his left, Elzbieta Lenkiewicz bites her lip.

Mr. Dobrowolski salts. He lifts a single french fry from the platter and holds it to the light. He rotates it. He breaks it in two and follows the rising steam.

Then he puts the potato into his mouth. He holds it there for a long moment. He tilts his head and thinks. Seated opposite, Jan Masternak leans forward, hands clasped prayerfully under his chin.

"H'mm," says Mr. Dobrowolski.

This is the most important moment in the entire crisis-ridden history of the McDonald's Polish potato project. McDonald's Corp. wants to grow potatoes here; it wants to serve them in its restaurants in Western Europe. The Poles want to grow them. But can they accept the immutable world-wide anti-deviationist standards of the golden french fry? Can McDonald's impose its system on Poland?

That is what Mr. Dobrowolski has come to find out. He was born in Poland 66 years ago. But since 1956 he has lived in the U.S., and for 18 years his office has been on Ronald Lane in Oak Brook, Ill. He is the man from McDonald's.

On a gray morning in Warsaw, when Mr. Dobrowolski climbs into a car for his excursion to Guzow, he wears a blazer with a Golden Arches pin in the lapel. His tie has a Golden Arches motif. He has a Golden Arches ring on his finger.

"He is very loyal to his company," says Jan Masternak, joining him in the back seat. "He loves it."

As a representative of Interpegro, Poland's agricultural trading company, Mr. Masternak is also loyal. His tie has the Interpegro logo. For six years, he has toiled together with Mr. Dobrowolski in the potato struggle.

"Polish people tell me, 'You crazy Masternak. Stop it. What are you doing? Why do you cooperate with American people?' I say, 'Slowly, slowly. We will see what will be.'"

"Listen to me," Mr. Dobrowolski says. "Some people don't see the benefits. But in life you must always have challenges. These potatoes are important—important to McDonald's."

Riding down a country highway, past horse carts and along fields dotted with crows, Mr. Dobrowolski fills in the background.

The Poles made the first move. In 1978, they revealed a desire to give communism its first taste of special sauce. They were talking restaurant. "A tremendous possibility," Mr. Dobrowolski says. "We have millions of people here to feed with hamburgers."

Talks began. Papers were drafted and redrafted, an announcement readied, a reception planned. It was August of 1980, the month the Solidarity free trade union came into being. The Poles sent McDonald's a telex: reception canceled, project suspended.

But "I didn't want to give up," says Mr. Dobrowolski. "Maybe, I thought, Polish farmers could grow something McDonald's could use."

Potatoes. McDonald's needs potatoes. Polish farmers grow potatoes. They grow 36 million tons of potatoes a year. And Polish people eat potatoes: dumplings, cutlets, pierogi, pancakes. In a year, they eat 330 pounds of potatoes apiece. Poland has a potato institute, a potato festival. The town of Monki has a potato monument—a huge concrete potato.

Could McDonald's use Polish potatoes?

No. Mr. Dobrowolski ran tests. Polish potatoes, he found, don't have what it takes to make golden french fries. They get soggy. They don't slice up in rectilinear tidiness. Only one potato truly does. It is called a Russet Burbank and it comes mainly from Idaho.

McDonald's has never shipped Russets to Europe from America. It would cost too much, and the European Community wouldn't let them in anyway. At the moment, McDonald's settles for less-than-perfect potatoes in its restaurants around Europe. But what would stop it from raising Russets in Poland? If the EC wouldn't take them raw, they could be cut, cooked and frozen first—most likely at a McDonald's-blessed plant in Turkey.

To begin with, though, McDonald's had to teach Polish potato farmers how to grow them. Thus began what Mr. Dobrowolski calls "the fiascoes."

"The potato has been grown in Poland for four, five hundred years," he says. "Polish farmers think they know all about potatoes, and nobody's going to teach them. Then comes this American and says do it this way, do it that way."

Polish farmers plant potatoes in narrow rows; Russets have to be planted in wide rows. Russets have to be weeded; Poles don't weed. Russets are susceptible to black blight. If they get too wet and then get too dry, they explode. Russets have to be pampered.

"After the farmers found out this was a demanding potato, they refused to grow it," Mr. Dobrowolski says.

"We tried Lublin," says Mr. Masternak. "We tried Bialystok."

But in five years, five crops failed to make the McDonald's grade. "We produced nothing for export," says Mr. Dobrowolski as the car turns into Guzow Vegetable Experiment Station. Forsaken by the farmers, he has cast his lot with the scientists.

Mrs. Lenkiewicz stands in the drive as the car pulls up. She wears hoop earrings and white rubber boots. She runs the place.

"We have planted 15 acres," Mrs. Lenkiewicz says, squeezing into the back seat for a short ride to her potato patch. "We are excited." She rubs her thumb and forefinger together. "The most important thing is money, money, money."

The car stops at the edge of the field. Mr. Dobrowolski alights, puts on a pair of galoshes, and walks out onto the soft, dark earth. A truck stands in the middle distance. Around it, a few dozen young people in jeans and quilted vests load the crop into plastic crates.

"We have sprayed against black blight," Mrs. Lenkiewicz says. Mr. Dobrowolski nods and walks on. Near the truck, he stoops to pick up a potato. He runs a finger over its skin and drops it.

"The rows are proper!" calls Mr. Masternak, running up.

Mr. Dobrowolski gets out his pocket knife and cuts a tuber in two. "This is normal," he says, and returns to the car.

In a while, the scent of deep-frying Russet Burbanks fills the dining room of the Vegetable Experiment Station. Mrs. Lenkiewicz and her guests sit. Waitresses serve the main dish: ground beef with onions.

"A hamburger," Mr. Masternak ventures.

"You might say," replies Mr. Dobrowolski. And minutes later, with a french fry in his mouth, he says:

"H'mm. This is not a McDonald's french fry. Absolutely not. It's an inexperienced way of making french fries. But we should not make an issue of it. The potato is OK."

Mrs. Lenkiewicz beams. Mr. Masternak seizes the bottle of vodka on the table, pours everyone a glass, and stands for a toast.

"To McDonald's and the good french fries," he shouts. "To the golden orchards!"

"Arches," says Mr. Dobrowolski, standing himself and raising his glass. "To Poland." Then he takes the McDonald's shield from his lapel and pins it to Mrs. Lenkiewicz's sweater.

"I'm touched," she says, blushing.

Mr. Dobrowolski kisses her hand.

If Fitness Matters, Shouldn't a Chicken Do a Workout Too?

'Free-Range' Fowl Are Billed As Hardy and Thus, Tasty; But Look Inside the Coop

By Kathleen A. Hughes

7/16/86

In the old days, chickens were tough. Descendants of jungle fowl, they strutted about the barnyard, chasing bugs, scratching for bits of grain, perhaps climbing into a haymow to lay an egg. At dusk they would flutter up to a low tree branch to roost without fear of foxes. It all made for a pretty full day.

Commercial farming has taken the spice out of chickens' lives. It breeds them to do nothing but sit around and get fat. They don't leave their climate-controlled coops until their time is up, and the coops are jammed.

But the American chicken's story isn't quite over. Something called free-range chicken has been showing up on menus at trendy restaurants and gourmet shops, often at a breathtaking premium over sit-around-and-get-fat chicken.

Diners are told these birds roam the prairie and fend for themselves as their forefathers did, and so have firmer muscles and more flavor. "A free-range chicken runs around free and is allowed to feed freely," says Scott Smith, a waiter at 385 North Restaurant in Los Angeles.

All this is adding mystique to "poulet ordinaire." The Quilted Giraffe in New York serves a dinner of grilled free-range chicken for $75. "Before they became available we never deigned to serve chicken," says Noel Comess, the chef. "If it didn't have that cachet there's no way we would have the nerve to sell chicken at that price."

Epicures are eating it up. William Pope, a Los Angeles cameraman, goes to a gourmet shop for a brand called Rocky the Range Chicken, depicted on the tag with a cowboy hat, boots, spurs and a smoking gun. "It's the John Wayne of chicken," says Mr. Pope, who pays more than twice the price of a more timid fowl.

In fact, a peek at Rocky's daily routine reveals a surprising serenity for such a dashing bird. But first a bit of background.

It was about six years ago that some U.S. chefs began to complain that the American chicken had gone soft. Lawrence Forgione, the owner of An American Place restaurant in New York, upon discovering some unusually tasty eggs laid by hens that got to run around, asked the farmer if he could produce a meat chicken the same old-fashioned way—outdoors. The producer, Paul Keyser of Warwick, N.Y., now supplies fancy New York restaurants like Lutèce and the Odeon with free-range chickens. But when asked exactly how much freedom and range they have, he won't say.

Rocky the Range Chicken is a later arrival, the creation of two California food marketers, Bart Ehman and Patricia Bridges. They asked a commercial chicken farm, Lakeville Growers in Petaluma, Calif., to divert some chicks into a free-range program. So Lakeville cut chicken-size doors in some coops and added back yards of one to three times the coop's size. Indoors, it gave Rocky two square feet instead of the usual one.

But that doesn't quite mean Rocky is on his own. Since his feed trays are kept filled, there isn't much incentive for him to do a lot of ranging, and he doesn't. During a reporter's visit to a coop of 3,500 free-range chickens, only about 500 waddle outside when the doors open at 7 A.M. A few peck at the dry grass, but most just sit around.

"It's not exactly a blaze of activity," concedes Alan Johnson, head of the operation. "I don't think any of them forage very much. They have all the food they need. It's eat, drink and sit down." Inside, many of the others have their beaks buried in the feed trough.

By about 9 A.M., the chickens that went outdoors waddle back in to escape the sun. A few venture out again for a while in late afternoon. At night the manager locks them inside.

Mr. Ehman blames Rocky's lethargy on his pedigree. As a chicken of a fast-growing type called Hubbard, the free-ranger is "genetically bred not to run and not to get nervous," he says, adding that he is experimenting with a more ambitious breed.

Habit may also be a factor. After arriving from a hatchery, Rocky lives in a regular closed coop the first four weeks or so. That's about a third of his life.

There can be slippage in the regimen, too. Though brochures boast that Rocky doesn't eat animal fats or proteins, feed supplier Richard Krengel says "it does happen from time to time" that Rocky chicks get the same feed as others for the first few weeks. And Mr. Johnson concedes "there are a few extra birds" in one coop, giving each somewhat less than the prescribed two square feet.

Though Rocky's workout program is hardly what you'd call aerobic, certain chefs insist it firms him up. "Tom Snyder walks in and says, 'Give me some of that tough chicken,' " says Roy Yamaguchi, the chef and proprietor of 385 North Restaurant. "He asks for a steak knife, but he likes the flavor."

Not every palate is so discerning. At a reporter's dinner party, guests are asked to taste four unmarked chickens—two regular roasters and two

Rockys. Four of the six guests prefer what turns out to be the ordinary homebound chicken.

"It tastes like a bird that flies around. It tastes happier," says Marina Kieser only to learn that her choice is a chicken that never got to go anywhere. Another guest, Robert Leighton, thinks the supposedly well-traveled Rocky "tastes bland," while the stay-at-home chicken "has more character."

Even educated palates don't always get it right. Wolfgang Puck, the chef at Los Angeles's Spago, serves grilled Rocky for $16.50. But in a blind taste test with chickens done by a cook at his restaurant, Mr. Puck and three others all prefer the plain chicken over the free-ranger. On a scale of one to four, four being the highest, Mr. Puck rates Rocky a mere two for taste and one for texture.

Mr. Puck's wife, Barbara Lazaroff, suggests a second blind test, with chickens grilled the way the restaurant normally serves them. But again, Mr. Puck and a party of three all pick an unassuming supermarket chicken over Rocky.

The chef is a bit unsettled. "I definitely think we should find out why they charge so much money," he says.

But Mr. Ehman, Rocky's marketer, has an explanation. He says it's all because the grass in the yard turned brown, leading Rocky, too, to go a little flat. Mr. Ehman has a remedy, though it's hardly one that an independent chicken of yore would ever require. He has tossed some green hay into Rocky's pen.

How the Swiss Try
To Regain Attitude
Of Holier Than Thou

———

Case of the Disappearing Holes
In Gruyere Cheese Leads
To a Wholly Holey Quest

———

By Roger Thurow

6/19/85

DIETISBERG, SWITZERLAND—Hans Schwab, an official cheese inspector and therefore a mighty important man in this land of milk and cheese, knows a good chunk of Gruyere when he hears one.

Among cheese connoisseurs, Gruyere gets high marks for its taste, smell and looks. Mr. Schwab and his fellow cheese inspectors care about how it sounds.

Working quietly in his white lab coat, Mr. Schwab is listening to a round slab of Gruyere in the cellar of Robert Boschung's small cheese dairy here. With the wooden end of his special cheese tester, which looks like an old-fashioned corkscrew, Mr. Schwab taps the surface of the cheese, like a doctor tapping the back of a patient. He hears a welcome sound, sticks the tester into the cheese and pulls out a thin, tubular strand of Gruyere.

Hallelujah, a hole! He had heard right!

"It's a good one," beams Mr. Schwab, breaking off a bite of the sample and plugging the rest back into the slab. "It's clean, pretty. It's pea-sized; not too big, not too small."

Such is the beauty of Gruyere and other Swiss cheeses. In the hundreds of cheeseries nestled in the picturesque Alps, there is little that matches the sight, or sound, of a perfect hole.

Unfortunately, this pleasure is getting ever rarer among Gruyere makers. Mr. Schwab is hearing fewer and fewer holes. Never mind that the cheese tastes the same with or without the holes. People expect holes in Swiss cheese.

The cheese inspector doesn't know just why the cheese is becoming less holey. Nor does the cheese maker, who has been churning out hole-pocked Gruyere for years just as naturally as the cock crows each morning. Nor do the cheese scientists toiling at the Federal Dairy Research Institute outside Bern.

"Traditionally, the holes just came, and no one knew why," says Hans Schaer, one of the scientists. "Now the holes are disappearing and no one knows why." He has already spent a couple of years trying to find out why, and he reckons it will be another few before he knows.

Some people have blamed the cows, but if their milk has changed, it's clearly not their fault. It could be the new, improved fertilizer. Or maybe those newfangled machines, both in the barn and in the dairy. Most people, however, point their scrubbed fingers at the better hygiene in the production process. Something in the milk, the air, the machines has changed. The hole-making bacteria that had always appeared from somewhere are mysteriously disappearing.

Today, as much as half of Swiss Gruyere is considered to have too few holes, which are formed through the appearance of carbonic acid in the early months of ripening. In an ideal 24-inch-long slice of Gruyere, there should be about 12 to 15 pea-sized holes. These days, a cheese maker is lucky if he gets three or four. Or any, for that matter.

In a world of nuclear tension, this may seem a trivial matter. But in Switzerland it is a situation that truly stinks. For in this persnickety country, cheese is not only holey, it's holy. Cheese is the country's best-selling agricultural product, and, as the promotional film in the cheesery in the medieval town of Gruyere says, cheese is Switzerland's "ambassador" to the world.

Thus, a problem such as disappearing holes is tantamount to a serious diplomatic crisis. "For us, Gruyere without holes is like a bar of soap," says Mr. Boschung, who has been proudly making cheese, not soap, for the past 30 years. Put another way, Mr. Schaer, the scientist, says, "Swiss cheese without holes is like champagne without bubbles."

Heinrich Glaettli, a colleague of Mr. Schaer, peruses his bookshelf and pulls out an album filled with colored photos of Gruyere. He turns to some with improperly shaped holes, and worse, some that are totally bald, or blind, as he puts it. "Now, who would eat this?" he asks. "The consumer decides not only with the mouth but also with the eyes," Mr. Glaettli says. "Who would buy Swiss cheese without the holes?"

For the Swiss Cheese Union, which oversees the country's cheese business, this is a most troubling proposition. Officials insist that Gruyere sales haven't fallen since the holes began disappearing several years ago. Gruyere is the cheese of choice among the Swiss—particularly for fondue, because it doesn't get all chunky when it melts—and they apparently are continuing to gobble it up, holes or no. Of the 23,000 metric tons of Gruyere produced annually, 6,000 are exported, and the union says its export sales haven't slipped, either.

But the image problem remains, and the Swiss worry that people might think the holes are also disappearing in Emmental, the most-famous variety of Swiss cheese—the one with the cherry-sized holes. A 24-inch-long slice of Emmental has about 60 holes, and they are all there. At one time, earlier this century, they were disappearing, too, but the scientists plugged that problem. Emmental holes today are created with the help of a drop or two of special bacteria.

Since 60,000 metric tons of Emmental are produced a year, and 41,000 are sold for export, consumer perceptions are important. So the Swiss Cheese Union has begun a public-relations campaign to deal with the problem.

The first objective is to clarify the all-encompassing label "Swiss cheese." Emmental, Sbrinz, Royalp and Appenzell are made in the German-speaking part of Switzerland. Gruyere, Raclette, Vacherin and Tete de Moine are made primarily in the French part. And then there are the cheeses made high up in the Alps, with each peak having its own specialty. Among the more than 100 varieties, only Gruyere has a hole problem. Some Gruyere is made outside Switzerland, including a little in the U.S., but the problem is primarily Switzerland's.

The union also wants everyone to wholly understand that Gruyere still tastes the same. In fact, look at the bright side: fewer holes, more cheese.

This doesn't do much to lift the spirits of the puzzled cheese maker, whose well-being is tied to holes. The producers receive a set price for every 100 kilograms, or 220 pounds, of cheese, and then receive additional money based on a rating scale. A perfect 100-kilogram chunk of Gruyere—worthy of a top-scale 20 points—receives an extra $10.90. If a cheese has too few holes, it may receive only 19 points, and only $6.60 extra.

Mr. Boschung, who makes about 175 kilograms, or 385 pounds, of Gruyere each day of the year, says he used to get a perfect 20 nearly all the time. But since the holes started disappearing, he has been receiving a batch of 19.5s and 19s. "You notice the difference in income," he says.

Eager to find a solution, the Gruyere makers turned to the Federal Dairy Research Institute for help. There, 15 scientists are wrestling with the problem of creating holes in Gruyere. The experience with Emmental doesn't help much, because the bacteria that make the holes in Emmental also produce the distinguishing taste. This time the scientists are looking for a "taste neutral" bacterium—one that produces carbonic acid to make the holes but doesn't affect the taste.

The scientists have taken samples of ideal Gruyere, isolated the bacteria and produced about 1,000 vials of freeze-dried cultures that are locked up in a freezer in the laboratory's basement. The scientists are confident of finding a solution, but it's a bit like looking for the Holy Grail. They have to wait out the entire nine-month ripening period for each experimental cheese before testing the results, so the quest may take another three to five years.

A Moment of Glory
With a Zucchini Pie
Is Oft Remembered

Millicent Nathan Won Big
In the Pillsbury Bake-Off;
Her Originality Endures

By Robert L. Rose

2/18/92

BOCA RATON, FLA.—Millicent Nathan cherishes every detail of her proud moment 12 years ago in the grand ballroom of Miami Beach's Fontainebleau hotel.

There she stood, smiling before a cheering crowd. Photographers snapped her picture. Someone handed her a bouquet of red roses. And Bob Barker, the TV game-show host, put his arm around her and handed her a check for $40,000. "I felt like I'd won the gold," she says.

What she actually won was the Pillsbury Bake-Off. Her prize-winning entry: a zucchini quiche that Pillsbury christened "Italian Zucchini Crescent Pie."

For Mrs. Nathan, these memories are as real today as the tiny Pillsbury Doughboy propped on the counter in her sparkling kitchen overlooking a private golf course here. "They don't give them to just anyone," she says of the pudgy vinyl doll the food company gave the finalists.

In 1949, Eleanor Roosevelt was among the guests at Pillsbury's first annual Grand National Recipe and Baking Contest, held at New York's Waldorf-Astoria hotel. By 1976, the Bake-Off was so popular that Pillsbury decided to skip every other year. Today, the company hires a judging agency to screen tens of thousands of entries. Pillsbury home economists cook up the most promising recipes, then choose the 100 finalists.

Early next week, 91 women and nine men will strut into a Disney World convention hall lined with row upon row of mini Kenmore kitchens. A band will toot "When the Saints Go Marching In," and the finalists will go to work on their favorite recipes. Munching in a separate "jury room," a panel of food experts will select the winners. In this 35th Bake-Off, the grand-prize winner will walk away with $50,000 and a $10,000 kitchen makeover from Sears' Kenmore.

For the triumphant, the afterglow never fades. Elizabeth Meijer of Tucson, Ariz., still bakes the Almond-Filled Cookie Cake that won the Bake-Off two years after Mrs. Nathan's quiche. At Christmas, Mrs. Meijer sends her cake to friends around the country via Priority Mail. Men like it, she says, because "there's not a lot of gooky, icky stuff on it."

Mary Lou Warren (Apple Nut Lattice Tart, 1986) subscribes to a newsletter for food-contest aficionados and keeps up a chain letter with other devotees. Her confidence was shaken, though, after a friend cooked up Salmon Burgers with Cilantro Kiwi Sauce and Hazelnut Crusted Lamb Burgers. "I'm thinking I'm not innovative enough anymore," Mrs. Warren says.

That's not a problem for Mrs. Nathan, a diminutive, red-haired 68-year-old. She has baked, sauteed, pan-fried and broiled since she was an eight-year-old farm girl in New Jersey, and she's always popping with ideas and opinions on the cooking and presentation of food.

For instance, she likes to pepper shoppers in grocery stores with cooking tips. One favorite: Give rice extra bounce by cooking it with water and chicken bouillon cubes. Then toss in tiny frozen peas.

At lunch at the country club, she compliments the waitress on the artful way a leaf of lettuce has been introduced into her tuna pita sandwich. When she and her third husband, Sigmund, dine out in this affluent community, they informally rate restaurants on a scale of one to 10. A local seafood place gets a "seven or eight," losing points for charging extra for salad. The chocolate-chip cookies don't impress her, either. "Mine are better," she declares.

With this kind of cooking self-confidence, it's no wonder she entered the Bake-Off. In fact, she says she thought of her zucchini quiche the minute a contest entry form fell out of a bag of Pillsbury flour. "Why not?" she recalls thinking. "It's such a good recipe." Members of her bridge club in Tamarac, Fla., where she then lived, agreed. And agreed, and agreed again, as she refined her entry on their palates.

Like thousands of others, her recipe was sifted through the Bake-Off judging process. Many are thrown out immediately because they don't follow the rules. For example, if flour is used, the recipe must call for at least one cup. Others are tossed because they lack clarity, appeal or originality. "It's hard to have an original white bread," says Marlene Johnson, a Pillsbury publicist.

Pillsbury even sends recipes for baked goods to Colorado, so a freelance home economist can test their performance at high altitudes. Another crew checks cookbooks, magazines and computers to make sure contestants haven't "borrowed" recipes.

Mrs. Nathan admits she had a few things going for her the year she cooked up the winner on range No. 26. One, presentation: She placed the round zucchini slices in concentric circles, and garnished it with parsley. Second, versatility: The zucchini quiche can be served as an hors d'oeuvre, a first course or a main dish, cut in wedges and complemented by a fresh green salad. (Indeed, her prize winner appears in the Pillsbury Bake-Off Cookbook under "Main Dishes and Side Dishes," on page 59.) Third, and perhaps most important: "It was timely," she says. Two in-

gredients—zucchini and fancy French mustard—were then in vogue, and
so was the quiche.

Winning made her an instant celebrity—and, says Gertrude Jaffee, a
veteran of Mrs. Nathan's dinner parties, "gave her whole life a great zip."
She was written up in newspapers, and appeared on ABC's Good Morning
America. "Everyone knew who I was," says Mrs. Nathan. "Everyone was
talking about me."

Not one to rest on her laurels, she dug into her jackpot to treat herself
to two weeks at La Varenne, a cooking school in Paris. She brushed up on
basic principles, such as the importance of matching the serving platter
to the shape of the food, and learned to employ a little truc, or trick, with
each recipe.

The highlight came when the owner asked her to address fellow students on winning the Bake-Off. A lower moment came when she had to
confess that the crust for Italian Zucchini Crescent Pie wasn't from
scratch, but from Pillsbury crescent dinner rolls. Contest rules require
that contestants use at least one Pillsbury product. "I had to tell them it
came out of a can," she says.

Mrs. Nathan pulled out all the "trucs" for a recent dinner party, her
first since moving to Boca Raton several weeks ago. She set the table on
Monday. On Tuesday, she bought fresh vegetables; on Wednesday, the
day of the party, she dashed out for fresh raspberries.

Back home, Mrs. Nathan put on one of her favorite cotton dresses, the
kind she can wipe her hands on. She flipped on the telephone answering
machine so she wouldn't be interrupted. She whirled around her spotless
new kitchen, rinsing spoons and cleaning counters along the way.

Precision reigned. For the mustard dip, Mrs. Nathan cut the raw string
beans and carrots to the same lengths. For the lemon chicken, she made a
sauce of chablis, lemon juice and chicken stock. She dipped the chicken
into seasoned bread crumbs and flour. The trick though, was to heat the
olive oil before adding margarine and sauteeing the chicken. That way,
the margarine won't burn before it has a chance to cook into the chicken.

And how did the party go?

One guest, Helen Budd, raved about the warm fruit compote, and
called the next morning for the recipe.

Mr. Nathan was appreciative. "Love goes through the stomach," he
says.

And Mrs. Nathan, was she pleased? The party was, well, "just beautiful," she reports. "Apart from being hostess, I was the star."

Millicent Nathan's
Prize-Winning Recipe

4 cups thinly sliced zucchini

1 cup chopped onions

2 tablespoons margarine or butter

2 tablespoons parsley flakes

½ teaspoon salt

½ teaspoon pepper

¼ teaspoon garlic powder

¼ teaspoon basil leaves

¼ teaspoon oregano leaves

2 eggs, well beaten

8 ounces (2 cups) shredded Muenster or mozzarella cheese

8-ounce can refrigerated crescent rolls

2 teaspoons prepared mustard

Heat oven to 375 degrees F. In large skillet, cook zucchini and onions in margarine until tender, about 8 minutes. Stir in parsley flakes, salt, pepper, garlic powder, basil and oregano. In large bowl, combine eggs and cheese; mix well. Stir in cooked vegetable mixture.

Separate dough into 8 triangles. Place in ungreased 10-inch pie pan, 12x8 inch (2-quart) baking dish or 11-inch quiche pan; press over bottom and up sides to form crust. Seal perforations. Spread crust with mustard. Pour egg-vegetable mixture evenly into prepared crust.

Bake at 375 degrees F. for 18 to 22 minutes or until knife inserted near center comes out clean. Let stand 10 minutes before serving. *6 servings.*

VIII

THE
SPORTING
LIFE

It's a Bloody Business
Being a Baseball Fan;
Ask Mr. Giampietro

*He Runs the Ambulance Corps
That Helps the Mets Fans
Who Are Beaned at Shea*

By Timothy K. Smith

7/15/92

NEW YORK—Michael Giampietro, having studied the incidence of foul
balls at Shea Stadium for 17 years, has figured out the difference between
men and women:

"A girl normally gets hit in the chest," he explains. "Why? Because
she wants to protect her face, and she puts her hands up. The guy don't
give a damn, he's looking to catch that ball, so he winds up hit on the
head with it."

When that happens, things often get disgusting. "That ball is doing 70,
80, 90 miles an hour, am I right? The stitches on the ball, it hits you right,
the stitches rip your head right open. And that's an area where it bleeds
like crazy," Mr. Giampietro says.

There hasn't been any question about how dangerous a major-league
baseball game can be since Aug. 16, 1920, when New York Yankee
pitcher Carl Mays hit Cleveland shortstop Ray Chapman in the head with
a fastball, killing him. But American boys still are taught that it is abnor-
mal to fear a baseball, that "ball-shyness" is to be subdued. So they tend
to be astonished later in life when they go to a game, take a seat behind
third base, make a play for a fly ball and regain consciousness in a hospital emergency room.

"People get surprised," says Jeffrey Crianza, a volunteer in Mr. Giampietro's Corona Community Volunteer Ambulance Corps, the group that
ministers to the sick and wounded at Mets home games. "When you get
hit in the head by a fly ball, you have sustained a head injury."

"Guy in the Merrill Lynch box a couple of nights ago, best seat there is,
he caught a foul ball in the neck," says Edward Bernstein, also of the
ambulance corps. "Here's this yuppie, probably been begging his boss for
tickets for the last six months, finally gets tickets and I think we took him
to Booth Memorial," one of the 10 nearby hospitals to which the corps
delivers baseball fans.

This isn't the kind of thing television cameras linger on, and the baseball commissioner's office says it doesn't keep statistics on fan injuries. A Mets spokesman says spectators are hit by baseballs "I would say every game," but adds that "usually the injuries are not major." Mr. Giampietro says that "two or three" fans are struck in the course of an average game, and that others may sustain fly-ball damage indirectly: "Sometimes you get somebody, they go for a ball and they reach over BOOM go through the seats with their foot and rip their legs open, or fall out of the box onto the field."

The Mets organization, like most major-league clubs, has a doctor and a nurse in attendance at each game. But most of the legwork is done by Mr. Giampietro's volunteers, an arrangement that works out well for the Mets and the ambulance corps. In the Mets, Mr. Giampietro gets a sponsor for the old-fashioned, free-of-charge, community-based ambulance service that he runs out of a converted fishing club in Corona, Queens. In Mr. Giampietro, the Mets get a first-aid provider who looks like Father Christmas.

Mr. Giampietro's job with the Mets may sound like one of those rare and perfect combinations of social utility and fun, like driving the back end of a hook and ladder, and he does get two free seats behind home plate for every game. But he and his volunteers owe their first allegiance to the ambulance corps, not to the Mets, who are currently in fourth place in the National League East.

The corps, founded in 1960 with an old hearse and $500 donated by the local undertaker, is a vestige of the days when New York neighborhoods were cohesive enough to finance and staff their own emergency services. Mr. Giampietro, a former airplane mechanic and sanitation worker, is 68 and the last of the original members. With donations from neighbors and the Mets, he has expanded the operation to include some 30 volunteers and four ambulances—five if you count his old orange-and-white Cadillac, which had a bit part in the movie "The Thin Blue Line" but is now in storage at corps headquarters.

There, hours before a game, volunteers load oxygen bottles onto an ambulance; three dogs charge around in circles; two cockateels make a racket in a cage; a TV set murmurs and an alligator turtle crawls around under the furniture somewhere. "You should have been with us yesterday, we had three guys hit by the same ball and nobody caught it," Mr. Giampietro says.

And what sorts of curious medical cases has Mr. Giampietro seen at the ballpark over the years?

"Over the ears? We've had a spider in the ear, a cockroach in the ear, a big moth in the ear, a tick in the ear, and the stupid things stay alive. Generally you just pour a little alcohol in there and they walk right out."

This night the Mets are playing the Chicago Cubs, formerly managed by a beanball victim with a metal plate in his head (Don Zimmer, struck by a pitch in 1953). At the stadium, the volunteers take their stations: two in the mezzanine first-aid room, two in a blue-and-white striped tent at field level, and two directly behind home plate to watch where the foul balls go. "If they get hit with it, you run," Mr. Giampietro says. "You grab a wheelchair and an oxygen tank, and the trauma bag you take with you."

Mr. Giampietro calls his volunteers "peasants" until they complete their Emergency Medical Technician training, at which point they become something like family. Six of them are people he took in off the street. "If it wasn't for this, I'd probably be dealing drugs," says Louis Calderon, a 16-year-old who lives in the neighborhood and works for the corps after school.

Mr. Giampietro calculates that 32 million people have trooped in and out of Shea stadium since he started working Mets games, and he has seen all the ailments you would expect in a transient community that size. There have been deaths—a fatal heart attack roughly once a season, and two years ago a naked suicide leap—but so far no births. "We almost had a set of twins," Mr. Giampietro says. "We want to nail one baby, name it Shea."

But the commonest event requiring medical treatment is foul-ball trauma. "I've had a couple times in this place where a kid got hit with a foul ball, a line drive, and the imprint of the stitching was right on the head," says volunteer Robert Crews.

Occasionally a bloodied fan will sue, but the Mets organization says it has never had a foul-ball judgment against it. Such lawsuits are rare in the major leagues, and victories rarer, because the clubs provide some screened seats and disclaim responsibility on the backs of tickets.

But baseball clubs are keeping a wary eye on a decision in May by the appellate court in Cook County, Ill., reinstating a lawsuit against the Chicago White Sox by a woman whose jaw was broken by a foul tip in 1986. The appeals court overruled a lower court's summary dismissal.

This night at Shea, however, things are relatively peaceful. A small boy gouges a hole in his knee on the teeth of an escalator step, an old man has his finger slammed in the door of a station wagon, a young woman suffers a dizzy spell, and both baseball teams empty the benches for a make-believe rumble after Mets rightfielder Bobby Bonilla is struck on the elbow by the first pitch of the fourth inning. Nobody is seriously hurt.

And in the bottom of the sixth, with the Mets on their way to an 8-to-2 victory, a hot-dog vendor named Richard Salay turns his back on the game to sell a frankfurter and is whomped in the back of the head by a foul ball. It is a weak pop fly, and all he needs is ice. Says Mr. Giampietro: "Good thing he didn't drop that hot-dog box."

Mr. Giampietro waits till the stadium has emptied and leaves for the corps's headquarters, where he will let the birds out of their cage, try to get them to sit on his finger, and stay up most of the night in case someone in Corona needs an ambulance. Tomorrow he will be back at Shea, tending to the wounded and contemplating the truths of baseball. "Like sometimes a bat breaks in half and goes flying into the seats," he says. "That bat is solid, you know."

This 50-Year-Old Sees His Idol as Last Of the Sports Heroes

How a Home Run Hit in 1951 Has Engaged the Life Of One Albert Engelken

By Albert R. Karr

10/27/89

Albert Engelken and Robert Thomson had never met, though for 38 years their lives had been intertwined in a way peculiar to the sports world. Mr. Engelken, now a transit-association executive in Washington, D.C., and Mr. Thomson, a paper-products salesman in Montvale, N.J., hadn't even talked to each other. But one recent day, they became much closer.

Mr. Engelken, a rabid baseball fan, pores over the sports pages to chart the exploits of "my favorite and not-so-favorite teams and players." He often groans, he says, at the "clutter" of sports stories about drugs, alcohol, gambling and some player's lament "about the miserly millions he is offered to play the game." His morning paper, the Washington Post, even carries a sports column called "Jurisprudence" that recounts the latest arrests and convictions of players and team managers. Like many sports buffs, Mr. Engelken has turned cynic.

But his is a story about a hero in an era of sports anti-heroes, and about what Babe Ruth, Mr. Engelken reminds us, once called "the only real game in the world." To Mr. Engelken, it is also a story "about love, because I'm blessed to have a wife who still thinks her slightly eccentric husband's 50th birthday deserves the ultimate present."

To understand what Mr. Engelken means, one must go back to a sunny October afternoon in 1951 at New York's Polo Grounds stadium, where, it can be argued, the most dramatic moment in baseball history was played out.

It was the ninth inning of the third game of a three-game playoff between the Brooklyn Dodgers and the New York Giants. Baseball fans throughout New York had sweated out a long summer with their teams, and now it had come to this: a battle between the two for the National League pennant—down to the last inning of the last game, no less.

Some 34,320 fans jammed the stands, and shouted at the top of their lungs. Mr. Engelken was doing the same across the Hudson River in New Jersey, where, with his nose pressed against the front window of the Passaic-Clifton National Bank, he watched the duel on a television set the bank set up for the event.

The playoff series had riveted the 12-year-old Giants fan. "The Giants struck first, winning the opener, 3–1, on a two-run homer off Dodger right-hander Ralph Branca," Mr. Engelken recalls with precision today. "The Giants got swamped in the second game, 10–0, and trailed 4–1 going into the bottom of the ninth of the third and deciding game. The Giants scored once and had runners on second [Whitey Lockman] and third [Clint Hartung] as Bobby Thomson advanced to the plate."

The rest, as they say, is history. Mr. Thomson, a tall, Scottish-born, right-hand hitter, stepped into the batter's box. "Thomson took a called strike," Mr. Engelken recounts. The tension mounted as Ralph Branca, again on the mound, stared down the batter. He wound up and let loose a fastball. The pitch sailed toward Bobby Thomson high and inside and then, with a crack of the bat, was sent rocketing back into the lower left-field stands. "Giants fans went into euphoria," says Mr. Engelken.

And Bobby Thomson was made a legend. The same Bobby Thomson, it turns out, who sells those paper goods today.

There can't be an older baseball fan alive who doesn't clearly remember that Bobby Thomson homer, who can't tell you where he was when he heard the famous Russ Hodges radio broadcast—the one that concluded with Mr. Hodges shouting, over and over, "The Giants win the pennant, the Giants win the pennant!"

Mr. Engelken and Mr. Thomson drifted in different directions in the subsequent years, and the Polo Grounds, located under Coogan's Bluff in upper Manhattan, was replaced by a public-housing project. Mr. Thomson played outfield and third base until 1960, posting a lifetime .270 batting average and chalking up 264 home runs before retiring and going into paper-goods sales.

Mr. Engelken moved south to Washington, but he took with him enduring memories of the homer of 1951. When his wife, Betsy, came down the aisle on their wedding day in 1966, Mr. Engelken—no slouch on the romantic front—gave her the ultimate compliment: "You look prettier than Bobby Thomson's home run." The couple's first dog, Homer, was named after the Great Event, though unwitting friends assumed he was the namesake of the poet.

And when Mr. Engelken's sister, Martha, who was born two days before the home run, reached her 25th birthday, Mr. Engelken wrote his sports hero to tell him of the coincidence of events. Mr. Thomson sent off a card to Martha: "It doesn't seem like 25 years since I hit that home run to celebrate your birth," it read. Martha was pleased, but nowhere near as much as Mr. Engelken.

The family license plate reads "ENG 23," the first three letters of the family name and—no surprise here—Bobby Thomson's uniform number.

And on Mr. Engelken's 40th birthday, his wife bought a book detailing the big homer and sent it off to Mr. Thomson to be autographed. "What could have been better?" asks Mr. Engelken.

Betsy Engelken asked the same question earlier this year, when her husband was about to turn 50. She had an idea.

On her husband's 50th birthday (after an auspicious 23 years of marriage, it should be noted), Betsy, Al and their college-bound son set out for New York to visit Fordham University. Mrs. Engelken had scheduled a stop on the New Jersey Turnpike, she told her husband, to pick up some papers for a neighbor. The papers would be handed over at a bank of telephone booths just off Exit 10.

"It sounded like something out of Ian Fleming," Mr. Engelken recalls.

At the appointed exit, the family pulled over, and Mrs. Engelken went to get her papers. Mr. Engelken turned off the motor and rolled down the window.

In a matter of minutes, she was back, with a tall, silver-haired man in tow. She crouched down by the car window and addressed her husband with her favorite nickname: "Bertie," she said, "Happy 50th Birthday. This is Bobby Thomson."

"And there he was," recalls Mr. Engelken. "The hero of my youth, the one person in history I'd most like to meet. Keep your Thomas Jeffersons, or St. Augustines or Michelangelos; I'd take baseball's Flying Scot without hesitation."

They talked of the home run. "I thought it was in the upper deck," said Bobby Thomson, now 66 years old. They talked of the aftermath. "I never thought it would become so momentous," Bobby remarked. Mr. Engelken, says his wife, "was overwhelmed by the whole thing. It was worth it, just for the look on Albert's face."

The two men spent an hour at Exit 10, rehashing the event, "fulfilling the lifelong dream of a young boy now turned 50," Mr. Engelken says. His hero signed photographs of the homer and diplomatically called Ralph Branca "a very fine pitcher." And when Mr. Engelken asked him why he took time off from work for somebody he didn't even know, Bobby Thomson replied: "You know, Albert, if you have the chance in life to make somebody this happy, you have an obligation to do it."

In an interview, Mr. Thomson, who is married and has three grown children, says he has few ties to baseball these days, other than playing old-timers games now and again. But his fans, to his constant amazement, never let him forget the famous four-bagger. His mail regularly recalls "my one event," and has been growing in recent years.

In response to the letters, Mr. Thomson usually sends an autographed photo with a polite note, and rarely arranges a rendezvous. But when Betsy Engelken wrote him, saying she could stop near his New Jersey home, it seemed different. "What a good feeling it would be for me to do that," he says he thought.

When the Engelken family got back from its trip up north, Mr. Engelken wrote it all down, just to make sure no detail was missed. "On the way home," his notes recall, "it took concentrated effort to keep that car pointed south. My mind was miles north at a place called Coogan's Bluff, where a real sports hero had captured the imagination of a kid who never fully grew up and is all the richer for it.

"Take heart, sports fans," he wrote. "Real heroes exist. You might not find one in the 'Jurisprudence' column. But who knows? You might meet up with him at that bank of telephone booths just off Exit 10 of the New Jersey Turnpike."

Imagine Romania,
Of All Places, Having
A Shortage of Bats

Ceausescu Would Turn Over
In His Grave If He Knew
That Baseball Had Arrived

By Roger Thurow

4/8/91

BUCHAREST—As a new major-league baseball season opens with million-aire outfielders whining about their measly wages, spare a cheer for a league so impoverished that the batters have to wear their own motorcycle helmets to the plate.

"We would have liked to start our season in April or May, but we don't have enough equipment yet. So maybe we will start in June," says Christian Costescu, the president of the Romanian Baseball Federation. "Some teams have only one bat. We need more balls. But our biggest disaster is gloves. Some teams don't have a full set. It is very difficult to practice when you have to share gloves."

As spring comes to the Balkans, Romania is taking its first swing at America's national pastime. The league president is a former national champion swordsman who has never played an inning of baseball. Enough coaches have signed up to form 29 teams around the country, but there are only six proper fields. The amateur players are veterans of "oina," the beloved sport of Transylvania that is played on a rectangle instead of a diamond and bears as much resemblance to baseball as Babe Ruth does to Dracula.

But never mind all that. "What the Romanians lack in equipment and expertise, they make up for in desire to play," says Allen Docal, the American Information Center director in Bucharest and unofficial talent scout. "They know they aren't Reggie Jackson and the New York Yankees."

They aren't even the Chicago Cubs. But at least it is a start, which, given baseball's history here, is quite an achievement.

"We are orphans in Romania, too," says Mr. Costescu, comparing his fledgling league to the thousands of babies abandoned during the Communists' reign, when both birth control and baseball were officially banned. "As we start with our baseball activity, you can put a big 0 on our scoreboard."

Pitching the shutout was that renowned spoilsport, Nicolae Ceausescu, the Communist dictator who feared that if baseball came to Romania, capitalism would be sure to follow. For various other reasons, he also banned Scrabble, bridge, martial arts and field hockey.

Mr. Costescu, a stocky man with silver hair, lives, eats and drinks baseball in a little office at the end of a dark corridor on the seventh floor of the gloomy Ministry of Sports building, where the elevator rarely works. A miniature cardboard cutout of former New York Mets Manager Davey Johnson looks on from the bookshelf. A wooden ball sits on the desk, like a paperweight. On the wall behind hangs a banner from Topps, the American baseball-card maker. "Team U.S.A. today, big leagues tomorrow," it says.

Even though it is only 8 in the morning, Mr. Costescu offers an American visitor a glass of plum schnapps. "A Romanian tradition," he explains. He proposes a toast to baseball and settles into his chair.

"I saw my first game in 1985. It was in Italy," he says, beginning the saga of baseball in Romania. Mr. Costescu, then the head of the oina federation, returned home with tales of what he had witnessed, a baseball instructional video and a rule book, all of which he shared with a couple of physical education teachers. For the next two years, this group covered the rudiments of the game, translating the rules into Romanian, scouting potential fields and publishing some articles in the local sports newspapers to whip up interest. A few trial games were even played under the nose of the security police, who figured it was a mutant strain of oina.

In 1988, Mr. Costescu committed an error. He boldly approached Romania's sports officials with an application to set up a baseball federation, which would have made the sport eligible for government funding. He didn't get to first base.

"They told me, 'No, baseball is a capitalist sport and we will never allow such propaganda for capitalism in Romania,'" recalls Mr. Costescu. "You see, the government knew baseball is a sport very much loved by American people. It isn't a Soviet sport, but an American sport. And America is the No. 1 capitalist country."

The baseball advocates argued that the game is also the national sport of Cuba. They also pointed out that Romanians play volleyball and basketball, two other American sports. To no avail. "After that, we had to go underground," Mr. Costescu says with a conspiratorial grin. Clandestinely, he and the others continued to plan for the day when baseball would be free. They drew up a mock schedule based on a fantasy league. It was the longest off-season in history.

Then, during Christmas of 1989, a popular revolution overthrew the Communists and Mr. Ceausescu was executed. On Feb. 4, 1990, the Romanian Baseball Federation was born.

Soon, Mr. Costescu, with the sponsorship of the U.S. Information Agency, was off to Williamsport, Pa., home of Little League Baseball, to watch and learn. Next stop was Tennessee to visit the U.S. Olympic baseball training operation. Then it was on to Italy with 13 other Romanians for a two-week coaching clinic. Back in Romania, practice started for the first season. But the troubles weren't over.

"You know the economic situation in Romania," Mr. Costescu moans. "There isn't enough money for all the sports, so the authorities give aid only to federations with good results. They told us to find some sponsors, but the sponsors are only interested in championship teams. It is a vicious circle. Without sponsors there is no possibility to develop. Without development, there are no sponsors." He has the desperate sound of a man caught in an eternal rundown.

Enter the Americans. Mr. Docal, who has been named honorary president of the baseball federation, found some equipment in the attic of the embassy. The International Baseball Association, based in the U.S., sent some bats and balls. Mr. Costescu wrote letters to American sports-equipment companies. One replied. It sent umpiring gear.

Still woefully short of the basics, Mr. Costescu is now turning to the farm market, just as the old dictator feared. He has taken a bat to a Romanian wood carver and some gloves to a Romanian shoemaker and has asked them to see what they can do. He would like to work out a joint venture with an American partner to make sports equipment in Romania.

Why not just use oina equipment, he is asked. Mr. Costescu pours another glass of schnapps and proceeds to diagram an oina game. "It is difficult to explain to a foreigner," he cautions.

The oina bat is thin and equally proportioned, like a stickball bat. The ball is soft, stuffed with horsehair. No one uses gloves. There are two teams of nine players, one at bat, one lined up in three rows on a rectangular field. The batter hits the ball, pitched by a member of his own team, and proceeds to run between the rows of fielders. The fielders try to hit the runner by throwing the ball at him. If they do, they get two points. If they don't, the batter gets two points. When all the batters are out, the teams switch sides. They play one inning. Then the game is over.

Mr. Costescu opens a filing cabinet and retrieves a stack of papers that tells a curious story. It seems some military officers from Transylvania emigrated to the U.S. about 150 years ago. There, they put on an oina exhibition. Perhaps one of the onlookers, so goes the Romanian tale, was Abner Doubleday, a U.S. Army officer who is traditionally credited with inventing baseball.

"Maybe oina had some influence on baseball. Who knows?" says Mr. Costescu. "We say oina is the Romanian national sport, but we don't know who invented it. Some say it was invented in the Turkish empire."

Still, baseball has something oina doesn't. "From the beginning I loved baseball because it has a moral quality," says Mr. Costescu. "Fair play is the fiber of baseball. It is a game that can teach you many things."

He gets misty-eyed as he talks about his favorite element of baseball. "The sacrifice bunt," he proudly announces. "One player sacrificing himself to help another. I think it is a very nice play."

Buyers of Golf Art Want Lots of Golf, Not Too Much Art

Collectors and Artists Defend Game as Worthy of Both Masters and Masterpieces

By Cynthia Crossen

5/30/90

On the front wall hangs a picture of a hole with a little flag sticking out of it. On the side wall hangs a picture of a hole with a little flag sticking out of it. Across the room is a picture of a hole with a little flag sticking out of it. It is a sign of the times that James Olman's Cincinnati gallery is devoted exclusively to a genre conspicuously underrepresented in the nation's finest museums: golf art.

In the past few years, art depicting golf has been furiously painted, printed, reproduced and sold at ever higher prices. As a game, golf is enjoying some fresh popularity. Art prices have been rising. Link the two together and the result is expensive golf art, like the late 19th-century oil, "The Cheerful Caddy Boy," a portrait of a smiling urchin in baggy pants carrying a set of clubs. It recently sold for more than $15,000 to Jeff Jennings, a collector of golf art in Greenwich, Conn., who says with some pride, "I had a caddy boy like that when I golfed at the Gleneagles course in Scotland."

Modern golf artists are also cashing in on golf-art mania. Some say they have enough commissions to paint golf holes for the rest of their lives. Golf museums report increased traffic, and, says one curator, people stand longer in front of each golf painting.

Golf art strikes art purists as kitsch. "Golf art is for duffers who can't quite pull their britches up anymore," says W. Graham Arader III, a New York art dealer who specializes in European and American art of the 16th to 19th centuries. Golf art "can look horrible, but if Bobby Jones once rubbed up against it in a locker room in Brisbane, Australia, it's priceless," Mr. Arader says. "People pay crazy prices for this stuff, but I've never seen a piece of golf art I'd hang in my home."

Golf artists scoff at this misguided snobbery. "It's definitely art," says LeRoy Neiman, the sports artist whose own golf oeuvre includes the radiant "Arnie [as in Palmer] in the Rain." Taking a world view, he adds, "People are just going to have to adjust to it as they have to other modern problems."

The people who buy golf art tend to be the kinds of golfers who watch pro tournaments on TV, play at least 18 holes a week and are apt to relive great golf moments (their own) over drinks in the clubhouse—relishing the 300-yard drive, the brilliant seven-iron shot from the rough and the final victorious 20-foot putt that causes their opponents to weep from envy. To them, golf art is a kind of nostalgia trip, a chance to remember their own games on the world's great courses; or, having once glimpsed a golf god like Mr. Palmer, a chance to frame the magic of the moment in their office, den or rec room.

For this reason, most golf art depicts either the great players—Bobby Jones, Jack Nicklaus, Ben Hogan and Arnold Palmer are the most popular—or the great holes, the 16th at Augusta National or the 16th at Cypress Point, for example. (Actually, these holes are not necessarily the best ones, golf artists say; they're popular because they're short, treacherous and provide the most drama on televised tournaments.)

It also figures that the favored style of golf art is realism, although some artists have experimented with pointillism, surrealism and fantasy—four golfing dogs perched on hind legs or whimsical golf holes depicted in the Okefenokee Swamp or in the middle of Wall Street. Golf art also has its share of still lifes, such as Brenda Turner's watercolors of artfully arranged clubs, balls, tees and a blank scorecard on which a golfer can record one of his own memorable games.

But essentially, buyers of golf art want lots of golf and not too much art. "You get a little artist's license to move the odd tree or bush around," says Bill Waugh, a Scottish golf artist, "but basically it has to be the golf course as the golfer remembers it."

Mr. Waugh, a self-taught watercolorist, says that if anyone saw him at work, "they'd kill themselves laughing." With art texts at his side, Mr. Waugh works from photos or sketches, often for Japanese or American clients who commission him to paint their favorite holes. Mr. Waugh says he has heard of an American painter who, for $50,000, will paint a golfer playing his favorite hole. However, the artist will only paint a back view, Mr. Waugh hears, because he hasn't mastered face or hand technique.

Although Mr. Waugh claims never to get bored painting one golf hole after another, he does say that he could do it in his sleep. "You do do it in your sleep," volunteers Mr. Waugh's wife. On the subject of the color green, Mr. Waugh gets a bit testy. "I get fed up with green," he says. "I really get fed up with painting greens."

The success of people like Mr. Waugh has taken many other aspiring golf artists off the links and into the studio, with some unfortunate results. Mr. Olman, whose gallery receives scores of unsolicited pieces a year, points to a group of drawings that recently arrived of elephants swinging at golf balls. His critical eye immediately spots a serious flaw: The elephants are all swinging left-handed. "The market for left-handed golfers is much smaller than the right-handed market," says Mr. Olman, shaking his head in disgust. "The artist, clearly not a golfer, had no idea."

When confronted by art's equivalent of a whiff, Mr. Olman shows no mercy. One print, of a chubby little girl swinging a club in a field, didn't attract any buyers as art, so Mr. Olman slapped the prints on some wastebaskets and sold them as golf-theme trash receptacles, which have been moving quite nicely.

Early golf art (pre-1930) isn't necessarily better, it is just more rare, and expensive. Traditionally, golf art has hung in the clubhouses of country or golf clubs, and many of the old clubs have burned down at least once over the decades. (St. Andrews in Scotland, made of stone, is a notable exception.) Many paintings have gone up in flames.

Devotees of golf art say courses are beautiful landscapes, manicured and pampered like no other land on Earth. "Players and spectators walk out there wearing orange-and-green-striped shirts, purple shoes, red socks, and no one even looks twice," says Mr. Neiman. "So when the gallery rings the green, it's like a bed of flowers." Walking a misty fairway in the solitude of early morning is like walking through the pearly gates, golf artists say.

Golf is also exciting, argue the sport's fans, and there is a growing body of art to illustrate it. Austin Cragg, owner of Commemorative Golf Galleries in Greenwich, Conn., is creating a series of prints of 560 major moments in golf. Mr. Cragg's first such moment was a depiction of Gene Sarazin making his "Shot Heard 'Round the World." This is not to be confused with Tom Watson's "Chip Shot Heard 'Round the World," by artist Michael Lane.

Golf dealers, artists and collectors agree that golf is a game of the wealthy, the people who can most afford to collect art. "Golf is a major investment in a lot of respects," says Mr. Olman, "and people become more involved in it partly because of that." But it's not the only reason. Mr. Jennings, the collector, says he has a photograph of himself golfing at Muirfield in Scotland on his office wall. "I hit this great shot on the last hole," he remembers fondly. "It happened to be an important shot, and I won a lot of money. I have every intention of hiring an artist and saying, 'Do it up.'"

Dear Dad: At Last, Your Boy's Become A Real Professional

And in Wrestling, Unlike Journalism, People Ask Me for My Autograph

---

By Paul B. Carroll

4/12/89

GLASSBORO, N.J.—I find myself in a ring with a professional wrestler.

As a local cable-TV station's cameras roll and hundreds of people chant obscenities at me from the bleachers, "Tricky Nikki" and I are reaching our big move, a Suplex. I grab my partner's head under my left armpit, grasp his shiny black tights with my right hand and whisper, like a fifth grader at dancing class, "One, two, three." I fall backward: Nikki leaps up, flipping himself over my shoulder, and we bounce off the mat with a boom.

This is supposed to be the penultimate moment in our carefully choreographed four-minute match. But we have a problem. Just before our act began, we were told the concession stand had run out of soda, so we were to stretch our performance until someone could buy more. Having exhausted my repertoire of moves, I turn to the ref and ask, "Are we close?" He throws me a verbal Body Slam: "Five more minutes."

Can it be a coincidence that this is happening on April Fool's Day?

I landed in this predicament because of recent testimony in the New Jersey legislature that pro wrestling is all fake and isn't a real sport. Such comments outraged fans, delighted cynics and persuaded this reporter to investigate.

I headed straight to the Monster Factory, a training center set in a former pizzeria in Paulsboro, N.J., a refinery town outside Philadelphia. Run by "Pretty Boy" Larry Sharpe, a 38-year-old peroxide blond and former pro wrestler, this nationally known school has been "monsterizing" prospective behemoths for years.

After introducing myself as a reporter, I went through a tryout with two construction workers. We flipped and fell 20 times. It stung. I flubbed some falls. But I was pronounced "trainable."

Normally the course costs $3,000, comes with a guarantee that it will make the student a professional and lasts three to four months. Even a shameless correspondent will take just so much abuse, however. I signed up for a two-week sampler.

Not everyone immediately welcomed into their midst a 31-year-old, 160-pound reporter who was a mediocre high-school wrestler and never quite reached 5-foot-9. Acceptance came with bruises. When I told some of the wrestlers that I had to scrunch up my right side and hold my head in both hands to groan my way into bed, they chuckled and assured me that the pain usually disappears in a couple of weeks.

After learning how to fall, I began picking up the moves: the Front Face Lock, the Small Package, the Step-Over Toe Hold. But, for some reason, no one wanted to explain when to writhe in pain or punch the referee.

When one bystander pressed a wrestler to admit he faked pain, a colleague called "Hoss" invited the wrestler into the ring. Hoss obliterated him with a Splash, a sort of 440-pound swan dive that knocked the wind out of him. "Why don't you talk to your boy now and ask him how fake that felt?" Hoss taunted. He leaned his shaved head over the ropes and surveyed the room for his next victim. Not finding any takers, he said, "Hey, Wall Street Journal, what about you?" I demurred.

Instead, I sidled up to Joelle Heck, the tiny girlfriend of Frank "Frankie Angel" Dempsky. "He told me you'd ask me," she said with a titter, "and he told me not to say it's fake." She paused. "In my opinion, you have to be a moron to think this is real."

But the pain is. Frank, a 240-pound weight lifter said he had suffered three shoulder separations, broken both wrists and cracked five ribs twice during his 18 months of wrestling part-time. He said a doctor told him his right knee was so messed up it looked like a can of tuna fish, and he was once paralyzed for half an hour after being tossed out of the ring.

So why do it?

Mostly, these bouncers, bartenders and roofers wanted to be pro wrestlers ever since they were kids. Some said they wanted to be role models for today's children. Many talked of the joys of signing autographs and of chasing the "ring rats"—the women who can't seem to get enough of pro wrestling. Some full-time wrestlers said they earned $40,000 to $50,000 a year by spending less than an hour a week in combat, and there were tales that some of Larry's former students earned several times that. Most of the wrestlers at the school currently earn $50 to $100 a match, and the matches can be a few weeks apart. But each was sure he was the one who would hit it big.

Even if the dreams don't pan out, these guys seemed to be having a great time. After a recent match, a whole pack of them went to an Italian restaurant that locals say is run by a mobster. That didn't stop Chief Thunder Mountain, a 415-pound American Indian, from saying to the owner, "Hey, little man, where's the bathroom?"

When the owner arranged for a picture with the wrestlers, Larry waited until the picture was about to be snapped, then lifted the owner's toupee off his head.

The mood, alarmingly, was catching. By the middle of the second week, I began to envision myself clearing troublemakers out of bars. "Dynamite Dennis" Bunt confirmed the feeling on the last night of my training when he saw me chatting with some friends. "Just relax, and do what I tell you," he said. "I'm going to make you look goooood." The 200-pounder had me throw him all over the place. He writhed in pain and even kicked the mat a couple of times for emphasis. I felt great.

I told Larry I had decided to use the name of the New Jersey town where I live and wrestle as "Hulk Hoboken." But he said I had to have "Wall Street" in the name, and dubbed me the "Wall Street Warrior." I agreed, figuring that meant I wouldn't have to shave and tattoo my head as one of Larry's students did before he became World Wrestling Federation star Bam Bam Bigelow. (Larry, a shrewd entrepreneur, has produced enough stars that he and a partner have formed their own World Wrestling Association and are planning to take it and the school public. Larry figures that if a brothel in Nevada can sell stock, he can, too.)

Larry decided I'd wrestle in gray, pinstriped tights. He also picked an appropriately small opponent for me: "Tricky Nikki" Kasternakis, an 18-year-old, 150-pounder who delivers mail during the day for Johnson & Johnson. Larry labeled this an exhibition in the program, and we rehearsed everything.

On the night of my professional debut (I'm getting paid $50 for this), I sit in the locker room of the gymnasium at Gloucester County College. Two wrestlers called the "Pit Bulls" are donning their dog collars and chains. "The Mummy" is being wrapped in gauze and covered with baby powder. The referee assigned to our match asks Nikki and me who will win and what the pinning move will be. He also says, "I can't remember, are we on before the midgets or after the midgets?"

The announcer soon tells the crowd he is about to bring out "an actual Wall Street Journal reporter," and everyone cranes his neck. A bunch of guys in the front row start heckling me. "Go back to New York," one yells. "Hey, nice tights," another shouts. As the match starts, the obscenities begin.

I sling Nikki into the ropes, but he bounces off and knocks me down with a shoulder. (We're told always to hit left-shoulder-to-left-shoulder; that way, no one gets confused and gets hit head-on.) Nikki leaps over me and bounces off the ropes, but as he comes back I jump up and throw him with a Hip Toss. I hold on to his wrist, and Drop a Leg on his arm. Then I put one black, patent-leather boot under his arm and one on his chin, and pull on his arm.

I let Nikki get to his feet but hold on to his wrist and step under his arm twice as though twisting his shoulder into a corkscrew. He forgets a bit of the script, so I twist his arm a third time and whisper, "Take a bump." Nikki flips himself over and lands on his back.

The momentum shifts to Nikki, and he drops me on his knee in a Back Breaker. Nikki lets me up but then puts me in a Headlock and, with a little help from me, flips me over his hip. "What's next?" I ask Nikki. "Just lie there and rest a second," Nikki says.

Right about the time the referee shocks me with the revelation that we have five minutes to kill, someone starts a chant of "Wall Street, Wall Street, Wall Street. . . ."

When we move into unscripted territory, Nikki whispers guidance. He surprises me once, and I land on my face, but that does no particular damage. Soon enough, someone signals the referee that the soda has arrived. "Any time now," the referee whispers, and Nikki quickly pins me with a Small Package.

At Nikki's suggestion, I climb slowly up off the mat and tap him on the shoulder. He turns around, and the audience expects me to flatten him, in the time-honored tradition of professional wrestling. Instead, we shake hands, and Nikki raises my arm in triumph. A gnarled, old spectator tells me later that in all his years of watching pro wrestling, this is one of the nicest gestures he has ever seen.

As I leave the ring, kids flock around me, and I sign more than 50 autographs. It occurs to me that this has never happened following any of the stories I've written as part of my day job covering the computer industry. Nobody seems to mind that I have trouble signing "Wall Street Warrior" and sign my byline instead.

On a high, I bump into Larry in the locker room and ask him, "So, do I have a future in the business?"

"Yeah," he says, "the newspaper business."

Landlubber Reporter
Sails the Atlantic
And Survives, Barely

The 27 Days Before the Mast
Were Marked by Terror
And Make for a Good Yarn

By Paul B. Carroll

7/9/87

Call me Schlemiel.

With just two days' sailing experience, I blithely accepted a friend's invitation to join the crew on a 42-foot sailboat in the transatlantic Constitution Race, which began May 16.

It seemed like a good idea at the time.

Starting my first watch at 3 A.M. in the English Channel, however, I wasn't so certain. As I stepped into the cockpit, the first mate told me: "If you go overboard, the water is so cold you'll only last 15 minutes, and in the dark we'll never find you. If you go overboard, just take a couple of big gulps of water and go under. You'll save yourself a lot of time and trouble."

As the 4,000-mile trip progressed across the North Atlantic, we sailed into two weeks of storms so severe they nearly banged the boat apart. The bulkheads cracked, and the sails tore. Most ominous, the mast seemed to be pounding its way through the bottom of the hull as we were 1,500 miles from the U.S., heading into our third gale in less than a week and unable to raise help on the radio.

Some of the four European boats in the race—we were the sole U.S. entry—had it even worse than we did, and it isn't uncommon for sailors to be seriously injured or even to die in transatlantic races. Yet, for some reason, thousands of people, so they say, cross the ocean this way each year.

Back on land, where there's plenty of dry underwear and where beds don't move, I find it hard to explain the grim fascination that gripped the six of us in the crew. Bill Salvesen, the first mate, describes it as "a madness that afflicts me when I'm on land. . . . I kept a journal during my first two Atlantic crossings, but if I had read anything I wrote, there's no way I'd be here."

This race was to commemorate the 200th anniversary of the U.S. Constitution and the 30th anniversary of the treaty that established the European Community, and it began pleasantly enough, with a party.

But shortly after we put off from Nieuwpoort, Belgium, a spectator boat got a bit cozy with us and punched a hole through our hull, and that forced us back into port for 10 hours of repairs. By the time we got under way again, at around midnight, the crowd that had seen us off was long gone. We slunk away into the dark, and reality began to set in.

Long-distance sailboat racing, I quickly learned, is largely about realities—sometimes harsh, dangerous realities, but mainly just annoying, little ones. Take sleeping, for instance. The boat leans at a 25- to 30-degree angle much of the time, so crew members, who sleep on the high side of the vessel in order to minimize the leaning, must be strapped into their berths. Everything smells like a locker room, loose shackles bang, and leaks in the deck seem to be strategically positioned to drip on the sleeper's forehead. In the early going, I would often lose my grip getting out of my berth and go flying across the cabin.

Wetness was a constant. For anyone who would like to get a feel for this at home, I suggest a steering simulation: Sit in a rocking chair and wrestle with a truck tire, while every couple of minutes a friend throws a bucket of cold water in your face. If, after five hours of this, you find that you are enjoying yourself, then ocean sailboat racing is for you.

Eventually, we became jaded. At one point, in heavy seas, we needed sea water to wash vegetables for dinner. So Bill "B.T." Tattersall, our 21-year-old cook, who was at the helm, pointed the bow into a couple of big waves. Pierre Brihay, a 30-year-old Belgian doctor, caught the spray in a bucket.

Still, there were many amazements. One overcast night, though the clouds blocked all light from the moon and stars, the whitecaps seemed to flash light and the sea glowed an eerie green. Plankton, the old salts explained. The microscopic creatures glow when they move, and this was the one time each year when they flower and glow the brightest. Bob Cook, 43, our radio operator, hauled up some water and poured it into the cockpit; it was as if he had poured out embers on a dark night.

Later, a couple of packs of pilot whales swam lazily by, and dozens of dolphins would swim up to the boat to play with us. We had one warm, sunny day early on, with so little wind that we took down the sails and went swimming a thousand miles from the nearest land.

Then, two weeks of bad weather started. We headed south to avoid the worst of an approaching gale, but we still wound up in a 2½-day storm, with huge waves coming at us from all directions.

John Kalish, our 47-year-old skipper, had crossed the Atlantic twice before and once survived a capsizing that threw him overboard and knocked him unconscious. This time, he was worried. "There's only one word for these seas, and that's terrifying," he said. "I suppose that if I live to see seas like this 50 more times, they'll still terrify me."

I, at 29, spent an hour and a half of terror in the middle of the night in that storm as I fought the wheel and tried to keep us upright. I persuaded

Bob, my watch partner, to sit right behind me for the first half-hour so he could offer advice and grab the wheel if I made a murderous mistake.

That first storm was just a prelude. The second, which arrived after a day of mild weather, dished out its worst in the middle of the night, battering us with 55-knot winds and waves as high as 35 feet from the tip to the middle. (We later learned that the crew of the QE2 said the storm caused the ocean liner's worst crossing in 15 years.)

Bill Salvesen, a 30-year-old Belgian who is Scandinavian by birth and who looks—sails—like a Viking, began, uncharacteristically, to complain, yelling down into the cabin every few minutes to find out how soon his watch would end. He bellowed that the wind was blowing so hard he couldn't breathe and demanded that I not be one second late in relieving him. When I took over at midnight, the rain felt like birdshot in my face, and I took so many waves over the bow that the spray blinded me.

But then strange things began to happen. The rain stopped, and the wind slowed some. Next, stars appeared and the moon blinked on and off as clouds thundered past. When the moon was hidden, I couldn't see the waves until the whitecaps loomed a few feet from the boat, but that didn't seem to matter. The crazy, confused, conflicting patterns I had seen in the seas suddenly made sense, and so did all the advice people had given me about sailing. I developed the irrational but overpowering sense that I had conquered this huge storm. I felt that I had become part of the sea surrounding me and that I somehow was controlling it. This, I thought vaguely, makes it all worthwhile.

At 1:45 A.M., Bob brought me some soup and took the wheel. As my mind settled down, I realized I was exhausted. I went below. Within a few minutes, the wind had picked up again and a cold rain began to fall, and reality set in once more.

For one thing, the boat had begun to fall apart. The mainsail was ripped so badly that we had to take it down for two days of resewing. Cracks developed in the bulkheads; laminations in the hull separated, and the mast began vibrating ominously. We were also hearing a mysterious second bang when the boat pounded down off a wave, and Bob was convinced the mast was banging through the hull.

"I went to bed that night expecting to wake up dead," he says.

We had been rationing liquid since the fourth day at sea because we had inadvertently dumped three-quarters of the fresh water from our tanks, and now we found that some of our bottles of emergency water had cracked. Our main supply of cooking gas also ran out at this point. And we were about to hit another gale. Our skipper, ever the optimist, finally acknowledged that our three-week trip was becoming a four-week trip.

Our depression was such that if a glitch developed during a sail change, we would sit on our haunches on the deck, hoods pulled well down over our faces, staring at our hands until someone addressed the problem. Finally, John reached race officials on the radio and said that if the weather didn't improve quickly, we were going to quit the race and head for Bermuda, the nearest land. I liked that idea.

At that point, a rogue wave knocked Bob into the rigging hard enough that he suffered deep cuts in his forehead, nose and lip. Pierre ruled that the lip needed stitches; he sat there with a needle just below Bob's lip, trying (without anesthetic) to get into synch with the rhythm of the bouncing boat and then jabbing the needle into him.

That was the low point. Afterward, the weather cleared a bit, we missed a storm front we had been expecting, and the mysterious second bang disappeared. We pressed on, and each day became a little easier. Eventually, the sun came out, and finally we limped into Cape May.

As it happened, we finished third, but that no longer mattered much. We were just glad to be safe and dry after 27 days at sea, and to be able to eat something other than sausage and Snickers bars.

I have tried to put the trip out of mind, but every time I do I remember the orange moon rising large over the horizon. I feel a warm breeze coming up. I picture dolphins splashing through the moonlight. And I think I might try it again.

IX

UNCOMMON
LANGUAGE
AND NOVEL
WORDS

Urban Is In in Japan, Much to the Delight Of Urban, Himself

Urbs Seek Urb-Mates; Shoes Are 'Urban Epicurean'; And Urban's No Irwin

---

By Urban C. Lehner

12/6/90

TOKYO—Finally, a country where people really understand the importance of being Urban.

The Japanese, in their infinite wisdom, have decided that the English word "urban" has a nice ring to it, just as my mother did 43 years ago. I first noticed the trend a few months ago in Nagoya, when I boarded a train that, on close inspection of my paper coffee cup, turned out to be called the Urban Liner. Aside from musing momentarily on what a headline writer might make of the situation ("Urban Lehner Rides Urban Liner"), I gave the matter little thought. But soon I began to discover myself everywhere.

Here was Urban Wide 400 (a new Hitachi refrigerator) and New Era Air Conditioner Urban (Matsushita). There was Natural Urban Cosmetics, men's suits by D'Urban and buildings called Urbannet and Urban Court Moto Azabu and Urban Cloud 8. Cars have names like Urban Break (Mazda). Toyota even named one floor of a Tokyo showroom "Intelligent Urban Life," which some colleagues consider a contradiction in terms.

Soon it became clear that one of those inexplicable Japanese fads was building up around me, or at least my name. "Urban has become a very general word used for everything," confirms Kim Kawamura of ODS Corp., a Tokyo-based concern specializing in corporate and brand images.

In English, the word urban, which derives from a Latin word meaning city, appears frequently in negative contexts, like "urban blight" and "urban sprawl." Certainly the word has had some negative implications for me. My father, also an Urban, wanted to spare me the name, but my mother insisted that the only thing better than one Urban was two. In first grade, the class bully took a dislike to the name, which gave me my first opportunity to engage in hand-to-hand combat. My high-school Latin teacher, Sister Peter Verona, referred to me constantly as Urbibus (the ablative plural of my name's Latin root, if I recall correctly). As an adult, I've come to appreciate the name, though I know when I introduce myself on the telephone I'm doomed to be Irvin or Irwin unless I specify: "That's U-R-B-A-N, as in renewal."

By contrast, the Japanese treat urban (and Urban, for that matter) with the utmost urbanity. Linguistically, Urban is no odder to them than any other non-Japanese name. Conceptually, "tokai-teki"—the literal Japanese translation of urban—has overwhelmingly positive connotations.

"It suggests the cosmopolitan side of big-city life," says Kazuhiro Mawatari, a "corporate identity" expert at Tokyo-based Dentsu Inc., the world's largest advertising agency. "In our life style, 'inaka' [rural] is bad."

To many foreigners, the notion that Japanese love big-city life seems peculiar: The Tokyo-Yokohama metropolitan area, with its 32 million people, evokes images of rabbit-hutch housing and jam-packed commuter trains.

But let me assure you: If you have to be an Urban, this is the place. To the Japanese, "urban" is the Tokyo that is clean and safe and crisscrossed by trains that run on time; the Tokyo that caters to every taste, from Parisian bistros to smoky Korean barbecue places, from modern jazz hangouts to live sex shows.

"I'm from Tokyo," says Dentsu's Mr. Mawatari. "I think it's very hard to live in. The trains are crowded. The houses are small. But it has so much charm. It has so many faces."

But why use "urban"? Why don't the Japanese just say "tokai-teki?"

Actually, for most of recorded history they did. Even 14 years ago, when Osamu Yakou bought Urban, a coffee shop under a railway overpass near Tokyo's Kanda station, "tokai-teki" was the norm. But Mr. Yakou liked the English name that came with the Japanese shop because it sounded cosmopolitan. Just as Americans will drop a French word to show off their "savoir-faire", the Japanese drop English words as proof of their sophistication.

("Japanese English" or "Japlish" has its amusing moments. My personal favorite is a chain of coffee shops called, in English, Sports House Italian Tomato.)

Trouble was, when Mr. Yakou bought his coffee shop, "urban" wasn't well understood by Japanese coffee drinkers. Worse, Mr. Yakou relates, they had a hard time remembering the name because they couldn't pronounce it; in Japanese, the "R" sound never follows a vowel in the same syllable.

The solution was obvious and typically Japanese. Mr. Yakou kept the name, which is still written in roman letters on the shop and in red letters sewn on his white work shirt. But his business card is in Japanese, with "Urban" written in a syllabic Japanese script used for rendering foreign words. The effect is to radically change the pronunciation.

"It's not Urban," sniffs Dentsu's Mr. Mawatari. "It's Aaah-bahn." In Japanese, aaah-bahn is stunningly mellifluous.

Of course, creative uses of "urban" aren't exclusively Japanese. On a recent trip to the U.S., I counted 130 listings in the Manhattan white pages under Urban, including some intriguing ones, like Urban Bush Women and Urban Truffles Inc.

But to my knowledge, no one in America has named a product Urban Toilet. In American newspapers we do not see flyers advertising apartments headlined "Urbest Mansion Hot News." (Urban, Urbetter, Urbest?)

Nor does America have shoes touted as Urban Epicurean, nor cars hawked under advertising slogans like Urban Dry Stanza (Nissan), nor buildings called Urban Elegance, nor real-estate complexes described as Nice Urban (we Urbans especially appreciate the latter two sentiments).

And the U.S. certainly doesn't have Urb magazine, the bilingual Tokyo magazine for Urbies, which recruits staffers (some of whom are called Urb-mates) with the ringing slogan: "Urb Wants You!"

I admit I gagged when I saw that "Urbie." Urbie was a childhood nickname I'd like to forget. But to Kazuhiko Nishi, a computer-software mogul and Urb's publisher, an Urbie, or "Urb-type person," is a thing of mystery, someone who is "hard to define . . . different."

How different? Well, for one thing, an Urbie "doesn't read ordinary magazines," the publisher says. Mr. Nishi, who claims to read hundreds of magazines, is not himself an Urbie. "I have more sophisticated taste," he says. But he is convinced Tokyo is brimming with unworldly Urb-types, and he has big ambitions for Urb magazine.

Right now, Urb is an eight-page freebie handed out in coffee shops in Tokyo's Minato Ward, with an editorial content that veers between being an about-Tokyo guide and a classified advertising bulletin board, in which Urb-type people offer to teach each other languages or rent each other rooms.

To expand into more wards, Mr. Nishi admits that Urb needs a sharper editorial focus. But the fuzziness of the current concept is one reason Urb is an Urb and not an Urban.

"Urban is too specific," Mr. Nishi explains. "Urb is more abstract. We'd like to start adding meaning to it."

Actually, a starting point in the search for meaning is at hand. The magazine now offers Urb jackets and Urb T-shirts. Printed on the T-shirt is the Urb philosophy:

> *Look lively! Everyone's watching and you're the star.*
> *The show is called life so be who you want to be.*
> *A worker, a poet, a friend. You rule your destiny.*
> *Choose your part and play it well.*
> *Work together! You are not alone in a city of millions.*
> *There is no urb like Tokyo.*

A Story of the Type
That Turns Heads
In Computer Circles

Digital Smiley Faces Are Used
In E-Mail Conversations
By the Lateral-Minded

By Michael W. Miller

9/15/92

The subject is uncontrollable scalp flaking. On a computer bulletin board called the Well, "Casey," as she calls herself on-line, is proposing a novel remedy. "I found that rinsing my scalp with vinegar will cut down on it for a while," her electronic message advises. "If you don't mind smelling like a salad :-)"

Elsewhere on the Well, a debate rages over the rules of etiquette for newlyweds. Scott Marley of Albany, Calif., joins in: "I believe Miss Manners insists that the thank-you notes must be sent before the divorce :-)"

All over the country these days, electronic-mail messages are concluding with this odd little punctuation sequence :-) or one of its many variants, like :-(

These are "smileys," so-called because when you tilt your head to the left, they look like little faces with a colon for eyes and a hyphen for a nose. Thus, when a message ends :-) it means "just kidding." If it ends :-(it means "I'm depressed." If it ends 7:^] it means "I resemble Ronald Reagan."

You may have thought that the only people who use smiley faces in written communication are motivational consultants and teen-agers in love. But the electronic smiley is spreading like a virus in the new medium of e-mail, used by thousands as a form of emotional punctuation.

One smiley dictionary circulating on computer bulletin boards lists 664 distinct variations, including:

:-D I'm laughing.
B-) I'm cool.
:*) I'm drunk.
:-'| I have a cold.
{(:-) I have a toupee.
}(:-(I have a toupee and it's windy.

Smiley's started popping up on computer screens more than a decade ago. The MIT Press's "New Hacker's Dictionary" attributes the very first smiley to a 1980 message by a Carnegie-Mellon computer scientist named Scott Fahlman. "I wish I had saved the original post or at least recorded the date for posterity," he later wrote, "but I had no idea that I was starting something that would soon pollute all the world's communication channels."

Today it's hard to log on to a bulletin board without tripping over someone's electronic face. On some boards, it's de rigueur to use a noseless version known as "midget smiley," which looks like the original, ubiquitous 1970s happy face :) The CompuServe network, where 1.1 million computer buffs swap messages, has its own smiley alternative, representing the word "grin." A recent usage: "Women irrational? Nahhhhhhh! Can't be <g>"

"Dvorak's Guide to PC Telecommunications," a popular technical tome, devotes four pages to the symbols. It soberly explains: "These are called emotions and are used to express on-line the emotions of normal voice communication." The guide lists 105 essential examples, including :-8 (I'm talking out of both sides of my mouth) and =|:-)= (I'm Uncle Sam).

Why is this happening now, when for thousands of years writers have found it possible to express emotions without using little sideways smiley faces? The smiley's roots may well go back to the science fiction "fanzines" of the '40s and '50s, homemade cult publications such as "Spaceship" and "Rhodomagnetic Digest." The writer Harlan Ellison, a pioneering fanzine publisher, recalls that contributors commonly punctuated their inside jokes with a simple sideways smile in quotation marks, like so: ")"

Today smiley scholars (there are already a handful) attribute the trend to the hybrid quality of e-mail, which at times is less like an exchange of letters than like a telephone conversation. Without some device to suggest a tone of voice, they say, e-mail is uniquely ripe for misunderstanding.

In a computer conversation, "It is difficult for a sender to convey nuance, communicate a sense of individuality, or exercise dominance or charisma," write social scientists Lee Sproull of Boston University and Sara Kiesler of Carnegie-Mellon in a study of "electronic communities" that examines the rise of smileys.

David Gans, an Oakland radio producer and bulletin-board devotee, began using smileys when he found his "deeply sarcastic" tone was getting lost in transmission. "I found that if you're going to say something really rude, you damn well better defuse it," he says. Today, he sprinkles his messages generously with his favorite smiley ("sort of a three-quarters-view"):^)

Sometimes the smiley also helps in the difficult business of flirting via computer. Consider this exchange on the Well:

She: "In general I hate the smell of perfumes and deodorants, while the smell of certain people's fresh sweat turns me into a gooey gibbering mass of slithery lust."

He: "hmmmmm . . . i work out tuesday and thursday . . . :-)"

In the same context, a popular alternative is the "winky" ;-)

The world's most elaborate electronic flirting signal was invented in 1987 by a Silicon Valley engineer named Alan Chamberlain. It drew heavily on the appearance of its creator's own face. "In those days I had my hair real short, I wore shades, I had a brash in-your-face personality," Mr. Chamberlain recalls. He called his creation the "kissy" and typed it like this #!^ ~

There are computer users whose faces wrinkle with distaste at the whole smiley phenomenon.

"I cringe when I see them," says the movie critic Roger Ebert, a habitué of CompuServe, interviewed via e-mail. On the other hand, he adds, "smileys might be a real help for today's students, raised on TV and unskilled at spotting irony without a laugh track."

An even fiercer anti-smiley is the comedian/magician Penn Jillette, who runs a computer bulletin board with his partner Teller and writes the "Micro Mephisto" column in PC Computing magazine. His scornful verdict: "As soon as you put one in you've killed the joke." In a recent column, he described the smiley as "the hateful :) which means 'just kidding' and is used by people who would dot their i's with little circles and should have their eyes dotted with Drano."

Ms. Sproull and Ms. Kiesler, the e-mail scholars, discuss a limitation of smileys in their book "Connections: New Ways of Working in the Networked Organization." "Although such cues weakly signal mood, they are flat and stereotyped . . . . Mild amusement looks no different from hilarity," the scholars write.

Flat and stereotyped? Hey Sproull and Kiesler, do some real research! :-) Joe Flower, a Sausalito, Calif., writer, recently sent an electronic message about his brutal book schedule—"a chapter every ten days, counting weekends and holidays, for five months." Then he signed off by hanging his tongue out with exhaustion :-+

A Little Bad English
Goes a Long Way
In Japan's Boutiques

———

Used on Goods as Decoration
And for Trendy Reasons,
Language Sells but Suffers

———

By Yumiko Ono

5/20/92

TOKYO—Need a coffee break? Doutor Coffee Co. has a special brew for those who are . . . tense in the breasts.

"Ease Your Bosoms," is the fractured English slogan on a packet of City Original Coffee. "This coffee has carefully selected high quality beans and roasted by our all the experience."

What the Tokyo retailer really means to say is that its coffee is so relaxing, it "takes a load off your chest." Or so says a company spokesman. But copywriters hadn't been quite sure how to put the claim in English for their Japanese customers.

"Using English gives products a stylish image" in Japan, says the coffee man, whose product isn't exported. It's just easier to sell Japanese goods to Japanese consumers, using a little English as a come-on.

A couple of rambling English sentences on the label, typically arranged neatly in three lines, give a product a catchy, Western look. English is on juice cans, writing paper, T-shirts and $740 leather jackets (which is 98,000 yen to you). But messages ranging from cloying to racy to incoherent almost always baffle the discerning reader.

The legend on a T-shirt declares: "Snow is Popsy." A nylon fanny-pack announces: "I'm seeking for something on the street." The back of a jacket has this dynamic advice: "Vigorous throw-up. Go on a journey."

"There's more and more English that foreigners see and don't understand," says Tsuneo Kusunoki, the president of Global Educational Opportunities and Services, Japan's largest chain of English-language schools. Some call the genre "Japlish." Nobody sees a pressing need to correct it. In fact, many product designers (evidently inclined to think that the medium is the message) are surprised to see foreigners taking an interest in what the slogans have to say.

Even the growing number of goods with American cartoon characters on them need extra English writing when sold in Japan so they will look suitably American to Japanese consumers. A 350-yen Mickey Mouse pen, for instance, is attached to a little bio in swirly letters: "He is cheerful, warmhearted, sensitive, and generally likes people. Since 1928."

Theories abound about what is behind the silly English, especially in a country where most people study the exotic tongue in school for eight or 10 years. And product designers say they don't really intend their English to be so far off the mark—it just turns out that way.

One man's direct translation from Japanese is another man's gibberish. Part of the problem may lie in the nature of the two languages, says Ira Caplan, who recently resigned as vice president of the international division at Dai-ichi Kikaku Co., a Tokyo advertising agency. The Japanese language has a rich vocabulary with which to express feelings that are hard to turn deftly into English. Japanese copywriters tend to "try to expand on feelings rather than ideas," says Mr. Caplan, who has collected and analyzed myriad examples of Japanese English intended for domestic consumption. The legend on a ski jacket, for example, tries to stress long-term friendship: "Let's go skiing since 1886." A sports bag rejoices in good health: "A drop of sweat is the precious gift for your guts."

Still, why exactly would the cover of a black notebook urge users to "Be a man I recommend it with confidence as like a most intelligent stationary of basic design"? Only Kanako Wada, who wrote the run-on sentence, can fathom the description of manliness. "I wanted to say I'm proud to present the product to the consumer because it's got a simple, masculine image," says the 25-year-old designer for San-X Co.

Conceding that she is no linguist, Ms. Wada says she hired a translator, then tinkered with the copy "for space reasons," an old editor's excuse. But whether the writing makes sense is of next to no importance. The main purpose of the English is to be with-it, says Ms. Wada. "I don't expect people to read it."

Besides, look at it from this perspective: What would a sentence or two of Japanese mean on a T-shirt worn in New York? Not much and who cares? It's art.

Japan's merchants have long been mangling English for commercial purposes, particularly in the naming of products. A sports drink is called Pocari Sweat. Choco Sand is a cream-filled cookie, and a line of casual clothing is called Prankish Flandre. (French and German are in vogue here, too, by the way, and just as incomprehensible to all concerned.) But Sanrio Co., known throughout the world for its "Hello Kitty" cartoon-character products, isn't keen to be an English mangler. So the company, which for the past 30 years has been thinking up cute things to write on some 12,000 consumer items, has had Western English speakers on staff as proofreaders for more than a decade.

"We can't just write garbage," says Douglas Parkes, who approves writing such as "Duckadoo, the Stylish Duck of Today." He also blessed: "I guess I'm just a little softie," a line of copy to go with a fluffy white bear called Sugarcream Puff.

Mr. Parkes admits he sometimes has a hard time discouraging the company's 120 designers from writing things that seem off the wall to Western readers. But he also understands that the writing must appeal to the domestic Japanese market. "Some people in the U.S. subsidiary laugh when they see what we write." Sanrio drops much of the English from the products it exports to the U.S. and other countries.

Young Japanese consumers, it seems, aren't all that interested in grammar, syntax and picking nits. They just want to see English on the stuff they buy, and the more of it the better. Kaori Sugiyama, a 16-year-old from central Japan, says she bought her new red polyester jacket because it was drenched in English. On the back are such phrases as "style basic and many feels fine," and "standard dangeradventure good taste sportive wear." A tag on the sleeve reads: "Musical Architect" and "Fast Freddie's."

"I like clothes that stand out," says the shy high-school student. "I've never read this, but I still think it's cool."

Her mother, though, isn't too thrilled with the impression the jacket makes. "It's so showy," says Mrs. Sugiyama. "There are too many letters."

Young customers' insouciance about what all those words truly mean brings out the mischief in people like Nobuhiko Kitamura, a designer for a brand called Hysteric Glamour. Many teen-age girls buy his T-shirts because of their bright colors and artwork, he says, with no idea that they sport such messages as "Tonight's the Bitch!" and "All Kinky Hysterics Late Night Specialized Services." People have been known to call his office, bewildered about the snickering encountered in traveling abroad in their T-shirts.

"I'm not trying to be mean," he says. "But I feel like luring consumers by drawing a cute picture, and attaching copy that'll shock them," that is, if they ever find out what it says.

Designers even dabble in self-parody—and, in doing so, can be rather frank about what they are pandering to. The printing on a brown paper bag says exactly what Kokuyo Co. is up to—making "the very best stationery especially for people who get excited when they see English all over everything, for boys and girls who are fans of anything and everything American."

Hush Mah Mouth! Some in South Try To Lose the Drawl

'Accent Reduction' Becomes A Big Bidness in Atlanta; Searchin' for the Lost 'G'

By Daniel Pearl

12/13/91

ATLANTA—In the next sequel to "Gone With the Wind," will Scarlett talk like a Yankee?

Until recently, that question would have been as preposterous as a parade honoring Gen. Sherman along Peachtree Street. Meetings in Atlanta began with a round of "hey, hah yew?" and echoing refrains of "mahty fahn." A visitor was offered a "Co-Cola" before settling down to "do bidness." The only way to say yes was, "Yes, Ma'am" or, "Yes, Sir."

But then the Yankees came—wave upon wave of them, sent down by Fortune 500 companies during the 1970s and '80s to staff regional offices here. The meetings included more and more people from places like New Jersey and Wisconsin. Some people felt that a Southern accent went from a badge of honor to a liability. Some even began referring to it as "Magnolia-mouth."

Now, a lot of Atlantans are trying to rid themselves of this dreaded syndrome. They are spending $1,000 or more for private accent-reduction lessons, signing up for English classes aimed at foreigners and setting up group drawl-busting sessions. Rhonda Gilbert, a partner in an accounting firm, so wants to impress clients that she not only took an accent-reduction course herself, but would like to set up classes for the others in her office. "With a Southern accent, it's very difficult to make a good first impression," she says.

At one time, such a sentiment would have been unthinkable. People looked askance at the fast-talking, often ill-mannered Northerner, who pronounced "mother" with a final "r." But things have changed. Soon after Atlanta was awarded the 1996 Olympics a year ago, a column appeared in the Atlanta Business Chronicle exhorting people to "get the South out of our mouth" to impress all the expected visitors. The author, Susan Shulman Cox, a communications consultant from New Jersey, wrote: "By cleaning up our speech, maybe we can finally convince the world that we're not just a bunch of cow-tipping morons down here."

"Traitors," grumbles syndicated columnist and resident good ol' boy humorist Lewis Grizzard. "I personally think everybody that has a Southern accent and wants to change it should be flogged."

The problem, many people believe, is television. The Southern accent has sustained tremendous image damage from Hollywood over the years. Shows like "The Beverly Hillbillies" and "The Andy Griffith Show" made slow-talking practically synonymous with simple-minded. This has only reinforced the superiority Yankees feel at having won the Civil War, says Jim Sledd, a retired English professor who has studied Southern speech.

A Southern accent isn't always a handicap here, mind you. When John Joos, an Atlanta human-resources manager, is trying to break the ice with subordinates, he says it sometimes helps to sound like a "dumb good old boy." A disarming drawl can sometimes be a powerful weapon against an overconfident Yankee. And some Northerners even find it convenient to adopt the accent from time to time. Many start using "Y'all" with a passion, even when addressing only one person.

But mostly, Mr. Joos says, his Southern accent is giving him a complex. He notices Northerners talk slower and choose their words carefully when talking to him, as if they believe he just fell off the turnip truck. When he saw two Southern senators on television recently, he caught himself thinking their accent "takes a notch or two from their credibility." So now he is working to stamp out his own Southern phrases, such as "fixin' to go."

Regina Buice, a human-resources worker at Southern Bell, is trying her best not to sound like a Southern belle. She is sick of all those silly things that pop out of Yankees' mouths when they hear a Southern accent. (They have imitated her. They have told her she is sexy. They have remarked that she must be a "real Southerner.") What is more, she is up for a promotion, and she is worried the decision will be made by Northerners. So she has practiced saying "you guys" instead of "y'all," and is trying to exorcise "oh, shoot" from her vocabulary. She is also taking night speech classes at Kennesaw State College. Unless she can drop the accent, she fears, the promotion committee "might not think I'm so sharp."

At Kennesaw College, her instructor, Janice Monk, probes Ms. Buice's speech patterns for regional quirks. Like most Southerners, she stretches out certain vowels, explains Ms. Monk, a speech pathologist and a native of Pennsylvania. So "mine" ends up sounding close to "man," and "ice" sounds like something else altogether. Her prescription for Ms. Buice: Read ad nauseam from special word lists—in class, at home, commuting to work. Among the words: liar, dime, fighter and pie.

Others drop an "r" at the end of words. So "here" becomes "heahh" and butter becomes "buttah." To correct it, Ms. Monk tells her students to open their mouths wider as they speak—so wide that one student protests, "It makes my jaw hurt."

Of course, some people in town think that those who teach accent-reduction classes are just modern-day carpetbaggers. "It really is a scam," says Lee Pederson, an English professor at Emory University.

Beverly Inman-Ebel, a speech pathologist who is trying to sell accent-reduction courses to Atlanta businesses, got hate mail and found her yard strewn with toilet paper when she offered a class in nearby Chattanooga, Tenn., called "Southern Success Without the Southern Accent." (Ms. Monk changed the name of her evening class from "Say, What?" to the more respectable "Businesspeak.")

Richard Clary, a 70-year-old Atlanta businessman, got so irritated with a young acquaintance who was affecting a Northern accent that he wrote a three-page letter chiding her for putting on airs. People who pronounce "furniture" or "cotton" with a pronounced "t" sound, he informed her, are as ridiculous as "the young woman who knowingly puts too much body language into her hip movements as she sashays along the promenade."

In fact, a small pro-drawl movement seems to be developing. Elizabeth Blahnik helped start the Atlanta Natives Club—by invitation only, an Atlanta birth certificate required. Members gather regularly to enjoy one another's vocal inflections. "There's no way I'd try to change my accent," says Ms. Blahnik.

Ludlow Porch's radio talk show is at the center of Atlanta's Southern resistance. Mr. Porch, whose voice is as slow and sweet as molasses in January, gets a steady stream of female callers who call him "sweet thang" and male callers who call him "mah friend." When complimented, Mr. Porch is apt to say, "Well, ah'm tickled" or "Bless your heart."

But even Mr. Porch concedes things are changing. He lives in a suburb where he goes for weeks without hearing a Southern accent. And he admits that, sometimes, he even catches himself "doin' silly things like pronouncin' mah 'g's."

Does 'Iliad' Lose
A Little in Recital
By an Accountant?

*Mr. Powelson Can Reel It Off
In Greek, From Memory,
But His Audiences Yawn*

By Lee Berton

11/17/88

> The wrath do thow sing, O goddess, of
> Peleus' son, Achilles . . .

So begins Homer's 15,693-line "Iliad." It would take all day, from rosy-fingered dawn to dark-browed night, to recite the entire epic of the siege of Troy—just the thing, perhaps, to stave off boredom on a New York–Beijing flight or a Saturday night in the drunk tank.

If your muse isn't up to it, no matter. The bard of Les-Loges-en-Josas, France, Stephen Powelson, stands ready, able and more than merely willing to pour the first 14,300 lines into your ear, from memory—and in classical Greek. Soon, he hopes, he will have committed the final 1,393 lines to memory.

Mr. Powelson, a 70-year-old accountant, lives in the Paris suburb of Les-Loges-en-Josas, near Versailles. He has returned to the U.S. at least 40 times in the past 10 years to do the "Iliad" thing, usually for not more than an hour or two, at schools and colleges. At these exhibitions of mnemonic prowess, a resident classicist randomly picks a line from the epic, and Mr. Powelson takes it from there.

Awesome. Says Mr. Powelson: "Everyone I meet can hardly wait to see if I can meet all these challenges."

But don't roll over, Homer, not just yet. As you might have put it, not all men reckon as sweeter than honey the words that escape the barrier of the many-languaged Mr. Powelson's teeth. To put it more bluntly, some people, including several classicists, say Mr. Powelson comes off as a crashing bore, ruining the poetry of the "Iliad" by reciting it in a relentless, mind-numbing, mile-a-minute monotone.

Gordon Kirkwood, a retired classics professor at Cornell University, describes a Powelson performance as "an amazing tour de force." But, he says, "It's something to admire from a distance rather than hear." Mr. Kirkwood, an authority on Greek life some 3,000 years ago, says that "the original rhapsodists who recited the 'Iliad' did it with a lot of emotion. Some might even weep or cry, and it was a very lively experience as contrasted with what Mr. Powelson does."

Alice Bennink, whose husband was a 1938 classmate of Mr. Powelson at Harvard College, heard Mr. Powelson's recitation at a class reunion last June. "He's learned it by rote, so he rattles on very quickly and almost without any verbal or facial expression," Mrs. Bennink says. "I can't believe that the original bards of Greece narrated it like that."

Yet Mr. Powelson manages to keep the invitations coming. Z. Philip Ambrose, chairman of the classics department at the University of Vermont, says that "Steve Powelson is very singleminded, and he's a great promoter of himself." Mr. Powelson recited about an hour's worth of the "Iliad" from memory at the university in early 1987 before an audience of about 100.

"I'd heard about Powelson from another classicist at the University of Maryland, and then Powelson began to besiege me with letters asking for an invitation," Mr. Ambrose says. "Before he did the recitation, I thought I was going to be knocked out. But frankly, I found myself nodding at one of the greatest works of literature."

At dinner, Mr. Ambrose says, Mr. Powelson couldn't stop reciting the "Iliad." "It's an obsession with him," he says. "No matter what topic we brought up—when I told him someone I know had broken a leg—he would somehow relate it to the 'Iliad' and then begin his recitation all over again. I could hardly wait to get away."

Mr. Powelson says he isn't an "Iliad"-obsessed bore. "I participate in chess tournaments, play tennis and squash, and my favorite sport is water skiing," he says. "Why, I can even ski on one foot backwards." He does admit to running through the tale of the siege of Troy in fast-forward mode, "because that's the way I have to learn it. It's so long and filled with almost unending lists of proper names in some sections."

The "Iliad" has 24 books, totaling 600 pages. One section in Book II lists the names of 498 Greek ships and warriors in close order. Book XVIII contains 33 complex names of sea nymphs. When Mr. Powelson recites these names rapid-fire, he sounds like the late Danny Kaye reeling off the tongue-twisting names of 49 Russian composers in only 39 seconds in his novelty song "Tchaikovsky" in the 1941 Weill-Gershwin musical, "Lady in the Dark."

Various devices help Mr. Powelson retrieve long strings of names from his memory. "Three of the sea nymphs, for example, each has a name that involves water," he says. The syllable "cym" in Cymothoe means wave in classical Greek. "Actae" in Actaea means beach, and "limne" in Limnoreia means lake. Thinking of "a man with a fork of chrome who's an enemy" cues his recall of other names, Phorcys, Chromius and Enmemus.

Mr. Powelson began his bardship in 1977, when he was 60. Unemployed, with no job in sight, he decided to renew his interest in the classics and memorize the "Iliad" "as a mind exercise to keep me busy and from worrying about getting a job. For that sort of thing, my memory is good," he says.

At the age of 10, he says, he memorized in one week an entire year's homework in Sunday-school Bible studies. In prep school, he memorized the first 100 lines of the "Iliad," took three Greek courses in his senior year and won a national prize for his Greek. At Harvard, he studied Greek drama for only one semester and then had "nothing to do with Greek," he says, for 39 years.

Mr. Powelson eventually got the job he still holds, managing an office for an Arab businessman in Paris. Not long after, friends suggested that he go public with his feat of memory. "It sounded like a good idea," Mr. Powelson recalls. So he began soliciting appearances at colleges, prep schools and literary clubs in the U.S. and Europe. He has performed at the universities of Arkansas, Colorado and Massachusetts and at Tulane University, among other places.

His wife of 47 years, Esther, says that Mr. Powelson is constantly mastering new lines. "When we go to lunch and we're waiting for the check or on a station platform waiting for a train, he pulls out his copy of the 'Iliad,'" she says. "Sometimes he wakes up in the middle of the night, and leaves the bedroom to look up a word in classical Greek."

But, she says, "while my husband's memory is phenomenal, it is very selective. I still have to find his glasses and keys for him. He just doesn't remember where he puts them."

What Does an Ephah Have in Common With A Diaskeuast?

They Are Crossword Words, As Our Puzzling Reporter Discovers in Big Contest

By Michael W. Miller

9/2/86

NEW YORK—What on earth is a four-letter word for "Quarterback Brian"?

I need to know in a hurry. I have just the first three letters, S-I-P.

On a muggy summer afternoon, I have left the pace of daily journalism for some real deadline pressure. This is the fifth annual U.S. Open Crossword Championship, where a roomful of fiendish puzzlers squared off the other week in the Grand Prix of American word games.

For many people, solving crossword puzzles is a relaxing activity, something to do on a lazy afternoon in a comfortable armchair. Not at the U.S. Open. We are huddled tensely over a bank of long tables in a university auditorium, with a giant Seiko clock in one corner loudly counting off the seconds. In a few minutes a referee will yell, "Time's up!" and snatch all our puzzles away.

I glance to my left. A young woman is gliding through her puzzle using a black felt-tip pen. I glance to my right. A middle-aged man, already finished, is ostentatiously leafing through a morning newspaper. I glance back down at my puzzle. "Kin of the Potawatamis," it says. "Olive genus." "Ottoman chief." "Trypanosome carrier." . . .

This is the last of five puzzles in the tournament, with time limits ranging from 15 to 45 minutes. We get points for every correct word we fill in, with bonuses for finishing a puzzle before the clock stops. At the end of the day, the top three finishers will step onto the auditorium stage for a sudden-death final crossword, working with erasable markers on giant grids before a crowd of spectators. The champ will win $1,500, a dictionary and the U.S. Open's coveted trophy, a six-foot pencil.

My 249 rivals range in age from 18 to 82. They are from all over the country and work in all manner of jobs: a sociologist, a quilter, a nuclear-reactor operator, several accountants, and many computer programmers.

One contestant listed her occupation as "boat bum," another as "itinerant peddler" and a third as "diaskeuast," a crossword-puzzle word for editor.

All of us weathered a round of five preliminary puzzles, prepared by the monthly magazine Games, to qualify for this tournament. We all came here believing that we had a certain knack for filling in blank squares with obscure words.

But I have quickly learned that mere knacks count for little here. "A lot of people are really humbled," cautioned Will Shortz, the tournament's director and a Games senior editor, before the event began. "For most people, crosswords are a very solitary sport. They do them with their family and their friends, and they can be a star in their own small circles. Then they come to a tournament and they find they're not champions."

Several battle-scarred contestants echo this warning. "My first year here, I thought I was good," recalls Raymond Cotter, a Corning, N.Y., transportation executive vying in his fourth U.S. Open. "I thought I'd come out here and get in the top 10. I came to one word and the clue was 'mating game,' and I must have looked at that one word for five minutes." The answer turned out to be "chess." Mr. Cotter finished 176th.

"The top solvers here fill in the spaces as fast as my hand can write," laments Carolyn Bartlebaugh, a Camp Hill, Pa., high-school French teacher who has competed in all five U.S. Opens. "If I had the answer in front of me and I could just transfer all the letters into my puzzle, they still would win."

This tourney, in fact, has attracted some of the crossword circuit's most bruising competitors.

They include David Rosen, 33, and Ellen Ripstein, 34, a pair of New York insurance workers who regularly grab top spots at the U.S. Open and leading regional contests. Like many athletes who wear lucky charms when they compete, Mr. Rosen wears his lucky two-piece gray suit. "It goes with my type-A personality," he explains.

Four years ago, Mr. Rosen and Ms. Ripstein met at the first U.S. Open. He finished seventh and she finished 10th, and they have been dating ever since. "We're the Chris Evert and Jimmy Connors of crosswords," Ms. Ripstein says.

Towering over the field is Rebecca Kornbluh, a 35-year-old weaver from Mundelein, Ill., who basically owns the sport of competitive crosswords today. A tense, animated woman with a long braid down her back and a little enamel pig (her lucky charm) pinned to her dress, Ms. Kornbluh swept the last two U.S. Opens and has vowed to retire after this match.

Talking with Ms. Kornbluh, I begin to see what separates the giants from the duffers in this sport. My preparation for the tournament consisted of doing a few crossword puzzles on the airplane to New York and having a lot to eat and drink at a reception for entrants the night before the contest. Rebecca Kornbluh tells me she has been doing 15 timed crosswords a day for the last week, and she skipped the reception.

"I felt I needed a quiet evening, not a party," she says. "I stayed home, did some puzzles, and went to bed early."

The day begins with three unusually devious puzzles. Foxy wordplay lurks everywhere. One crossword is filled with puns on detergent brand names. (The answer to "supply the detergent" is GIVE ONE'S ALL; "print on a detergent box" is BOLD LETTERING.) Another features movie-star names turned into birds. (Answers include GEORGE SEA-GULL, STARLING HAYDEN and DONALD O'CONDOR.)

Every corner brings agonies of self-doubt. At 7 Down—"fake golds"—the intersecting across-words leave me with OROIDAS, which looks extremely dubious. Could "a little more than a bushel" really be EPHAH? Worst of all, for "site of Cybele's temple," I'm left with total gobbledygook: MTIDA.

My eyes glaze over. My mind begins to wander. Mtida. . . . Mtida. . . . "O Cybele, I have journeyed here to Mtida, bearing ephahs and ephahs of tribute, to pray for victory for quarterback Brian Sipo (Sipi? . . . Siph? . . . Sipu? . . .)."

At the lunch break, the auditorium breaks into a din of postmortems. "Dominique Sanda? Who ever heard of these people?" "Narwhal? A narwhal doesn't have tusks!" All around me, people are buzzing about the location of Cybele's shrine; it turns out to be Mt. Ida.

I compare notes with Martha Browne, a contestant who caught my eye by finishing all three puzzles early and then whiling away the remaining time with an Italian crossword magazine. Ms. Browne, a free-lance editor from New York, says, "I had a private smirk of pleasure at the detergent theme. For decades women have had to learn a lot of sports terminology to do puzzles. This morning I was pleased to hear a lot of men grumbling."

The afternoon features a puzzle with a twist: About a third of the words are defined with audio clues played on a loudspeaker, asking questions such as "Whose voice is this?" or "What work is this song from?"

Here my '70s upbringing slows me down. I have trouble identifying the singer of "Dream a Little Dream of Me" (MAMA CASS) and the theme song being played (from "LILI"). On the other hand, I quickly recognize the 10-letter deep voice hissing, "There will be a substantial reward for the one that finds the Millennium Falcon" (DARTH VADER) and the six-letter high, throaty voice warbling, "It's not that easy bein' green" (KERMIT; another hapless solver came up with VERMIN for this one).

The end of the day finds Ms. Kornbluh, the defending title holder, pitted in the finals against a New York pianist and a Virginia labor lawyer (a pair of dark horses who upset the Chris and Jimmy duo to claim the other two top spots). Ms. Kornbluh eats them alive. Pausing only once, to step back and double-check her spelling of "inimical," she sprints to a perfect finish more than a minute before her opponents, each of whom makes a couple of mistakes.

After her victory, Ms. Kornbluh puffs on a cigarette and reflects on what it takes to be a crossword champion. Is her secret a spectacular vocabulary? "I have a pretty good vocabulary," she admits cheerfully, "but it's passive. I don't know what half the words mean."

As for me, I wind up in 22nd place, an exciting finish as far as I'm concerned but a long way from the six-foot pencil.

Looking over my corrected puzzles, I see that "fake golds" turns out to be oroides, not oroidas. Amazingly, an ephah is indeed a little more than a bushel (it equals one-tenth of a homer, to be exact). And the quarterback's name is Brian Sipe, not Sipo, my eventual guess.

I should have suspected something was wrong there when the crossing word, "sunny vacation spot," came out as OSLO. The correct answer: ISLE.

A Fictional Library
Becomes a Real Place
With Unreal Fiction

———

Much Is Novel at Brautigan's,
Where the Unpublished
Go to Find Immortality

———

By Lawrence L. Ingrassia

5/28/91

"I don't know how to break it to you, but you've got a pretty far-out operation going on here. This library is a little on the whacky side."
—RICHARD BRAUTIGAN, "THE ABORTION"

BURLINGTON, VT.—As the inspiration for the Brautigan Library, the only library in America exclusively for unpublished books, the late author knew what he was talking about.

Let other libraries stock "Death of a Salesman," "Lord of the Flies" or "Lassie Come Home." Nowhere else but here can you find "Sure Beats Watching Trains," the tale of a "burned-out shoe salesman . . . overtaken by an alien persona." Or "Theories of Father," a "video-image script-novel narrated by a house fly, with help from Ed Sullivan." Or "Rory Stories, Vol. 1": the "humorous adventures of a talking Shetland sheepdog named Rory O'More."

No, at the Brautigan Library you will never find a book that is on the bestseller list or even at your favorite bookstore.

But so what? Says Sheri Vance of Salt Lake City, Utah, a visitor to the library, "There is some really horrific writing, but that's what's sort of fun. The pleasure of reading the stuff is really the pleasure of being a voyeur. There is an intimacy to it that you don't have with a book that is published."

Which is just what Todd Lockwood envisaged when he re-created the fictional library-of-the-unpublished described by Mr. Brautigan in "The Abortion." "We're trying to encourage works that share something personal," says Mr. Lockwood, a 40-year-old, long-time Brautigan fan who also runs a recording studio here. "To get beyond the notion of traditional publishing, we're going to get lots of not-so-well written novels. But we're getting interesting, idiosyncratic works."

Keeping with the spirit of Mr. Brautigan, even some of the authors see the humor of the place. In a letter mailed with his opus "Oedipus in America," an "adventure of misplaced libido," David Lee Johnston wrote, "I hope this book is worth including. If not, please damage it beyond repair."

Mr. Brautigan himself, though an icon of the 1960s counterculture, was never taken seriously by much of the literary world. His best-known novel, "Trout Fishing in America," which sold two million copies, is often mistakenly stocked in the sports sections of bookstores, although it's not about fishing. It's about America.

Indeed, not everyone thinks the library is such a great idea, even as a memorial to Mr. Brautigan, who committed suicide in 1984. Garry Trudeau refused to become a trustee, contending that there are too many good published books to waste time "poking through unpublished materials." Kurt Vonnegut's agent "burst out laughing" when informed of the idea, Mr. Lockwood says. But Jerry Greenfield of Ben and Jerry's ice cream is on the advisory board. So is author Thomas McGuane.

The nonprofit library greeted its first visitors a year ago in a long, narrow room in the back of a building that houses the Vermont Institute of Massage Therapy. It is a frugal, offbeat place, staffed by volunteer librarians and furnished with chairs that don't match (as required by its bylaws). Only open on weekends, the library is for readers; books can't be checked out.

Nor does the library use Dewey Decimal System for cataloging books. Instead, it runs on the "Mayonnaise System," which allows authors to place their works in categories like "Meaning of Life." (Mr. Brautigan ended one book with the word mayonnaise because, he noted, he always wanted to.)

And it is one library where the cliché "you can't tell a book by its cover" is true, literally. All manuscripts get a blank binding in one of five colors. Authors pay a fee of $50 a book, for the binding and to cover expenses, like rent.

The Brautigan isn't the only unusual library in the country, of course. There's the American Nudist Research Library in Osceola County, Fla., where all the books are about nudism, but nudity is optional; the Library of Natural Sounds, at the Oakland [Calif.] Museum, featuring recordings of insects, birds, mammals and thunder; and the American Philatelic Research Library in State College, Pa., which offers 60,000 publications on stamps.

By contrast, what the Brautigan lacks in quantity—it has only 180 books, so far—it makes up in variety. Its shelves offer everything from steamy erotica to poetry to children's books to a master's thesis ("Theory, Design & Application of a Photocombustion Reactor"). Works range in length from two pages (actually, two half pages) to 600 pages long, and they're written by bus drivers and hairdressers, corporate types and teachers, including some who worship Mr. Brautigan and some who have never heard of him.

Many have been snubbed by publishers. "I've been rejected by the best and the least," boasts Melvin Spivak, a short-story writer ("Fantasies II"), ex-dishwasher and ex-security guard. A. Alexander Stella, an electrical parts inspector and unpublished author, says of the library, "It's probably my one hope to achieve immortality."

The most prolific contributor is Albert Helzner, a retired engineer from Marblehead, Mass., who has sent in 20 books, mostly eccentric musings about life. In "Some Observations About the World," Mr. Helzner (who like reclusive author J.D. Salinger declines to be interviewed) describes a day in the lives of two wildebeests named Fred and Charlie: "Plenty of food here. Chomp. Chomp. Chomp. Looks safe, but I'll keep my eyes open for lions. . . . Boy, this is good eating. . . . They caught me. Help me, Fred. I can't shake them. I'm down. One's got me by the thr . . ."

Some of the fiction is equally, uh, zany. John H. Sullivan's "Dead Lines" is about a "smart but raunchy, married and womanizing newsman" who is having an affair with his editor's wife while the editor (a former all-pro football player) is having a homosexual affair with the town mayor. After their first tryst, the newsman tells the boss's wife: "I'll always remember tonight as my Super Bowl of sex." Mr. Sullivan, a 76-year-old retired press officer under former Secretary of Defense Robert McNamara, says the plot "just came out. I would sit down and say, 'What would these characters do in this situation next?' I didn't plan it."

But, if some of the works are a bit camp, others are touching and personal, written by people who don't much care whether they get published or not. There is a collection of poems written by a now-deceased mother and submitted by her daughter, memoirs of an elderly cancer patient living out his days in a convalescent home and the remembrances of a Pennsylvania teen-ager who realized his dream of becoming a cowboy in Wyoming during the Depression.

"Dying According to My Mom" is handwritten by a nurse, in a child's voice, to prepare her four-year-old son for an older brother's death. In "Another American Journey," the author tells of quitting his job at age 40 and traveling 22,672 miles in a van to all 48 states in the continental U.S., over 13 weeks, 5 days, 9 hours and 23 minutes. "I saw a highway stretching to a distant horizon, around a mountain curve, beside a flowing stream, along an ocean beach, through a fragile desert," he writes.

Having a place for books like this, where people pour out their hearts, say the library's fans, is what Mr. Brautigan had in mind. Says May Janko, 65, who sent in a children's book after it was rejected by innumerable publishers: "It has a home. In my mind, it's someplace, and that's a good feeling. It's not in oblivion."

Here's the Story
That Won the Nobel
For Best Writing

That's a Fib, but Competitors
For 'World's Biggest Liar'
Tell Even Taller Tales

By Ken Wells

11/26/91

Santon Bridge, England—Reg White is an engineer by profession, but a liar by inclination. So great a liar, in fact, that he was crowned the World's Biggest Liar last year in the 149th Annual World's Biggest Liar competition.

This being the 150th anniversary of the event, Mr. White, from the English coastal town of Blackpool, is back here in scenic Cumbria, the Ozarks of England, to defend his title. Competition is stiff: Eleven other world-class liars are rumored to be jetting in from around the globe. Loosening up at the Santon Bridge pub, where the finals are to be held, Mr. White admits he is feeling the pressure: "I'd be lying if I said I wasn't nervous."

Last year, Mr. White lied his way to the summit with a truly tall tale: All explorers who have ever claimed to have reached the top of Mount Everest have been lying. Why? Because Mr. White, during a two-week, $17.50 packaged tour to Katmandu years back, trekked up Everest, broke off its very tip and lugged it away in a plastic shopping bag. Natives, scoffing at his story, obliquely named the mountain range for him by chanting: "Him a liah! Him a liah!"

This is the kind of tale that would have enthralled the event's founder, Will Ritson, a 19th-century pub owner from nearby Wasdale Head. After a few pints of his favorite ale, Mr. Ritson would wax eloquent if untruthful about the virtues of his native Wasdale Valley and its agriculture. Among other things, he claimed to grow turnips so big that they had to be quarried instead of merely dug up. Locals swear the progeny of Mr. Ritson's turnips still thrive, and are being hollowed out and sold as condos.

For most of its life, the contest had been an informal gathering of local yarn spinners. In 1974, however, the competition was opened to global liars. Organizers also added a trophy and promised to make the winners rich for life. (The prize is actually about $45, but "this is a lot of money in India 50 years ago," notes one contest official.)

The event has almost always been held in a pub, except for a brief hiatus a few years ago, when reformers moved it into the civilizing influence of a convention center. But liars forced the contest back into the bar. "Lying is thirsty business," explains Adrian Hope, a contest organizer.

Mr. Hope, during pre-competition briefings, had also made much of the growing international nature of the event, noting past participants from Australia, Jamaica and Japan. But on competition night, Dorothy Graham, the event's chief historian, is leafing through a roster of past contests and can't seem to find a record of these lying foreigners. "Ah, but there was an American once, a fellow who had won the National Cherry-Spitting Contest in the U.S.," she says. Mrs. Graham can't remember his name, or his lie. But she does recall that the judges didn't care spit for his tall tale, and he didn't win.

This year—cross their hearts—organizers are bracing for a foreign invasion. Among the rumored finalists are an American savings-and-loan executive; a mysterious Frenchman said to be fond of British cooking; and the pre-coup editor of Pravda, the former mouthpiece of the now-defunct Soviet Communist Party.

Mysteriously, at contest time on a recent rain-swept night, the foreigners fail to appear. Stan McManus, the contest's master of ceremonies, explains their absence by noting the remoteness of Santon Bridge, a sometimes fogbound speck far from any major highway, and the persistence of a local legend. "Surely you've heard of the Good Shepherd of Wasdale Valley?" says Mr. McManus, an electrician by trade. "He is a kind, old shepherd who often appears out of the fog to greet lost travelers. Then he points them on their way—always in the wrong direction."

Although the Pravda editor hasn't made it, Tass, the increasingly independent Soviet news service, has sent a correspondent, Sergei Voitishkin, to cover the event. Mr. Voitishkin finds his presence something of an event itself. He is surrounded by envious liars wanting to know if there is truth to a recent British magazine report crowning Pravda, which means "truth," as the lyingist newspaper of all time.

"Yes, I guess you could say there were a lot of lies," says Mr. Voitishkin. But he promises to write the truth about the World's Biggest Liar competition.

The contest rules are straightforward. Each liar gets between two and five minutes to tell his tale. No props are allowed. And the contest is closed to professional liars—defined by organizers as lawyers, politicians and real-estate agents.

Of the seven liars who have shown up, the first to take the podium is the Rev. John Graham, sporting a somber gray suit and vicar's collar. He spins out a tale of leeks so big that they are used for forms in the construction of the English Channel tunnel, and of Australian rabbits found dangling on the end of carrots plucked from Cumbrian gardens. The Rev. Graham turns out to be a man of the lard, instead of a man of the Lord—actually a livestock farmer from a nearby village.

Another contestant, Dr. John Reeves, later admits that the M.D. attached to his name stands for "doctor of mendacity." He is actually an employee of a nuclear power plant who regales the audience with stories of clever Cumbrian animals.

One is of a farmer who pushes his sow by wheelbarrow over a steep mountain pass en route to breed her with a boar. The deed done, he returns home and puts the sow out to pasture, hoping she will begin nibbling on grass—the telltale sign that she has become pregnant. Nothing happens. After three such trips, he turns the sow loose, retires to his farmhouse and later asks his wife to check on the pig. "What's that sow doing now, eating grass?" he asks her. Peering from the window, his wife replies: "No, I think she's climbing into the wheelbarrow."

It is defending champion Mr. White, however, a deadpan 68-year-old with a quavering voice, who steals the show with his tale of his life as a party animal. Mr. White claims that in his early days he was a singer of such extraordinary talents that he was known as the "Sinatra of Santon Bridge." Thus, while pop star Tom Jones, a Welshman, claims credit for the "gimmick" whereby female fans fling their underwear at him during a performance, "it was really me who started it."

It happened one night during a performance for a prison reform society attended by a vast crowd of "at least 10 or 12 people." Mr. White, fearing he was losing his voice, refused to sing unless he could find a swatch of red flannel cloth to cloak his neck. In the audience was the "large and selfless" Agatha Ackroyd, a shepherdess from nearby Wynnrose Pass, who wore unmentionables made out of "double quality red flannel" to protect her during her frequent lunches on Cumbria's cold stone fences.

Upon hearing his request, Ms. Ackroyd "whipped off her knickers and flung them at me." They circled his neck three times, and "within seconds my voice was restored and I gave the performance of my life."

Judges again crowned Mr. White the Biggest Liar in the World, leaving Tass's Mr. Voitishkin scratching his head. "The story of the pig my readers will understand. But Tom Jones and knickers? I don't think it will translate."

Gender Bender:
A Boy Called Dana
Causes Confusion

———

People Think Our Reporter Is A Woman, Which He Isn't; Female Doug Has Trouble

———

By Dana Milbank

9/21/92

Oh, to be just another Tom, Dick or Harry. Even Bob, Fred or John would do.

But it was not to be. Instead, my parents got together 25 years ago and named their firstborn son Dana, a name so feminine that one baby-name book defines it as "mother of the gods" and another as a "sweet, willowy, statuesque dancer."

Ever since, life has been a series of little indignities. In grade school, when small boys try to be tough guys, I shrank in my seat as yet another substitute teacher, sensing a hoax, frowned during roll call because a boy had answered to Dana. Despite my protests, The Wall Street Journal's switchboard in New York continues to tell callers asking for me, "She's in our Pittsburgh bureau." I thought I had put a stop to it.

Such abuse is no doubt foreign to those fortunate, oblivious people whose names match their gender. But consider the plight of the stubbly-faced Evelyn, not to mention Courtney, Stacy, Tracy, Robin, Kim, Whitney, Dale, Toby, Kyle, Jody and Randy. And what about those Glenns or Darryls who need bras not neckties, not to mention the countless others cursing androgyny and the confusion it causes.

"Picture this," says one such victim, former Pittsburgh Steelers star Lynn Swann. "You graduate from college as an All-American, your football team wins the national championship, and how is the first letter from the alumni association addressed? 'Ms. Lynn Swann.' " Then, while the famed wide receiver was leading the Steelers to four championships, he got in his mail a free box of tampons.

Shirley Povich, the famous retired sportswriter of the Washington Post, was listed in the first edition of Who's Who of American Women. He appeared there between Louise Pound and Hortense Powdermaker in a blurb lifted directly from Who's Who in America. "It says there plainly that I'm a father of three and a husband of one," he says.

But Mr. Povich took the gaffe in stride. "This is no longer a man's world," he says. "I was glad to be listed on the winning side."

When Beverly Carter, who goes as "Bev," checks into hotels, the desk clerk hands his credit card back—to his wife. Even Eastman Kodak Co.'s chairman, Kay R. Whitmore, was turned into a "chairwoman" in this newspaper last year.

Occasionally, the confusion has its advantages. When I was in high school, the track coach at Mt. Holyoke College, a women's school, sent me a recruitment letter. In track, my times ranked me among the top girls in the state. For a boy, they were mediocre at best.

The trials are endless for the ambiguous. In summer camp, the laundry sent my name-tagged clothes to the girls' bunks. My girlfriend, Donna, complains that people think she is seeing another woman.

"Parents say only sticks and stones can break your bones, but of course names harm you," says Bruce Lansky, author of the Baby Name Personality Survey (and father of a 19-year-old daughter named Dana). "You're giving a child needless problems if you give the child a name with gender confusion."

Actress Michael Learned has the problem, and so does Michaele (pronounced Michael) Weissman who, as a child, was called Mike. "It was horrible," she recalls. "It felt so unfeminine." She says her father, a college athlete, had wanted a boy. She thought up elaborate self-justifying lies to explain her name, claiming, for instance, that the Puritan author Michael Wigglesworth, a man, was an ancestor. In college, some wag sent her on a star-crossed blind date with yet another Michael Weissman, a 5-foot-three dental student. Ms. Weissman, on the other hand, is 5-foot-8.

Albert Mehrabian, a psychology professor at UCLA and author of the book "The Name Game" says studies show that those with ambiguous names score lower on tests and are less popular socially. Perhaps that's why Johnny Cash's "A Boy Named Sue" vows to "search the honky tonks and bars and kill that man who gave me that awful name."

Says Dr. Mehrabian: "Parents give a boy a feminine name to make him appear warm and loving or give a girl a masculine name to make her more competitive in the professional world." But it often backfires: "These names have negative impressions in terms of success and morality."

Those of us with iffy names aren't always taken seriously. When Douglas Newsom, wearing a paisley dress, tried to board an airplane in Dallas recently, she was asked to show pieces of identification. When she complained, she says, the agent suggested she change her name. Of course, some people with ambiguous names actually do that. Gerald R. Ford might not have made it to the Oval Office with his given name, Leslie King Jr. And how many starring roles might John Wayne have lost had he not sloughed the name Marion Morrison? But being Dana Andrews didn't seem to hurt his acting career.

If there is any consolation for endangered male Danas, it's that female Danas have their troubles, too. As a girl, Dana Frost, who moved around a lot as a child, dreaded the first day of school each year. "They'd say,

'Dana Frost' and look at all the little boys," she recalls, "and I was saying, 'No, here, with the pigtails!' " When Ms. Frost turned 18, she started receiving draft-registration material in the mail, which she ignored until she was threatened with five years in prison.

The Selective Service admits it has sent notices in the past decade to 139,688 men who turned out to be women. "The system tries to be as friendly as possible," says spokesman Lew Brodsky. "But if there's any doubt, the piece of mail goes."

Like others who assign questionable names, my parents had expected something other than what they got. My mother wanted to name me David. My father, for his own reasons, preferred Quentin. They compromised with Dana Timothy.

But the fallout was immediately apparent. All the personalized baby stuff for Danas—from shoelaces to toothbrushes—came in telltale pink. When I selected a personalized license plate for my bike, I found it in the girls' rack between Daisy and Danielle.

I tried to ignore the D-name in school and write "D. Timothy," on homework assignments, but it looked terribly stuffy, and I didn't care much for the Timothy part, either. My mother to this day calls me "Dane," a pet name in both senses of the word. I associated it with the dog.

Actually, my parents aren't entirely to blame. The 1966 name book they used says Dana means "Man from Denmark" and doesn't even list Dana in the girls' section. A more recent name book, "Beyond Jennifer and Jason," lists Dana among girls names that are "so far in they're out."

Times change. In the 7th century, there was a king of East Anglia named Anna. The difference, of course, is that King Anna didn't have to argue, as I do, with a Blockbuster Video clerk who accuses me of using some woman's card when I try to rent a movie.

Occasionally, the insult is so keenly felt I can't just laugh it off. As a senior in college, after I got a rejection letter for a summer job addressed "Dear Ms. Milbank," I wrote an angry reply. Had I made so little impression on the woman who had given me the face-to-face interview?

She apologized, blaming the mistake on her secretary. I still didn't get the job.

X

THERE WILL ALWAYS BE AN ENGLAND

Endangered Feces:
Paleo-Scatologist
Plumbs Old Privies

———

It May Not Be the Lost Ark,
But Then, Andrew Isn't
Exactly Indiana Jones

———

By Tony Horwitz

9/9/91

YORK, ENGLAND—Below the Gothic spires of this postcard-perfect town, under its cobbled lanes and its beamed Tudor pubs, there lies a hidden world.

"Beneath us right now is about three meters of dirt from earlier settlement," says Andrew Jones, bouncing on a tourist-packed sidewalk in York. "I'd guess that one-third of it is excrement."

Historical records support his scatological analysis. King Edward III visited York in the 14th century and declared that "the abominable smell" from "dung and manure and other filth and dirt" was worse "than in any other city of the realm."

But what may have been a blight on medieval England is buried treasure for Dr. Jones. He is a paleo-scatologist, plumbing the depths of history for clues as to diet, health and sanitation in earlier times. In leading archaeological journals, such as Antiquity, he has pondered topics such as "The Worms of Roman Horses," while at scientific conferences, he gives an earthy lecture titled "Passed and Present: The Archaeology of Excrement."

Clearly, the sewer-level window he opens onto old English life is a far cry from the romantic idyll of Robin Hood. "The bottom line," he says, "is that people tolerated what would seem to us incomprehensible squalor. Time and again, you get a very strong picture of filth."

Dr. Jones's interest in the origin of feces is philosophical as well as scientific. He sees his work as an antidote to the fiction made famous by his Hollywood namesake, Indiana Jones, that archaeology is an exotic quest for holy grails or chests of gold. "This," says Dr. Jones, peering through his microscope at an oat grain scraped from the intestine of an Iron Age man, "is what really moves most archaeologists."

His philosophy is enshrined in the Archaeological Resource Centre, a prize-winning museum he manages here in York, housed in an abandoned Gothic church. At one exhibit, visitors use forceps to pick through soil samples from a site called Swinegate; petri dishes labeled "slag" or "fishbone" show them what to look for.

But perched on a small plastic mount is what Dr. Jones regards as the most significant find yet in York. It is a 1,000-year-old stool identified by the museum as the "Lloyds Bank Turd," after the bank building under which it was deposited by a Viking settler.

"This is the most exciting piece of excrement I've ever seen," Dr. Jones says. Fearing that the hazards of public display might render it endangered feces, Dr. Jones asked Lloyd's of London—the insurance agency, not the bank—to estimate the prize exhibit's value for a policy. The company came back with a figure of £20,000, equivalent to about $34,000. "This is insulting, really," says Dr. Jones. "In its own way, it's as irreplaceable as the Crown Jewels."

What makes the specimen so precious is that it is an almost undamaged "coprolite," the scientific term for a complete stool. Usually, Dr. Jones must analyze mere scraps with the patience and grit of a forensic detective.

"This sample is from a Roman-era cess-pit," Dr. Jones says, examining a grime-smeared slide. "See that brown blobby bit? Probably fungal spores. And that rod-like thing is a fragment of grass cells." He shakes his head, disappointed. "This is just ordinary soil."

Scanning another part of the slide, Dr. Jones hits pay dirt. "There's a brilliant one—a real classic!" he says, focusing on the egg case of the intestinal parasite "Ascaris lumbricoides", a.k.a. large human roundworm. Such evidence reveals that the leavings are indeed human. Some paleo-scatologists also make a "fecal odorogram," using chemicals to reconstitute the smell for more exact identification.

Food remains also are telling. The Lloyds Bank Turd and other specimens reveal curious clues as to the Vikings who occupied York a millennium ago. Contrary to popular myth, "Vikings weren't all warmongering, ale-swilling rapists," Dr. Jones says. In York, they were communal craftsmen and farmers who consumed a healthy, high-fiber diet of grains, fish, seeds and berries. "Hippies, really," Dr. Jones says.

On the other hand, their guts contained a staggering cocktail of parasites. The reason, says Dr. Jones, is that the floors of Viking homes were a mix of dirt and mouse droppings, pigs rooted in the yard, and latrines, if used at all, lay a few feet from wells.

Later settlers weren't much cleaner. Pausing at a quaint street of medieval butchers, known as Shambles, Dr. Jones sketches its appearance in former times. "An open sewer with workers pushing barrows of offal to dump in the river," he says, "and women emptying chamber pots from windows."

Even the grand manor where Henry VIII once stayed with Catherine Howard has only a chute through which sewage drained. "Piles of goo—just a few feet from the door," Dr. Jones says. "And they were royalty!"

Only the Romans, whose sewers still honeycomb subterranean York, escape his censure. He believes that Rome's sanitary engineers, rather than its legions, may have been the true secret to the empire's success. "Without clean water, Roman colonists would have been wiped out by epidemics," he says.

Back at his office, Dr. Jones riffles through the "Urgent" basket and finds a soil sample sent to him for analysis by a colleague in Scotland. As a research fellow at the University of York for 12 years and now a leading paleo-scatologist, Dr. Jones often receives such parcels, including ancient camel dung from Egypt, dog droppings from Thailand and wild boar stools from France. He also monitors academic papers relating to his field, such as "Gastrointestinal Transit Times" and "Latrines and Cesspools of Medieval London."

A zoologist by training, the 41-year-old Dr. Jones began his career studying fish bones. As part of his Ph.D. thesis, he trampled on fish heads and also ate large quantities of kippers, to study how the bones look crushed or digested—the way they typically are found on archaeological sites. Later, when his research turned excremental, Dr. Jones put himself on a high-fiber diet to see if he could match the ancient stools he studies.

"My current research," he adds, "is pretty horrible." In concert with a Dutch doctor, he's studying "nappies and potty training" to better understand the taboos surrounding defecation. Double-seated latrines found in York suggest that our forebears had little notion of privacy about their bodily functions. "Somehow, we lost our innocence," he says.

On Dr. Jones's impetus, a reconstruction of Viking village life in York now includes a figure crouching in the open air, clutching a piece of moss, a precursor of toilet paper. The designers, though, insisted on hiding the man behind a stalk screen, which Dr. Jones regards as "completely ahistorical."

He says America is even more squeamish about its scatological heritage. "In Williamsburg," he complains, "no one talks about latrines at all."

Karl Reinhard, a paleo-scatologist at the University of Nebraska in Lincoln, agrees. "Americans are more comfortable discussing sex than feces," says Dr. Reinhard, who has exchanged ancient samples with Dr. Jones. "People are kind of put off when I explain what I do."

Modern England is more forthright, and also has a long tradition of lavatory humor. Dr. Jones jokes that his ambition now is to found "The Institute of Higher Excrement Studies."

Even the starched-collar workers at the local Lloyds Bank branch take the eponymous excrement in stride. Asked how he feels about the name of York's most famous feces, assistant bank manager Kenneth Fenby just smiles. "We take it as a compliment," he says.

A Scud It's Not, But the Trebuchet Hurls a Mean Piano

Giant Medieval War Machine Is Wowing British Farmers And Scaring the Sheep

---

By Glynn Mapes

7/30/91

ACTON ROUND, ENGLAND—With surprising grace, the grand piano sails through the sky a hundred feet above a pasture here, finally returning to earth in a fortissimo explosion of wood chunks, ivory keys and piano wire.

Nor is the piano the strangest thing to startle the grazing sheep this Sunday morning. A few minutes later, a car soars by—a 1975 blue two-door Hillman, to be exact—following the same flight path and meeting the same loud fate. Pigs fly here, too. In recent months, many dead 500-pound sows (two of them wearing parachutes) have passed overhead, as has the occasional dead horse.

It's the work of Hew Kennedy's medieval siege engine, a four-story-tall, 30-ton behemoth that's the talk of bucolic Shropshire, 140 miles northwest of London. In ancient times, such war machines were dreaded implements of destruction, flinging huge missiles, including plague-ridden horses, over the walls of besieged castles. Only one full-sized one exists today, designed and built by Mr. Kennedy, a wealthy landowner, inventor, military historian and—need it be said?—full-blown eccentric.

At Acton Round Hall, Mr. Kennedy's handsome Georgian manor house here, one enters the bizarre world of a P.G. Wodehouse novel. A stuffed baboon hangs from the dining room chandelier ("Shot it in Africa. Nowhere else to put it," Mr. Kennedy explains). Lining the walls are dozens of halberds and suits of armor. A full suit of Indian elephant armor, rebuilt by Mr. Kennedy, shimmers resplendently on an elephant-size frame. In the garden outside stands a 50-foot-high Chinese pagoda.

Capping this scene, atop a hill on the other side of the 620-acre Kennedy estate, is the siege engine, punctuating the skyline like an oil derrick. Known by its 14th-century French name, trebuchet (pronounced tray-boo-shay), it's not to be confused with a catapult, a much smaller device that throws rocks with a spoon-like arm propelled by twisted ropes or animal gut.

Mr. Kennedy, a burly, energetic 52-year-old, and Richard Barr, his 46-year-old neighbor and partner, have spent a year and £10,000 ($17,000) assembling the trebuchet. They have worked from ancient texts, some in Latin, and crude woodblock engravings of siege weaponry.

The big question is why.

Mr. Kennedy looks puzzled, as if the thought hadn't occurred to him before. "Well, why not? It's bloody good fun!" he finally exclaims. When pressed, he adds that for several hundred years military technicians have been trying fruitlessly to reconstruct a working trebuchet. Cortez built one for the siege of Mexico City. On its first shot, it flung a huge boulder straight up—and then straight down, demolishing the machine. In 1851, Napoleon III had a go at it, as an academic exercise. His trebuchet was poorly balanced and barely managed to hurl the missiles backward. "Ours works a hell of a lot better than the Frogs', which is a satisfaction," Mr. Kennedy says with relish.

How it works seems simple enough. The heart of the siege engine is a three-ton, 60-foot tapered beam made from laminated wood. It's pivoted near the heavy end, to which is attached a weight box filled with 5½ tons of steel bar. Two huge A-frames made from lashed-together tree trunks support a steel axle, around which the beam pivots. When the machine is at rest, the beam is vertical, slender end at the top and weight box just clearing the ground.

When launch time comes, a farm tractor cocks the trebuchet, slowly hauling the slender end of the beam down and the weighted end up. Several dozen nervous sheep, hearing the tractor and knowing what comes next, make a break for the far side of the pasture. A crowd of 60 friends and neighbors buzzes with anticipation as a 30-foot, steel-cable sling is attached—one end to the slender end of the beam and the other to the projectile, in this case a grand piano (purchased by the truckload from a junk dealer).

"If you see the missile coming toward you, simply step aside," Mr. Kennedy shouts to the onlookers.

Then, with a great groaning, the beam is let go. As the counterweight plummets, the piano in its sling whips through an enormous arc, up and over the top of the trebuchet and down the pasture, a flight of 125 yards. The record for pianos is 151 yards (an upright model, with less wind resistance). A 112-pound iron weight made it 235 yards. Dead hogs go for about 175 yards, and horses 100 yards; the field is cratered with the graves of the beasts, buried by a backhoe where they landed.

Mr. Kennedy has been studying and writing about ancient engines of war since his days at Sandhurst, Britain's military academy, some 30 years ago. But what spurred him to build one was, as he puts it, "my nutter cousin" in Northumberland, who put together a pint-sized trebuchet for a county fair. The device hurled porcelain toilets soaked in gasoline and set afire. A local paper described the event under the headline "Those Magnificent Men and Their Flaming Latrines."

Building a full-sized siege engine is a more daunting task. Mr. Kennedy believes that dead horses are the key. That's because engravings usually depict the trebuchets hurling boulders, and there is no way to determine what the rocks weigh, or the counterweight necessary to fling them. But a few drawings show dead horses being loaded onto trebuchets, putrid animals being an early form of biological warfare. Since horses weigh now what they did in the 1300s, the engineering calculations followed easily.

One thing has frustrated Mr. Kennedy and his partner: They haven't found any commercial value for the trebuchet. Says a neighbor helping to carry the piano to the trebuchet, "Too bad Hew can't make the transition between building this marvelous machine and making any money out of it."

It's not for lack of trying. Last year Mr. Kennedy walked onto the English set of the Kevin Costner Robin Hood movie, volunteering his trebuchet for the scene where Robin and his sidekick are catapulted over a wall. "The directors insisted on something made out of plastic and cardboard," he recalls with distaste. "Nobody cares about correctness these days."

More recently, he has been approached by an entrepreneur who wants to bus tourists up from London to see cars and pigs fly through the air. So far, that's come to naught.

Mr. Kennedy looks to the U.S. as his best chance of getting part of his investment back: A theme park could commission him to build an even bigger trebuchet that could throw U.S.-sized cars into the sky. "It's an amusement in America to smash up motorcars, isn't it?" he inquires hopefully.

Finally, there's the prospect of flinging a man into space—a living man, that is. This isn't a new idea, Mr. Kennedy points out: Trebuchets were often used to fling ambassadors and prisoners of war back over castle walls, a sure way to demoralize the opposition.

Some English sports parachutists think they can throw a man in the air and bring him down alive. In a series of experiments on Mr. Kennedy's siege machine, they've thrown several man-size logs and two quarter-ton dead pigs into the air; one of the pigs parachuted gently back to earth, the other landed rather more forcefully.

Trouble is, an accelerometer carried inside the logs recorded a centrifugal force during the launch of as much as 20 Gs (the actual acceleration was zero to 90 miles per hour in 1.5 seconds). Scientists are divided over whether a man can stand that many Gs for more than a second or two before his blood vessels burst.

The parachutists are nonetheless enthusiastic. But Mr. Kennedy thinks the idea may only be pie in the sky.

"It would be splendid to throw a bloke, really splendid," he says wistfully. "He'd float down fine. But he'd float down dead."

Very Dark Plots Are Afoot in England, As Grouse Grow Fat

It's Gamekeeper vs. Poacher
In an Old Feudal Rite;
Dead Bird a 'Calling Card'

By Tony Horwitz

10/18/91

NOCTON, ENGLAND—Late on a dismal night, a man in jungle fatigues steps off 20 paces in his yard and fires into the mist. A lead ball zings through the dark and smacks the exact center of a can of car wax. "Haven't lost me touch," the poacher says, lowering his slingshot. "I hope ol' Alan heard that."

Alan Count is a gamekeeper who lives just two doors away. He, too, is plotting for the season ahead. "This time of year, you don't linger at the pub," he says, testing a high-powered lamp. "You don't want the poacher to know where you're lurking about."

In England each autumn, as pheasants grow fat and leaves fall from trees, gamekeepers and poachers begin a centuries-old rite. Prowling through the dark, deploying everything from horsehair to infrared beams, they duel over game that is reared for the sport of much richer men. At stake is their livelihood, and also their pride.

"The poacher knows most of my tricks and I know most of his," says Mr. Count, a keeper for 35 of his 53 years. "We're heads and tails of the same coin."

Mr. Count's role isn't the romantic one of the gamekeeper who beds Lady Chatterley in D.H. Lawrence's novel. He began his career trapping rats and selling their tails for a ha'penny bounty. Later, he toted bullets and bagged game for a rich huntsman with a waxed mustache and manners to match. "The only thing he ever said to me was 'don't drag them hares through the mud!' " Mr. Count recalls.

Even so, gamekeeping offered some escape from class-ridden rural life. "The land belonged to rich people, and much of it still does," he says. "But if you're a keeper, the land is your beat. It belongs to you."

It also is his to defend. For the gamekeeper, poachers are but one of many pests with which he must wage nonstop guerrilla war. By day he sets traps for stoats and weasels, and uses ferrets to flush out hares. By night, he stalks foxes, feral cats, badgers and other "vermin" that prey on game birds, their eggs or their food. His only ally is a hip flask of sloe gin, "the keeper's drink."

Picking up the potent, garlicky scent of a fox, Mr. Count pans his lamp and spots a pair of flame-red eyes in a beet field. To lure the fox closer, he makes a squeaky sound with his mouth and hands, mimicking a wounded rabbit. "I reckon every predator's entitled to his share," he says, raising his gun. "But the fox is a wanton killer. He'll take every bird he can."

So too does Mr. Count's neighbor in Nocton, a poacher whose nom de guerre is Charley Peace, a 19th-century cat burglar famed for eluding the law. The modern-day Mr. Peace once dreamed of gamekeeping, but when he couldn't find a post turned to poaching instead. He tries, however, to target vast estates.

"I loathe aristocracy," says the 44-year-old laborer, a grizzled man with graying mutton chops. "Game was put on this earth for every man. I'm just part of the natural balance."

The workshop behind his home is decorated with huge antlers. "Them's from the Earl of Ancaster's estate," he chuckles. "Took that stag with a wire snare." His armory also includes a rifle fitted with a home-made silencer, a dragnet for sweeping up partridges, and raisins threaded with horsehair, which catch in a pheasant's throat and leave the bird flapping on the ground.

But Mr. Peace's preferred weapon is a simple, hazel-wood slingshot. "Silent, deadly and efficient," he explains. On bright nights, he picks out the pheasant's silhouette and downs the bird with lead musketballs he crafts himself. "Simplicity itself," he says. "And no need to spit shot out at dinner."

For cover, he relies on a face mask and foul weather. "The only night to go out is when it's fit for neither man nor beast," he says. In the wet and cold, birds roost low in the trees, sound doesn't carry, and keepers are less likely to venture out.

Mr. Peace clears about $400 a week in season illicitly selling poached game on the cheap to willing dealers. And in 25 years, he's been caught only once, when a jittery accomplice turned him in. Reveling in his roguish success, Mr. Peace wears his poaching camouflage to the pub and often leaves a bird or musketball at the scene of the crime, "as me calling card."

Even so, stealthy loners like Mr. Peace are a dying breed. To some degree, gamekeepers tolerate local poachers, particularly "one for the pot" men who catch birds for their own consumption. But city gangs have been moving in, taking 1,000 birds a night and disregarding the small-timer's turf.

To defend against them, some keepers use night-sight binoculars, infrared beams to locate intruders, and rubber pheasants that set off an alarm when hit. The gangs, many of them from depressed mining and mill towns, also have a certain flair. Alan Edwards, a North Yorkshire gamekeeper, has found couples smooching in getaway cars—as decoys, while their partners poach game with lamps and dogs.

Mr. Edwards spends his Friday nights creeping with the fog across the desolate grouse moors. A light flashes in the gloom, shuts off, flashes again. Mr. Edwards checks his watch. "That'd be right," he says. "It's pub letting-out time."

Back in his jeep, he edges forward without lights. But the poachers hear him and break for a waiting car. Mr. Edwards hits on a spotlight and gives chase. "Jill, can you read me?" he yells into his radio phone. Jill is his wife, who relays messages from the Edwards's cottage to the police. On this night, though, she is sound asleep.

Mr. Edwards bluffs instead. "Give it up, lads!" he shouts. "The police are on the way!" The driver, a scowling young skinhead, waves his fist and shouts a threatening obscenity. Then the two men begin a high-speed chase across a wheat field, with the poacher trying to bump Mr. Edwards's truck.

"Not worth getting killed for," Mr. Edwards says, as the car vanishes in the fog. Though poachers only face a fine of about $75, many have criminal records and would rather fight than face the police. Mr. Edwards once was badly beaten; other keepers have been wounded with crossbows, and occasionally shot dead.

For gamekeepers, such risks bring modest rewards. Those on traditional landed estates earn about $300 a week, plus tips from hunters and a range of rather feudal perks: a lonely cottage, coal for the fire, work clothes and a tweed suit to wear on shooting days. Mr. Count, the Nocton keeper, prefers to work for "shooting syndicates" that rent or buy land for use during the hunting season. But to "keep the wolf from the door," he says, he has often had to take second jobs.

This fall, Mr. Count began teaching gamekeeping at the Lincolnshire College of Agriculture. While passing on the age-old wiles of his craft, he also teaches his students how to deal with animal-rights activists, who often appear at hunts, shouting "Scum! Scum! Kill For Fun!" and tootling horns to mislead dogs. If the Labour Party wins next year, it may well try to ban "blood sports," especially fox-hunting, which Oscar Wilde termed "the unspeakable in full pursuit of the uneatable."

"To most people now, we're cruel old bastards who murder and persecute every creature in sight," Mr. Count reflects, dropping a rabbit on the run at 75 yards. "I guess if there's justice in this world, I'll collapse out here one day, where the vermin can feast on me."

Gamekeeping also is under siege on other fronts. Many estates have broken up, thinning keepers' ranks to just 2,500, down from 23,000 in 1911. And as village life wanes, there are fewer men with the appetite or know-how for lonely patrol of woods, moors and fens.

But Mr. Count clings to one consolation: If gamekeepers go the way of the dodo, so too will his lifelong antagonist, Charley Peace. "He's not a villainous character, really," Mr. Count says, slipping out of the pub as his counterpart appears. "So in heaven, he'll still be poaching birds, and I'll still be there chasing after him."

Hapless Hedgehogs
Get a Helping Hand
At St. Tiggywinkles

The British Have a Soft Spot
For the Prickly Critters,
Therefore, This Hospital

By Glynn Mapes

1/8/92

AYLESBURY, ENGLAND—This hospital's intensive-care ward isn't for the spineless.

Medical charts attached to the beds of the 70-odd patients tell terrible tales: severed limbs, fractures, poisonings, internal injuries and brain damage. Some patients are blind, some are in shock. All endure their suffering silently, without complaint.

This is St. Tiggywinkles Hospital, and patients in the ward are hedgehogs. Animal lovers send the critters here from all over England and Wales, often by British Rail's overnight parcel service, which has a special rate for shipping injured hedgehogs here. The eight-year-old hospital opened a new $1.9 million building in November.

St. Tiggywinkles, named after a hedgehog washerwoman in the children's book "Tales From Beatrix Potter," exemplifies the growing affection Britons have for this cute but prickly beast. Informal networks of care givers are springing up throughout Britain. In their homes, they tend hedgehogs poisoned by pesticides, struck by cars or caught up in farm machinery. They feed baby hedgehogs so they will survive the winter.

"Everybody loves the hedgehog. He's a good chap, with nothing at all against his character," declares retired British Army Maj. Adrian Coles, head of the 10,500-member British Hedgehog Protection Society. "All he does is eat beetles, wood lice and slugs—and who likes beetles, wood lice and slugs?"

Indeed, in England hedgehogs are called "the gardener's friend," quite a compliment in this nation of gardeners and a big reason for hedgehogs' booming popularity. "They don't bark, they don't bite and they do good works right outside your backdoor," says Tim Thomas, wildlife officer of the Royal Society for the Prevention of Cruelty to Animals.

The hedgehog's appeal, however, isn't immediately apparent. It sports

5,000 or so sharp quills. It is half the size of a loaf of bread, very likely to be flea-infested and resembles a toilet brush. With its tiny feet hidden by the spines, the animal trundles along as if on wheels, looking like a windup toy. When in danger, it tucks in its head and rolls itself up into a ball, bristling. That usually discourages large hungry animals but has little impact on its biggest predator: the motor vehicle. Hedgehogs are the armadillos of England, flattened by the thousand on roadways. (In Surrey, drivers who hit a hedgehog can confess to a telephone hotline and pay a small, voluntary fine.)

Unrelated to porcupines, hedgehogs don't exist in the wild in North America. They first appeared in Europe 15 million years ago—well before saber-toothed tigers and woolly mammoths—and have always managed to survive their enemies. One was Queen Elizabeth I, who declared them vermin and put a three-pence bounty on their heads, falsely accusing them of sucking milk from cows' udders and stealing grain.

Nonsense, says Elaine Drewery, postmistress of tiny Authorpe, Lincolnshire (pop. 100). "These animals are our heritage—we should be nurturing them."

Considered the doyenne of England's hedgehog ladies, Ms. Drewery, a 52-year-old grandmother, runs Hedgehog Care, a network of about 150 volunteers in the English Midlands who nurse injured and orphaned hedgehogs in their homes. Her cottage, which is also Authorpe's post office and dog-clipping parlor, is teeming with the creatures.

"I regard hedgehogs as a priority—humans take potluck here," she says emphatically, leading a visitor through the kitchen (diagnosis and de-fleaing), the TV room (surgery and antibiotic treatment) and the bathroom (postoperative recovery). At the moment, 72 hedgehogs, in various stages of recovery, are in the house; more are in pens in the garden. Those that recover are set free; the less fortunate get a proper funeral, and Ms. Drewery sends a bereavement card to human benefactors.

Ms. Drewery has no regrets about the sacrifices she has made for hedgehogs. "It may seem like sentiment and sop," she says, "but I've gained from these animals. I haven't given up anything." After a moment's pause, she adds, "Well, I guess I've given up my bathroom."

When tough medical problems arise, however, Ms. Drewery and other hedgehog fanciers turn for advice to Les and Sue Stocker, who run St. Tiggywinkles Hospital. Mr. Stocker, 48, a former accountant, does most of the minor surgery and bone-setting himself in a well-equipped operating room, complete with mini anesthesia machine and heart monitor. A veterinarian, paid on an hourly basis, comes in for amputations and complicated operations. Hernia surgery is often needed for road accident victims. Bad teeth plague all hedgehogs, so patients here get their teeth scaled before they are released.

A few patients even undergo brain surgery. Consider Hercules the hedgehog, who was kicked in the head by a rhinoceros in an English safari park. He survived the operation but is brain-damaged and walks in circles. Hercules is cared for in a volunteer's enclosed garden.

But why all this medical attention for such a common animal?

"A broken leg hurts an ordinary animal as much as it does an endangered species," says Mrs. Stocker, who handles fund raising for the hospital. This kindly approach goes down well with the animal-loving British public. St. Tiggywinkles, which has no government financing, operates in the black.

Schoolchildren are big contributors, so are some major companies: British Petroleum, for example, last year gave $98,000 to equip an operating-room suite. Mr. Stocker also contributes proceeds from wildlife books he writes, including "The Complete Hedgehog," the U.K.'s No. 2 nonfiction best-seller in 1987. Mr. Stocker last week was awarded the M.B.E. (Member of the Order of the British Empire) by Queen Elizabeth II for his work with hedgehogs.

The hospital has expanded into the treatment of all forms of wildlife, from sparrows to deer. Some 10,000 animals were treated last year. In its new facility, the hospital aims to handle 50,000 a year, while offering courses for paramedics as Europe's first wildlife teaching hospital. Atop the new building is a hedgehog weather vane, "so we don't forget our roots," says Mrs. Stocker.

Brits definitely bristle when they think hedgehogs are being mistreated or merely treated with disrespect. Three months ago, bulldozers about to break ground for a nursery school in London's Chelsea district were turned back by irate hedgehog fans. This was the site of Beatrix Potter's childhood home, which was destroyed in the Blitz. The author's beloved pet hedgehog, Tiggy, is buried in the former garden. (Tiggy became Mrs. Tiggy-Winkle in the Potter book.) Because of the furor, the nursery school found another building site.

Hedgehog mania has accounted for at least one business success story: Hedgehog Foods Ltd., one of Europe's biggest makers of organic potato chips, or crisps as the British call them. In 1981, Philip Lewis, a pub owner in Wales and devotee of hedgehog jokes, decided as a lark to produce "hedgehog flavored" crisps. Sales boomed, but it didn't take long for angry hedgehog lovers to blow the whistle, fearing that the crisps actually were made from hedgehogs. In fact, they were flavored with pork fat.

But then, in 1982, Britain's Office of Fair Trading hauled Mr. Lewis into court for false advertising. A settlement ultimately was reached under which Mr. Lewis interviewed gypsies, who actually do eat baked hedgehog, ascertained what hedgehogs taste like and commissioned a flavorings firm to more or less duplicate the flavor. He changed the labels from "hedgehog flavored" to "hedgehog flavor," and all interests were satisfied.

Last year Hedgehog Foods had sales of $3.6 million and is now a major contributor to St. Tiggywinkles Hospital, plugging the hospital on every package. "Looking back, it was a bit gruesome, that flavor," Mr. Lewis concedes.

British Run Mowers
For 12 Long Hours
But Cut No Grass

If You Think That's Strange,
You Haven't Yet Heard
Of Annual Sports Classic

By Glynn Mapes

8/6/90

WISBOROUGH GREEN, ENGLAND—It's a balmy Saturday, the grass needs cutting, and—like suburbanites everywhere—Dan Steward is having trouble starting his lawn mower. Again and again, he yanks on the rope. Finally, the riding machine's engine sputters to life. Mr. Steward leaps aboard, adjusts his crash helmet, checks his headlights and roars off, waving to the cheering crowd.

Crash helmet? Headlights? Cheering crowd?

Welcome to the annual 12-Hour Endurance Classic of the British Lawn Mower Racing Association.

If hell has a suburb, it looks like this. Thick billows of smoke and dust roll across a 20-acre pasture as nearly 60 lawn mowers, souped-up and de-mufflered, scream around at speeds approaching 50 miles an hour. Drivers take corners on two wheels, sometimes leaving the ground altogether as they bounce over ruts and potholes.

The din is brain-rattling, more like chain saws than lawn mowers, with backfires that sound like cannon. From 9 P.M. Saturday to 9 A.M. Sunday, the mowers race through gloom and early morning mist, with only brief pit stops for fuel and repairs. Most diabolical of all, not a blade of grass gets cut: The mower blades have been removed for safety reasons.

Recognized by Britain's Royal Automobile Club as the governing body for lawn-mower racing, the BLMRA has been staging such events for some 18 years. Nearly every summer weekend finds the 200-member group zooming around some farmer's field in England or Wales. Ordinarily the weekend meets consist of 10-minute speed sprints along a "track" marked with bales of straw. High point of the season is the grueling 12-hour event, raced relay-style by teams of three drivers.

This, a BBC commentator observed during the one and only telecast of a race, "is a classic British sport: played by fanatics, under absurd rules, generally in the rain."

If not absurd, the rules are certainly elaborate. Three pages of fine-print dictate everything from the height of front-mounted grass catchers to the shape of the seat. Most importantly, the mowers must have been manufactured and sold to mow home lawns (". . . not golf courses, public parks or the rolling prairies of the American Midwest," the regulations caution) and the engines must be identical to those originally sold with the machine. Among the few modifications allowed are changes in the driving gears or pulleys to send more power to the wheels. In addition to wearing crash helmets, contestants must attach ignition cut-off switches to their bodies so that if they are thrown off, the mower stops.

Lawn-mower races have the festive air of a county fair. Tents and caravans line the track, families lounge in beach chairs and tend barbecues while children and dogs run about. At the 12-hour race, elaborate, flood-lighted pits line the track, each with stocks of spare parts and even arc-welders for repairs. That race draws hundreds of paying spectators. The proceeds go to charity, and commercial sponsorship of individual mowers is prohibited.

Off the track, mower racers are a friendly, easygoing bunch, as befits an organization that had its start in a West Sussex pub. Jim Gavin, general secretary of the BLMRA, recalls that over numerous beers in 1972, he and several other motorsports fans were trying to come up with something different to race.

"All we could think of was combine harvesters, but there were only three or four in the county," says Mr. Gavin, 52, a travel consultant. "Then we realized that, after all, this is England—everybody has a lawn and something to cut it with." Thus was born "the noble sport," as adherents call it. And it soon acquired a proper Latin motto: "Per Herbam ad Astra"—"Through the Grass to the Stars."

The motivation? "It's the cheap man's motor sport, an easy way to get into something very competitive," says Howard Annett, a 40-year-old engineering-firm executive, as he tinkers with his Atco mower. "I'd always been interested in motor racing but never had the money or the courage to do it." Though most of the racers are male, at least four women drive their own mowers and others take part in teams.

The lure of the lawn occasionally draws big names, like former Formula One champion Stirling Moss and sports-car racer Derek Bell, five-time winner of the Le Mans 24-hour endurance race. Teammates Moss and Bell have won the BLMRA's 12-hour race twice.

"It's a great feeling on a fast lawn with the wind at your backs," Mr. Moss says, fondly recalling his team's first win a few years ago. Mr. Bell has some painful memories. "Absolute agony is what it is, bouncing around some great bumpy field in clouds of dust!" he says. "It's like being beaten about by a prizefighter for 12 hours."

It is indeed rough going. Many of the racers wear eight-inch-wide body-builder's belts to keep their innards in place. Minor injuries abound. This year's 12-hour racers suffered several sprained ankles, a dislocated shoulder and numerous bruises and burns. Even the scorer, with a laptop computer, was injured. He had dashed onto the track to pull a driver from under an overturned mower and had grabbed a hot exhaust pipe. He was rushed to a hospital with burns on both hands.

Mower racing shows signs of spreading to the Continent. Last fall, at the invitation of the mayor of Limoges, France, 30 BLMRA drivers hauled their machines across the Channel to race a newly formed group of French mower enthusiasts. What they encountered was a shock, a classic confrontation of the precise English with the free-form French.

Among the machines trotted out by the French: a racer powered by a motorcycle engine, another invention constructed from parts of a Land Rover, and a "mower" built from the bodies of two Citroen 2CVs with a grass catcher bolted to the front. One other French machine had a beach umbrella welded to the back, along with a vase filled with flowers.

"Our first reaction was, 'Hold on, chaps, these things aren't built to our rules and regulations,' " recalls English racer Mr. Annett. More worrisome, the English thought the monster French machines might topple over on them during the race. "We were terrified they would flatten us," says the BLMRA's Mr. Gavin.

Anglo-French diplomacy produced a compromise: The larger French machines would race separately in a newly created class called "super prototypes." The "entente cordiale" resumed, and a good time was had by all.

"The French are all daft as brushes," says Pete Hammerton, another English racer. "But they were great to us, and the food was terrific." The second annual international race is set for Limoges, Sept. 29–30.

In the most recent 12-hour race here, the first-place team racked up 277 miles, more or less without mishap. The Ant Hill Mob team, headed by Dan Steward, the racer who had trouble starting his engine, finished fifth in its class. At the end, however, the engine died again—after 213 miles—and the mower had to be pushed across the line.

The big news of the day was a new world's record set by the Flying Doctors team of Group 1. This special class, which races only once a year in a track adjacent to the riding mowers', is for self-propelled "walk-behind" machines, though "run-behind" would be more apt. A British sportswriter described a Group 1 racer as "a demon nanny being towed by a runaway, supercharged pram."

The 15 members of the Flying Doctors team, aged 12 to 45, managed 105.1 miles during 12 hours, including pit stops for rewelding of chassis and handlebars. This supplants the team's previous record, listed in the Guinness Book of Records, of 101.1 miles, set in 1984.

A Transporting Love
Of Toads Is British
To the Very Core

————

Folk Help Toads Cross Roads
During Mating Season:
Thousands Still Get Squished

————

By Glynn Mapes

3/27/91

HENLEY-ON-THAMES, ENGLAND—Why does the toad cross the road?

For love. And therein lies a tale of woe for the toad—and a story of the compassion of British animal lovers.

We're on toad patrol this miserable, rainy March evening, 30 miles west of London. All around us, thousands of lovelorn toads, awakened from hibernation by the suddenly warm weather, are making a beeline to their ancestral breeding pond, just across the two-lane road running between the towns of Marlow and Henley.

That road is the problem. When the toads are running, cars are running, too, often at speeds unsafe for amorous amphibians. The carnage is dreadful: toads squished by the hundreds, making a sickening mess of the highway. It's a scene repeated throughout Britain every March when, toad experts say, some 20 tons of toads are run over by cars.

But the British are a people concerned with all creatures great and small—especially small. So here on the Henley road, and at 400 other designated toad-crossings in the U.K., some 4,000 volunteers of the national Toads on Roads Campaign slop through the mud with their rain gear, rubber boots, flashlights and plastic pails to carry the toads to safety.

"I don't really like doing it," confides Michael Irwing, a 24-year-old gardener who often stops here on the way home from the local pub to carry toads across the road. "But otherwise, they'd get flattened, and that shouldn't be." Adds Roland Laycock, busy patrolling the side of the road with his two young sons: "It's just great when you hear the toads talking to each other in your bucket—well worth coming out on a night like this."

The toads of Henley are fortunate in more ways than one. In 1987, Toads on Roads volunteers constructed England's first toad tunnel here to help the creatures pass under the highway. Since then, five other toad tunnels have been built in the U.K., not counting one designed for newts. The 10-inch-high tunnels, made of plasticized concrete, are buried shallowly with air vents at road level to maintain a user-friendly degree of dankness.

(To answer the obvious question, toads don't bang their heads on the roof of the tunnel as they hop along. Toads waddle; it's frogs that hop. And toads don't croak like frogs: They peep like chicks.)

Germany, with fewer volunteer groups than Britain, instead applies Teutonic efficiency to its squashed-toad problem: It has built 150 toad tunnels in the past 12 years. The catalyst for the tunnel program was a car accident in Bavaria, where several people were killed or injured when a motorist skidded on rain-soaked toad bodies. New roads near toad breeding ponds are required to include tunnels; in Britain, there is no such law, and the few tunnels that exist have been built largely with donated materials and volunteer labor.

Toad tunneling has become a science. The world's first International Toad Tunnel Conference took place in Rendsburg, West Germany, two years ago. Amphibian specialists, known as herpetologists, presented papers from 10 countries discussing such toad-tunnel arcana as "overshoot" (when the toad misses the tunnel entrance), "drift fencing" (tiny fences designed to overcome overshoot), "the rumble factor" (road noise that disorients the tunnel traveler) and, most mysterious of all, "tunnel hesitation" (why some toads sit for hours at the tunnel entrance, reluctant to enter).

All the concern about toads on roads has improved the critter's lousy public image. The word toad has long been a term of abuse; even Shakespeare dismissed the toad as an ingredient in a witches' stew. Its Latin name, Bufo bufo, and its Greek zoological classification, herpes, haven't helped matters. And many people firmly believe that touching a toad causes warts (not true).

Mr. Toad, the lovable rascal in Kenneth Grahame's "The Wind in the Willows," published in 1908, helped give the toad a better name. (The author lived only a few miles from where the Henley folks carry toads today.) Toads also eat insects and grubs and play an important role in the food chain. But what's really helped their image is the Toads on Roads Campaign and its organizer, Tom Langton, Britain's unofficial toad czar.

"When you get close to toads, you just become very fond of them," says Mr. Langton, a young and very earnest conservation biologist. "We aim to give the toad as much popular appeal as the robin." To that end, boosters distribute such trendy toadiana as bumper stickers, posters and T-shirts emblazoned "Help a Toad Across the Road."

Mr. Langton certifies newly discovered toad crossings for the Department of Transport, which then authorizes erection of traffic-hazard signs bearing a toad silhouette in a red triangle. He also helps organize an annual toad census and maintains a computer data base of the volunteer groups. Last year, he figures, Britons carted some 250,000 toads across the road.

Wyllan Horsfall of Thurgoland, England, has carried her share for some 24 years. She and her group of toad bearers, aged eight to 70, patrol Cote Lane, near her home. "People thought I was a nut when I first started. Now they all join in," Mrs. Horsfall says. The toads made their presence known right after she moved to Thurgoland. She had left her front and back doors ajar while working outside. Suddenly, hundreds of toads were ambling through her house, which apparently lies astride the quickest route to the breeding pond. "I hauled bucketfuls out of my dining room," she recalls grimly.

Not all toads that get hit by cars are goners. A few survive, and of these, the luckiest must be in Aylesbury, England, home of St. Tiggywinkle's Wildlife Hospital. The hospital specializes in patching up road-injured hedgehogs (Mrs. Tiggy-Winkle is a hedgehog in Beatrix Potter's beloved children's books), caring for about 3,000 a year, along with thousands of other animals ranging from birds to deer. Staffers man a toad patrol near the hospital during the mating season and stitch up as many as 20 toads a night—plus the odd frog—in the hedgehog intensive-care ward.

Frogs occasionally pop up in the buckets of toad carriers, much to the delight of any youngsters around. Daniel Laycock, 10, though an enthusiastic member of the Henley toad lift, confesses to being a frog fanatic. "Frogs are prettier," he explains, holding a toad in one hand and the lone frog of the evening in the other.

A visitor this night, however, finds it hard to tell the difference: Both creatures look an unpleasant warty brown; neither is anything like Kermit-green.

Janice Laycock, Daniel's mother and a schoolteacher in Marlow, provides some guidance. "Frogs are long and pointy. Think Fred Astaire," she advises. "Toads are squat. Think Jabba the Hutt."

XI

AFTER
THE FALL

The Nelsons Take In Albania and Find A Singular Souvenir

Land of Zog Isn't at All Like Virginia, Which Is the Point For These Spunky Tourists

By Barry Newman

6/17/92

TIRANA, ALBANIA—"We went on Star Wars," Elizabeth Nelson says.

"Star Tours," her son, Jeff, corrects.

"What others? Oh, I know, It's a Small World."

"The Mad Teacup."

"And the Castle. We covered the whole thing. We went to all the different lands."

Mrs. Nelson, who is 66-years-old, and her 33-year-old son are on a 15-day vacation in Europe. They've just done Euro Disney. Next they'll do Italy, Corsica and Spain. Now they're doing Albania.

"We're on the 11th floor," Mrs. Nelson says in the lobby of the Hotel Tirana after her first night's sleep. "We walked down. The elevators are kinda weird. We don't mind. We slept comfortably. It was very peaceful, except for those gunshots."

Buying stamps at the souvenir stand, Mrs. Nelson encounters a fellow American. "I'm Albanian," he says. "I live in Michigan." He has come to search for his relatives. "Are you Albanian by origin?" he asks.

"No."

"Then what brought you here?"

"Oh, tourism." The man pauses and looks Mrs. Nelson over. She has on a crisp blue-and-white striped blouse, soft-cotton trousers and sneakers. She has short white hair and a friendly smile.

"Are you a sort of missionary?" he asks.

"No," says Mrs. Nelson. "We just came over."

Genc Caushi, one of Albtourist's two guides, stands chewing a toothpick. "Let's move!" he says. The Nelsons heft their bags, push through the crowd of beggars, and get into a chauffeured red Peugeot for one ride Euro Disney didn't have: Communism's Haunted House.

Albania has nice mountains. It has the Albanian Riviera—miles of empty beach stretching from civil war in Croatia to package tours in Greece. It also has chaos. Ending a gruesome tyranny this past year, the people ran amok. Democratic government has only just taken hold. Law and order—for example, persuading people not to shoot off guns in the middle of the night—is one of its goals. So is growing food.

Someday, Albania is sure to be a pleasant place for tourists to go. At present, most Albanians consider it an ideal place to get out of. Jeff and his mother aren't totally up on this. Mrs. Nelson's only guidebook is Nagel's Albania, which describes the dead dictator, Enver Hoxha, as "a man of luminous intelligence imbued with French humanist culture." Riding north on the road to Shkodra, she has a lot of questions for Mr. Caushi.

"All these people standing around, they don't have jobs?" Right. "The animals look small—is that nutrition?" Correct. "Do you have free lunches at schools?" No. "Do you have pasteurized milk?" What's that?

Jeff looks out the back-seat window while Mrs. Nelson, sitting behind the Peugeot's driver, leans up and feeds questions into Mr. Caushi's left ear.

Why are so few trucks on the road? "Very little to deliver." Why have so many buildings been pulled down? "Anarchy."

The Nelsons notice the rounded concrete pillboxes that cover Albania like a pox. Mr. Caushi tells them how Hoxha had them built to ward off an imagined Soviet invasion.

"What are they used for now?" Mrs. Nelson asks.

"Toilets."

"Did you say storage?"

"Toilets!" Mr. Caushi explains.

Mrs. Nelson turns to a traveler tagging along and says, "I hope you won't make us look shallow." Perish the thought. Anybody who goes to Euro Disney and then Albania may be kind of weird, but not shallow. The Nelsons get around.

They went to Saigon in 1964, when Jeff was five; Mr. Nelson was captain of a destroyer. They moved to Arlington, Va., in 1969, where Mrs. Nelson taught elementary school until she retired, at 62, in 1987. At home, she makes dinner, walks the dog. "It's kinda dull." Her husband likes group tours. But once a year of late, Mrs. Nelson flies someplace, gets a car, and just goes.

Jeff has her spirit. He was born deaf and is blind in one eye, but that didn't stop him getting on his bike in 1987 and cycling around the world for 1,274 days. He hit Indonesia, Nepal, Jordan, Uganda and 52 other countries. Albania was one of the few that didn't let him in; he's making up for that now. His mother, who has been to Norway, Russia, Greece and Kenya, came partly because she remembers Albania's King Zog, but mainly to get out of the house.

"I just think it's very difficult," she says, "to be around the same kind of people all the time."

The car pulls up to the 15th-century tomb of Skanderbeg, a rare Albanian hero whose bones weren't dug up this year, and then pushes on to the day's second and last historic site—the Rozafat Citadel, a weedy ruin where several families are having a picnic.

"The foundations were laid by the Illyrians," Mr. Caushi says, walking the ramparts. "And with the split of the Roman Empire . . ."

"Italiano!" a young man shouts, rushing up to Mrs. Nelson. She smiles and says, "American." The man is thunderstruck. "Thank you very much!" he screams. "Washington! Bush!" More young people run up. "Where you from? Why you here?" One yells, "Cigarettes!"

"Sorry," Mrs. Nelson says, "I don't smoke." But the youth won't let up. Shouting, "A gift!" he pulls out two cigarettes and presses them on her. Mrs. Nelson blinks and takes them. "Thank you very much," she says.

"There was never much to see in this castle," Mr. Caushi says back in the car. He has a problem. Leading tours of foreign fellow travelers in the old days, he'd point out such sites as the Karl Marx Hydroelectric Station and the Friedrich Engels Power Station. With those off the tour, he has to improvise, as in: "This area stinks because of chemical plant. All the time stinks."

Riding into Shkodra, which resembles South-Central Los Angeles, Mr. Caushi says, "This is Shkodra, founded 3rd century B.C., and that is Communist Party building, burned in act of revenge." "You mean recently?" Mrs. Nelson asks. The car brings them to Shkodra's one restaurant for a lunch of salty meat washed down by the contents of a familiar-looking bottle labeled "Joke" instead of "Coke."

"This is smuggled from Greece," the guide explains.

And there ends day one. Over the next four, the Nelsons will travel south, where Mrs. Nelson will meet an English ambulance driver and pick up her only souvenir: "The best composite rock I've ever seen." But now, she and Jeff are hurtling toward tonight's hotel, 65 miles away in the port of Durres.

The driver seems intent on simulating Big Thunder Mountain. Squealing around a bend one wild moment, he opens his door to check for a flat. Jouncing in back, Mrs. Nelson comes to a judgment about this country. "A travel agent," she says, "wouldn't recommend it to an ordinary tourist." Beside the driver, Mr. Caushi sleeps.

"So, we are here," he says, waking up to the flaky seafront facade of the Adriatic Hotel. The Nelsons lug their bags up to the lobby. On the wall hangs the slogan of the country's first private airline: "You need to leave Albania?"

They check in and walk out onto the empty verandah. The beach is pretty, except for those pillboxes. Jeff takes off his shoes and goes down to test the water.

"Very peaceful," he says, coming back. "Ten years from now, it'll be crowded, totally different. Just like Katmandu."

Russian Psychiatrist Tries to Make Sure Cosmonaut Stays Up

But the Last Soviet Is Down About His Long Flight; An Odd Victim of Politics

By Adi Ignatius

2/5/92

MOSCOW—Whenever Sergei Krikalev gets on the phone, a little man with glasses and a beard listens in. He's Alexander Slyed, Mr. Krikalev's psychiatrist.

It isn't an ideal arrangement, because Dr. Slyed's patient is always off in space—quite literally.

Dr. Slyed is Russia's psychiatrist to the stars, the psychological link to the two cosmonauts aboard the Mir space station orbiting high above his office at Spaceflight Control Center outside Moscow.

It's never an easy job, and these days it's particularly delicate. Mr. Krikalev, who has been in space for eight months, is dying to come home to be with his wife and two-year-old daughter and to see the enormous changes that have taken place in his country.

But space officials pressured Mr. Krikalev, a flight engineer, to agree to remain for another four months in what cosmonauts refer to as the "tin can." How does Mr. Krikalev feel about that? "He isn't exactly thrilled," says the doctor. "Let's just say he's nostalgic."

On May 18, 1991, when the cosmonaut left the planet, Mikhail Gorbachev still ruled something called the Soviet Union. Communism held sway. Prices were low. Ukraine was called "The Ukraine." And Mr. Krikalev's hometown was named Leningrad. It's St. Petersburg now.

Today, Mr. Krikalev, whose uniform bears the insignia "U.S.S.R.," is the last Soviet. He has a colleague in the space station—flight commander Alexander Volkov—but Mr. Volkov just rocketed in last October. Mr. Krikalev "will have big problems adapting when he gets back to earth, especially dealing with the market economy," says Dr. Slyed. "Emotionally, I doubt he's ready for this."

When anti-reform elements in Moscow launched the coup attempt in August, Mr. Krikalev, 32, was noticeably upset. After hearing the news, he refused to make contact with mission control for two consecutive orbits. Finally, Mr. Krikalev spoke in a bitter, metallic tone. "Yes," he said. "We've heard the news."

That piece of conversation was easy for Dr. Slyed to interpret: "How could you jokers on earth have allowed this to happen?" But it's not always so simple. Every 90 minutes, traveling at a speed of 14,000 miles an hour, the Mir completes an orbit and comes into contact with ground control. For just 10 minutes or so, there is phone contact, and then nothing for another 90 minutes. Mr. Krikalev has made about 4,200 orbits so far.

"As a psychiatrist, you have to develop a sensitivity to sound and intonation," says Dr. Slyed. "Normally, you see people and you get information from their body language and appearance. We have to compensate, like blind people do. It's an art form, really."

And an important one, too. Soviet officials discovered how important when they had to bring a pair of cosmonauts home early during a flight in the '70s. They fought "like a cat and a dog," Dr. Slyed says, and finally one declared: "If you don't bring us down to earth now, I'm not going to work with this corpse anymore."

Sitting in the vast control room, Dr. Slyed listens to every word from the cosmonauts. He makes judgments about their visual memory and their capacity for logic. He advises commanders on what experiments the cosmonauts can handle that day. He also has access to a soundproof room, in which he can speak privately with the cosmonauts. He does that only about twice a week, though. "People in the space center get all worried if they see the psychiatrist talking to the cosmonauts for long," he explains.

During his sessions, the cosmonauts generally don't take well to direct questions about their problems. So Dr. Slyed tries indirect routes, opening a conversation, for example, with an observation such as, "Boy, the weather in Moscow sure is crummy." If the cosmonauts leap in—"Things are bad here, too"—the session is under way.

Boredom is a big problem. The two men work most of their waking hours, taking some time off for meals and a spin on the exercycle. "Free time basically consists of looking out the window," says Victor Blagov, deputy director of the space flight. For kicks, Mr. Krikalev sometimes entertains TV viewers at ground control by squeezing his coffee out of its tube. It forms a ball and hangs in front of him until he moves forward to gulp it down.

There is particular concern about Mr. Krikalev because of the unusual length of his flight. Mr. Blagov says it generally takes three months just to get used to things. The initial sensation, he says, is of being in a bottomless elevator shaft after the cable breaks. The next three months are the best. "The cosmonaut gets the sense that he is in heaven," Dr. Slyed says. "He closes his eyes and knows exactly where his instruments are. He looks down at earth and knows where everything on the planet is."

But soon after, problems begin to develop. "The constant anticipation that something bad is going to happen begins to work at their subconscious," says Dr. Slyed. "Every one of them knows that three millimeters separates him from a vacuum. If, God forbid, those three millimeters were to be punctured, there is basically nothing that could save them."

As a result, six months in space is considered optimal. But Mr. Krikalev's desire to return fell victim to political and economic pressures.

The political pressure originates in Kazakhstan, the former Soviet republic that is the base for much of the space program. Even as Mr. Krikalev orbited the earth, the leader of Kazakhstan pressured Russia to send the first Kazakh cosmonaut to space. So a flight was hastily arranged in October, which normally would have included cosmonauts to relieve those on the Mir. Unfortunately, because of the big rush, there wasn't time to find an engineer to replace Mr. Krikalev.

So Mr. Krikalev's original partner in space came home. The Kazakh cosmonaut just went up and came right back down. And Mr. Volkov, who flew into space with the Kazakh, remained at the Mir station. So did Mr. Krikalev.

It would cost perhaps $3 million to send a rocket to get Mr. Krikalev. That's a lot of money to the Russian space program, which is actively courting U.S. investment to overcome its cash woes. While Mr. Blagov insists that Russia would send up a rescue rocket, the pressure on Mr. Krikalev to stay is strong. "He doesn't want to hurt his chances of continuing to work in this field," says his wife, Elena Teryokhina, who speaks to her husband about once a week.

Mr. Krikalev did, however, negotiate a deal: He agreed to stay longer in return for permission to undertake another space walk. Normally, cosmonauts are permitted to perform the dangerous, but prestigious, walks only once per flight. Mr. Krikalev will soon do his second.

If all goes well, Mr. Krikalev will finally return to earth in springtime, barely missing the record of 366 days in space set by two cosmonauts in 1987–88. There was little fanfare when Mr. Krikalev took off, and there will likely be even less when he lands. He'll probably touch down in the barren fields in Kazakhstan, where he'll be met by a small group of family members and officials, who will put him in a wheelchair and take him away for observation.

Gypsy Peddler Goes
From the Frying Pan
... To the Frying Pan

———

Wladyslaw Misiel Sees Warsaw
Through Years of Change
And Just Takes the Heat

———

By Barry Newman

10/19/92

WARSAW—A thoroughfare called Marszalkowska traverses the heart of Warsaw between two Communist eyesores, the Sezam department store and the Palace of Culture. Its wide sidewalk was a placid promenade until swarms of traders descended on it in 1990. In 1991, the city shooed the traders away, making the new order a little more orderly.

But Wladyslaw Misiel stood his ground.

"Things around here change," he says. "I don't change. I've been here all the time, and I'm still here."

Mr. Misiel, who is 45, has black hair and a black mustache. He wears patched, shiny blue trousers and a jacket with the English words "Selection of Fashion" stitched on the front. He staked out his spot, a few yards down from the entrance to Sezam, 20 years ago. Mr. Misiel is a Polish-born Gypsy. He sells frying pans.

A good frying pan was a thing of rarity in people's Poland. I learned this in late 1986, when my landlady gave me one made of aluminum that bonded chemically with kielbasa. The state allegedly made Teflon pans under license from DuPont Co., but hardly anybody had seen one. Searching the sagging shelves of Sezam's housewares floor was like mining bauxite. Only the state dollar shop, Pewex, sold Western pans. On my way there from Sezam, I came across Mr. Misiel.

Marszalkowska's one private retailer stood against a blank wall with three pans at his feet. I picked one up. It was made of thick steel. It had heft. Mr. Misiel wanted $8, a fortune in Poland at the time. I offered $1.70, and he settled for $2.50. I took the pan home, seasoned it and fried happily ever after.

Then came capitalism. By late 1990, Marszalkowska's sidewalk had turned into a souk, lined end to end with blue-and-yellow tents and metal stalls. On a windy evening in November, the stall keepers had hung out lanterns and stayed open late. The crowds moved past them like lava, picking up shoes, jackets, jeans, books, tapes, toys, toiletries. And midway along the street, near the entrance to Sezam, there was Mr. Misiel.

"It has changed," he said. "It was forbidden to trade before. The militia chased you. Now, you can sell anything."

He sat on a stool, his pans set out on a small folding table. More pans were stacked on the ledge behind him.

"Sales are up, three times at least," he said. "I sell 60 a day right here. I make these myself. I have materials and machinery. Ten of us are making 1,000 a day. We sell all over Poland. We'll make big pans as well, copper pans. Nothing's stopping me now."

Except, perhaps, force of habit.

In March 1991, Warsaw's city fathers decided to eschew downtown Dhaka as their urban ideal. "People selling, dirty streets," an official said then. "It is absolutely unacceptable if we are coming back to Europe." The police went in and swept the traders of Marszalkowska away. Some scattered to other streets. Some took over vacated state shops. Mr. Misiel just folded his table and stood up.

Today, Marszalkowska's sidewalk isn't much more crowded than it was in 1986. A glass-walled McDonald's has opened to the right of Sezam. To the left, people gather at Warsaw's first outdoor cash machine; it looks as if a vandal, or maybe a frazzled customer, has taken an ice pick to its bulletproof window. Mr. Misiel stands next to the machine, three pans at his feet and one twirling in his hand.

He bangs the pan as a possible customer walks up, then turns cool when he learns we've met before. "You mean I gave you the same name?" he says. He steps into the flow of strollers, sidles up to a small woman and bangs his pan.

"How much?" she says. He wants $6. She offers $3. He sighs and says, "All right." Then he moves into the path of a large man. "How much?" Mr. Misiel wants $7. "Expensive," says the man. Mr. Misiel differs. "It's steel. Feel how heavy." The man says, "Does that mean it's good?" and brushes by. Mr. Misiel pursues, whispering that he will take $5. The man shakes him off and walks on.

As Mr. Misiel has noted, things have changed. Three years after the revolution, a frying pan from which food can be removed without a chisel is no longer the holy grail of Polish kitchenware.

In Sezam, where the shelves still sag under a ton of state-made aluminum, the mythical Teflon pan has materialized. It comes in two colors, has a see-through lid and sells for $11. The Olkusz Plant of Enameled Dishes makes it. The plant employs 3,200 people and is due to go private. It used to ship Teflon pans to Poland's fraternal partners. Now that the brotherhood has dissolved, the Poles have so much Teflon they could ski on it.

"A lot of people," says a woman shopping in Sezam, "think our Teflon is better than the Teflon in the West."

Pewex, the state shop where Poles once paid dollars for Western pans, has fallen on hard times. It was set to open a glamorous department store in a new building with blue-tinted windows, next to the Holiday Inn. But Pewex couldn't afford the rent, and the space was snapped up by Zbigniew Bogusz, Warsaw's trader of traders.

Mr. Bogusz was already a busy man when I met him in 1987. He lived in a whitewashed house on the city's edge, employing 30 people to make jewelry in his own workshop. "Things are changing here," he said even then. "You have to earn profits." In 1991, he leaped into retail, and opened Warsaw's first private department store—in the Stalinist Palace of Culture. This year, he jumped to his new, untainted location, christening it the Bogusz Center.

On the fourth floor, he sells $8,500 fur coats from Italy and, on the first floor, German frying pans of cast iron and surgical steel with a layer of copper sandwiched between. They go for $85.

Besieged by salesmen, Mr. Bogusz has no time for a frying-pan interview, but his manager, Ludwik Nowakowski, says "ours sell very well." He adds, "They're made of a composition of metals. My grandmother had a Gypsy frying pan. They're totally different. Now you can fry without fat. Steel needs fat. Gypsy frying pans have never changed."

On Marszalkowska, the sun has broken weakly through the clouds. A beggar kneels on the sidewalk holding a sign that says, "Help me." Near Mr. Misiel, a man opens a case of cloths that resemble napkins; when slept on, his literature assures, they emit energy that "removes fatigue, exhaustion and apathy."

Reluctantly, Mr. Misiel lights the man's cigarette. In the old days, he at least had the sidewalk to himself.

"In communism, there was no Teflon," he says glumly. "Teflon is bad for the health. And these Western pans—yes, they're good, but that's a pan for a lifetime. I could eat for a month for what they cost."

Far down the street, two policemen come into view. The beggar and the man with the miraculous napkins disappear. Shouldering his carryall, Mr. Misiel says, "That's enough talk for today, OK?" And until the policemen pass, he mixes with the crowd, banging the bottom of his steel pan.

After Being Lenin
And Stalin, It's Hard
Being Merely Igor

––––––

He Posed for Statues of Greats;
Now Russian Model Wants
Acclaim as Model Russian

––––––

By Adi Ignatius

12/7/92

MOSCOW—Igor Basanko stands at the base of "The Worker and Collective Farm Girl," a 75-ton monument to socialist realism that towers above a Moscow exhibition ground. Fifty-five years ago, he posed as the worker in the sculpture.

"I used to look like that, no kidding," says the heavily bundled old man, gazing skyward at the impossibly muscular proletarian hero. "Well, maybe the artist added a few things."

Mr. Basanko thrusts his right arm back and lifts his left arm skyward, imitating the statue's pose. "Every time I look at this monument, I see myself and I remember the pride we used to feel in our country," he says. "I also remember how hard it was to stand like this."

For decades, Mr. Basanko was the premier male model for the Soviet art machine's obsessively produced inspirational works. A simple man with little education, the then strapping six-foot, 183-pound weight lifter was ideally cast as the virtuous and muscular paragon of the Soviet era.

Mr. Basanko stood for the country's most prominent sculptors and painters in the poses of Lenin, Stalin, assorted workers and peasants and—in his most challenging assignment—each and every one of the "26 Commissars of Baku." His likenesses appeared in bronze and granite in factories and parks across the country and even overseas. "They turned them out like pancakes," Mr. Basanko says.

"Basanko has always been able to capture the essence of the great Soviet heroic figures," says Vladimir Zhuchkov, an instructor at Moscow's Stroganov Arts-Industrial School. "And he's got great legs."

As a young man, Mr. Basanko dreamed of becoming a circus strongman. But in 1932, a professional photographer caught sight of the youthful athlete with the golden smile and bulging biceps, and invited Mr. Basanko to pose for a studio session. Mr. Basanko was a natural, and a career was born.

But time is quickly passing Mr. Basanko by. The body has aged, turning Mr. Basanko—still fit, however—into a hulk of sagging muscle. Moreover, the proud spirit of the Soviet masses that Mr. Basanko once captured in his poses now is generally dismissed as anachronistic or as crass propaganda.

"It upsets me that no one is doing socialist realism nowadays," says Mr. Basanko, who speaks with a booming voice. "Those works inspired the Soviet people with positive feelings."

It's especially distressing that some of the most prominent statues— the Lenins, the Stalins, the Felix Dzerzhinskys (organizer of the Soviet secret police)—have been torn down by officials and angry mobs alike in the post-Communist era. "You can't destroy history," says Mr. Basanko. "Those idiots! They know nothing about art."

Maybe not. But there is little demand nowadays for the heavy-handed, didactic art of the Soviet era, especially art that would demand a wrinkled, 78-year-old model. Nonetheless, Mr. Basanko remains loyal to his craft and scrambles to find what work he can. Five days a week, he takes the bus to the In Memory of 1905 School of Arts, where he poses for art classes.

On a recent morning, Mr. Basanko is hard at work, sitting stiffly in a chair, fully clothed. In his left hand is a cement scraper: He is a construction worker. For this, Mr. Basanko makes 25 rubles (six cents) an hour.

Across the room is another model: an aged babushka. She sits stone faced, bundled up in a heavy overcoat, her head wrapped in a dark scarf. Between the pair stand a dozen students in their 20s, each with a paint brush and an easel, studying these elderly visages and trying to capture something of their essence. Mr. Basanko maintains his expression, displaying the purposeful, but blank, look that characterized Stalinist socialist realism.

"There's something wrong with the heat in the school," Mr. Basanko complains when the session is finished. "I've been sitting in the cold for four days."

Back home, Mr. Basanko has to walk the one flight up to his apartment. "The elevator doesn't work," he says, gasping for breath, as he fumbles for his door key in the grimy unlit corridor.

Inside, he takes a seat at the table in his simple, sparsely furnished living room. A statuette of Lenin, for which Mr. Basanko once modeled, stands on a shelf.

Mr. Basanko picks up the statuette, which depicts the Soviet leader studying a book. "I always wondered," Mr. Basanko says, " 'What is he supposed to be reading?' But it would have been rude to ask."

When Mr. Basanko posed as Lenin, artists generally deleted a few muscles, to replicate the slight revolutionary's frame. "I didn't really have the right body for Lenin," Mr. Basanko says. "But I used to love to do him. He was more dynamic than Stalin, always moving."

Mr. Basanko never made much money for his work. But posing as Stalin offered certain privileges. "They would press the uniform really well before I put it on," Mr. Basanko says. He begins to reminisce, and adopts the Stalin pose: head back, eyes wide, right arm bent across his chest.

"While I was posing as Stalin, a sculptor once told me to live the image," Mr. Basanko says. "I recalled having seen Stalin at a military parade talking to the soldiers. It almost brought me to tears." After a pause, he adds: "I would gladly do Stalin again, any time."

Mr. Basanko recalls, too, posing for the statue of the Russian warrior-liberator, which still stands in Berlin's Treptow Park. The figure grips a sword in his right hand, and is smashing a swastika with his boot. Under his left arm, the soldier is cradling a young girl.

The sculptor, Yevgeny Vuchetich, had Mr. Basanko pose for long hours in a hot studio in full military dress, including an overcoat. Initially, Mr. Basanko was clutching a doll. "Then Vuchetich's maid volunteered to bring in her baby," he says. "So there I was, in stifling heat, trying to hang on to a squirming baby. But the sculpture turned out beautifully."

For all the success that Mr. Basanko has had in pretending to be someone else, he has failed to win much glory for himself. For years, he has been petitioning the state to recognize him as an "Honored Worker in the Cultural Sphere." To make his case, he carries around a stack of old letters from institutes and artists he has worked for. They praise his dedication, his posture, his muscles.

The official recognition, if it ever comes, would have little value in post-Soviet Russia, though it might boost his modest pension slightly. Nonetheless, he spends most of his idle hours trying to persuade the cultural bureaucracy to grant it to him. "I've worked so long," he says. "It would be an honor to me."

He recalls the well-known model, Sonya Osipovich, who in the 1950s was bestowed a medal of labor, one of the highest honors a Soviet worker could receive. "There was never another model like her," says Mr. Basanko. "Even during the war, even when it was freezing, she would agree to pose in the nude."

XII

PORTS
OF CALL

How Khartoum
Won No. 1 Ranking
As a Hardship Post

Floods, Famine and Pestilence
Give Sudan a Bible Flavor;
A Place to Escape Phones

By Tony Horwitz

4/26/89

When Allah created the Sudan, Allah laughed.
—SUDANESE PROVERB

KHARTOUM, SUDAN—At Sudan's Natural History museum, the Living Collection is mostly dead.

Rusted pipes recently poisoned the tank of Nile fish. A snake, starved for lack of rabbits, decomposes in its pen. Nearby, an uncaged monkey forages through heaps of jagged metal, discarded jawbones and dead birds. "It is hard to run a museum without any resources," says the acting caretaker, Fathi Al-Rabaa.

Mr. Al-Rabaa's office has seven phone lines, all dead. This is usual; many phones in the capital city of Khartoum haven't rung for years. On the street outside, one of Khartoum's main arteries, potholes are big enough to swallow pedestrians. Power lines droop on broken sidewalks, a hazard when there is power, which there often isn't. During a typical week this month electricians were on strike, as were bank workers, bus drivers, pilots, postal workers, doctors, pharmacists, engineers and university staff.

"In most African cities, you can bribe your way through the chaos," says Geoff Bulley, a British relief worker. "Here, it's so far gone that you often can't find anyone to pay."

Even in good times, this nation of 25 million people, 500 tribes, 115 languages and 60 political parties is almost unmanageable. In bad times, like the past 12 months, Sudanese also must endure war, floods, famine, locusts and pestilence. "It's like living in the Bible," says American aid worker Wendy Wakeman, who recently had malaria.

Yet much of Sudan's misery is man-made. Last year's floods produced a bumper grain harvest, but problems with labor and transport wasted half. Khartoum's whimsical parliament reshuffles ministers and laws so routinely that planning is impossible; the last coalition fell after just six weeks. The infrastructure is so neglected that walking is the only reliable transport, walkie-talkie the only sure way to communicate.

"It's hard to call this a developing country because most of the movement is the other way," says Abdul Rahman Abu Zayd, a political analyst.

State-owned Sudan Air typifies the country's chaos. The airline's timetable is meaningless; flights routinely skip scheduled stops, make unplanned layovers of several days, leave without passengers—or most commonly, don't leave at all. In late March, Sudan Air pilots went on strike. It was an empty gesture; the airline's entire fleet was already grounded due to maintenance problems and lack of jet fuel.

In 1983, a Sudan Air 707 landed at night in the White Nile. Though accounts differ, pilots say the navigator mistook the river for the runway; miraculously, everyone made it ashore. Last year, officials in London declared a Sudan Air plane unfit and sent it home empty. Passengers joke that the airline's international code, SD, stands for "sudden death."

"No sensible person flies Sudan Air unless they absolutely must," says John Pott, an engineer with the World Health Organization. "Of course, when you absolutely must, you can be sure the plane won't take off anyway."

Sudan pays little on a foreign debt of $14 billion and the country is responsible for a third of all overdue payments to the International Monetary Fund. The value of imports is treble that of exports. Many factories crawl at 5% capacity while inflation rages at 100%.

Sudanese with skills quickly flee overseas. "Those without skills stay to run the government," says Ali Abdalla Ali, an Oxford-educated economist.

Last year, Mr. Ali founded a newspaper called Sudanese Business. "We posed ourselves the question, 'Is there a meaningful private sector in Sudan and what are its prospects?' " he says.

After six months, he thinks he has found the answer: "Sudan has no stability, no private initiative, no hard currency and not a single clear policy." Asked what he would advise foreign investors, Mr. Ali responds: "I'd have to tell them, 'Please, go away.' "

For Khartoum's 4,000 or so Westerners, the capital can be dreary. A once-lively nightlife ended abruptly in 1983 when officials dumped the city's alcohol supply in the Blue Nile and instituted Islamic law. Even venturing out at night is hazardous; trigger-happy soldiers lurk in the unlit streets, and there is an 11 p.m. curfew (though, like all else in Khartoum, laxly enforced).

Before the U.S. closed its embassy in Afghanistan, Kabul was widely regarded as the world's worst posting. Now it's Khartoum.

"No matter what index you use—weather, isolation, health, access to Western amenities—it ranks at or near the bottom," says one American.

Adds an unhappy Marine: "Except for the North Jersey shore, it's the ugliest place I've ever seen."

Asked if there's anything they like, some Westerners say they get a lot of reading done, or that they enjoy the fact their phone hasn't rung in years. Americans also receive a pay raise of 25%—the State Department's maximum level of hardship bonus.

The city's three to four million Sudanese don't have that cushion. Their life is a ceaseless grind of bread lines, gas lines, strikes and power outages. Unlike most Third World capitals, Khartoum residents often suffer more than town and village dwellers.

"The further you are from the bureaucracy, the better off you are," says Bona Malwal, editor of the Sudan Times. Also, black marketeers siphon off goods to the hinterland, where profit margins are higher. Shortages in Khartoum are so acute that rural visitors often bring food and other supplies with them to the city.

"People don't live here, they just manage," says Mr. Malwal, as the lights in his office flicker. "If it gets any worse, there could be anarchy and bloodshed."

Most would say anarchy already has begun. Price rises in December sparked three days of rioting and rumors of coups. Hundreds, perhaps thousands, sleep on downtown streets each night, defecating in vacant lots and begging passersby for money.

Hundreds more stream in each day from the war-torn south, or from the eight bordering countries, some of which are in as much turmoil as Sudan. They settle in garbage dumps, in stripped cars, or with luck, in camps run by aid groups.

"I've been here since I lost my fingers in 1969," says Hassan Hamid, who commutes from a lepers' colony to beg at downtown mosques. "Life is hard, but we Sudanese are very patient people."

Khartoum is a city of glaring contrasts. Huts of straw and cow dung abut neighborhoods filled with vast brick villas and new Mercedes, often paid for with black market profits or with funds sent by the 300,000 Sudanese working abroad.

Last year, when an estimated 250,000 civilians starved, diplomats say that a government minister collected $4 million in "signature bonuses" for authorizing export of half the country's sorghum harvest.

"No one was embarrassed about it—that's just the way things are done," says a Western diplomat. Says another: "Pressuring this government to reform is like trying to pressure Jell-O."

Few analysts offer any notion of how to turn Sudan around. Most agree that an end to the civil war and efficient use of the country's vast resources would be a start. But many wonder if Sudan, the product of colonial map-making, makes sense as a nation.

"You can't decree national identity," says Mr. Abu Zayd, the political analyst. "Unless people put Sudan before tribe and religion, we'll be left as we are, with everyone living by their own wits."

Others believe that only a strongman, such as the exiled military leader, Jaafar Numeiri, can set the country straight. More than a century ago, the British general Charles George Gordon came to a similarly despairing conclusion, but doubted there would be any takers.

"I do not advocate the keeping of the Sudan by us, it is a useless place and we could not govern it," he wrote in Khartoum, shortly before Sudanese insurgents killed him and kicked out the British. "The Sudan could be made to pay its expenses, but it would need a dictator, and I would not take the post if offered to me."

Iceland Has Elves,
Who Live in Rocks,
Nowhere to Be Seen

Roads Are Diverted to Avoid
Disturbing Elf Dwellings;
'Odd Shapes in the Stone'

By Tony Horwitz

7/13/90

EGILSSTATHIR, ICELAND—It is a mile between farms in this bleak outpost of fog and stone, but just a few paces to the nearest hidden home.

"A family moved in here years ago," says Helgi Hallgrimsson, tapping a large boulder. "They raise cows, I think." A family down the road herds sheep. They live in a tree trunk. Generally, though, elves prefer stones. "It is easier to find such housing," Mr. Hallgrimsson says, standing on a hill that is bare except for a few Siberian pines.

Returning to his own simple farmhouse, Mr. Hallgrimsson dines on bread made with sheep's blood, and curdled milk mixed with moss. Asked if the rock dwellers eat similar fare, he responds: "Probably so. But you know, they have never invited me to visit."

Mr. Hallgrimsson's neighbors are "huldufolk," a word meaning "hidden people." They also are known as "alfar," or elves. While Iceland isn't the only country with elves—Ireland and Sweden have them, too—few are so accommodating to unseen citizens. Icelandic highways dogleg to skirt large rocks, lest engineers dislodge the occupants of "enchanted spots." Farmers politely leave fields unplowed because hidden people need hay for their hidden cows. Huldufolk homes appear on environmental-impact statements, and factory construction can sometimes halt while elves find someplace else to live.

"The only thing we haven't done is give huldufolk the vote," says Stefan Stefansson, a fisherman in Reykjavík, the nation's capital. Like many Icelanders, he is slippery on the subject of elves. "Do I believe in huldufolk?" he asks, staring into his beer. "I am one."

When more than 900 people were asked the question in a University of Iceland survey, 55% said the existence of huldufolk (and fairies) is possible, probable or certain. Only 10% answered, "impossible." Erlendur Haraldsson, the psychologist who conducted the survey, wasn't surprised.

Nor does he think Icelanders are particularly superstitious. "This isn't America," he says. "We have very few UFOs."

If aliens ever should land here, they would no doubt feel at home. When work began last year on an asphalt path in Reykjavík, surveyors' instruments vanished and computers developed glitches. The landscape architect directing the project suspected supernatural mischief. She called in a well-known psychic, Erla Stefansdottir, to investigate.

Visiting the site, the 53-year-old piano teacher pats the top of a rock mottled with lichen. "Just knocking to see if anyone is home," she says. Thereupon a man with a long beard and breeches emerges from the rock—visible to her though not to this reporter. "He's laughing at us," she says. "He thinks we're crazy to be standing here staring at him."

On her advice, the city rerouted the path to skirt this and another inhabited rock. In the nearby town of Kopavogur, "Elf Hill Road" narrows to one lane as it passes a rocky outcropping. An attempt last year to widen the road ended abruptly when a new jackhammer broke on the first day of work. Town officials refer to the unseen rock dweller on an adjoining lot as "the old man at No. 102."

Elves in Iceland are as old as the hills. According to Nordic lore, some of them are hills. Elves arrived in Iceland with the Vikings and Celtic slaves who settled here 1,000 years ago. Extreme isolation, and Iceland's sagas and oral lore, kept supernatural beliefs alive. So did Iceland's weird landscape. Bubbling with volcanoes, geysers and boiling mud pits, Iceland is so lunar in parts that it has been used to train astronauts.

Iceland also is sparsely populated, with just 250,000 people occupying an area the size of Ohio. "In such a lonely place, it is natural to fill out the landscape with elves," says Hallfredur Eiriksson, a leading Icelandic folklorist.

Perhaps it is only natural that Icelandic elves resemble humans, rather than the dwarfish, often malevolent goblins of Scandinavian legend. Country huldufolk fish for herring, raise sheep and attend church, just like other folk. And in a society so peaceful that it has no army and few police stations open on weekends, humans and huldufolk usually get on well. Midwives have told Mr. Eiriksson about delivering elf babies. Farmers say they have milked elf cows. Sometimes, the two peoples fall in love, though affairs of the heart often end badly.

"It should be nice to have invisible in-laws, but really it can create problems," says Mr. Eiriksson.

Icelanders who are skeptical about elves treat the issue delicately, as an American parent might field a child's questions about Santa Claus. Haukur Gudmasson, a Shell Oil salesman, is that rare Icelander who openly declares: "This talk of huldufolk is nonsense." But, later in the conversation, he recalls his 16 years in the merchant marine: "Whenever I worked in the engine room," he says, "there was another man—not a real person—there at my side." The fellow was blond, wore a wool sweater and helped Mr. Gudmasson with his work. Could he have been an elf? The salesman bristles. "A ghost, maybe," he says. "But I certainly don't go around seeing people in stones."

Very few Icelanders do, but almost everyone can tell when elves are about. Guthmunder Svafarsson, a veteran road engineer, remembers the time he tried to blast through a ridge while building a highway in the north. Bulldozers broke down, and residents had nightmares. Normally, he says, a simple elf-diversion would have done the trick. But this was a major project, with an added complication: The rock wasn't merely occupied, it was cursed.

"We had discussions," the engineer says, by which he means that a medium contacted both the elves and the deceased woman who had hexed the rock. They were of one mind: Build over, rather than through, the ridge. "I was furious," says Mr. Svafarsson, who has encountered elf delays on other occasions. "But what could I do? Everyone except me believed in elves."

Work on a fish-meal factory in nearby Akureyri also ceased when elves sabotaged machines. In that case, however, talks proved fruitful. The elves said construction could resume, but that they first needed three weeks to vacate. Workmen obliged.

Through one man's efforts, elf advocacy is becoming a sophisticated science. Mr. Hallgrimsson, the farmer in stony Egilsstathir, began his career as a botanist, specializing in mushrooms. While gathering fungi, he collected folk tales as well. Drawing on oral testimony and written records, he now is mapping Iceland's supernatural population.

He presented road builders in Akureyri with a detailed map of the elf harbor and metropolis their highway would bisect (they built it anyway). When plans were drawn up for an aluminum smelter, which has yet to be built, he inserted a map with a legend that includes: "Huldufolk Dwellings, Other Spirits, Odd Shapes in the Stone." In Egilsstathir, he has also gathered data on dwarfs, trolls and a humped serpent, called "the Worm," that lives in a lake.

Mr. Hallgrimsson, a 55-year-old with merry blue eyes and a pointy gray beard, looks rather like a storybook elf himself. Oddly, given all his research, he remains an agnostic on the question of whether huldufolk truly exist. As a scientist, he is most comfortable with empirical evidence, and so far all his information is secondhand.

"It would be enough," he says wistfully, "to see one elf."

The 70 Million Sheep Roving New Zealand Create Quite a Stink

Fluffy Ruminants Produce Enough Gas to Run a Car Or Ruin the Atmosphere

---

By Geraldine Brooks

6/30/87

WELLINGTON, NEW ZEALAND—The sun eases up over a lush horizon, turning blades of grass into filaments of gold. Sheep, fluffy as cotton balls, gleam in the early morning light.

It's the kind of scene that makes you want to throw back your head and take a deep breath of fresh air. Don't. What you're likely to get is a mouthful of methane.

New Zealand may pride itself on its pristine landscapes and its rigorous environmental standards. It may eschew nuclear energy and build clean hydroelectric plants instead of dirty smokestacks. But that hasn't saved the country from the ravages of polluters.

The villains aren't cigar-chomping industrialists plotting in some multinational boardroom. They're sheep, millions of them, munching away on New Zealand's verdant hillsides.

Flatulent sheep, to be blunt about it. "Sheep are very efficient methane producers," says David Lowe, a geophysicist with the New Zealand Institute of Nuclear Sciences. Humans, he says, produce very little.

"If you could hook up a sheep to the carburetor of your car, you could run it for several kilometers a day," Mr. Lowe says. "To power the same vehicle by people, you'd need a whole football team and a couple of kegs of beer."

Trouble is, scientists haven't figured out how to hook sheep to cars, so instead of being a useful power source, the ruminants' copious methane output simply creates pollution.

The problem is particularly acute in New Zealand because the country of three million people has more than 70 million sheep. Each produces about five gallons of methane a day.

That means the local sheep population is producing almost 2.5 billion gallons of foul-smelling gas every week, making New Zealand a big contributor to potentially serious environmental hazards.

Analysis of ancient air bubbles trapped in Antarctic ice shows that 30,000 years ago the concentration of methane in the Earth's atmosphere was only a third as much as it is today.

Along with carbon dioxide, whose atmospheric presence also is increasing alarmingly, scientists fear methane will contribute to the phenomenon known as the greenhouse effect, which could cause a dangerous rise in the Earth's temperatures and even a melting of the polar ice caps. While scientists know that higher levels of carbon dioxide are caused mainly by industry, the source of all the methane remains mysterious.

"One thing's for sure, it isn't just New Zealand's sheep," says Mr. Lowe. Other ruminants, such as cows, have in their digestive systems the same cellulose-eating bacteria, which produce methane. But the methane rogues' gallery also includes rice paddies, fossil fuels, volcanoes, Amazonian swamps and termites.

But why the drastic increase over the years in methane? Mr. Lowe and his colleague Rodger Sparks, a nuclear physicist, are trying to find out.

Through radiocarbon dating, the scientists can determine the age of various types of methane in the air, distinguishing recently produced gas from methane that is eons old. And by taking atomic "fingerprints" of methanes from various sources, the scientists hope to pinpoint which methanes come from sheep, swamps, people or industry.

But collecting methane samples isn't for the queasy. Sheep methane comes from a local agricultural university that is conducting research into the animals' digestion. The unfortunate sheep in these experiments have tubes protruding from their intestines, which makes methane collection simple, if unpleasant.

"It's horrible to look at and horrible to smell," says Mr. Sparks, who leaves most of the sample-collecting to Mr. Lowe.

When the scientists need human methane, Mr. Lowe calls at the local sewage-treatment works. The centerpiece of the plant is a 33-foot-high tank, filled to the brim with what the plant superintendent, Chris Butler, politely calls sludge.

The methane that rises from the mess is drawn away down a wide pipe and used to heat boilers that power the plant. Mr. Butler has his own hypothesis about the sudden increase in atmospheric methane. "It must parallel the rise of modern-day politicians," he says.

To get his specimen, Mr. Lowe, armed with a half-gallon vacuum flask and a dishcloth, gingerly approaches a valve in the pipe. "I've done some strange things in this job, but this is the strangest," says the scientist, wrapping the cloth around the valve to form a seal as he turns the tap.

A powerful burst of methane hisses forth. The smell is just about as bad as you would expect. Mr. Lowe's face crumples. "One of these days I'm going to have to talk Rodger into doing this," he gasps.

Mr. Lowe's next sample-gathering task isn't as malodorous, but it can be just as onerous. It requires a trip to what he calls the clean-air factory—a bleak outcrop named Baring Head, where winds from the Antarctic first hit land after howling across thousands of miles of open sea.

Mr. Lowe gets his cleanest samples during southerly gales. That means he must do battle with blasts of icy wind as he sets up an array of flasks and pipes to trap air samples. "It's probably the cleanest air in the world," Mr. Lowe boasts. "In the Northern Hemisphere there isn't any clean air left."

To prove the point, the clean-air factory exports its product. It is hard to know what customs officers make of the apparently empty flasks regularly dispatched to destinations such as the Scripps Institution of Oceanography in San Diego, Calif., where the air is used in carbon dioxide research.

Back at the Institute of Nuclear Sciences, Messrs. Lowe and Sparks reduce the air samples to carbon particles that can be dated. So far, the scientists have found that about 75% of methane in the atmosphere is biological and of very recent origin.

Over coffee in the lab's cafeteria, the two researchers ponder a solution to the world's methane problem. "We can't just continue to use the atmosphere as a garbage dump for five billion people," Mr. Lowe says.

But a growing world population has to be fed, and that means more rice paddies, more livestock and more methane. "It's hard to figure how you cut down methane emissions," Mr. Lowe muses glumly. "About all we can do is stop eating."

Mr. Sparks stares into his coffee cup. "People will resist that," he says.

For the Bushmen, It's Not the Gods That Must Be Crazy

Tribesmen in Namibia Smoke Winstons and Drink Coke, But Politics Baffles Them

---

By Roger Thurow

7/13/89

BUSHMANLAND, NAMIBIA—In the precious shade of a gnarled Combretum tree, two dozen Ju/wa Bushmen, squatting in the dust like baseball catchers, pass around metal pipes stuffed with tobacco and talk about forming a government. In bush politics, this is as close as you get to a smoke-filled room.

"The white man has spoken for us too often. We must have a government to speak for ourselves," says one of the men in the gentle clicking language of the Bushmen. "Yes, yes," clicks another. "We must be organized, we must make our own laws."

Suddenly, in the nearby village, a man running on high-octane bush beer bursts out of a mud hut and begins chasing his wife, threatening to shoot her with his bow and arrow. The gathering disperses; the man's aim isn't to be trusted. Politics, centuries late in coming to Bushmanland, will have to wait.

For many millennia, the Bushmen had no need for governments or laws, or even for leaders, as they roamed freely across southern Africa, hunting and gathering in the Kalahari region of what is now Botswana and Namibia. But in the past several decades, the politically mute Bushmen have seen their once-vast foraging territory whittled down to a rectangular-shaped piece of earth called Bushmanland, in northeastern Namibia.

They lost 70% of their territory with a stroke of a white man's pen when South Africa applied its apartheid policy to Namibia and carved out homelands for various non-white ethnic groups. Now, with these homeland borders sure to fall away as Namibia gets its independence from South Africa later this year, the Bushmen fear that their little rectangle will be grabbed by covetous trophy hunters, conservationists and cattle ranchers.

This is what brought the wizened elders together under the spreading shade tree, and it is what brings them back after the bow-and-arrow chase. They represent about 1,000 Ju/wa (one of seven linguistic groups among the Bushmen) who are struggling to make a go of sedentary village life on the hardscrabble plains of eastern Bushmanland—the last group of Bushmen in southern Africa still living independently on a slice of their ancestral land. The 40,000 Bushmen still in Botswana are working for cattle ranchers who have moved in on their land. The rest of Namibia's 33,000 Bushmen—out of a total Namibian population of 1.2 million people—labor for white or black masters on commercial farms across the country, or they work as janitors or cooks or carry guns in the South African army. Or they starve.

"We must have a law among ourselves to protect our land. This will give us strength," says Tsamko Toma, who is emerging as the spokesman of the Ju/wa. He is 49 years old and can neither read nor write. But, in his clicks, he speaks with the eloquence of a Jefferson or de Tocqueville. "We do not seek the strength of the strong arm," he tells his people. "We seek the strength of thought."

The deep furrows in Mr. Toma's wrinkled face suggest that this will be a difficult quest, for it requires a fundamental change in this ancient culture. For the supremely individualistic Bushmen, seeking consensus beyond the immediate hunting party and extending their everyday concern beyond the next meal is as foreign as snow.

"Each of us just can't think of his own problems as we have in the past," warns Mr. Toma. "We must begin to think together. We must think as a group for our own survival." He shakes his head, out of both frustration and desperation.

Those gathered under the gnarled tree don't at all fit the image of Bushmen popularized in the film "The Gods Must Be Crazy"—bow-and-arrow hunters dressed only in loincloth and beads and so out of touch with the modern world that a Coca-Cola bottle is a mystery. These Bushmen are fully clothed; some of the men wear ties and jackets for the occasion. They smoke Winstons and Benson & Hedges (in addition to the metal pipes). Crushed Coke cans litter Bushmanland as they do other parts of the world. Bushmen still hunt, but mainly to supplement their farming and cattle raising.

Of the Namibian Bushmen, several thousand have become reliant on the South African army in the past decade, either as soldiers or their dependents, and now are accustomed to earning a salary and simply buying their food. But as the army pulls out of Namibia under the independence plan and the Bushman Battalion is broken up, they are back on their own and facing starvation in western Bushmanland, which is so dry and desolate that wild game rarely ventures there. Those working on the commercial farms aren't much better off. Government and anthropological research several years ago revealed that the annual per capita income of these Bushmen was less than $30, and that only 10% of the children attended school.

Down through the years, as progress swept through southern Africa, Bushmen were routinely shot as if they were vermin by white hunters and developers. But the modern tragedy of the Namibian Bushmen goes back to 1960, when the government set up a special department to deal with Bushman affairs and began luring them into Tsumkwe, which was created as the department's headquarters in Bushmanland. Soon, the Ju/wa were abandoning the hunter-gatherer life to become janitors and mechanics and cooks for the white administrators, and by the time the army arrived in 1978 there were no Bushmen in the bush. (The star of "The Gods Must Be Crazy" was working as a janitor in Tsumkwe when the movie's director put him in loincloth and made him an actor.)

The most devastating blow came with the homelands policy, which officially made the Bushmen wards of the state. While all the other ethnic groups were allowed to set up their own local governments and represent themselves at the national level, the Bushmen were kept under the control of the central government.

"It is a little bit paternalistic, but the Bushmen don't have the education or development to have their own government," says Johannes Swanepoel, an ordained minister of the Dutch Reformed Church who is the commissioner of Bushmanland. "They're not used to this type of politics; they don't understand it. It's no use just catching someone in the bush and telling him he's a politician."

Instead, other politicians decided for the Bushmen, and rarely in their best interest. They decided, for instance, that trophy hunters from Europe and the U.S. can use rifles to hunt game across Bushmanland, but the Bushmen must use only bows and arrows, and can only hunt on foot. As a result, Kgao Debe, who is 56 years old, spent two days in jail in Tsumkwe after being accused of killing a giraffe while on horseback, and Mr. Toma can't get a rifle license to protect his cattle from lions.

"The life of a Bushman depends on the animals," says Mr. Debe, burying his head in his hands. "Why should a white man with a gun be allowed to come and shoot animals that we can't?"

In 1981, small groups of Ju/wa began moving out of Tsumkwe, which they call "the place of death," and resettling in the bush. There, with the aid of the Ju/wa Development Foundation, which is funded by various religious and charitable organizations in Europe and North America, they have established 15 small villages, each with its own farming area and cattle herd. New villages are being planned as fast as water bore-holes can be drilled.

But already these settlements are under threat. Trophy hunters and conservationists alike want to claim a chunk of Bushmanland for a wildlife reserve, and the Herero cattle ranchers to the south covet a wide area of Bushmanland for its virgin grazing land. "Everyone wants a piece of Bushmanland," says Megan Biesele, an American anthropologist who is the project director of the development foundation.

To keep these hands off their land the Ju/wa are trying to stake a claim to their villages now. They have drafted the preamble to a Bushman constitution—"The land of our villages belongs to us because it belonged to our fathers' fathers and our mothers' mothers. No one can just take it from us"—and invited Namibia's two main political parties, the South-West

Africa People's Organization (Swapo) and the Democratic Turnhalle Alliance (DTA), for discussions under the Combretum tree. There, they have tried to reserve a place for themselves in post-independence Namibia and have sought to ensure Bushmen representation in whatever government is formed.

So far, neither party has committed itself to a firm land-use policy, but they pledge to keep the Bushmen in mind. "All of us have become conscious of the fact that the Bushmen have been pushed around for too long," says Katuutire Kaure, a DTA leader. Daniel Tjongarero of Swapo says the Ju/wa made a good case under the Combretum tree. "Everyone was sitting around, participating in the discussion," he says. "It was democracy at work."

Still, it's taking a while for the Bushmen to learn the new political language. "What does this Swapo and DTA mean?" asks an old man named Xashe. "I think they are all my enemies." He is wearing a U.N. T-shirt pledging "free and fair elections" for Namibia, but he confesses to not knowing what an election—free, fair or otherwise—is.

Such ignorance fills Mr. Toma with a sense of urgency. As he makes the rounds of the villages in a rickety blue pickup truck, collecting representatives for the meeting under the Combretum tree, he often looks at his watch and repeats the only English phrase he knows, "Let's go." In a rush of clicks he tells his people, "Time is leaving us."

Life Is No Breeze
When Winds Blow
In the Shetland Isles

Where the Tanker Foundered,
Cats, People, Even Cows
Are Known to Take Flight

By Ken Wells

1/13/93

SUMBURGH HEAD, SCOTLAND—Alexandros Gelis, captain of the oil tanker Braer, and John Rowland, a security guard, have something in common. They've both been mugged by the fiercest denizen of the Shetland Islands: the wind.

The wind blew Capt. Gelis's powerless 797-foot, 45,000-ton tanker onto the rocks near Fitful Head, unleashing a major oil spill. Mr. Rowland's encounter, though not nearly as disastrous, was still hair-raising. On New Year's Day, 1992, the wind picked up the local resident—all 250 pounds of him—and blew him into a ditch about 10 feet away.

He had an inkling this might happen after seeing a 15-foot fishing boat sail through the air above his head. Shetland winds occasionally turn humans, and even cows, into kites. Still, the flying boat, previously strapped down in a neighbor's yard, surprised him. "When a Shetlander ties down a boat," Mr. Rowland explains, "he really ties it down."

In most of the world, winds come and go. Here they blow, blow, blow. They have blown fiercely and unceasingly, with gusts of 100 miles per hour, since the Jan. 5 wreck of the Braer. Visitors are astonished. Locals are not.

In January 1983, gale-force winds blew for 29 straight days. The New Year's wind that blew Mr. Rowland off the ground reached gusts of 201 mph on the Isle of Unst north of here. This is an unofficial reading: The official weather-service wind gauge blew away.

If accurate, the gust easily surpasses the 177 mph wind that the Guinness Book of World Records says blasted the Shetlands in 1962. Few quarrel with the 201 mph figure, since that same gale blew a bird-watcher out of a stone hut and over a cliff several hundred feet away. She died.

The winds begin blowing here in September and often don't stop until April. That's the official gale season. "Of course, we get gales at other times—June, July, at any time," says Alen Gair, a Lerwick weather forecaster.

The reason why gales lash this place is no mystery, though the gales themselves often do mysterious things. The Shetlands sit squarely in the path of choice for icy storms that blow out of the sea near Iceland and howl across the North Sea before slamming into Europe. They usually hit the Shetlands just about the time they've gained full speed.

"Oh, it's a lovely place to fly," says Bill Roy, a helicopter pilot for British International Helicopters, which ferries workers to North Sea oil rigs near here. "I like the fogs that move at 80 mph. They make life interesting."

Then there's the phenomenon called "vortex ring"—a hellish downdraft. It was blamed for the crash of a helicopter offshore here last March that killed 11 people. Computer simulations based on the chopper's data recorder showed that, theoretically, the craft was flying with enough power to safely navigate prevailing gales. But it was suddenly batted out of the air and into the ocean by a huge fist of wind.

Over at the lifeboat station at Lerwick, the Shetland's biggest fishing port, the wind is the main source of business. "Most of our rescue calls are in Force 8 (about 50 mph) winds or better," says Magnus Shearer, secretary of the local lifeboat association. This means putting a 52-foot rescue boat into seas that commonly run to 50 feet, though the odd 100-foot wave is a well-known phenomenon here.

"Yes, you could say it gets rough out there," says Mr. Shearer. Of course, it can even get a little rough onshore. Mr. Shearer has an acquaintance who had a cow blown out of a pasture a few years back. "Maybe there should be signs on Shetland: Beware of flying cows," he adds.

"Oh, sure, my cats fly all the time," says Stephen Chambers, a research scientist who lives in a stone house perched on a bluff over the sea near here. "You kick them out the door for a little exercise and, poof, they're gone. It's quite funny to see."

How far do cats get before landing? Mr. Chambers, quaffing a pint of ale in a local pub to escape a blizzard that is blowing over the Shetlands at this very moment, gestures to a wall about 15 feet away. "But it depends on how strong the wind is, really." (Yes, the cats always land on their feet.)

Mr. Chambers, a physicist, explains a preflight phenomenon that affects humans shortly before they are swept off their feet here. "We call it Shetlands Dancing. You are grabbed by the wind and twirled round-and-round. Then you're usually blown over." This is why wind-wary Shetlanders always walk downwind of roads, so as to not end up in the path of oncoming cars.

Drivers also take peculiar precautions. Mr. Chambers, whose vehicle is a two-ton Land Rover, says he drives with a quarter of a ton of coal in the trunk. "Most people have something similar to keep them on the road," he says. Mr. Chambers added the coal after a recent flying experience in his Rover. "I was airborne for at least 15 feet," he says. "That was enough."

Houses seldom blow over here because ancient Shetlanders, realizing that the wind wasn't to be trifled with, built them out of stone with walls two to three feet thick. Boats don't fare as well. Wrecks on the shore here are battered to smithereens by winds and waves, usually within a day or two, and then disappear.

The tanker Braer was made of slightly sterner stuff. She lasted for a week before being pounded into four pieces yesterday. The same wind that is being blamed for the wreck, however, may yet get credit for limiting the damage of the ensuing 25-million-gallon oil spill. A lot of the oil is being churned up, broken down and blown away into the air.

Dressing for Dinner
Remains an Issue
In the Naked City

In Koversada, Yugoslavia,
It Is Those Still in Clothes
Who Raise the Eyebrows

By Barry Newman

9/9/88

KOVERSADA, YUGOSLAVIA—There are 24,000 naked people in this city, on and off, and that's a story.

"I need a pair of trousers," says a Yugoslav named Alojz in front of the Galanteria Boutique one warm afternoon. He and his girlfriend have on matching sandals. That's all. He carries a bag of empty bottles. She has a filling in her left incisor.

It is past lunchtime, and the crowds are out along Koversada's shopping strip. Like vegetarians in a meat market, they admire shirts and shirts in nicely dressed windows. Down the street is the duty-free shop, then a sports shop and a post office. There's a disco on the corner. Around the corner is a pizzeria, then a restaurant where patrons wear nothing but their starched white napkins. A supermarket is up the hill.

"I like having people around," Alojz says. "At home, I live in a quiet neighborhood."

Here on the west coast of Istria, in the Socialist Republic of Croatia, the hostels, campsites, miniature-golf courses, casinos and wind-surfing schools fuse into an Adriatic sea wall. The trade calls this industrial tourism. What goes on in Koversada and its four suburban camps might be called industrial nudism.

A socialist enterprise of associated labor runs Koversada. It also packs 10 million tins of fish a year, owns a neon-sign plant, a woolen mill and 2,000 sheep, plus 59 hotels, campsites and apartment complexes. They sleep 800,000 guests in a season. Koversada, maybe humanity's greatest undraped conurbation, sleeps more than 100,000. Most of these people come from the well-heeled climes of capitalist Western Europe, making for a profitable mingling of the naked and the red.

Past the main gate on Koversada's broad peninsula stands a row of warning signs. They show a lighted match, a camera and a bikini, all with diagonal lines through them. Morning traffic creeps behind a garbage truck and a man pushing an inflated dinghy. Horns honk. Cars park at odd angles on the roadside, some with tops down, some veiled in canvas against the sun. Trailers fan out for a mile, cheek by jowl, some of them as big as houses, with curtains in the windows.

What shocks a new arrival in Koversada, naturally, are the people, swarms of them, trundling down to the rocky shore: teen-agers on skateboards, old women on bicycles, families toting water wings and umbrellas—a good quarter of them brazenly strutting about in a flagrant state of dress. No kidding, they have clothes on.

"Nobody can force you to take your clothes off," says a man standing by the road in a wristwatch. He is Viennese, has a sacher-torte belly and clearly can't see what the fuss here is all about.

Yugoslavia's leading naked man can. He is Jerko Sladojev, the nation's first dyed-in-the-wool naturist, who keeps his distance in a tourist office seven miles away. To him, nakedness is an all-or-nothing proposition, and Koversada gets his dander up.

"In a naturist camp, everybody doesn't dress," he says. "From morning to night and all night long, they are nude. It's a kind of obsession. But not in Koversada. They are not naturists. They are naked, that's all. I used to try to change it, but the managers don't care. It's commercial. I'm too revolutionary for them."

In 1960, Mr. Sladojev helped found Koversada on a piney islet off the coast. It drew a modest tribe of believers whose uniform lack of uniform reminded Communists, in a way, of the Mao jacket. But soon Koversada expanded to the mainland and turned into a resort for the sort of people who will don shorts at the drop of a hat. Once again, the market triumphs over ideology.

"You have to maintain a certain respect," says Valter Velenik, Koversada's camping director, explaining why he has on a silky black shirt and white slacks. He sits at a table in a busy outdoor cafe, discussing his business.

"Profit," he says, "that's our stimulus here. In a season, we have sales of"—he pulls out a pocket calculator—"$7 million. We make a 30% profit. Camping, you know. Very profitable. We sell the sun. Twenty years ago, you didn't see anybody here in a bathing suit. Now you do. It's more modern, a modern town. We used to have a philosophy; now we have a democracy."

Even so, it can be mortifying for a newcomer to tour Koversada with clothes on. This is one town where the final event in the local beauty contest is not a swimsuit competition. Doctors here, who wear white coats, routinely treat barbecuers for burns in strange places, and male athletes for a certain kind of accident involving a tennis racket. Uniformed police nab intruders by checking for tan lines. If you aren't naked, you could be covering something up.

"I tried to keep my clothes on," says a rare visitor from elsewhere in the East bloc, a woman from Budapest named Zsusza. She came to stay with her elderly parents in one of Koversada's 1,000 motel rooms, where she dresses for an interview. "I tried for 24 hours. I felt an outcast." So she threw in the towel, even for wind surfing.

But some people here are completely uninhibited. "I was embarrassed the first time," says Isabelle, a Dutch tour guide who has stopped her motorbike at the entrance to a mobbed arrival hall. "I had on my uniform and my helmet. It was just the same as when 40 people are dressed and one isn't."

Isabelle removes her helmet. "Now I just don't care anymore," she says. A young man wearing a pair of sneakers walks by and looks her over. Isabelle blushes, but she keeps her shirt on.

The only pure naturists encountered on a trek from end to end through Koversada are Dorothy and Charles Garoutte, members of the American Sunbathing Association from Fresno, Calif. For $1,200 they have bought two weeks in a villa, plus two meals a day and round-trip airfare from London. It's called a "Skinny-Dip Tour."

"I thought about naturism since I was a boy," Mr. Garoutte says on his balcony, looking out over the treetops through tinted glasses. The Garouttes are both 60, but it was 1977 before they took it all off in public. "We joined a camp in Bakersfield," he says, "and stayed until it lost its permit." Mrs. Garoutte adds, "There's always somebody tells you how to live your life."

Mr. Garoutte says, "Some back home said, 'Why go to a Communist country?' As far as I can tell, the place is nice. France is real windy. They have that mistral."

His wife says, "Nobody over here drinks iced tea, though."

The Garouttes are among the few in Koversada who never worry about what, if anything, to wear and when, if ever, to wear it. Some babies wear diapers; others don't. One kid takes his shirt off to swim; his friend puts one on. Some women wear bottoms and no tops, others tops and no bottoms. One man wears a tie.

Most people climb into at least half a bathing suit before they set foot in a supermarket. As they walk out, fumbling with bundles of Band-Aids, bead curtains, clothespins and plucked chickens, they climb back into the altogether. The naked lunch is in fashion here, hard as it is to know where to tuck the napkin. But in Koversada, one dresses for dinner.

"If someone comes in naked, we say nothing," says Peter Lovic, the very-correct headwaiter of Restaurant Koversada. "Most people don't. It's the usual thing in Europe. I really don't know why."

He might check the thermometer. As the sun goes down, so goes the temperature.

Careful cooks slip on aprons. Women collect unmentionables from the launderettes and start ironing evening frocks. A man on a beach chair sits up and puts on an undershirt, sits up again and pulls on his socks. The two Yugoslavs who had gone shopping earlier at the Galanteria Boutique pass by, barely recognizable—he in his new trousers, she in a summer blanket.

Late in the evening, bulkily clad adults pack the disco to watch a bulkily costumed folk group perform. They know no shame. "When it gets cold," says a man, with primordial logic, "you get dressed."

By the time the folk group finishes, it is less than 60 degrees, and the wind is whipping. Now the real Saturnalia begins. All the oldsters go home. A rock band takes the stage. And the lithe, tanned teen-agers of Koversada put on their clothes and go wild.

More Sleaze, Please: Olongapo City Isn't What It Used to Be

Visit to the Philippines Raises
Doubt About Evil Repute
Of a Navy Liberty Town

By James P. Sterba

6/12/85

OLONGAPO CITY, THE PHILIPPINES—Let's talk sleaze.

Connoisseurs of this commodity, who are said to grace the ranks of the U.S. Navy in abundance, will tell you that you haven't graduated beyond the merely indelicate until you've experienced this place. On the fringe of the Subic Bay naval base, Olongapo (pronounced uh-LAHNG-uh-poe) is a pit stop for the Seventh Fleet and reputedly the hottest little liberty port on the entire planet.

Veterans of Tijuana and Times Square may think they know debauchery, but they are in the training-wheel stage when they get here, the experts assert. They say that the reason it took so much work to make "an officer and a gentleman" out of Zach Mayo in the recent movie is because he grew up here amid 500 or so bars, brothels, massage parlors, dives and sideshows where more than 15,000 Filipino "hostesses" do wonders for swabbie morale and the local balance of payments—not to mention the pharmaceutical industry.

They say all this, and some of it may still even be true. But talks with experts, as well as on-site inspections, raise serious questions about the continuing reputation of both today's Seventh Fleet sailors and today's Olongapo City.

Example: A veteran Navy chief, whose eyes seem to mist over when he starts telling stories about the bad old days, swears he recently witnessed two young sailors pick up two bar girls at the Stoned Crow saloon on the Magsaysay Avenue strip and take them back to the base to go bowling.

Example: Surrounded by virtually empty bars, the Big Circus snack bar on a recent afternoon was bustling with sailors and their local "dates." It was "Smurfy Day," and the snack bar was offering a special on Coca-Cola by the pitcher.

Example: At midnight one night, with two supply ships in port, the

Pizzahaus restaurant and bar is where the action is. There is a line outside for tables. A nine-piece show band called the "Heartbeats" is on stage playing bubble-gum rock. A Filipino Marie Osmond look-alike sings and dances, fully clothed, on stage with her two cousins. Her father is the bass player. Her uncle is on rhythm guitar. Sailors are invited on stage to join hands and sing "We Are the World." Manager J. W. Opoy says hard liquor doesn't sell here anymore. Beer, iced tea and soda are the favorites, he says.

To be sure (for those who don't believe any of this and are waiting for the good stuff), Olongapo City retains remnants of raunchiness. And when one or two aircraft-carrier battle groups dock and disgorge 10,000 to 20,000 all-American sailors, the market manages to adjust to meet most demands. Hint: Follow the Marines.

But along the once-notorious Magsaysay Avenue strip, just outside the naval base's main gate, sin is surprisingly subdued, the Navy is well-behaved, street crime has plummeted, and the streets themselves are probably the cleanest in the Philippines. Gone are the squalid brothels (hotels serve as discreet substitutes), the con artists, and what were the most talented 10-year-old wristwatch thieves east of old Saigon. For out-and-out sleaze, you have to hop a bus for Manila.

The man who doesn't hesitate to take credit for this new, relatively wholesome state of affairs is Richard J. Gordon, the 39-year-old mayor. His father, Olongapo's first mayor, was gunned down in 1967 while waging war on the town's "sin city" reputation.

Elected in 1980, Richard Gordon continued the fight and won. He closed the brothels, banned minors from the strip, cracked down on drug dealers, ran gangsters out of town and cleaned up the local police. He organized street vendors to finger pickpockets, teen-age hookers and con men. He organized some 300 bar and club owners into a civic association. He required them to send their bar girls to health clinics twice a month.

The mayor lives in the center of the action, next to Slim's Tavern on Gallagher Street just off the strip. From there he prowls the streets almost nightly, dropping into clubs unannounced, turning up at traffic accidents or arbitrating the occasional bar fight.

Trailing him around takes stamina. One night, after a full day of mayoral duties, he starts touring the strip at 9:30 P.M. and is still at it at 3 A.M., when a visitor cries uncle. At Trax nightclub, his first stop, girls gyrate in bikinis—toplessness is banned—as a band called the Soul Jugglers belts out top-40 rock. The trumpeter plays in the mayor's brass band at local festivals.

Then it's on to the Hot City Disco and Strawberry Fields Disco, where sailors and dates dance and carouse with less lewdness than could be found in suburban Des Moines. Prices are posted: 80 cents a beer; a $2 cover charge on weekends.

"A lot of Manila people are coming up here now," says the mayor. "It's cleaner, safer and cheaper. They bring their families, use the beaches, and come for the festivals we've organized."

The Showboat Supper Club, the mayor promises, has risque comedy. "Hi, Mayor," the comedian shouts as Mr. Gordon sits down. Johnny Carson tells raunchier jokes.

At Zeppelin, the owner has just made a $150,000 investment in strobe lights and renovations to cater to punk rockers. A mean-looking band with Mohawk haircuts, dark glasses and black-leather garb blasts heavy metal sounds through gusts of smoke. The band finishes its number, then invites the mayor to stand up and take a bow. The bar girls scream and applaud the mayor.

For the suspicious, it should be said that a tour of the strip without the mayor revealed similarly placid play, although a few dancers do let their tops down. Part of the reason for this relative wholesomeness, the mayor acknowledges, is that today's young American sailors seem to be a cut above the raucous, Vietnam-hardened escape-seekers of the past. Their officers say they are more dedicated and professional. Old-timers at the chief petty officers' club on base say they're wimps. In any case, they've changed.

T-shirts offer another example. In the old days, collectors could count on the grossest T-shirts imaginable being on sale at the shops in Olongapo. But now the stencils used to print the old favorites hang on the back-room walls of most shops gathering dust. They have to be special-ordered now, but most aren't.

Shirts Syndicate, the biggest shop on the strip, hasn't sold some old favorites in over a year. But it did recently sell one that has a mushroom cloud in the background, a bomber in the foreground and the caption "Now comes Miller time." And it sells several a week captioned "If the good Lord made anything better than San Miguel Beer and Filipino women, He keeps it to Himself."

Across America
In a Rolling Hotel:
Not for the Finicky

Sleeper Buses Give Germans
A Porthole on the World;
1 Dressing Room Fits All

By Ellen Graham

8/19/85

MICHIGAN CITY, IND.—It is 3 A.M., and we are camped beside a pasture in the nation's heartland. Beside me and below me, in the posterior of a 14-ton Mercedes-Benz bus, are 23 sleeping West Germans here for a four-week swing around the United States.

A thunderstorm is raging outside, but my traveling companions slumber on, tucked beneath eiderdowns in three neat rows of eight sleeping compartments, each about the size of a roomy coffin. The bus sways gently with their collective snores and snufflings.

Our home away from home is das Rollende Hotel, a "rolling hotel" operated by Rotel Tours, a privately held travel company in Tittling, West Germany. Filled with budget-minded tourists, 70 of these hulking, portholed sleeping buses crisscross the globe each year, from Katmandu to Machu Picchu and most points in between.

This is how 40,000 Germans each year see the rest of the world.

Whether on the steppes of Afghanistan, the freeways of Los Angeles or here in Indiana, the buses draw incredulous crowds. "The questions are always the same," says David Spaght, our 38-year-old American guide. "First they ask, 'What is it?' Then how we got it here and how many can sleep in it." It is often taken for a horse van, he says, and in New York's Chinatown recently, some men hopped aboard and demanded to be taken to Yonkers Raceway.

For sound sleepers who aren't squeamish about close quarters, a rolling hotel offers one of the world's cheapest outlets for organized wanderlust. This group has paid about $2,000 each for its coast-to-coast U.S. trek, including airfare to and from Frankfurt. I am going along for the three-day New York-to-Chicago leg of the trip. Union regulations prevent Rotel from accepting Americans on its U.S. tours, though they can travel elsewhere with the company. "Most Americans," Mr. Spaght says, "wouldn't find this adequate."

We rendezvous at daybreak one Sunday at a suburban New Jersey trailer park. The "guests," as Rotel calls its clients, have already learned the ropes. Semi-supine in their berths, they wriggle into robes and then descend narrow ladders onto a draped platform that serves as a common dressing room. (By day, the platform folds up to become one side of the bus.) At one time, the dressing area was bisected into male and female sections, but no more. "Europeans aren't as bashful as Americans," Mr. Spaght explains.

The group is a young one for Rotel, which caters to pensioners, and is split about evenly between men and women, adults and students. Among them are an aircraft mechanic and his Elvis Presley–smitten son; a retired Stuttgart journalist and her 14-year-old granddaughter, and an insurance man and his schoolteacher wife.

Early risers help Rudolf Kurz, an unflappable giant of a man who serves as driver, cook and mechanic, prepare a breakfast of coffee, bread and jam.

Mr. Kurz knows the world like the back of his hand. Except for brief annual layovers in his Munich apartment, he has spent the past 21 years driving Rotel buses. He knows how to cadge spare parts in Guatemala and how to set up camp in the shifting winds of Tierra del Fuego. He has strong opinions about the world's best driving conditions (the U.S.) and its worst (Tehran). Once, he says, he crossed the Sahara in 10 days without meeting another vehicle.

He met the company's founder, Georg Hoeltl, back when Rotel was busing pilgrims to Lourdes and Jerusalem, where they camped in tents. But one fateful night in 1958, known in company annals as die Katastrophen-Nacht, a group of campers was swamped by a downpour outside Nice.

Within a year, Mr. Hoeltl had patented his rolling hotel. Its design, Mr. Kurz speculates, may have been inspired by the stacked tombs found in some Italian cemeteries.

Today, Mr. Kurz steers west on the New York Thruway. Later will come Yellowstone and the Grand Canyon, Las Vegas and Disneyland, but now he must push along with 12 hours of hard traveling each day.

To break the monotony, Mr. Spaght lectures. "Germans like thoughts," he says. "Superficial chat won't do. You have to take one topic and stick with it for 15 minutes." As Albany, Schenectady and Syracuse roll by, he discusses, in fluent German, the construction of the Erie Canal, the plight of the U.S. farmer and what loosely translates as "carnivorous capitalists": the Astors, Rockefellers and Vanderbilts. There is a quick quiz on converting miles to kilometers.

No teacher could ask for more diligent students. On small tray tables, many guests take notes as Mr. Spaght talks, usually for 30 minutes at a stretch. Several of them have asked for an explication of the U.S. Social Security system. But because of the length of his planned remarks, Mr. Spaght explains, "I'm saving that for South Dakota."

A snag develops at the Canadian border outside Niagara Falls. Helen Treusch, the retired journalist, lost her passport, visa and $200 when her purse was snatched in New York City. She was issued a new passport there, but without a visa she can't accompany the group into Canada for fear she would be barred from reentering the U.S.

The group appears to take this brush with U.S. street crime in stride. "It can happen anywhere," a businessman shrugs.

While the Germans don slickers to view the falls, Mr. Spaght recrosses the border to help Frau Treusch. He finds her a cheap room and arranges for her to fly the next morning to Detroit, where she can rejoin the tour. She is downcast, for she must leave her granddaughter behind and has to pay the $130 airfare to Detroit.

Guests are told to allow $10 a day for expenses, including the midday meal, and they are frugal. At one Howard Johnson's, a couple and their teen-age son share a chef's salad for lunch. Cheap souvenirs hold little interest, though one teen-ager, to his father's dismay, spent $150 on old rock 'n' roll records in Manhattan.

The night air is abuzz with mosquitoes when the group reassembles at the falls. As usual, there are no stragglers. Horst Maas, the insurance man, is the last to board, and though he is a minute early, the others chide him amiably, pointedly consulting their watches. Teutonic punctuality is "nothing short of phenomenal," says Mr. Spaght, who spent several years studying and teaching in Germany. Scattered to the winds on unfamiliar turf, the guests always manage to regroup on time, the last to appear invariably apologizing, "Oh, am I the last?"

At camp near a neon strip of honeymoon cottages, the men unfold the bus in 10 minutes and everyone scrambles into an assigned berth. As the lights on the shuffleboard court dim, someone warns in German-accented English: "Watch out for grizzly bears!"

Each compartment has a reading lamp, a mesh basket for personal effects and a porthole to admit air. Because guests have access to their luggage only once every three days, they also stow a ration of clothes and underwear, shoes, bathrobes and toiletries in their bunks. At night, most such gear is transferred to the dressing platform, making for congestion rarely seen outside a college dorm.

Claustrophobia is fairly common, Mr. Spaght says. In extreme cases, guests sometimes sleep outdoors until they get over it.

The next morning the bus departs in drizzle, and Mr. Spaght launches into his "Canada in a nutshell" talk to while away a flat stretch of Ontario. During a two-hour lunch break at Detroit's Renaissance Center, the Germans unhesitatingly choose a McDonald's over a Burger King—"because we know what we get there," explains Adam Hueber, the aircraft mechanic. They are enchanted with the John Portman–designed glass elevators and gasp when told a room at the center's Westin Hotel goes for $110 a night.

After a detour to the airport to pick up a visibly relieved Frau Treusch, we press on. "I wish we could have visited an auto factory," one man says wistfully. Even though his charges are prone to doze after lunch, Mr. Spaght proceeds to lecture on urban blight, American cars and Lee Iacocca. He is pleased that the group is warming to his subjects, asking more questions: "What is the average factory wage?" "The cost of an American car?" "Must cars use turn signals?" Money—how Americans make, spend and save it—"is big," Mr. Spaght says. As for 20th-century American history, "they don't need reminding."

During a half-hour tour of a shopping center, a silver-haired American points to the portholes and confesses: "At first I thought it was a bus for dogs." Wherever they go, the Germans are bemused and a bit put off by Americans' instant familiarity.

That night in Michigan City, Mr. Kurz prepares a dinner of fresh vegetable soup, hard-boiled eggs and chocolate pudding. The texture and taste of American bread come in for a lot of criticism. "It just about finished the last group," Mr. Spaght says.

The next day, in blistering heat, the Germans rush a Chicago cop on a Harley-Davidson sidecar motorcycle, snapping pictures as he warns them to guard their wallets. ("Like in Italy," he says.) I depart as the group files into an unprepossessing steakhouse for the much-awaited "T-bone" they have been promised. Awaiting them are La Crosse, Wis.; Deadwood, S.D.; Cody, Wyo., and points west. Then, the flight home from Los Angeles.

For the two guides, however, there will be yet another planeload of Germans waiting in Anaheim, Calif., to be escorted overland back to New York. They are eager to keep moving. Mr. Spaght glances at his partner, grinning: "We are gypsies, eh, Rudy?"

Hate Winter? Here's A Scientist's Answer: Blow Up the Moon

Prof. Abian Says It's Time To Rethink the Cosmos; Others Say That's Lunacy

By *Judith Valente*

4/22/91

AMES, IOWA—Oh, sure, the moon seems nice enough. It illuminates dark nights, makes a wonderful backdrop for lovers and has inspired some fine poetry. "What is there in thee, Moon, that thou shouldst move my heart so potently?" pondered Keats.

But there's a definite dark side to the moon, too, says an Iowa State University mathematics professor named Alexander Abian, and he's not just talking about werewolves. According to the professor, the moon is the source of lousy weather on Earth. So, he says, we should blow it up.

That's right. Blow it up. If the moon's a balloon, we should pop it. No more moon over Miami. No more moonlight serenade. No more moon hitting your eye like a big pizza pie.

Clearly, there's no amore lost between Prof. Abian and the moon. He says he's making this suggestion with the utmost gravity. In fact, he says that's exactly the problem. The moon, he says, exerts a pull on earth that helps tilt the globe on a 23-degree axis. That, in turn, alters the angle that rays from the sun hit earth, causing scorching summers in one part of the world and stormy winters in another. If the moon were gone, earth would rotate more evenly, the sun would warm the planet more evenly and the world would bask in what Prof. Abian calls "eternal spring."

Mr. Abian is no lunatic. He's a respected 68-year-old mathematician who has three theorems named after him, including Abian's Order Relation and Orthogonal Completions for Reduced Rings. He has taught at Iowa State for 24 years and has published more than 200 papers. He says it's time to question the existing order of the solar system and wants scientists to start devising computer models on how to rearrange the universe.

"From the earliest traces of primate fossils some 70 million years ago, no one, but no one, has ever raised the finger of defiance to the celestial organization," he says. "We have been like blind slaves obediently being rotated without our consent." A reduction of the mass of the moon, splitting the moon into two or more pieces or what he calls a "controlled total elimination" of the moon would have immediate effects on earth's weather, he says.

How to accomplish this? Shoot the moon, quite literally. Blast it with nuclear-powered rockets. The moon's distance from earth, about 240,000 miles, would keep any nuclear fallout from contaminating the planet, Prof. Abian says. Plus it would make a great show for a few minutes.

Wouldn't blowing up the moon melt the polar ice caps and cause massive flooding? No, the professor says; ice at the North and South Poles would simply melt more evenly. What would happen to the tides, which the moon governs? They would be "more predictable, with much less fluctuations," he says.

And, most important, what about love? Prof. Abian brushes off the notion that a moonless earth would be a less romantic one. "In some cultures, the moon is associated with ugliness and plainness," he says. "In Russian, there is even an expression: 'To be as dull as the moon.' "

Anyway, he says, once human beings learn the secrets to rearranging the universe, scientists will be able to pluck moons from other planets and bring them closer to earth—but not so close that they interfere with weather. "To those romantics, I say, "OK, you love the moon? I will give you two.' "

Outlandish as this may be, his ideas are actually sparking interest in scientific circles. "The task seems to be feasible and we have many reasons to take it up," beams Jan Kadrnoska of the Czechoslovak Academy of Sciences, one of several foreign scientists who has written seeking more information from Prof. Abian.

But while scientists concede that Prof. Abian's "eternal spring" theory may have some theoretical validity, they also say it's a bad idea to fool Mother Nature. "We all know what are the consequences of many other projects when a man tried to intervene in the natural course of events," warns Soviet Professor E.M. Drobyshevski. Still, Prof. Drobyshevski says he would be willing to pursue Prof. Abian's ideas "with great pleasure" because Soviets suffer some of the worst winters on Earth.

There are other problems, too. "I'd hate to write the environmental-impact statement on this one," says Bevan French, a lunar expert at the National Aeronautics and Space Administration and the author of a book all about the moon called "The Moon Book."

Mr. French thinks several aspects of Prof. Abian's proposal are a bit out of this world. He disputes whether the technology exists to eliminate even a portion of the moon. Even if it did exist, it would first have to be tested somewhere closer to home, he says, "and I don't think the people on earth would like that much."

And what if a large chunk of the moon ended up hitting earth, Mr. French asks. "Sixty-five million years ago, a mere asteroid hit the earth and wiped out the whole dinosaur population," he notes.

Not only that, but Lowell Smith, a senior scientist with the Environmental Protection Agency, worries that the use of nuclear force to blow up parts of the moon would probably violate treaties between the U.S. and the Soviets.

Environmentalists are also concerned about what would happen to living things such as the poor Palolo worms of the South Pacific. The worms rise from the ground to mate only during full moons in October and November. And what about the grunions, those sardine-shaped fish that live in the seas off California? They spawn their eggs on sandy beaches during certain lunar cycles.

Prof. Abian, who has also taught at Oxford and Ohio State, dismisses such concerns. "It has never been proven that our life on earth depends on the presence of the moon," he says with an agitated wave of the hand.

An intense man with a half-moon of wispy white hair, Prof. Abian is no stranger to contrariness. He once considered a career as a classical pianist, but refused to play musical pieces the way their composers intended. "If a passage called for pianissimo [very soft], I'd want to play it fortissimo [very loud]. I knew I'd never succeed."

But the reaction to his proposal, from an angry public that seems positively moonstruck, eclipsed anything he could imagine. He first published his ideas in Abstracts of the American Mathematical Society. Since then, he was interviewed by a German television station and two London newspapers and was featured in a supermarket tabloid with the front-page headline: "Scientists Plot to Blow Up the Moon."

Karen Clute, a teacher at Mound Elementary School in Miamisburg, Ohio, took up the issue with her fourth graders after reading about Prof. Abian's ideas in Omni, a science magazine. Their overwhelming response: To the moon, Alice. "I don't want to hurt your feelings, but the moon is by my window every night. My little sister loves the moon and so do I," Danielle Sugarman wrote to the professor.

She also suggested that having nice weather all year long could get a bit boring. "If a child was born and had never seen snow in his or her life, how do you think they'd feel?" she asked.

But among older students—Prof. Abian's—the tide seems to be turning in his direction. "His theory has been widely misrepresented," says Paul Hertzel, a doctoral student. "He's not simply suggesting 20th-century man blow up the moon. He's saying don't be stagnant. Consider everything. Question everything."

Indeed, "they laughed at Galileo and Copernicus in their day too," Prof. Abian likes to remind others. "The fact of the matter is, the genius of mankind will not tolerate being hostage to the earth's existing orbit forever."

Juliet of Verona Gets a Lot of Letters From the Lovelorn

Her Correspondence Secretary Shepherds All Her Replies; Star-Crossed Saudi Romeo

By Lisa Bannon

11/10/92

Any man that can write may answer a letter.
—WILLIAM SHAKESPEARE
ACT II, SCENE IV "ROMEO AND JULIET"

VERONA, ITALY—Fate bequeathed a strange legacy to this small city in Northern Italy.

As the setting for Shakespeare's 16th-century tragedy "Romeo and Juliet," Verona inherited the curiosity of literary scholars, a celebrated theatrical tradition and several hundred thousand tourists a year.

In the bargain, the city also became the star-crossed lovers' capital of the world.

"We don't know how it started exactly," explains Giulio Tamassia, the bespectacled city spokesman for matters relating to Romeo and Juliet. "But one day in the '30s, these letters started arriving—unprompted— addressed to Juliet. At a certain point somebody decided Juliet should write back."

What began 60 years ago as an occasional correspondence has grown into an industry. This year more than 1,000 letters from the lovelorn will arrive in Verona addressed to Shakespeare's tragic heroine. Many of them land on Mr. Tamassia's desk, with no more of an address than: Juliet, Italy.

"They tend to be sentimental," says Mr. Tamassia, riffling through stacks of musty air mail in the cramped studio that serves as Juliet headquarters. Inside big pink folders are thousands of sorrowful letters, break-your-heart tales of love and loss. They come from all over—a teen-age girl in Guatemala, a businessman in Boston, a high-school teacher in London. Some but not many are written by students in Shakespearean language. About 2% of letters received are addressed to Romeo, but Juliet replies.

"Writing the letter itself is really the first step toward solving the problem," says Mr. Tamassia, a 59-year-old retired businessman who wants it known at the outset that he himself is not Juliet. He is more her correspondence secretary.

"People express feelings in the letters that they would never admit to the person they love. Juliet's story inspires them," he says.

After much rummaging, he pulls out one of his favorites—describing a modern equivalent of the Montague-Capulet family rivalry.

Hala, an 18-year-old Saudi Arabian, wrote in March that she had fallen in love with the only son of her family's mortal enemy. Years ago, in Pakistan, her great-grandfather was responsible for the execution of a man who was using his property for smuggling heroin. From that time on, war was declared between the two families.

Now Hala is in love with a descendant of the executed man. "I am torn between the love for my family, who has made me what I am today, and my love for Omer, the man of my dreams," she wrote.

"Please reply quickly . . . my love, my life and my future all depend on your answer."

Mr. Tamassia shakes his head and exhales a long stream of cigarette smoke. "That one was really dramatic. Do you hear the tone? Juliet didn't know what to say at first." The response Juliet finally hit upon gave Hala several options, one of which was to flee Saudi Arabia with her Romeo. Similar advice might have spared Shakespeare's Juliet from her ultimate demise had she just followed Romeo into exile. Mr. Tamassia says Juliet is still waiting to hear how things turned out for Hala and her true love.

"Juliet tries not to give concrete solutions, but helpful advice and a sense of confidence to help the person discover the solution on his own," says Mr. Tamassia. "It's like talking to a friend."

For traumatic or serious psychological problems, Mr. Tamassia says Juliet seeks advice from a local psychiatrist. A local priest—not unlike Juliet's faithful Friar Lawrence—provides insights into matters spiritual.

A German girl writes mourning the death of her beloved in a recent car accident. "I'm completely desperate, and I can't eat or drink or sleep. What must I do? My life no longer has sense," she writes.

"With letters like this," Mr. Tamassia says, "it's important that the person doesn't feel alone. Juliet would write back that there are difficult moments in life that do not last a whole lifetime, and it is important to have friends to help you through. She should feel like Juliet is her friend."

Many letters, most in fact, are lighter and even playful. "It's a big moment for China right now," he says. "Lots of them are students who want stamps from Italy, or a pen pal, or they want to practice their English." But only about one in 200 is a joke, Mr. Tamassia estimates.

Juliet treats real problems seriously. A Turkish airline steward wrote asking for help in getting a visa for his Chinese girlfriend so she could come to Istanbul to marry him. Mr. Tamassia says Juliet wrote to the

Turkish Embassy in Rome to see what could be done. "We're still waiting to hear what happened," he says, adding that sometimes Juliet will continue a correspondence until a problem is resolved.

Juliet may have been only 12 years old when she pledged her love to Romeo, but Mr. Tamassia nevertheless believes her to be a wise counselor. "She had a very clear idea of her will and desire. She was a mature girl."

He also believes in Juliet's actual existence; she isn't just a fictional creation. Historians disagree among themselves about whether the Shakespeare play is grounded in fact, but the Veronese claim that the presence of Montagues (Montecchi in Italian) in Verona through the centuries lends credence to the story.

Mr. Tamassia, who is married and has two daughters, just happened into his involvement with Juliet and the heartsick. A Verona city clerk who had helped Juliet answer letters for years quit suddenly in the mid-1980s. In the absence of city money to continue the job, Mr. Tamassia, who had retired from the candy business, volunteered to fill the void.

He and Juliet have four student volunteers from the University of Verona who translate English, French, German, Spanish and Russian letters. Turkish and Chinese are more of a problem. "I found a Turkish NATO commander who helps out when he's not too busy," he says. "The local Chinese restaurants will usually lend a hand for Chinese."

Mr. Tamassia himself picks up the tab for postage, office rent, Juliet stickers, post cards and lunch for visiting journalists.

"Destiny left us this responsibility—somebody's got to do it," Mr. Tamassia says.

A foreign correspondent for an American newspaper recently decided to give Juliet a try and wrote a letter asking advice on the difficulties of maintaining a long-distance relationship. Three weeks later, there came the following reply:

"If your Romeo is cast in the same mold as you are, there are no distances. And it's not a given that your two careers will always be in different places. You will have an intense life of work, of expectations, of enthusiasm that only love can offer. Yes, it will be hard to have a happy ending, but I almost envy you the chance."

Juliet's signature on the letter bore a resemblance to Mr. Tamassia's own scrawl.

"It doesn't matter who writes the letters," Mr. Tamassia says, giving away nothing. "It matters what they say."

Lawrence Welk Slept Here; That's Enough For These Visitors

They Stream to His Birthplace
In North Dakota to Soak Up
The Timelessness of It All

By Eric Morgenthaler

8/20/92

STRASBURG, N.D.—Taped accordion music floats from the barn as Jack McDonald wheels his long silver bus, towing a maroon Chevy pickup with a gleaming Harley-Davidson motorcycle in its bed, into the parking lot of the farm where Lawrence Welk was born.

The bus door pops open, and Jack's wife, Yvonne, descends.

A delicate woman in sunglasses, she is, in addition to being a biker, a pianist and a collector of sheet music. And today she is also a pilgrim, having persuaded Jack to interrupt their trip home from the annual Sturgis, S.D., motorcycle rally to visit the birthplace of the late bandleader, whose relentlessly wholesome music has been a television institution since the 1950s.

"I have always been interested in Lawrence Welk," Yvonne explains. She likes to play his music on the electric organ Jack installed in their bus, an erstwhile Greyhound.

It has been almost two years since Mr. Welk's birthplace, just outside this sleepy farm town in the middle of nowhere, became notorious as a symbol of federal spending run amok, with the disclosure that Congress had approved $500,000 to help restore it and set up a settlers museum. The grant was mocked by politicians from President Bush on down, and eventually canceled.

The uproar led to a lot of hurt feelings in Strasburg, a proud little Plains town of 600 people that's so peaceful its police department has an answering machine. Restoration went forward anyway, with private funds, though plans for a museum (where most of the grant money was to be spent) were dropped. And now, seven days a week from May 15 to Sept. 15, the faithful come—6,000 of them in 1991, the first year the farm was open. They turn off Route 83 in their campers and cars and drive up a gravel road lined with barley and wheat fields to the font of champagne music. They pay their $2.50 a head, and they take the tour.

"There's the outdoor privy," says guide Edna Schwab, who is a cousin of Mr. Welk and was raised on the farm. "It works: It doesn't flush."

For all the national criticism, the birthplace, in fact, is nicely done. It is a small prairie farm, with a simple house built nearly a century ago of sturdy sod bricks and later covered with wood siding. The handful of out-buildings includes a "summer kitchen," where the cooking was done this time of year to keep from heating up the house. Many of the furnishings are original. Family pictures, including many of Lawrence, are on the ta-bles. Lawrence's suspenders hang in an armoire.

The tours, conducted by volunteers, often take on the air of a family reunion, as visitors discuss their favorite Welk-show performers as though they were kin.

"What was that girl's name that danced with Bobby?" Doris Andersen, a farm wife from Stratford, Iowa, asks of no one in particular as she in-spects a photo of the orchestra from years ago.

Her husband, Ivan, ponders the question, as does tour guide Elaine Wald, but Mrs. Andersen is first with an answer.

"Bobby and . . . Cissy," she announces.

"Barbara," Mrs. Wald interjects. "Bobby and Barbara."

Mrs. Wald adds: "Bobby married Myron Floren's daughter." And ev-eryone nods.

And everyone is right, so let's translate: Bobby is Bobby Burgess, a dancer on "Lawrence Welk" and one of the original Mouseketeers. His first Welk partner was Barbara Boylan and his second was Cissy King. Myron Floren, Bobby's father-in-law, played accordion with Lawrence Welk for more than three decades.

As long as we're doing trivia: Before hitting upon the phrase "the champagne music of Lawrence Welk"—in 1938 at Pittsburgh's William Penn Hotel—Mr. Welk called his band the Honolulu Fruit Gum Orches-tra and, earlier, the Hotsy Totsy Boys. And despite the champagne music, Mr. Welk was a teetotaler.

Not that any of this would be news to Welk fans. The show long has had almost a cult following. Mamie Eisenhower was a fan. It was first broad-cast nationwide on July 2, 1955, and stayed on the air for 27 years—16 on ABC, then another 11 in syndication. In 1987, the Public Broadcast-ing Service began showing reruns, and 272 stations now carry it every week, making it one of the network's most-watched programs.

"He had a clean show, and that's what people wanted," says Katherine Kramer, who with her husband, Al, owns the Pin Palace, a restaurant and bowling alley where Lawrence, on trips home, used to commandeer the kitchen and cook scrambled eggs for everybody. A sign in the Pin Palace reads: "Don't criticize the coffee—you may be old and weak yourself someday."

The Welk show's vision of America—cheerful and folksy—echoes throughout Strasburg, a nice little town where more than half the resi-dents are retirees and at least that many seem to be related to Lawrence Welk. Lawns are manicured. The four houses on one side of a block on

Main Street have among them nearly 40 lawn ornaments—flamingos, ducks, butterflies, windmills, swans—plus countless wooden tulips. Another house, nearer the highway, has a zebra in front.

Police Chief Greg Brower, asked to name Strasburg's last serious crime, can't come up with one. Chief Brower is virtually a one-man department—he has a part-timer for "street dances and that sort of thing"—which explains the answering machine, turned on when he is on patrol. For emergencies, there's an 800 number.

Folks here are upbeat, even about the winters. "They're not nearly as bad as most people think," says Harvey Mattern, who runs an equipment-leasing service. "Sure, we have our 30 below, but maybe five or 10 days in a year, that's the most."

Lawrence Welk's parents, descendants of German farmers who had migrated to Russia, arrived in this lonely land in 1893 as homesteaders. Lawrence was born 10 years later, the sixth of eight children. When he left the farm at age 21, accordion in tow, to seek his fortune as a musician, he had a third-grade education and spoke only German. When he did learn English, he was embarrassed by his accent. In time, it became his hallmark. His autobiography, published in 1971, is entitled "Wunnerful, Wunnerful!"

Lawrence Welk never saw the restored homestead, which is run by a nonprofit group called Pioneer Heritage Inc. He died May 17 at his home in California, aged 89. The Lennon Sisters, who got their start on his 1955 Christmas show, sang at his funeral.

Three weeks later, the dedication of the homestead went ahead as scheduled. Among the speakers were two stars of the show: "Champagne Lady" Norma Zimmer and Myron Floren, who also played the accordion for the crowd. More than 2,000 people showed up, and traffic backed up for miles. It was, say locals, the first traffic jam in Strasburg's history.

OK, Brett, So It
Isn't Exactly Bulls
Loosed in Pamplona

Still, the Running of the Sheep
In Tiny Reedpoint, Mont.,
Does Have Its Moments

By Eric Morgenthaler

8/30/90

REEDPOINT, MONT.—Before Montana, there was Spain. And in Spain, there is Pamplona. And in Pamplona each July, there is the running of the bulls, in which the mighty animals tear through city streets, from corral to bullring, while thrill-seeking humans try to dodge or outrun them.

Ernest Hemingway used Pamplona as a backdrop for "The Sun Also Rises." As a symbol of adventure and romance, the running of the bulls there is world-famous.

Which brings us to Reedpoint.

Reedpoint isn't world-famous. It is hardly even Montana-famous. It has 96 citizens and seven businesses, and its high school this year should have a graduating class of one, assuming Robert Ulmer doesn't stumble along the way. It is in the wide-open ranch country of the Yellowstone River valley, where the access ramps to Interstates have grates to keep the livestock off the four-lane. Reedpoint has no water system, sewer system, mayor, police force, city government or city taxes. The signs on the highway south of town spell its name as one word; the signs on the railroad north of town spell it as two.

Nonetheless, little Reedpoint has at least one thing that puts it squarely, if gently, in the heroic tradition. As surely as July means Pamplona and the bulls, September means Reedpoint. And the sheep.

Next Sunday, thousands of people are expected to flock to Reedpoint for what is being billed as the "101st Running of the Sheep." (It is actually only the second running of the sheep, but more about that later.) The festivities stretch from morning until midnight, but the main event comes around noon, when a thousand or so sheep will be herded the four blocks down Reedpoint's main street, from the abandoned grain elevators at the north to the Conoco service station at the south, threading their way through the humanity. People can race or pet or mingle with the sheep.

The sheep, unlike the bulls at Pamplona, don't seem to mind.

"The sheep are so docile," says Russell Schlievert, an organizer of the event, which is a civic fund raiser sponsored by a group called the Reedpoint Community Club. "It's a very hands-on thing."

Last year's thing started as a low-budget spoof of a high-priced cattle drive that was the biggest event of Montana's 1989 centennial celebration. Reedpoint ended up attracting an estimated 12,000 people, and it raised enough money to pay for doubling the size of the Reedpoint Memorial Library, to two rooms from one. This year's proceeds will go toward buying a used fire truck and emergency medical equipment for the town.

No one knows how big a crowd to expect this year—or what to expect from the crowd. Last year, many people arrived with their favorite sheep in tow and in costume. One sheep wore tennis shoes. Another was painted to resemble an American flag.

The winner of the Prettiest Ewe contest wore red-and-black satin garters on her legs and a lacy bonnet on her head; her owner, who led the sheep on a leash, wore a matching bonnet and turn-of-the-century satin dress. The Ugliest Sheep winner, by contrast, had a polka-dot look, its shaved coat punctuated with unshorn clumps of wool, which were dyed various colors.

Aside from the beauty pageant, events this year range from a parade to a street dance to a "sheep-to-shawl" contest, which is exactly what it sounds like and is expected to take six hours or so; the shawls will be auctioned. On the cultural front, there are sheepherder-poetry readings. (Sample from last year: The place I lived in wa'nt too clean / It smelled like somethin' died / When I talked to other people / They'd stay on the upwind side.)

And there's the Smelliest Sheepherder event. Last year, it began as a joke, with a few adequately groomed sheepmen gamely getting up on stage to the hoots of the crowd. Suddenly, the real thing—a herder named Festus, straight from the hills—pushed his way through the crowd, climbed up on stage—and literally overwhelmed the competition.

"Everybody else on stage just turned around and walked away and said, 'Hey, it's his,' " says Mr. Schlievert, who emceed the contest. "Then he got up and talked about living on the range with the sheep." (Festus couldn't be located for comment or for determining his last name. He's out with his herd.)

The idea for a sheep drive came when the Reedpoint Community Club began looking last year for a new gimmick to liven up its annual Labor Day weekend fund raiser, Bachelor Daze. That event, which included the auctioning of bachelors, usually attracted a couple of thousand people to town, but the idea was getting old, as were the bachelors.

At the time, the Montana press was playing up something called the Great Montana Centennial Cattle Drive, a six-day extravaganza in which anyone could ride along with the herd and play cowboy at a price of not much more than, say, six days in Paris or Rome. Reedpoint decided that it might be fun to have something a little more down-to-earth. Sheep are about as down-to-earth as you can get; here in cattle country, they're treated as rather a joke. Soon, the Great Montana Centennial Sheep Drive was born.

The parallel with Pamplona's bulls was pointed out by a newspaper reporter in Billings, about 60 miles east of here; Reedpoint folks hadn't heard of Pamplona. But the small-town promoters proved adept at big-city media manipulation.

"We took our sheep to downtown Billings, unloaded them right in front of the TV stations and let them eat their flowers and stuff until they came out and interviewed us," says Chery Leicht, who was secretary-treasurer of the Community Club last year.

The word spread, and on Labor Day weekend, people descended on Reedpoint. Vendors ran out of food by midafternoon. Connie MacLean, the official silk-screener, ran out of T-shirts; after selling 560 of them that day, she later had to print up and mail another 400 to people who left orders. The event was thoroughly homespun: One old ranch lady set up a gas stove on a corner and made fried bread for passersby.

"The Great Montana Centennial Sheep Drive must be the most successful spoof since Orson Welles's 'War of the Worlds' was broadcast in 1938," an editorial in the Billings Gazette declared. "Certainly it was the most fun."

It also brought money into a town that doesn't have much of its own. The high-school girls' basketball team made enough from its hamburger stand to pay for new jerseys and a trip to Billings for the district tournament. And the Community Club netted enough—$9,131—for a 20-by-22-foot addition to the library, a former one-room schoolhouse roughly 12-by-14 feet.

"It was unbelievable," says Librarian Evelyn Burton, a retired schoolteacher, whose house is next door to the library. (People don't have library cards in Reedpoint, because Mrs. Burton knows everyone by name.) Mrs. Burton says that as a result of the expansion, she is considering increasing the library's hours—or, more precisely, hour: It's open from 3 to 4 every Wednesday afternoon.

Given the success of last year's event, there was no question but that it would be revived this year. Indeed, the only issue was what to call it. The organizers settled on the "101st Running of the Sheep"—even though it's only the second—because it's Montana's 101st birthday. "It didn't make much sense to me," says Ms. MacLean, the silk-screener. "But I think they just liked the sound of it."

It sounds like a tradition, an end-of-summer celebration that every year should give Reedpoint its moment in the sun. It might even become a continuing boon to the town's coffers. At least, say many residents, isn't it pretty to think so?

XIII

PERSPECTIVES ON ART

Upon Reflection, High-School Movies Really Were Bizarre

Educational Film Collector Finds Gold in the Oldies; Teens Still Hate Them

By Andrew B. Cohen

1/3/90

Phil has a problem. He can't seem to make friends at his new school. He is a "shy guy," so he tinkers with radios alone in his basement. His father tells him to "pick out the most popular boys and girls and keep an eye on them." Following Dad's advice, Phil becomes a good listener, helpful and polite. By the next class mixer, Phil is Mr. Popularity. And guess what? Seems the gang at school is interested in radios, too!

Thank Richard Prelinger for preserving "Shy Guy," a 1947 educational film that starred Dick York, later Darrin on the television series "Bewitched." Mr. Prelinger, a film collector and media archaeologist, estimates that nearly 600,000 such short films—most shorter than 10 minutes—were produced for schools and businesses between 1920 and 1980, when videotape took over.

Mr. Prelinger, 36 years old, began acquiring these films in 1982 after realizing that no one else was preserving them. He now has more than 20,000. Most came from bankrupt production companies and film labs eager to give them to anyone willing to cart them away.

His library now ranges from camp curios like "Dating: Do's and Don'ts" (1949) and "The Wonderful World of Wash and Wear" (1958) to graver, government-made films like "Sucking Wounds of the Chest" (1952) and "What You Should Know About Biological Warfare" (1951). A few deliver Manichaean lessons—such as "We Drivers" (1936, remade in '49, '55 and '62), a Chevrolet-sponsored cartoon in which Sensible Sam and Reckless Rudolph battle in a "Rocky"-style prizefight for the soul of a motorist.

Mr. Prelinger calls these works "ephemeral films," because they have outlived their original purpose, whether it was helping teen-agers overcome shyness or using silent comedy to show Frigidaire dealers that good service puts "Sand on the Slippery Sidewalks of Sales" (1927).

But, he adds, they are also ciphers to "everyday history," to the mores and values of American society. "I'm interested in finding films that show the conflicts and contradictions of their time," Mr. Prelinger says.

One favorite is a teen-guidance film called "A Date With Your Family" (1950). Ostensibly a lesson in dinner-table etiquette, it asserts that mealtime should be treated as if it were a social event of one's choosing. But under a veneer of prandial pleasantries lies what Mr. Prelinger calls a "really creepy" portrayal of suburban family life.

"These boys greet their dad as though they are genuinely glad to see him, as though they had really missed being away from him during the day and are anxious to talk to him," says the narrator of this unintentional film noir. "The women of this family seem to feel that they owe it to the men of the family to look relaxed, rested and attractive at dinnertime."

The narrator advises "pleasant, unemotional conversation" for the family gathering and subtly warns the viewer to "Tell Mother how good the food is. Maybe Sis rates a compliment, too. It makes them want to continue pleasing you."

Another Prelinger favorite is "From Dawn to Sunset" (1937), a big-budget documentary that depicts a day in the life of workers at a dozen General Motors facilities around the country. To the rhythm of martial music, masses of stone-faced workers march through factory gates, where men and machinery unite in productive harmony. Later, at home, the workers use their well-earned GM dollars to buy goods for their families, enriching the community in the process.

Mr. Prelinger notes that GM was fighting unionism at the time, hence the company's stirring appeal to worker loyalty.

Mr. Prelinger's firm, Prelinger Associates, sells the use of footage from his collection for up to $90 a second. He sold "From Dawn to Sunset" footage to Drexel Burnham Lambert Inc. for use in "Drexel Helps America," a film promoting junk bonds, as well as to Michael Moore, whose new film, "Roger and Me," blames GM's restructuring for the economic woes of Flint, Mich., the auto maker's birthplace.

Recently, Mr. Prelinger contracted to market his collection through another stock footage house, Petrified Films Inc. He is at work on other projects: producing segments for "Buzz," MTV's new "magazine" program, helping HBO find appropriately ironic footage for its new Comedy Channel and assembling a videodisk for scholars of "original visual research material" on the history of suburbia.

Some of his best clips are available on two home-video samplers from Voyager Co. of Santa Monica, Calif. Other volumes to come have such themes as car culture, gender roles and educational "misinformation."

The material for these categories is rich and ridiculous. Car culture alone spawned a particularly melodramatic genre: high-school safety films. As Mr. Prelinger puts it, "With safety films, you're always rooting for the accident to happen."

"The Last Date" (1950) is a "scare" film classic. Pretty Joanne could date any boy on the football team, but she ignores warnings that Nick (Dick York again) is a "teenicide" waiting to happen. "It would have been better if I'd died in the hospital rather than look the way I do. I couldn't even go to Nick's funeral," she sobs, her face teasingly hidden from the camera. "I've had my last date.

Makers of educational films say that "The Last Date" would no longer play in Peoria. The genre is now all but extinct, and the few driver's ed films still available are notable for a lack of gore and grief.

These days the emphasis is on bolstering "self-worth and teaching positive values," according to Joe Elliott, president of Chicago-based Encyclopaedia Britannica Educational Corp., the film-making unit of Encyclopaedia Britannica Inc. "A lot of what the films are doing is helping kids cope with very complicated lives. The pressures these kids face are a lot different from what we experienced."

Evidence of these changes can be seen in the latest Britannica catalog, where films for high-schoolers address up-to-the-second concerns in films like "Steroids: Shortcut to Make-Believe Muscles," "When Romance Turns to Rape" and "Coping with That Thing Called . . . Stress!"

Whether these films have ever made a shy guy popular or kept a kid from trying drugs is debatable. What's not is how many teens respond to them.

Jennifer Gravitz, a 17-year-old senior at Sachem High School (one of the nation's largest) in Lake Ronkonkoma, N.Y., undoubtedly speaks for millions of her peers, past and present, when she gives a big "thumbs down" to most educational films.

She cites one health film, "Natural Highs and How to Get Them," as one "really stupid" example, typified by platitudinous advice on staying sober. "You think, this is boring, and you just block it out," she says. The films "try to prove a point, but they treat you so stupidly. Students will fall asleep no matter what."

But time and nostalgia work wonders. Mr. Prelinger has screened his films at museums, universities and film festivals from San Diego to the Hague, usually to enthusiastic sell-out crowds. Though some of his audience derives from what he calls the '80s "camp and kitsch boom," he declares himself firmly anti-nostalgia and avers that others are ready to view ephemeral films seriously.

"What's really neat is to know how to look at media from some critical way," he says. "On the other hand, I don't think that watching films will change the world."

Amid L.A.'s Sorrows, Black Comedians See Shards of Laughter

Their Jokes—Tasteless, Angry, Forgiving—Help to Heal Their Listeners' Wounds

---

By David J. Jefferson

5/11/92

LOS ANGELES—"Some friends called me up," says Air Samuels as he launches into his comedy act. "They said, 'Move to California where a man can live like a King.' So I did. But I didn't know they was talkin' about Rodney."

The nightclub fills with laughter. It's a smaller audience than the Comedy Act Theatre in the riot-torn Crenshaw district usually gets on Friday nights, but the mainly black audience is no less eager for a good joke. As the community struggles to recover from the sorrows of the Rodney King verdict and its violent aftermath, black comedians are doing their part in inner-city clubs, finding shreds of sometimes-borderline, sometimes-tasteless humor in the devastation. All over town, black comedians are using black humor.

The recent mayhem illustrates "the trickle-down theory of looting, because for the last 10 years rich people have ripped off the savings-and-loans and the stock market, and now poor people are finally getting their chance to steal bread," says Jeff Joseph, a one-time writer for "In Living Color."

Jimmie Walker, who starred in the 1970s television series "Good Times," is telling audiences that "suddenly, because of the riots, every black actor in America is getting a new TV show. Even me. I'll be on the spinoff of 'Beverly Hills 90210,' called 'South Central, 911.' "

The comedians' interpretations of the verdict and the rioting are, by turns, politically charged and self-deprecating, funny and vulgar, angry and forgiving. Above all, they're brutally honest. If humor mirrors reality, these comics are reflecting the shattered images around them.

"The riots showed them that we won't take this ____ anymore," Comedy Act Theatre emcee Keith Morris tells the cheering audience. "And it showed them that you're all stupid ____ because you burnt down your check-cashing places." Like most club comedians, Mr. Morris loves a good expletive.

"Comedy is basically a release," says Michael Williams, the owner of Comedy Act Theatre. "The comics are the voices that help us ventilate some of the anxiety that was built up, some of the pain that was built up, some of the hurt and frustration that was built up."

Raw as it sometimes seems, such gallows humor allows people to take a traumatic event and "put it back to where they can control it," says Chaytor Mason, a psychology professor at University of Southern California. "Some people think it's in bad taste, but we actually need it."

Indeed, it sometimes seems as though everyone in town has become a stand-up comic. "The rioting stopped because they had to figure out how to program their new VCRs," goes one popular joke. At Verbum Dei Catholic High School in South Central, any student with new shoes gets teased by others, who demand, "Where's your sales slip?" Looters heading down Sunset Boulevard during the riots were greeted by a sign on the marquee of the Laugh Factory comedy club that read, "All the jokes were stolen. Please don't break in."

"I needed a release," says Myra Bauman, who is sitting in a small crowd of mostly professional people at the Fun House Comedy Club, near the burned-out hulk of Crenshaw Square mall. She'd spent the day at a local church, handing out groceries to riot victims.

Comedienne Jedda Jones was headed from South Central to perform at the Laugh Factory the night rioting broke out, and she witnessed some of the violence firsthand. Yet she also saw humor. "I was so hurt that my people had such bad taste," she says. "They were stealing crushed velvet sofas and swag lamps, and taking them back to places where they already had crushed velvet sofas and swag lamps."

Black comedians now find themselves part of a kind of group therapy.

"I'm gonna sue the city of Los Angeles for malpractice," says comedienne Dawn Keith. "They talk about rebuilding the community, but they should start with rebuilding my mind. I'm a wreck." Joking about the riots can be like navigating a mine field, Ms. Keith confesses before the show. Most of the jokes aren't really funny, she says. "What it boils down to is that the comedy is still preachy or pathetic. It's a very bitter taste."

Many comics are wriggling around the touchier points by sticking to looting jokes. "I know you," says Fun House host J. Anthony Brown, pointing to a young woman in the front row. "Channel 2 Action News. Compton Swap Meet." He then singles out a woman dressed in cutoff jeans and long black-and-white stockings and tells her, "Next time you're stealing stuff, turn the lights on."

At the Comedy Act Theatre, model-turned-comedienne Angela Means gets roars with her looting routine. "What's this with these people taking this stuff back to the church?" she asks, referring to a plea from the city's ministers. "If I'm not mistaken, shouldn't this be going back to the store? You have the preacher saying, 'Yes, come right on in, put that TV console right over there in the corner of my office.'"

But the comedians aren't without their anger. "'White Men Can't

Jump,' but they can beat the _____ out of a brother and get off for it," comedian Chris Tucker tells the Fun House crowd. Brandon Bolden, comic for the black radio station KJLH, asks, "What was the use of Bush coming down here? He didn't even bring a broom."

Others are using their acts as a rallying cry for black pride. The Fun House had T-shirts printed that read, "100% Black Owned," mimicking signs that spared some businesses. Several comics joke that white people are treating them differently since the riots. "I come to work now, and white people are playing rap music, serving watermelon buffets," says Reuben Paul.

Comedian Ricky Beecham's routine warns against the encroaching commercialization of Martin Luther King Jr.'s birthday. "You all will be driving down the street and turn on the radio and hear the commercials: 'Free at last. Free at last. Not free, but 50% off. Yes, he had a dream, but he never dreamed prices would be this low.' "

For some black comedians, any political correctness they might have felt before the violence went up with the flames. And the audiences are lapping it up. "It's easy . . . to find out who was looting. Any Mexican with new shoes," a comedian named Pierre tells the cheering crowd at Comedy Act Theatre.

"The comics are just bringing up what people are thinking anyway," Pierre says later, defending the racial humor. But he concedes that racist jokes can drive people apart. "The comedians are taking sides," he says.

Yet some black comics are choosing to stay away from such hot topics. "I decided to let others tell the story," says Wan Dexter, a schoolteacher and part-time comedian. Likewise, comedian Ralph Harris has put a lid on the riot act. "My job is not to get someone inflamed over what happened," he says. "If I'm gonna address my personal feelings, I should go to a different forum."

But back at the Fun House, Dawn Keith launches into a routine where she plays psychologist to Stacey Koon, one of the four policemen acquitted in the King beating. "Now I know you didn't really mean to do that," she tells the imagined Sgt. Koon. "You're under stress about these gangs. You lost control. So you go straight to jail, baby." No one laughs, but the silence is broken by the soft whir of a police helicopter.

It Is Hard to Play, Can Imitate a Duck And Isn't a Bassoon

*It Is the Little-Known Oboe,
And Its Soulful Tones
Take Their Toll on Oboists*

By Meg Cox

10/29/86

NEW YORK—It's no wonder oboe players have a reputation for being the curmudgeons of the orchestra.

You would be nasty, too, if your instrument were commonly called "an ill wind that nobody blows good." The oboe is devilishly difficult to play and has a limited solo repertoire. It demands laborious hours preparing reeds, the inch-long pieces of cane that create the instrument's sound. Hernias are just one of the ills that oboists are heir to.

All that, and no glory. The casual concertgoer tends to confuse the oboe with the bassoon. If asked to name a single oboe player, he will surely draw a blank. And if he can recall any oboe music at all, it is probably "Peter and the Wolf," in which an oboe plays the duck.

The cumulative impact of all this has sent some oboists into a permanent funk. The late Harold Gomberg, long the lead oboe with the New York Philharmonic and one of the most irascible oboists ever, once said to a famous conductor who complimented his playing: "Thanks, but you're the biggest bore I ever played for."

Harold's brother, Ralph Gomberg, who is now the principal oboe for the Boston Symphony, says: "It makes a beautiful, poignant and distinctive sound, but the oboe can destroy you. Some oboists are crazy, really. I meet them and I walk away."

Whatever the instrument's drawbacks, several oboists are struggling to improve the oboe's image and have embarked on solo careers. Ever hear of Humbert Lucarelli or Heinz Holliger? Perhaps you will one day, though both have a long way to go before achieving the culthood of flamboyant soloists like flutist James Galway.

Mr. Lucarelli, an energetic, 50-year-old American who would have chosen baseball over music if he hadn't been hit by a car in childhood, is the grandstander of the two. Last January, he booked Carnegie Hall for a special concert to celebrate the 100th anniversary of the modern oboe. (The oboe's ancestors can be traced back to 2800 B.C., but the modern concert version was developed in the 1880s in France.) Mr. Lucarelli also formed a nonprofit organization called Oboe International Inc. to promote his instrument and held the first Lucarelli International Competition for Solo Oboe Players, whose winner performed at the Carnegie concert.

Oboists got free tickets to the event if they agreed to participate; many agreed. At the finale some 75 oboe players dashed onto the stage, joining Mr. Lucarelli in special variations on "Happy Birthday." Although he has made a number of recordings under serious classical labels, Mr. Lucarelli's biggest success to date was a mail-order record called "The Sensual Sound of the Soulful Oboe," which sold about 80,000 copies. He gives many oboe recitals, but much of his time is spent as chairman of the woodwind department at Hartt School of Music in Hartford, Conn.

Heinz Holliger, a balding, 47-year-old oboist and composer from Switzerland, has made at least 100 recordings, including transcriptions of many pieces originally composed for other instruments. Many fellow composers have written works specially for Mr. Holliger. Many music critics consider him the world's top virtuoso of his instrument in technical areas like fingering and breath control.

But fellow oboists suspect neither man is cut out for stardom. Mr. Holliger, for one thing, is a shy, scholarly fellow who mumbles during interviews and disdains self-promotion. "I would rather quit my profession than appear on a talk show," he says in his thick Swiss accent. "For me, giving concerts isn't just having success, or show business."

But the oboe's limitations may be the biggest obstacle to celebrity. A major handicap is the repertoire. Though there are hundreds of oboe works, "we don't have a lot by the meat-and-potatoes composers," admits Mr. Lucarelli. "We don't have a concerto by Schumann, Schubert or Brahms, and only one by Mozart." Beethoven wrote one oboe concerto, but it has been lost, while Debussy died before starting a planned oboe piece.

Then there is the instrument's instability. The oboe itself, made of heavy, hard African blackwood, or sometimes rosewood, and overlaid with silver-plated keywork covering about 20 tone holes, isn't terribly temperamental. The wild card is the reed, a doubled-over piece of cane (bamboo), usually imported from France, that makes music as it vibrates.

Mr. Lucarelli, in a reed-making demonstration at his New York apartment, sits at a roll-top desk cluttered with a dozen varieties of knives and more exotic tools. He starts with little hollow tubes of cane he has soaked for hours; after cutting and splitting the tubes, he uses a $1,000 machine called a gouger to shave layers from their pulpy insides. Mr. Lucarelli gouges most of his reeds to exactly 0.6 millimeter in the center and 0.45 millimeter on the sides. But those he plans to use at high altitudes he gouges narrower to compensate for reduced air pressure.

After being gouged, the cane is doubled over, so it is about an inch long, and sculpted at the fold with a special knife. Next, the reed is tied with thread onto a "staple," a reusable tube made of cork-covered metal, which holds the reed in the oboe. Last comes more whittling, including clipping to create the tiny opening for blowing. Oboists spend up to 10 hours a week making reeds, often an hour on each, only to have them give out after a few performances.

But that is only one of their instrumental problems. At one recital, Mr. Lucarelli's oboe wouldn't make a sound because a morsel of food clogged it up. He said to the audience, "The sound you have just heard is a lamb sandwich stuck in a reed."

Even when conditions are perfect, playing an oboe isn't easy. The problem is that the instrument requires so little air, which is blown through an opening the size of a needle's eye. The rest of the air in a player's lungs just has to sit there, going stale, which creates "a strangulating effect," says Ray Still, the principal oboe with the Chicago Symphony Orchestra.

Considering the unsung hardship of their profession, you might think that other oboists would laud Messrs. Lucarelli and Holliger for giving their instrument a higher profile. Think again. Says Mr. Still: "Holliger is very skillful with his fingers, but his nasal, thin sound is from the duck-and-bagpipe school of oboe playing. He sells because he puts on a good show."

That opinion of Mr. Holliger's tone is shared by many American oboists, who prefer a fuller, more resonant sound. But they don't go wild over Mr. Lucarelli, either. Says Leonard Arner, the principal oboe with the New York City Opera, "He is one of our better oboists, but I think he's a self-promoter. If you want to be the Bruce Springsteen of the oboe, fine."

It might seem that all these woes would eventually drive musicians away from the oboe. But after all, the oboe is the instrument most like the human voice, and it is the oboe that sounds the pre-concert "A" that all the other musicians tune to. There is no shortage of young oboists stubbornly embracing the instrument.

"When things go wrong, the oboe sounds so horrible you just want to die," says James Bulger, a 25-year-old oboist in Boston. "But when everything goes well, there is nothing like it. The oboe gets all the slow, expressive solos in symphonic works that get you right in the heart."

It's the Immortal,
The One, the Only:
Ol' Brown Eyes!

If Frank Sinatra Is Salieri,
Jimmy Roselli Is Mozart,
Say Long-Suffering Fans

By Timothy K. Smith

7/8/91

NEW YORK—Maybe if his ears had been bigger, Jimmy Roselli's singing career would have been different, and it would have been he, not Frank Sinatra, who ascended to the show-business pantheon. Mr. Sinatra's ungainly ears, after all, were an essential part of the vulnerable image that made teen-age girls hysterical and teen-age boys so jealous that one Alexander J. Dorogokupetz hit him with three flung eggs at a concert in 1944, explaining, "It seemed like a good idea at the time."

Or maybe if their nicknames had been reversed, and Mr. Roselli had been billed as "The Swooner" while Mr. Sinatra labored as "The Dynamic Belter of Song," things would have turned out differently. Sinatra's sibilant sobriquet lent itself naturally to the formation of fan clubs like the Sighing Society of Sinatra Swooners (although alliteration sometimes took a back seat to forthrightness, as with the Flatbush Girls Who Would Lay Down Their Lives for Frank Sinatra Fan Club). Mr. Roselli's fans have been less well organized than Mr. Sinatra's, though no less ardent. "Jimmy," declares Doris Lardie, 62, of Fallbrook, Calif., "is better than Frankie. I mean it."

As it happened, though, Mr. Sinatra became the most famous Italian-American balladeer born the only son of a prizefighter on Monroe Street in Hoboken, N.J., and Mr. Roselli the least famous. Not too surprisingly, Mr. Roselli has little use for Mr. Sinatra. "He looks like a cab coming down the street with the doors open," Mr. Roselli says, alluding to Mr. Sinatra's ears.

Readers involved in loan-sharking may have heard Mr. Roselli's music (his rendition of "Little Pal," not Mr. Sinatra's "My Way," is the authentic wise-guy anthem, according to law-enforcement officials), but many more may not have. Mr. Roselli, a 65-year-old whose high tenor voice is still intact, has for the past 22 years been packing aficionados into sold-out dates while being completely ignored by the public at large. And he has had to watch while his former neighbor—singing many of the same songs in much the same idiom—married Ava Gardner, capered with a Rat Pack of Hollywood sybarites, earned more money than he could count and was the subject of biographies by, on the one hand, his adoring daughter and, on the other, Kitty Kelley (whose "His Way" is considered definitive and is the source of the silly names in the story thus far).

Mr. Roselli's destiny is all the more curious because he embodies aspects of the Sinatra myth more thoroughly than Mr. Sinatra does. "They say Sinatra was a saloon singer," Mr. Roselli says. "I sang in saloons. In the Bronx. In the cellar. Believe me. I worked in joints they used to have to have intermission to take the wounded out."

They say Mr. Sinatra grew up a tough urchin in Hoboken, but he was actually the neighborhood rich kid, sometimes called "Slacksie" for his fancy taste in clothes. Mr. Roselli, who was raised by his grandfather after his mother died in childbirth and his father ran off, used to lug his shoe-shine box into local bars and sing for change.

They say Mr. Sinatra is the mob's entertainer of choice. But it was Mr. Roselli who sang last year at the Helmsley Palace wedding reception of John A. Gotti, son of the reputed crime boss. Mr. Roselli says he has never done business with organized criminals, but he is resigned to the association between the Mafia and his music. "Every time they write a book, by the time you get to the fourth page there's a dead guy in a car with my tapes beside him on the front seat," he sighs.

By now Mr. Roselli is trailed by myths of his own, spun by fans to explain how a man can fill the Trump Plaza in Atlantic City with screaming, stomping fans one week and retreat into perfect obscurity the next. Some say he is afraid of flying (he isn't). Others say he got into a tangle over a mob-financed Carnegie Hall concert (never happened, he says). And they all say there is a sinister Sinatra influence at work. Mr. Sinatra declined to be interviewed.

Mr. Roselli actually is famous in some precincts. A magazine survey last year found that his photograph is the most commonly displayed celebrity headshot on the walls of restaurants in New York's Little Italy. Residents of Melbourne, Fla., recently collected 2,018 signatures on a petition imploring him to sing a benefit concert there.

There are people who believe that Mr. Roselli's eclipse is deserved. "You play his records in the zoo, the animals will climb the walls," says Pat Cooper, a comedian who used to work with Mr. Roselli. "He's performing in London now because they're tone deaf over there."

But others are quite serious about Mr. Roselli's musicianship. "He has a larger, richer voice than Frank," says Sammy Cahn, the legendary song-writer. "He's a miracle."

" 'Mala Femmena,' that's his song, that's the Italian-American national anthem," says Ernest J. Naspretto, a 32-year-old Queens police lieutenant. "The Neapolitan national anthem is 'Come Back to Sorrento,' and he owns that song, too."

Critics were as enthusiastic in 1965, when Mr. Roselli packed the

Copacabana, appeared on the Ed Sullivan Show and sold out Carnegie Hall. "Roselli is the gamest, most thrilling new talent I've heard in months," wrote the New York World-Telegram and Sun. "You're going to hear more and more of Jimmy Roselli," wrote the New York Journal-American.

Mr. Roselli signed a contract with United Artists Records, appeared with Jimmy Durante and worked with 50-piece orchestras, often in the presence of guys with bent noses, according to arranger Ralph Burns. "We used to record and they'd have the wine and the pastry set up, and the musicians loved it," Mr. Burns says. "There was never any question about budgets."

And then, in 1969, Mr. Roselli all but disappeared. What happened, he says, was this:

Mr. Sinatra's mother, Dolly, was organizing a benefit concert for the St. Joseph's School for the Blind in Jersey City in 1969. She wanted Mr. Roselli to donate his services, but instead of asking him herself she sent two proxies to track him down at his tailor. "I was a little insulted, so I said to the two guys, tell her I've got to get $25,000 and she's got to pay for the orchestra, 25 men," Mr. Roselli says. "Oh, she blew a fuse. She went and told Frank."

And does Mr. Roselli conclude that Mr. Sinatra, or Mr. Sinatra's Mafia admirers, torpedoed his career? "I know I used to get played quite a bit on WNEW" in New York, he says after a long pause. "To get a record of mine played on that station now, the Lord has to intercede." (Mrs. Sinatra died in a plane crash in 1977. WNEW station manager Gray Brandt confirms that Mr. Roselli doesn't get air time but says "I seriously doubt" that the mob ever had anything to do with what the station plays.)

"Sinatra supposedly had him blackballed," says Al Glasgow, a casino consultant in Atlantic City.

"The Sinatra story is real," says Lt. Naspretto of the Queens police department. "That was the end of everything. It totally ruined his career."

"We believe it was the Gambino family," says Joseph Coffey, a top investigator at the New York State Organized Crime Task Force.

But there is good news, according to the transcript of a conversation taped in Atlantic City last year by law-enforcement officials looking into the activities of an allegedly misbehaving high roller. On the tape, the high roller suggests in language we can't reproduce here that John Gotti has offered to settle any disagreements between Mr. Roselli and Mr. Sinatra.

"Whether [Mr. Roselli] has made peace with Sinatra's [admirers] I don't really know," says Mr. Coffey of the Organized Crime Task Force. "But recently he's become hot again."

Mr. Roselli has his own record company in Jersey City now. He has just released a new album, and he is selling his 31 previous recordings by direct mail and on late-night cable television. In the past few years he has sung for standing-room-only crowds at the Palladium in London, and last year he performed six shows at the Trump Plaza.

But whatever his chances for a comeback, certain show-business opportunities are lost to Mr. Roselli forever. If things had been different, Lt. Naspretto says, "I think he would have been part of the Rat Pack. I really do."

Violin Makers Fret As Musicians Fiddle With Their A-Strings

Demand for Modern Sounds From Ancient Instruments Arouses Fear of Damage

---

By Philip Revzin

7/5/88

CREMONA, ITALY—The 80 master violin makers of this North Italian town share a collective nightmare:

A famous violinist is midway through a vigorous Beethoven cadenza on a priceless Stradivarius. The 300-year-old instrument—its strings stretched taut to produce a strong, brilliant sound—begins to groan, then cracks. Suddenly, it explodes.

"It could happen," warns violin maker Stefano Conia as he fondly strokes the belly of one of his glistening new violins in his crowded workshop.

So far, it apparently hasn't, at least like that. But that's irrelevant. This is where Antonio Stradivari, Nicolo Amati and Giuseppe Guarneri del Gesu made their world-renowned stringed instruments in the 17th and 18th centuries. And that imposes a special burden on residents. So Mr. Conia worries. "What people are doing to these old violins is crazy," he says.

Calmly stated, what people are doing is tuning old violins according to new musical fashion. A more passionate view might be that musical treasures are being dangerously souped up to keep pace with unreasonable competitive demands.

The problem begins at A. In fact, that's pretty much the whole problem.

When the first Cremonese masters were making their violins, violas and cellos, everybody agreed that the pitch of A above middle C was around 420 cycles per second, or 420 hertz. Since A is the tuning note on which other notes—up and down—are based, first A is tuned in, then all strings are tightened accordingly. With A at 420 hertz, these instruments, which many say are unequaled for tone quality, sounded warm and rich among the few other strings in a small chamber orchestra.

But as orchestras and concert halls got bigger, musicians started to tune their instruments sharper, raising the pitch of A and thus all other notes. The more brilliant, more piercing sound could be heard above other players and delight listeners even at the top of the third balcony.

The more that violinists tightened their strings, the more pressure they put on their violin bodies. Singers had to reach for higher notes, putting more pressure on their bodies, too. By the time Giuseppe Verdi was writing his operas in the mid-19th century, A had sharpened to 435 hertz. That, Verdi thought, was enough for both man and machine. He got an international meeting in Vienna in 1885 to fix A at that level.

It didn't last. In 1939 another international meeting set A at 440 hertz, which is what comes from Mr. Conia's tuning fork. He takes it off a peg on the wall and bings it on his chair. "Even 440 is too much, but okay, let's stop there," he says.

Few have. Many orchestras tune today to 443, 445, or even 450 hertz, stretching strings ever tighter. Sergio Renzi, director of Cremona's violin-making school, says he has heard of tunings of 460 hertz.

That's just "murderous" for any violin, he says, and especially so for the 500 to 600 old Cremonese violins still being played (out of a couple of thousand produced by the masters). These instruments are usually on loan to stellar soloists from investors who buy them at auction or privately. Values range from six figures into the millions. A Stradivarius cello used by Yo Yo Ma went for $1.2 million last month.

The idea is that the instruments are kept healthy by use; stashed away unplayed, their vitality withers. But what kind of use? "The strings are now pulled so tight that they put enormous strain, driving the bridge [the small wood piece that holds up the strings] right down into the belly," Mr. Conia says, pressing on the midsection of his violin. He argues that even reinforcements and alterations made to most old Cremonese instruments over the years won't stand much more.

"New violins are built for this, but 300-year-old wood can't take it," he says.

So concerned are the Cremonese that at a recent conference to mark the school's 50th birthday and the 250th anniversary of Stradivari's death, experts called for a return to 432 hertz as the standard A.

So far, reaction has been akin to the sound made by a violin with no strings at all. "There's no crisis, just a problem that has been around for 100 years," says Laurence Libin, curator of musical instruments at the Metropolitan Museum of Art in New York. "The Italians are always issuing grand statements but nobody pays much attention to them."

Says conductor George Solti: "I've never seen or heard of a violin breaking because of the pitch, but it is pretty high today and it's very bad for the singers—they can't reach the high notes." He prefers 440, no higher. Some say that while there may not yet be cases of catastrophic breakage, they have seen gradual damage. Higher tuning is championed by orchestral players who want to stand out in the middle of the second violin section, but disapproved by some soloists who want to safeguard their investments.

Yehudi Menuhin, the violinist, conductor and teacher, plays a 1742 Guarneri known as "the Lord Wilson" and valued at $2.5 million. He favors a lower tuning but thinks the proposed pre-Verdi-era 432 hertz is unrealistic. "Our modern ears would consider that rather flat. The consumer wants his music brilliant and glossy."

That's too bad, too, Sir Yehudi feels. "Our ever more competitive age has not only pushed up inflation, it's pushed up the pitch. The Viennese are the guiltiest, the British the gentlest. A British oboist will often give you a nice, low A, so you can tune right down."

These days, as soon as he comes offstage, Sir Yehudi loosens his violin's A and E strings completely. But he has given up arguing with conductors about tuning. "It's hopeless. The most you can hope for is that the orchestra plays in tune at all."

Conductor Antonio de Almeida, though himself a proponent of lower tuning, maintains conductors can't do much anyway, given commercial considerations. "Music has become such a business, everybody says to hell with what comes naturally. If it sells, let's do it," he says. "Any move to a lower A would run into tremendous resistance. If a record company gets better compact-disk recordings with a higher A, that's what they'll go for."

That's fine with some people, too. "Life is hard enough. Brilliance is what it's all about," says Elmar Olivira, a prize-winning soloist who plays a 1692 Strad worth about $400,000. "Nobody can stand up in front of the Philadelphia Orchestra and hope to project and stand out at 435 hertz."

He says his violin is in "wonderful shape" despite centuries of playing, and he's comfortable at tunings between 442 and 447 hertz. "Violins don't exist in isolation, they exist to be played," he says.

In Cremona, however, the goal is brilliance without side effects. Most makers produce a couple of dozen violins a year, priced from $5,000 to $10,000. Mr. Conia's workshop, typically, is littered with bits of violin bodies, reeks of resinous varnish and hums to the sound of violin concertos played continuously over the stereo system. He painstakingly shapes thin strips of pine and maple, and applies 30 coats of varnish, as did Stradivari.

And he continues to battle. He often plays in local churches and town halls. The churches he prefers are ones with old, slightly flat organs. "I can tune way, way down, and be nice to my violin," he says, giving it a pat. "And nobody can tell the difference."